THE QUEEN'S KNIGHT

The Queen's Knight Volume 11
Created by Kim Kang Won

Translation - Sora Han
English Adaptation - Lacey Harris
Copy Editor - Shannon Watters
Retouch and Lettering - Star Print Brokers
Production Artist - Lucas Rivera
Graphic Designer - Monalisa De Asis

Editor - Hyun Joo Kim
Digital Imaging Manager - Chris Buford
Pre-Production Supervisor - Lucas Rivera
Production Manager - Elisabeth Brizzi
Managing Editor - Vy Nguyen
Creative Director - Anne Marie Horne
Editor-in-Chief - Rob Tokar
Publisher - Mike Kiley
President and C.O.O. - John Parker
C.E.O. and Chief Creative Officer - Stu Levy

A  Manga

TOKYOPOP and  are trademarks or registered trademarks of TOKYOPOP Inc.

TOKYOPOP Inc.
5900 Wilshire Blvd. Suite 2000
Los Angeles, CA 90036

E-mail: info@TOKYOPOP.com
Come visit us online at www.TOKYOPOP.com

ISBN: 978-1-59532-267-8

First TOKYOPOP printing: May 2008
10 9 8 7 6 5 4 3 2 1
Printed in the USA

THE QUEEN's KNIGHT

VOLUME 11

BY KIM KANG WON

HAMBURG // LONDON // LOS ANGELES // TOKYO

LAST TIME IN...

THE QUEEN'S KNIGHT

Yuna is a normal girl who visits her mother in Germany when a terrible disaster befalls her. After she returns home from her accident, she begins to have strange dreams. In her dream, a knight who calls himself "Rieno" tells Yuna that she is his Queen and that he is her knight. Yuna's brothers send her back to Germany, where she meets the knight from her dreams--who then promptly kidnaps her, taking her to Phantasma.

Phantasma is a world covered entirely with snow, and Yuna is forced to live with Rieno. But just when Yuna was getting used to being with him, spring arrives, and Yuna is taken to Elysian to be properly installed as the Queen of Phantasma. Once there, Yuna befriends the Queen's Guardian Knights, Ehren, Leon and Schiller, the hateful Chancellor Kent, as well as the Queen's rival, Princess Libera.

Yuna almost immediately begins to shake things up, as she not only repeals the taxes and declares slavery illegal, but insists on creating new policies and institutions like schools and hospitals.

As she settles into her new gig as the queen, she discovers that the queen's main duty is to maintain springtime in Phantasma and that can only be done if she's happily in love. As all her predecessors had fallen for Rieno, who would never reciprocate the sentiment, spring had all eventually come to an end...till now. Speculators, and even Yuna herself, are convinced that Yuna's object of amore is Ehren and that this is fantastic news for Phantasma as spring can be eternal again.

Later, Yuna learns of the doomed romance between Rieno and Eli, the Queen before her. At the same time, Ehren gets a brief history lesson of Phantasma and how Rieno, when he reaches age nineteen, will come to rule the land as lord of darkness. In order to prevent such travesty, Ehren is entrusted with a critical assignment: He must persuade Queen Yuna to drive the Mistletoe Wooden Dagger into Rieno's heart...

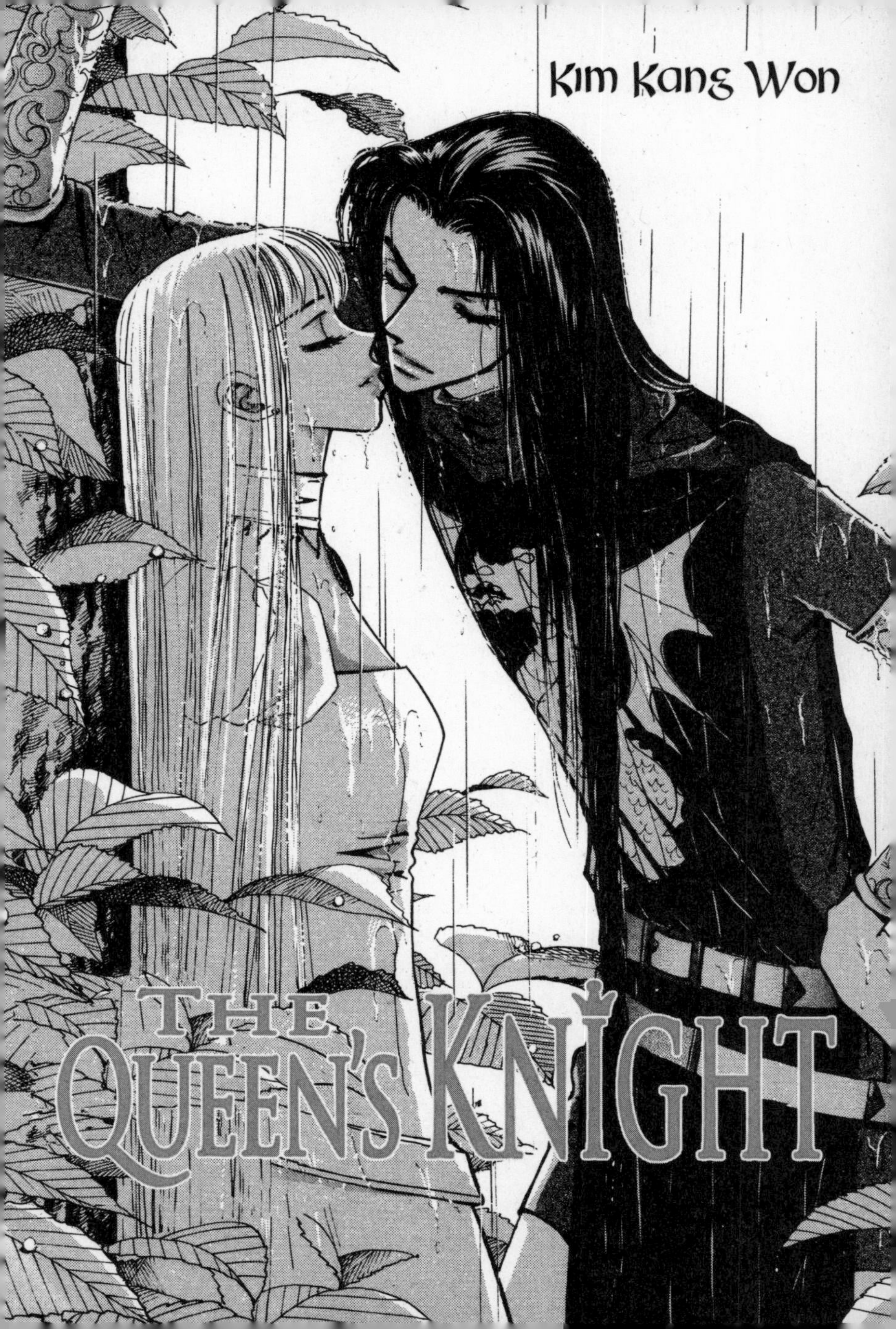
Kim Kang Won
THE QUEEN'S KNIGHT

Curse

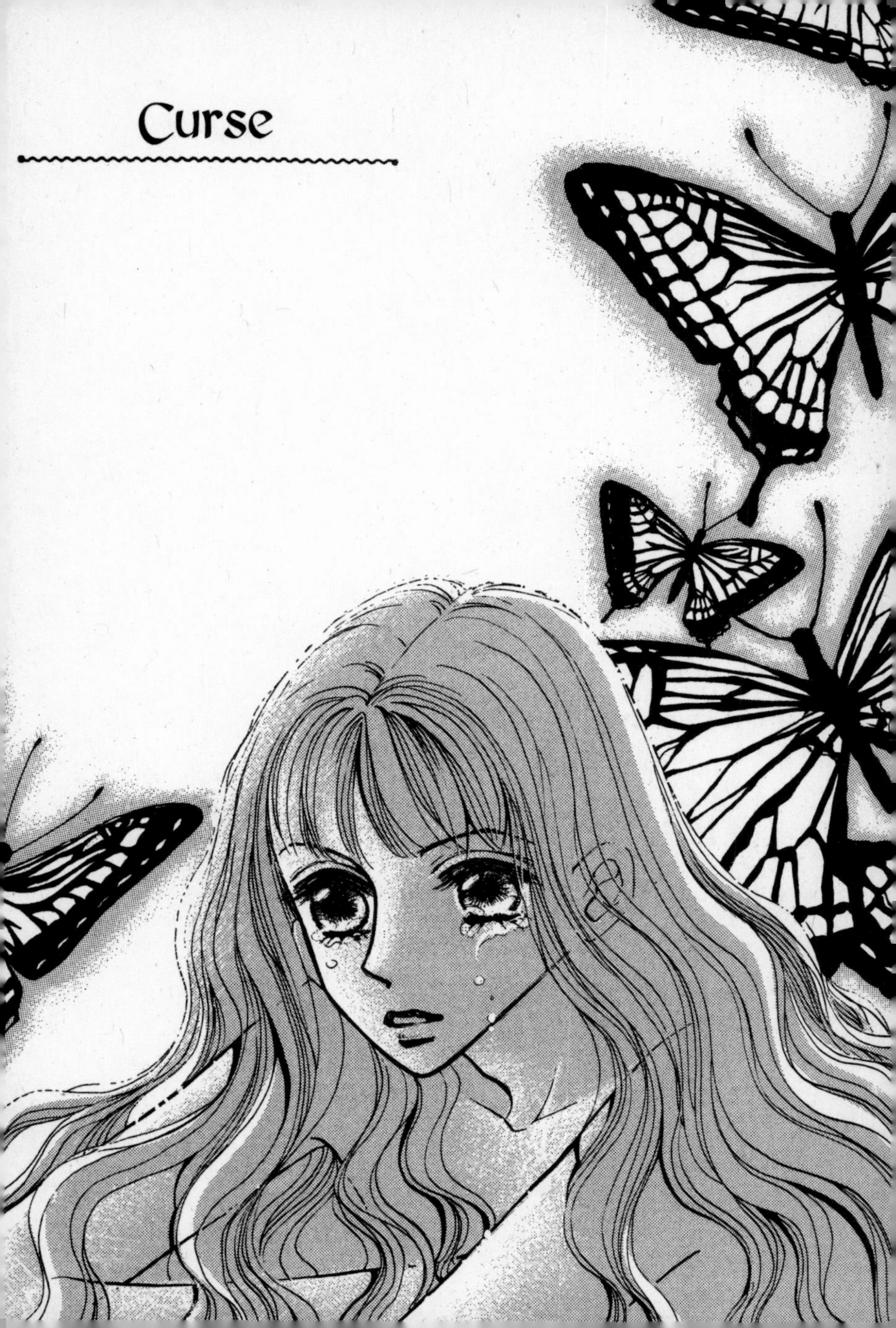

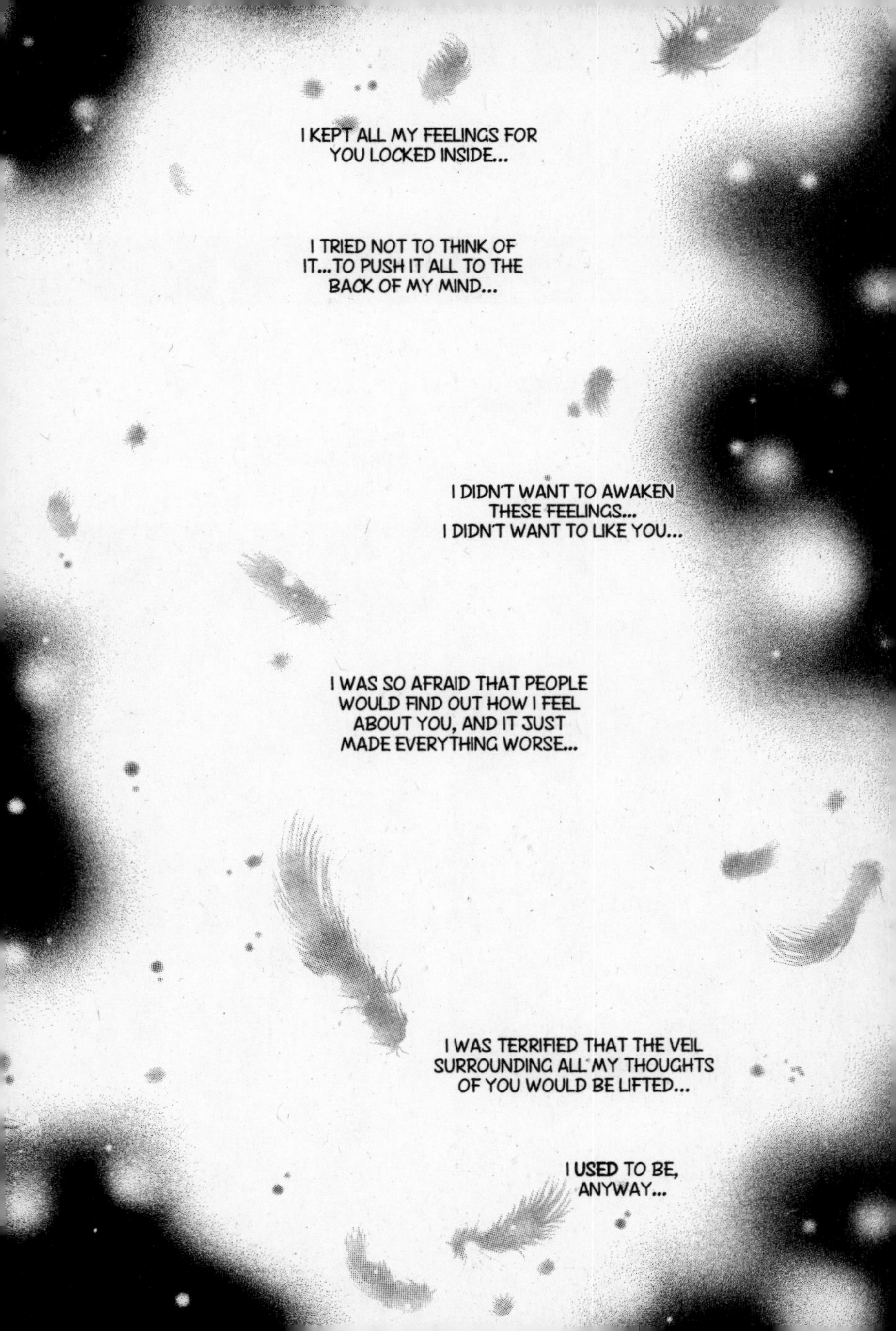
I KEPT ALL MY FEELINGS FOR YOU LOCKED INSIDE...
I TRIED NOT TO THINK OF IT...TO PUSH IT ALL TO THE BACK OF MY MIND...
I DIDN'T WANT TO AWAKEN THESE FEELINGS... I DIDN'T WANT TO LIKE YOU...
I WAS SO AFRAID THAT PEOPLE WOULD FIND OUT HOW I FEEL ABOUT YOU, AND IT JUST MADE EVERYTHING WORSE...
I WAS TERRIFIED THAT THE VEIL SURROUNDING ALL MY THOUGHTS OF YOU WOULD BE LIFTED...
I **USED** TO BE, ANYWAY...

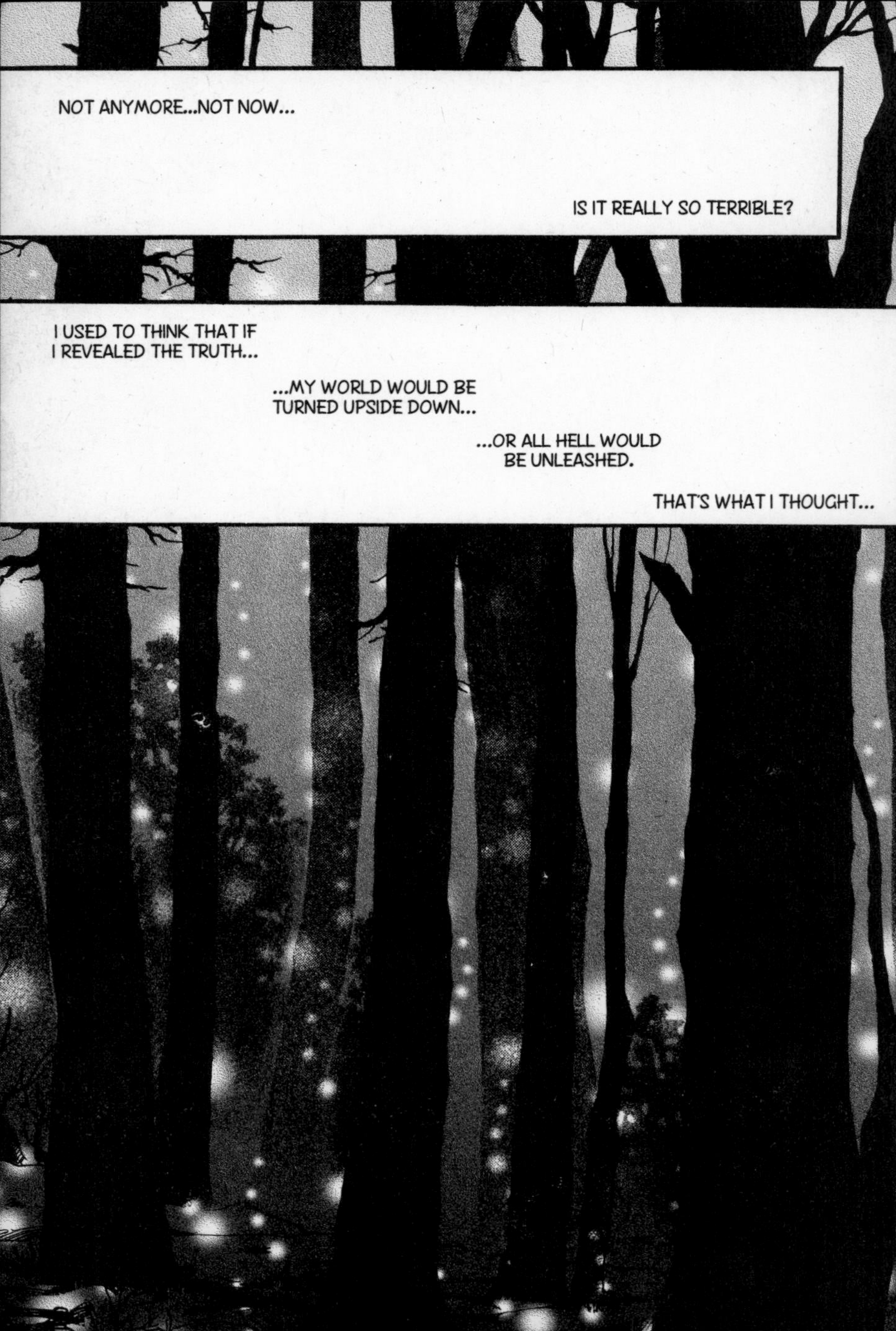
NOT ANYMORE...NOT NOW...
IS IT REALLY SO TERRIBLE?
I USED TO THINK THAT IF I REVEALED THE TRUTH...
...MY WORLD WOULD BE TURNED UPSIDE DOWN...
...OR ALL HELL WOULD BE UNLEASHED.
THAT'S WHAT I THOUGHT...

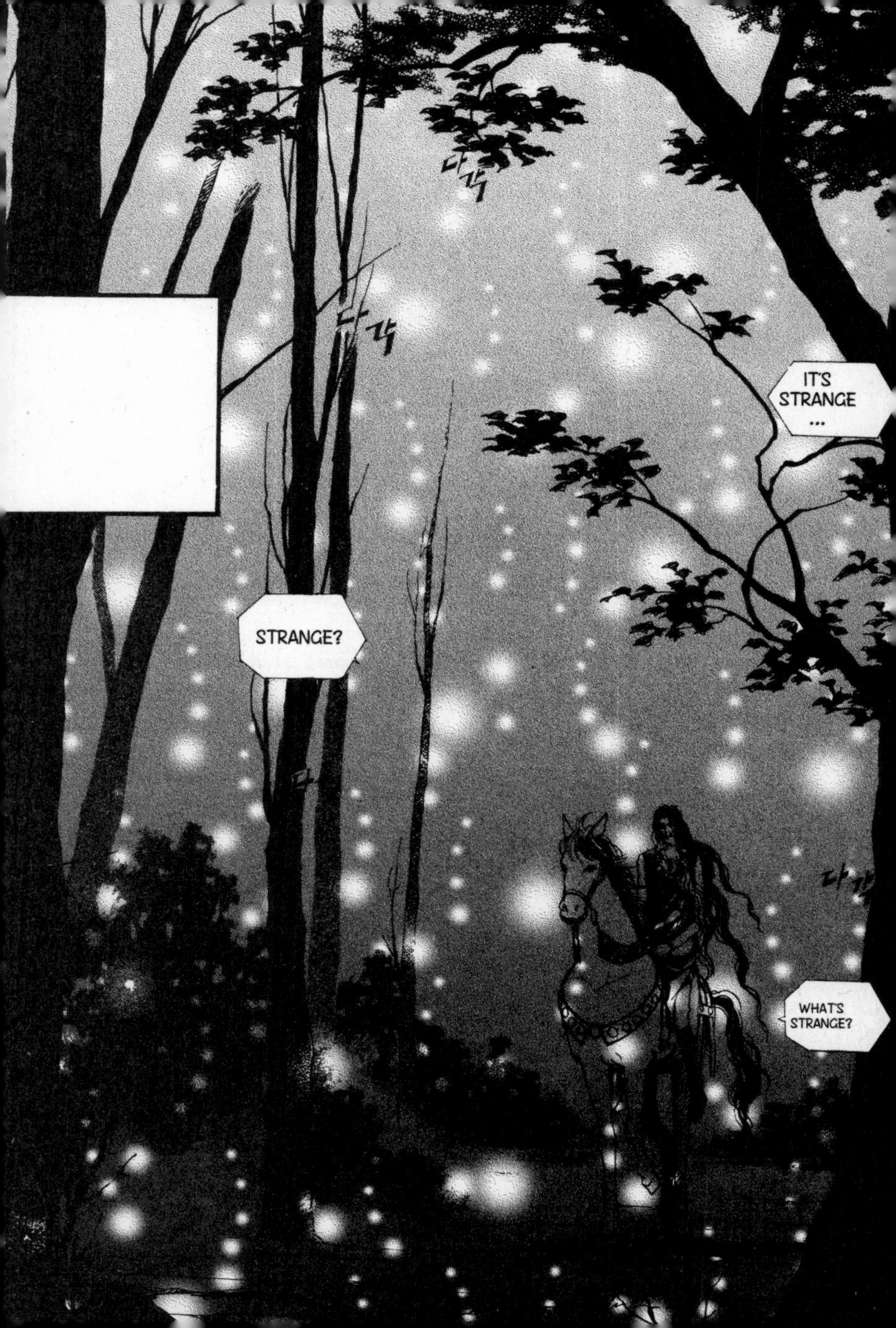
IT'S STRANGE ...
STRANGE?
WHAT'S STRANGE?

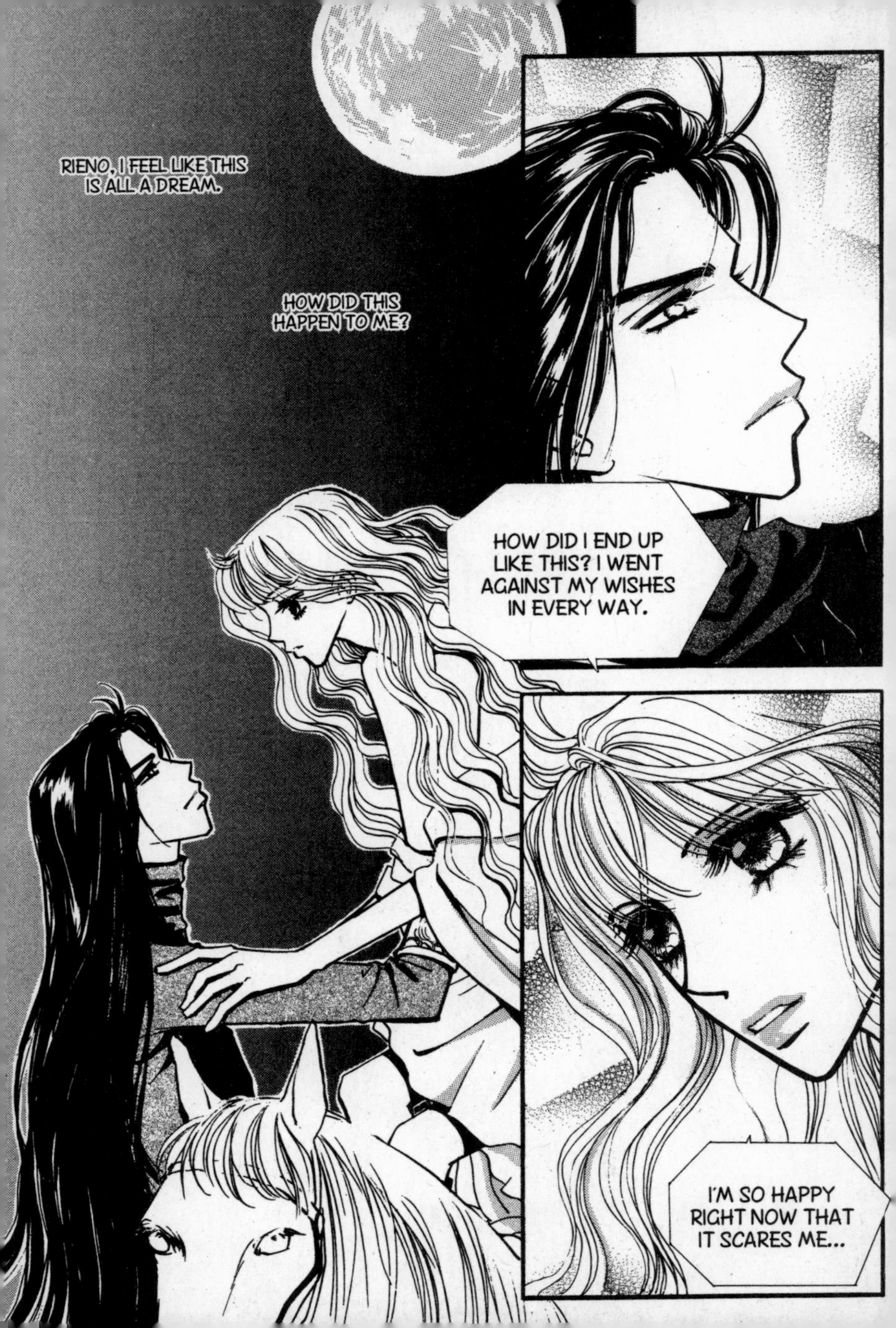
RIENO, I FEEL LIKE THIS IS ALL A DREAM.
HOW DID THIS HAPPEN TO ME?
HOW DID I END UP LIKE THIS? I WENT AGAINST MY WISHES IN EVERY WAY.
I'M SO HAPPY RIGHT NOW THAT IT SCARES ME...

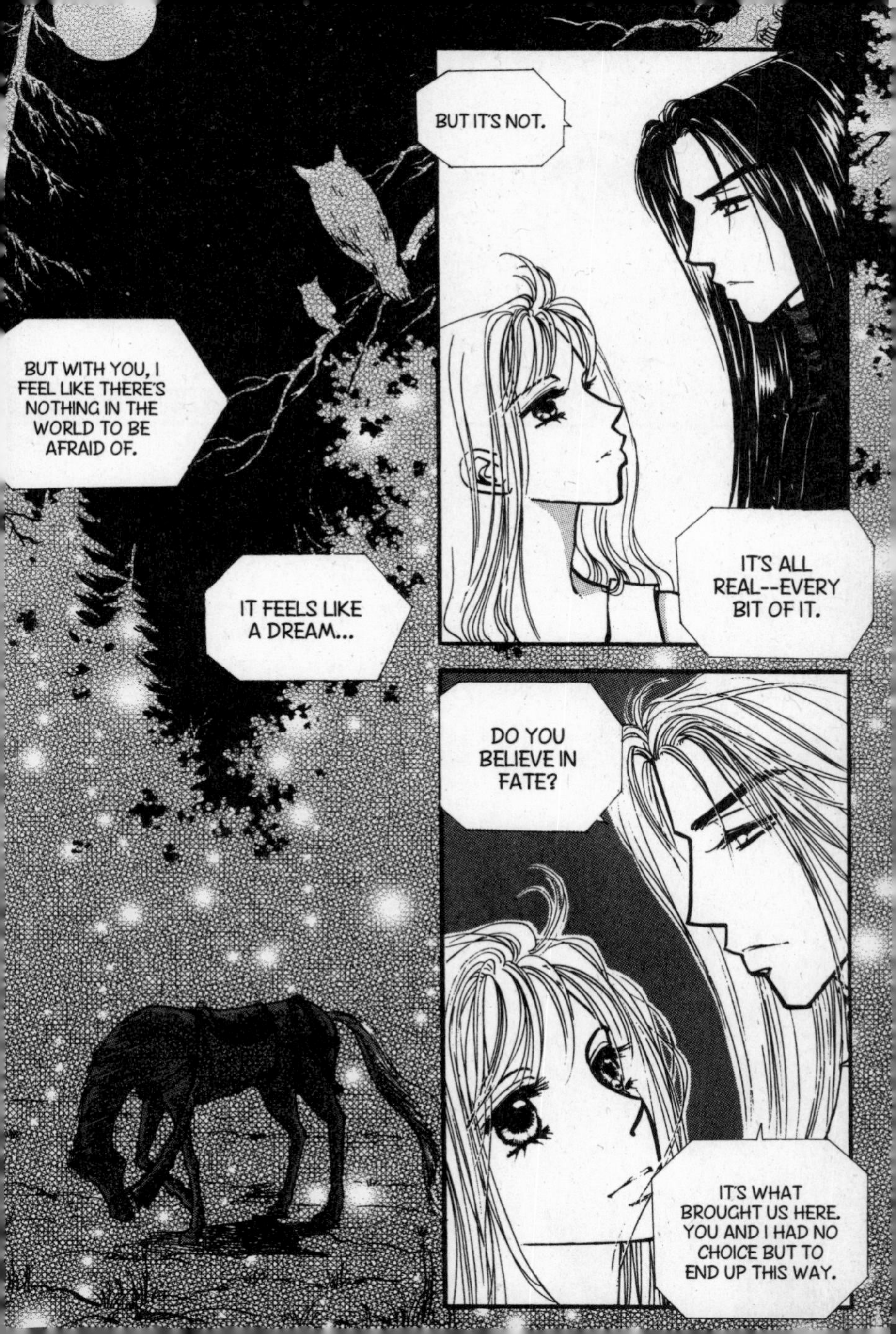
BUT WITH YOU, I FEEL LIKE THERE'S NOTHING IN THE WORLD TO BE AFRAID OF.
IT FEELS LIKE A DREAM...
BUT IT'S NOT.
IT'S ALL REAL--EVERY BIT OF IT.
DO YOU BELIEVE IN FATE?
IT'S WHAT BROUGHT US HERE. YOU AND I HAD NO CHOICE BUT TO END UP THIS WAY.

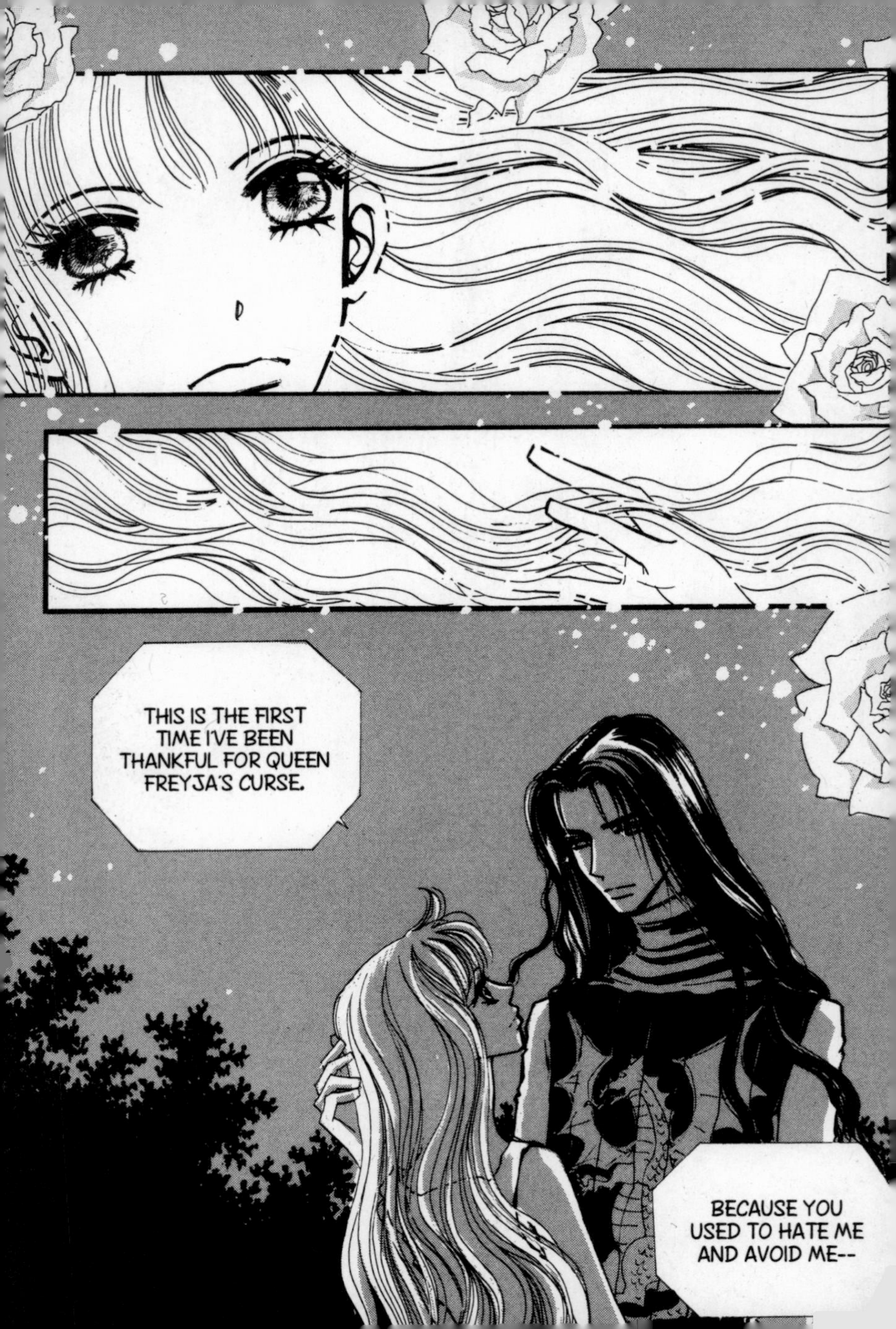
THIS IS THE FIRST TIME I'VE BEEN THANKFUL FOR QUEEN FREYJA'S CURSE.
BECAUSE YOU USED TO HATE ME AND AVOID ME--

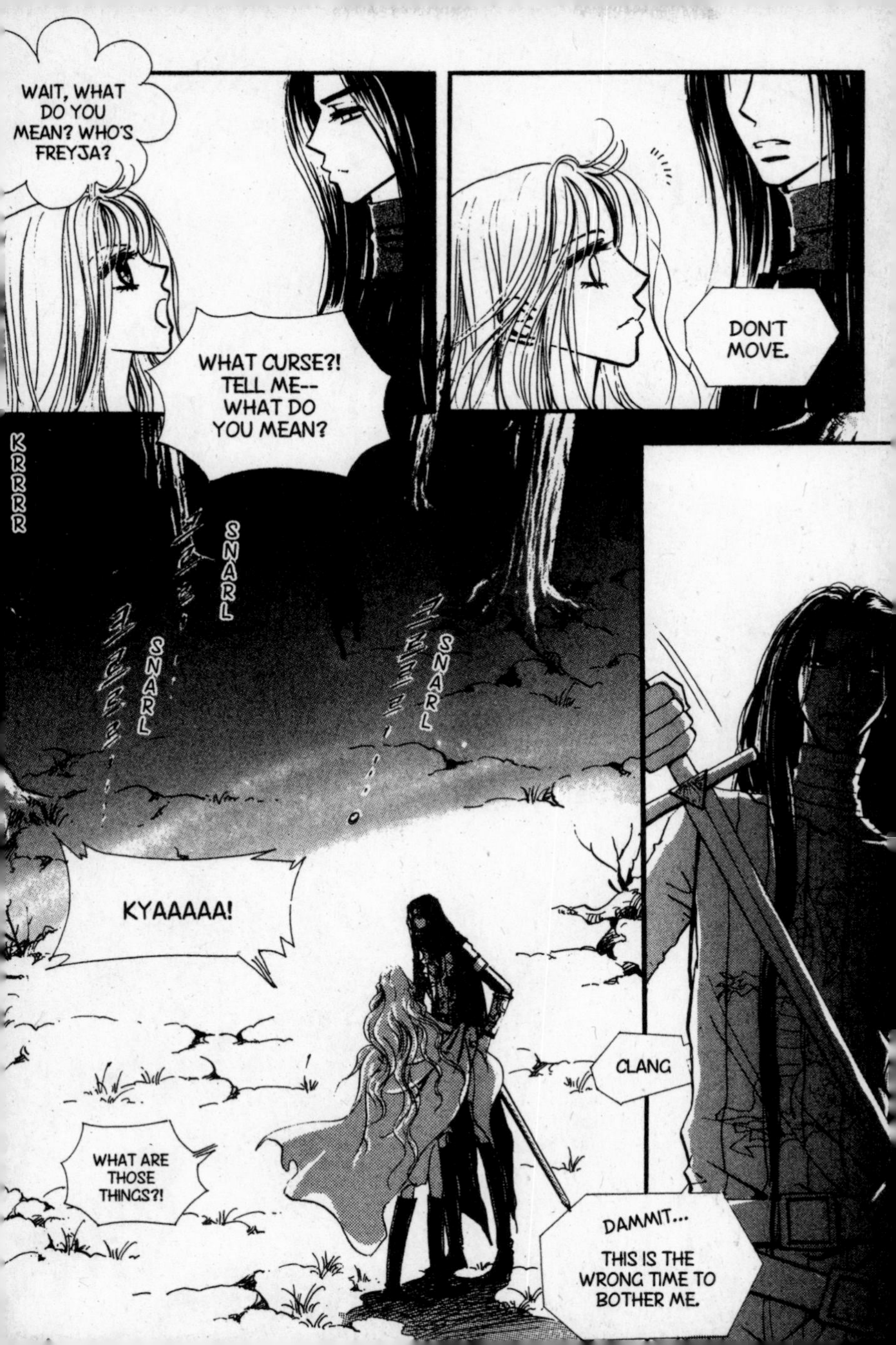

WAIT, WHAT DO YOU MEAN? WHO'S FREYJA?
WHAT CURSE?! TELL ME-- WHAT DO YOU MEAN?
DON'T MOVE.
KRRRR
SNARL
SNARL
SNARL
KYAAAAA!
WHAT ARE THOSE THINGS?!
CLANG
DAMMIT...
THIS IS THE WRONG TIME TO BOTHER ME.

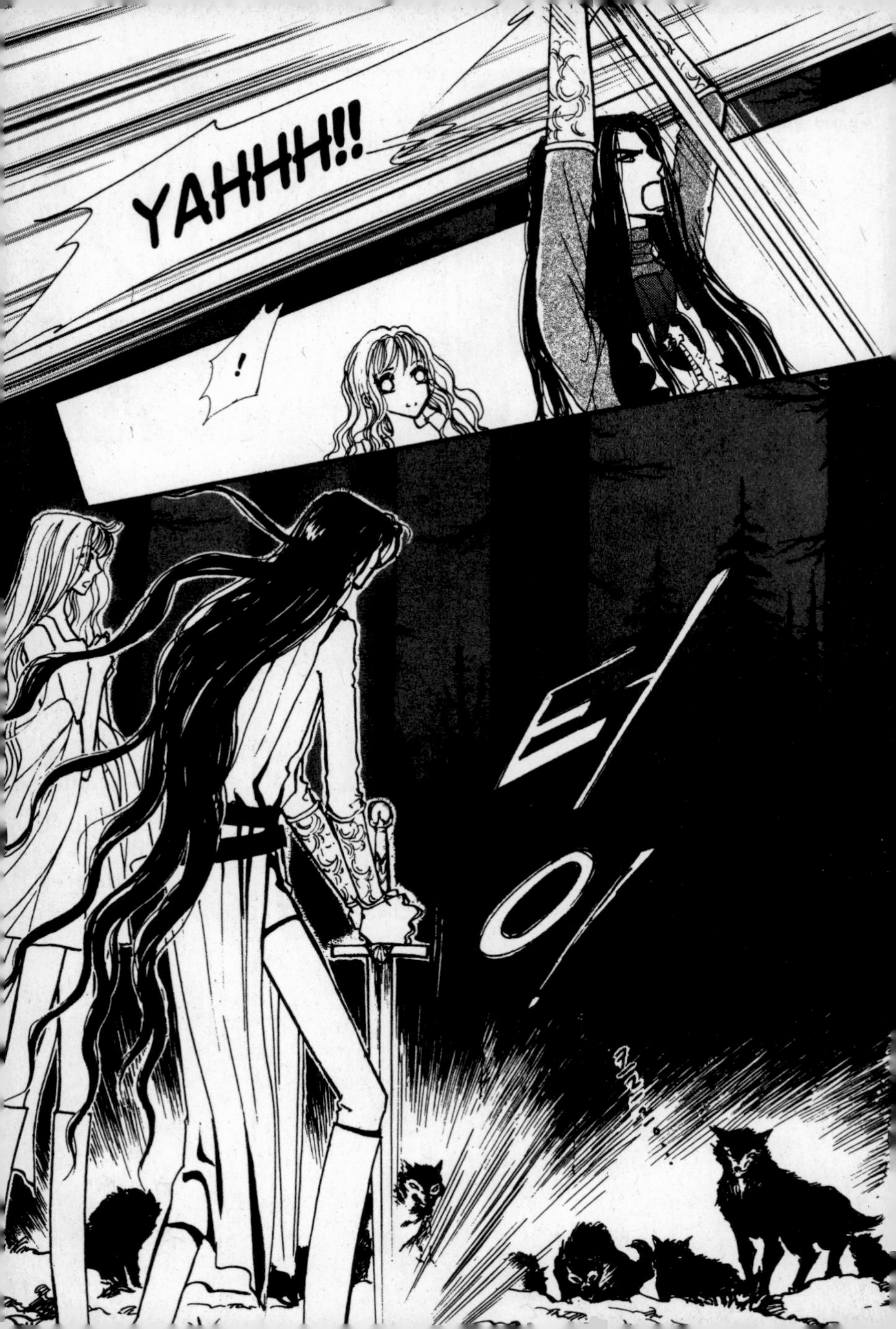
YAHHH!!
!

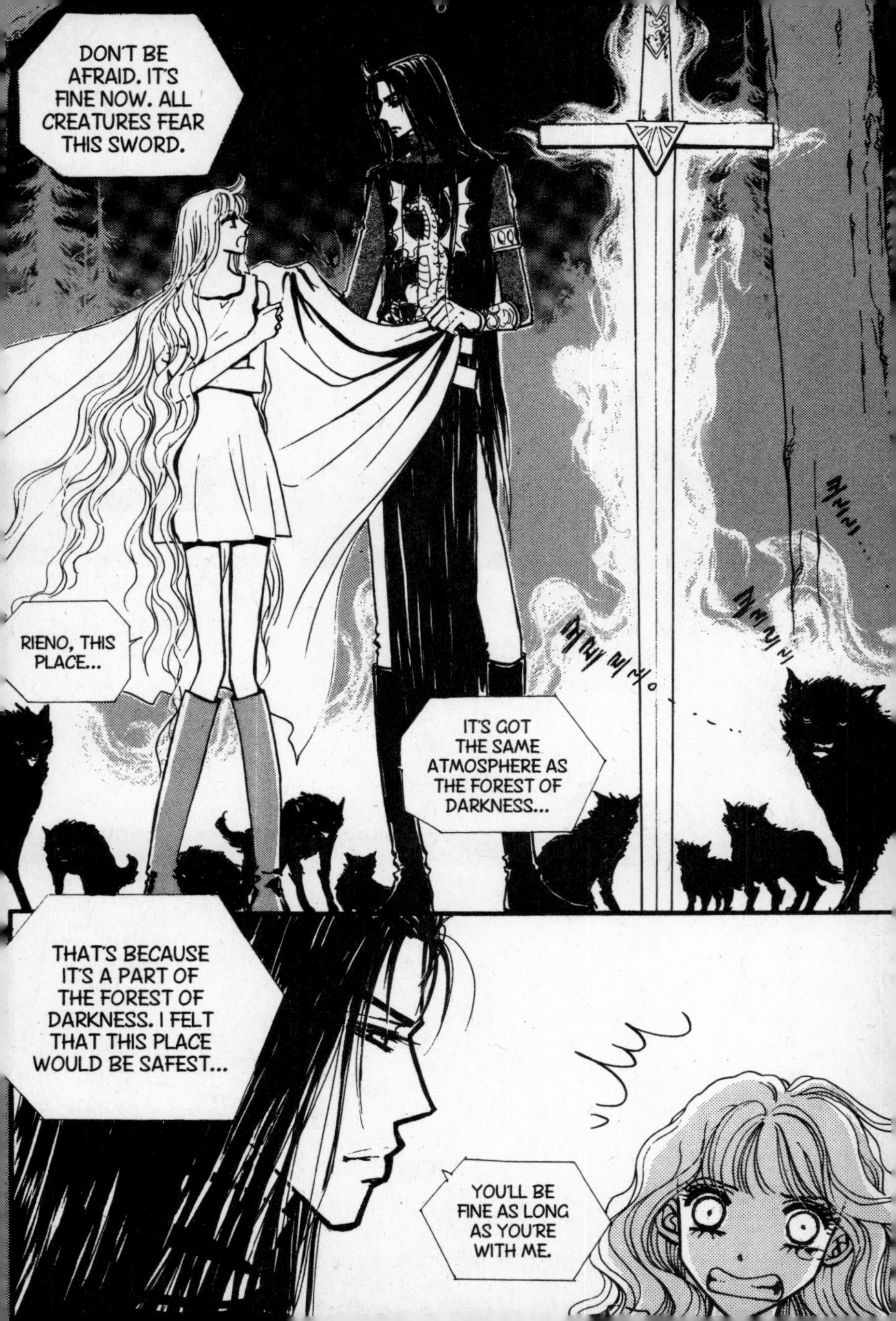
DON'T BE AFRAID. IT'S FINE NOW. ALL CREATURES FEAR THIS SWORD.
RIENO, THIS PLACE...
IT'S GOT THE SAME ATMOSPHERE AS THE FOREST OF DARKNESS...
THAT'S BECAUSE IT'S A PART OF THE FOREST OF DARKNESS. I FELT THAT THIS PLACE WOULD BE SAFEST...
YOU'LL BE FINE AS LONG AS YOU'RE WITH ME.

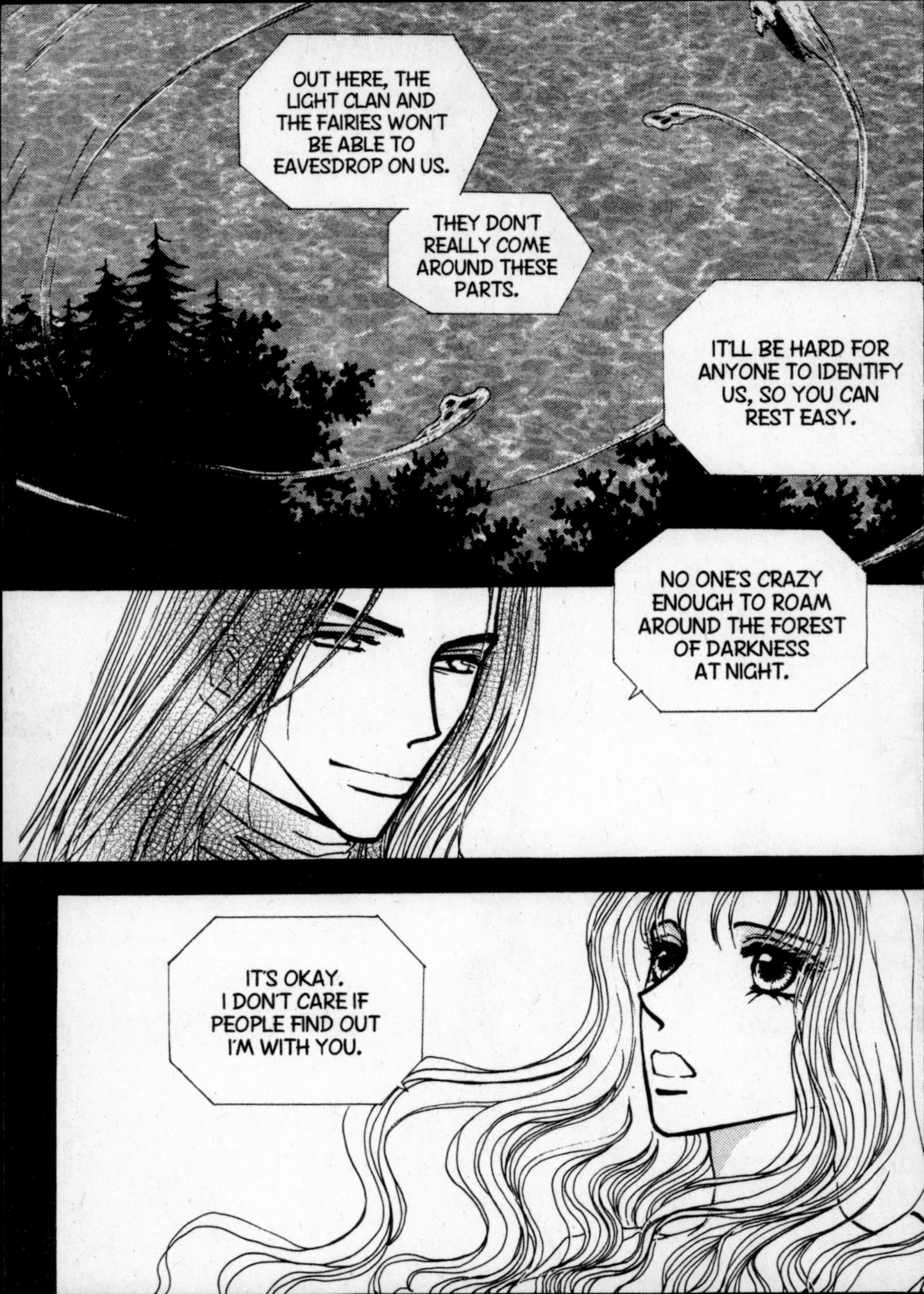
OUT HERE, THE LIGHT CLAN AND THE FAIRIES WON'T BE ABLE TO EAVESDROP ON US.
THEY DON'T REALLY COME AROUND THESE PARTS.
IT'LL BE HARD FOR ANYONE TO IDENTIFY US, SO YOU CAN REST EASY.
NO ONE'S CRAZY ENOUGH TO ROAM AROUND THE FOREST OF DARKNESS AT NIGHT.
IT'S OKAY. I DON'T CARE IF PEOPLE FIND OUT I'M WITH YOU.

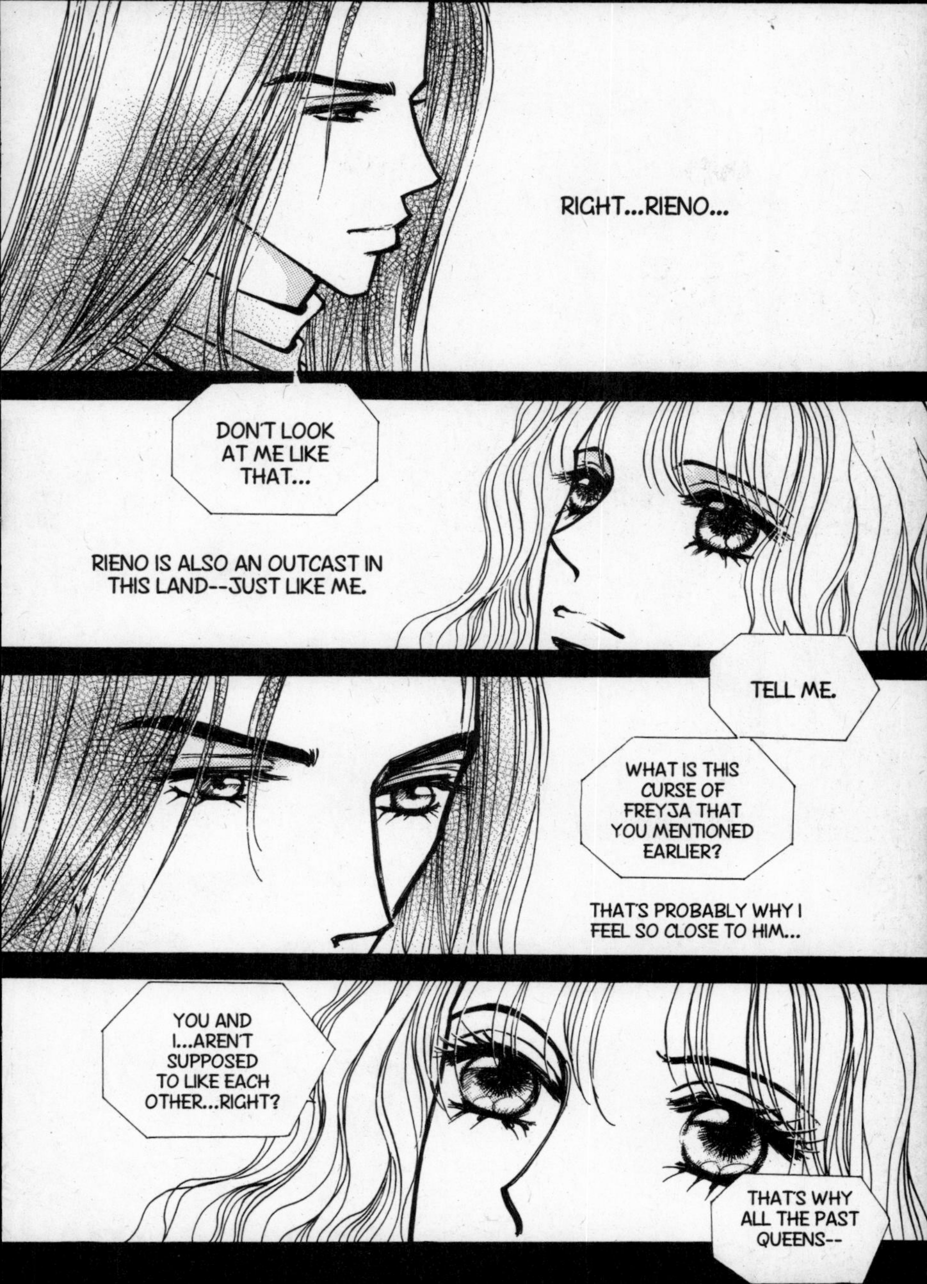
RIGHT...RIENO...
DON'T LOOK AT ME LIKE THAT...
RIENO IS ALSO AN OUTCAST IN THIS LAND--JUST LIKE ME.
TELL ME.
WHAT IS THIS CURSE OF FREYJA THAT YOU MENTIONED EARLIER?
THAT'S PROBABLY WHY I FEEL SO CLOSE TO HIM...
YOU AND I...AREN'T SUPPOSED TO LIKE EACH OTHER...RIGHT?
THAT'S WHY ALL THE PAST QUEENS--

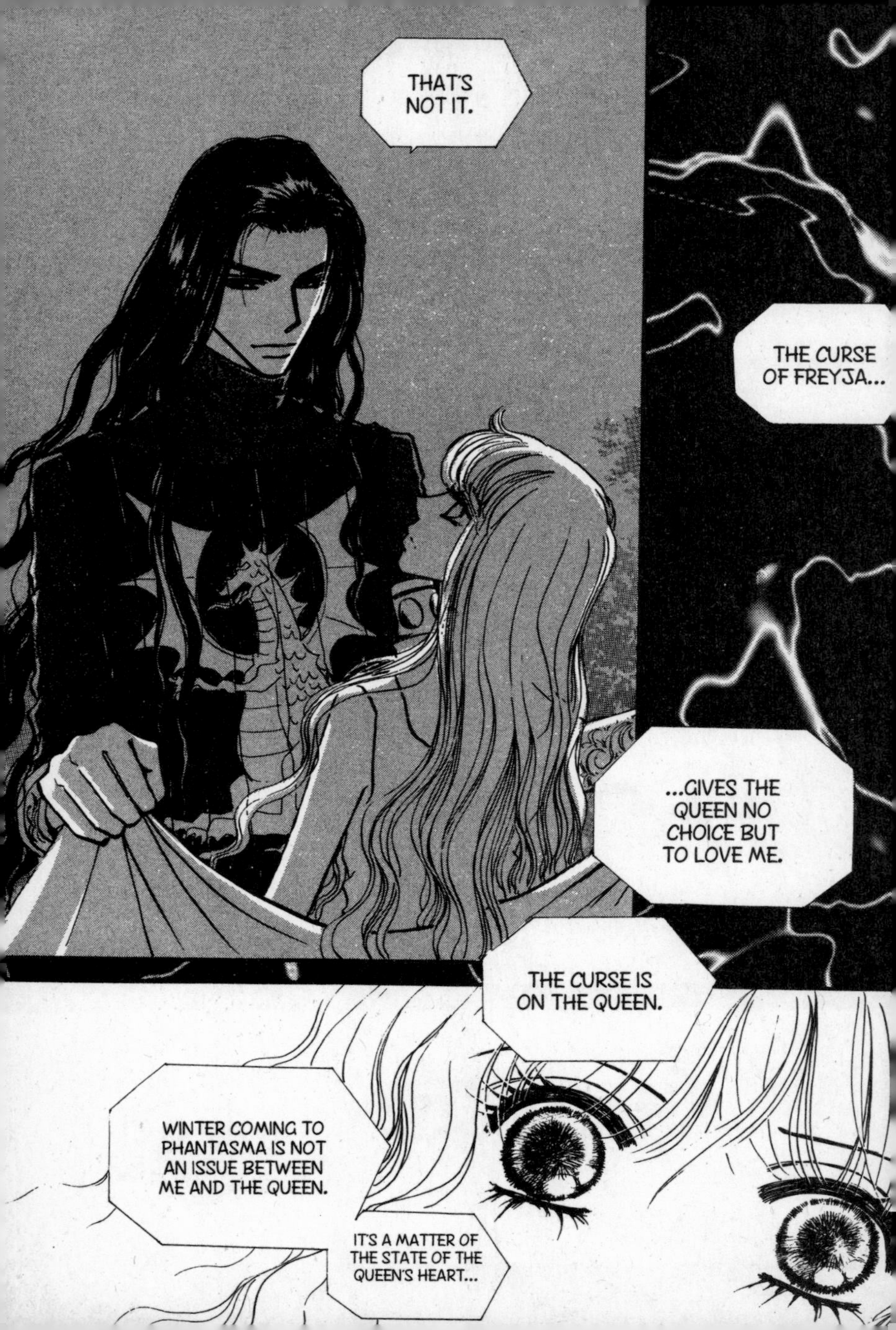
THAT'S NOT IT.
THE CURSE OF FREYJA...
...GIVES THE QUEEN NO CHOICE BUT TO LOVE ME.
THE CURSE IS ON THE QUEEN.
WINTER COMING TO PHANTASMA IS NOT AN ISSUE BETWEEN ME AND THE QUEEN.
IT'S A MATTER OF THE STATE OF THE QUEEN'S HEART...

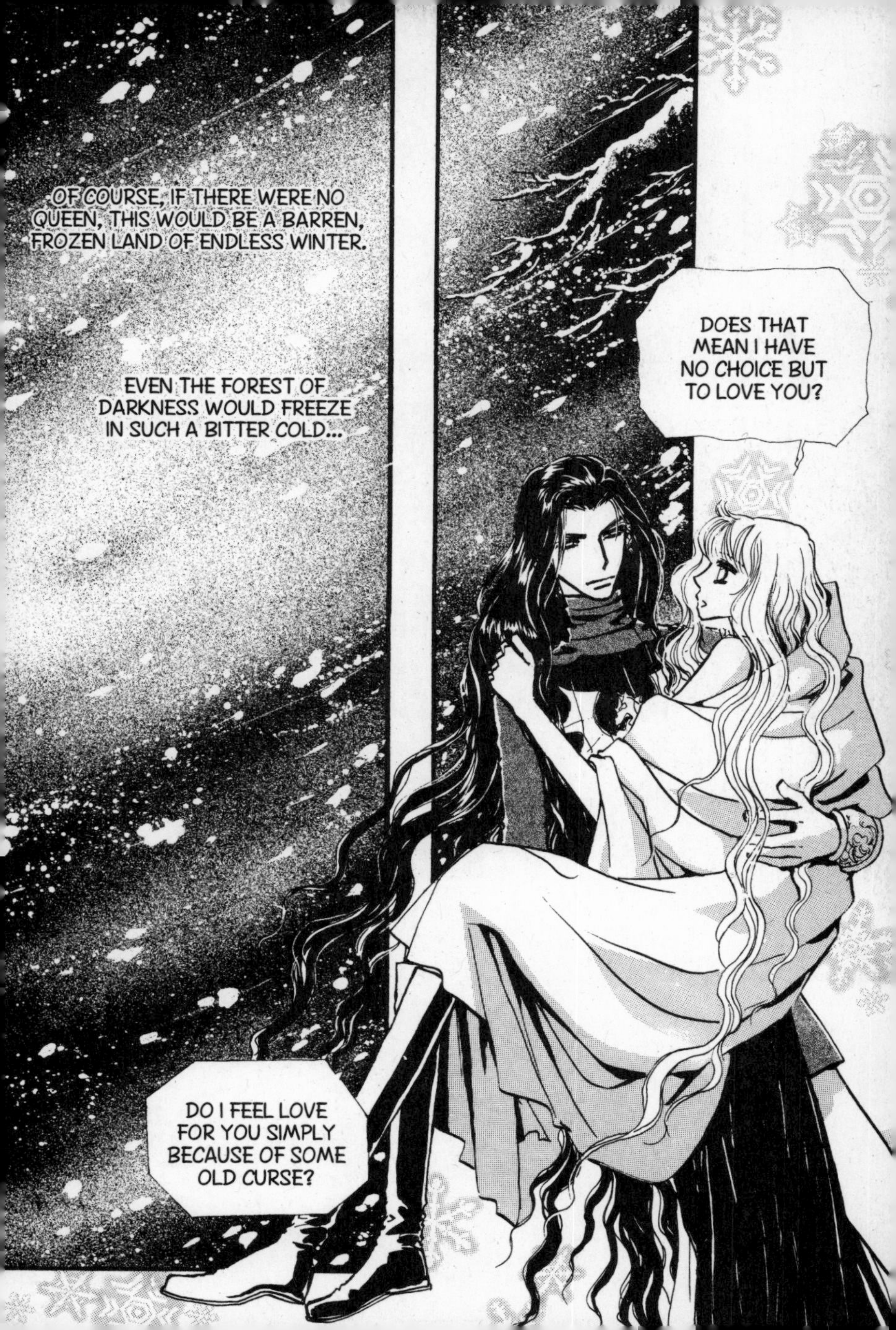
OF COURSE, IF THERE WERE NO QUEEN, THIS WOULD BE A BARREN, FROZEN LAND OF ENDLESS WINTER.
EVEN THE FOREST OF DARKNESS WOULD FREEZE IN SUCH A BITTER COLD...
DO I FEEL LOVE FOR YOU SIMPLY BECAUSE OF SOME OLD CURSE?
DOES THAT MEAN I HAVE NO CHOICE BUT TO LOVE YOU?

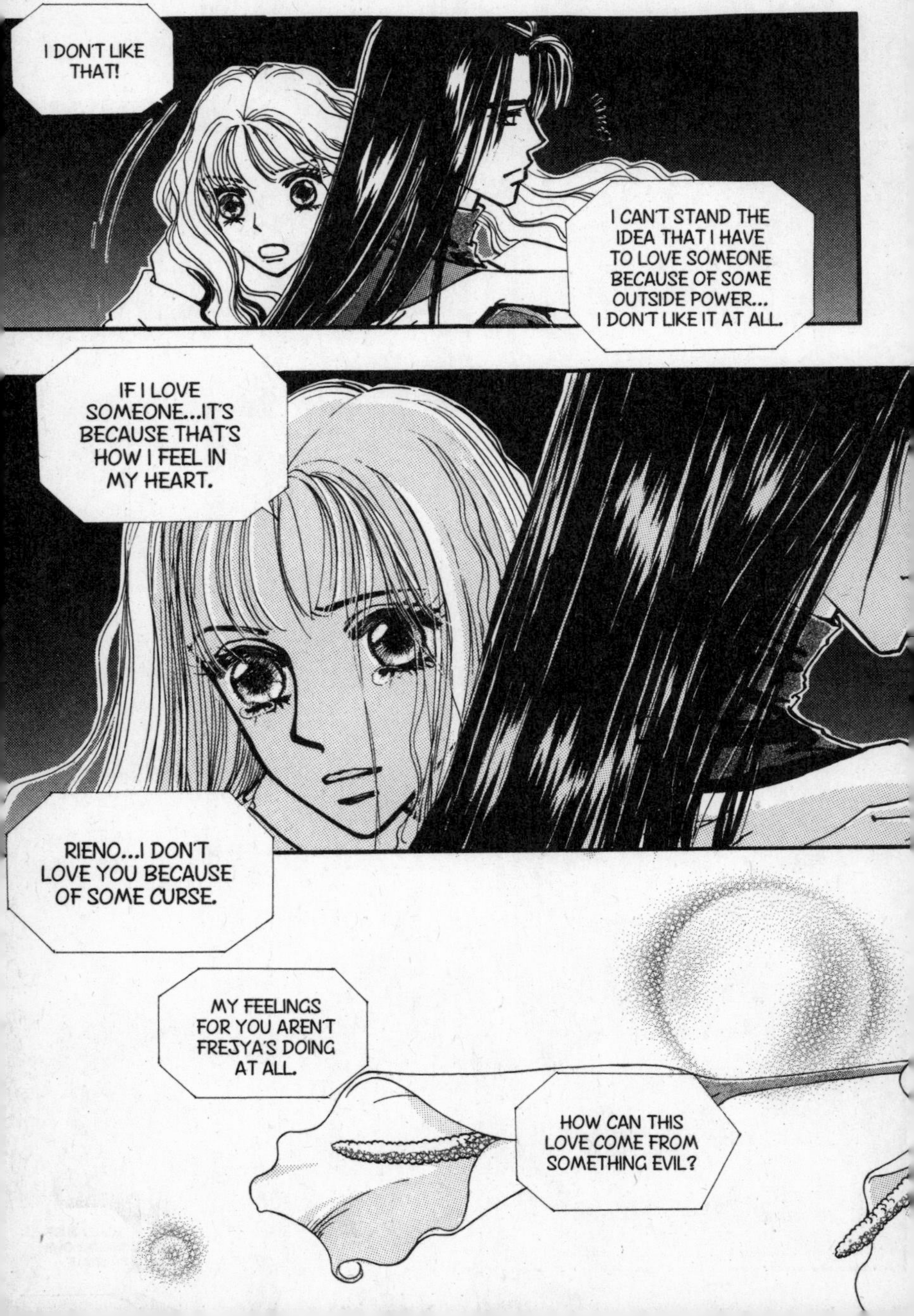
I DON'T LIKE THAT!
I CAN'T STAND THE IDEA THAT I HAVE TO LOVE SOMEONE BECAUSE OF SOME OUTSIDE POWER... I DON'T LIKE IT AT ALL.
IF I LOVE SOMEONE...IT'S BECAUSE THAT'S HOW I FEEL IN MY HEART.
RIENO...I DON'T LOVE YOU BECAUSE OF SOME CURSE.
MY FEELINGS FOR YOU AREN'T FREJYA'S DOING AT ALL.
HOW CAN THIS LOVE COME FROM SOMETHING EVIL?

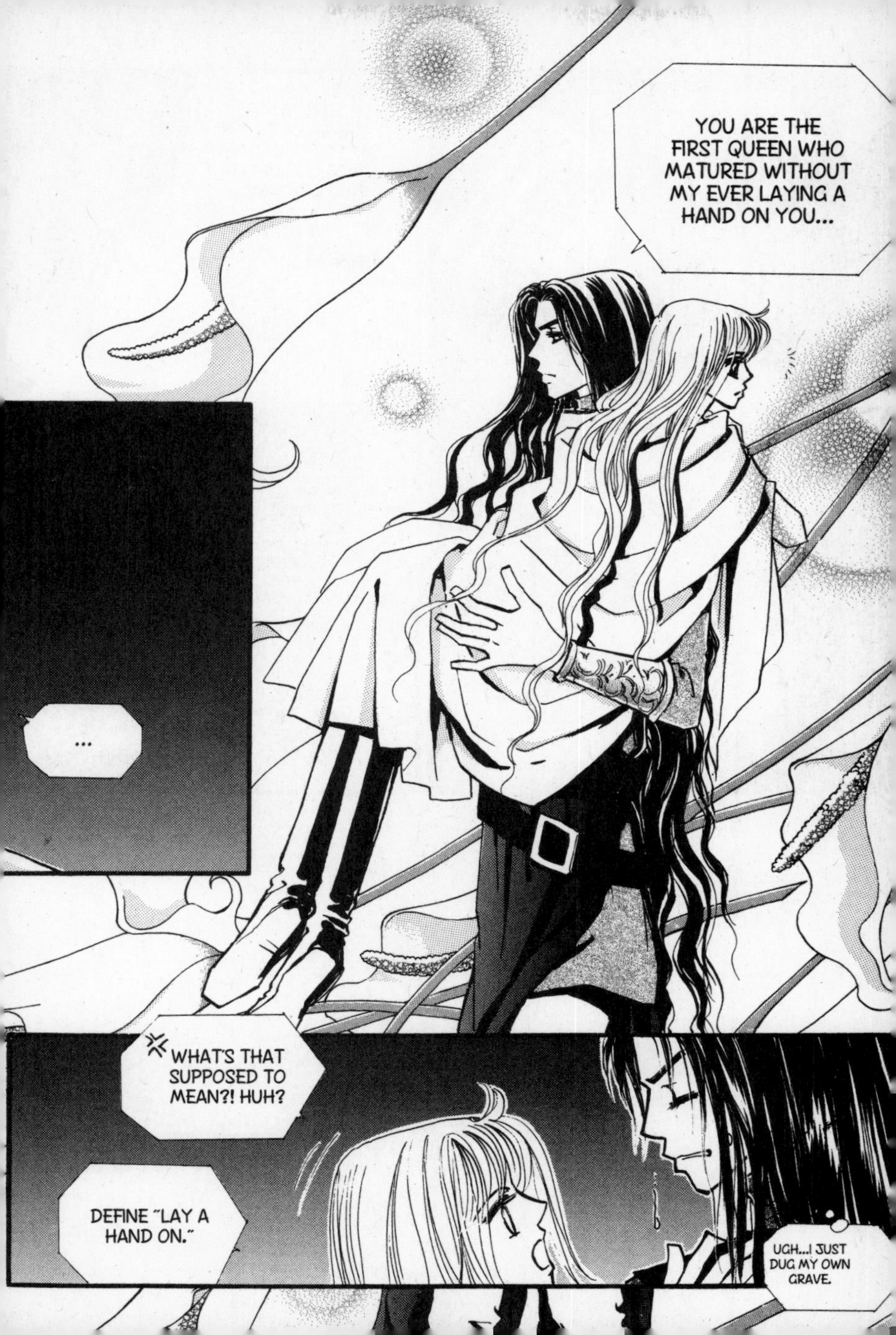
YOU ARE THE FIRST QUEEN WHO MATURED WITHOUT MY EVER LAYING A HAND ON YOU...
...
WHAT'S THAT SUPPOSED TO MEAN?! HUH?
DEFINE "LAY A HAND ON."
UGH...I JUST DUG MY OWN GRAVE.

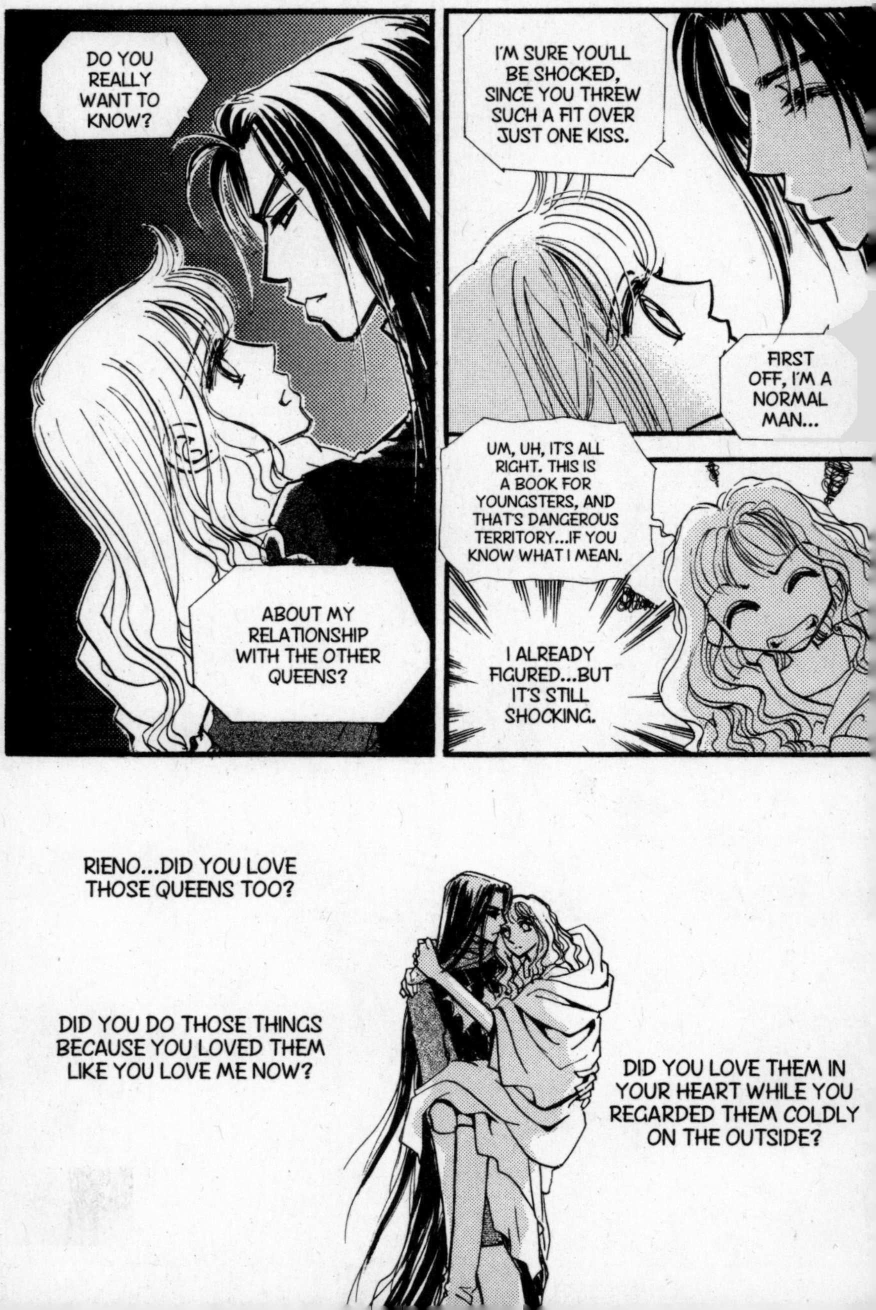
DO YOU REALLY WANT TO KNOW?
ABOUT MY RELATIONSHIP WITH THE OTHER QUEENS?
I'M SURE YOU'LL BE SHOCKED, SINCE YOU THREW SUCH A FIT OVER JUST ONE KISS.
FIRST OFF, I'M A NORMAL MAN...
UM, UH, IT'S ALL RIGHT. THIS IS A BOOK FOR YOUNGSTERS, AND THAT'S DANGEROUS TERRITORY...IF YOU KNOW WHAT I MEAN.
I ALREADY FIGURED...BUT IT'S STILL SHOCKING.
RIENO...DID YOU LOVE THOSE QUEENS TOO?
DID YOU DO THOSE THINGS BECAUSE YOU LOVED THEM LIKE YOU LOVE ME NOW?
DID YOU LOVE THEM IN YOUR HEART WHILE YOU REGARDED THEM COLDLY ON THE OUTSIDE?

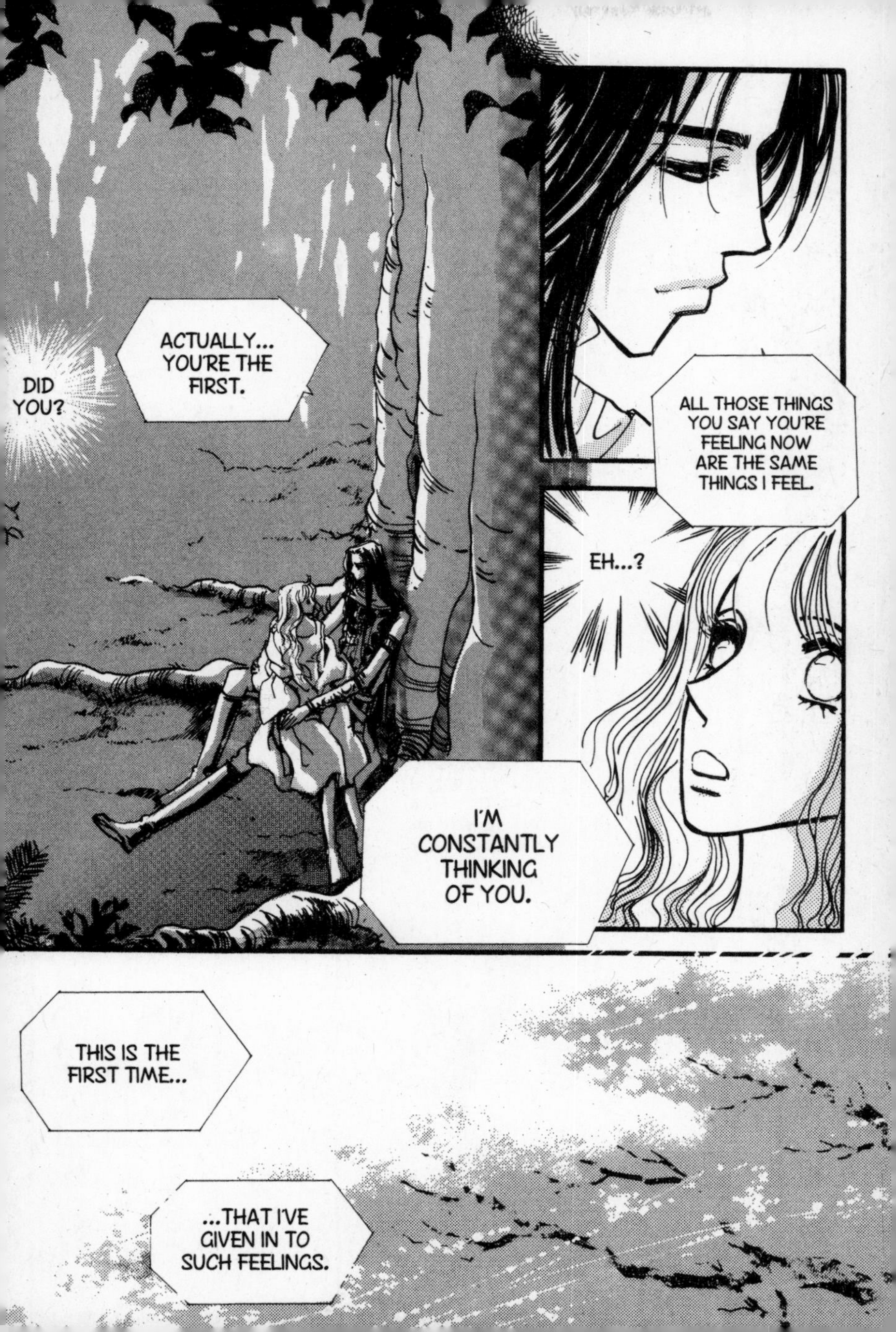
DID YOU?
ACTUALLY... YOU'RE THE FIRST.
ALL THOSE THINGS YOU SAY YOU'RE FEELING NOW ARE THE SAME THINGS I FEEL.
EH...?
I'M CONSTANTLY THINKING OF YOU.
THIS IS THE FIRST TIME...
...THAT I'VE GIVEN IN TO SUCH FEELINGS.

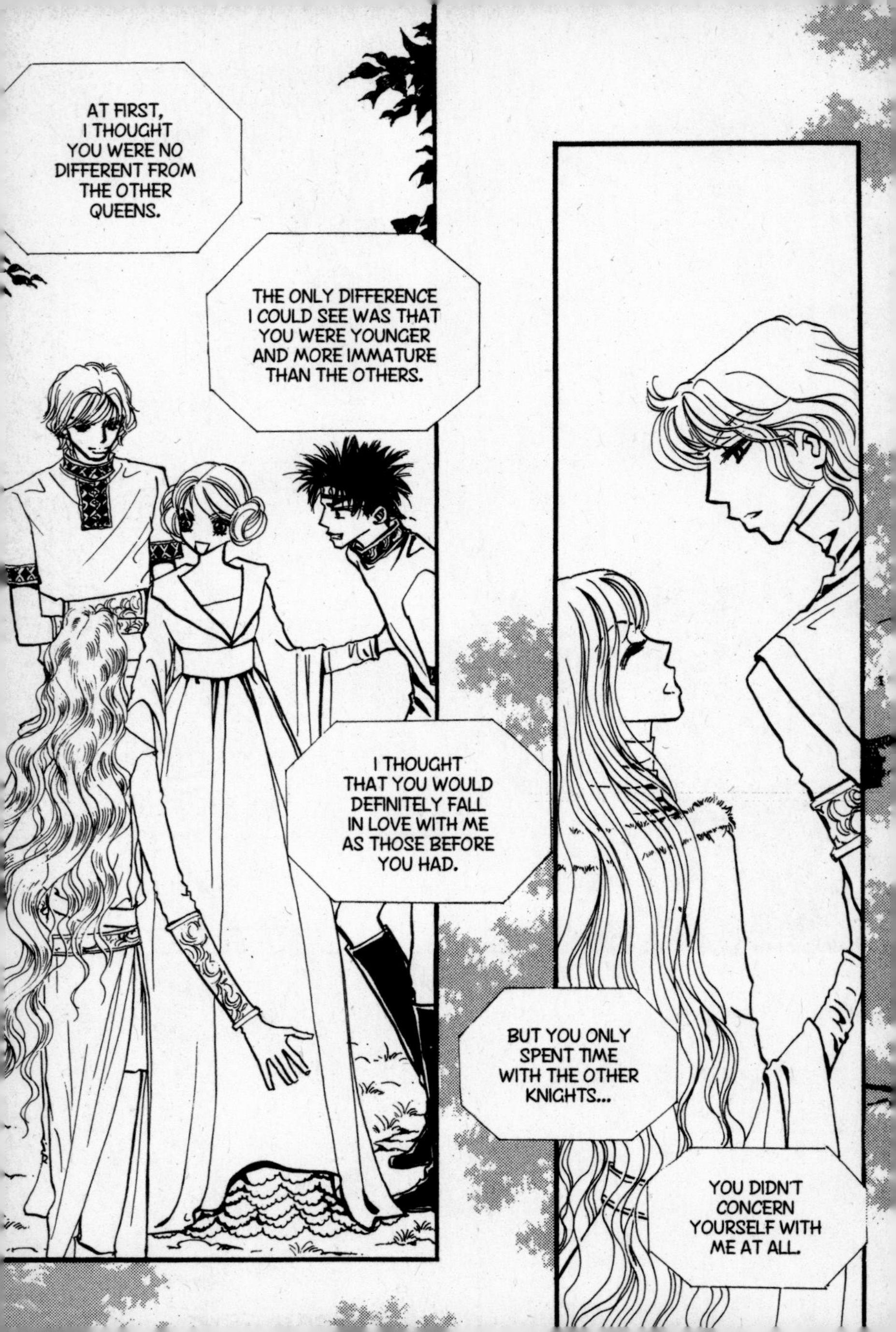
AT FIRST, I THOUGHT YOU WERE NO DIFFERENT FROM THE OTHER QUEENS.
THE ONLY DIFFERENCE I COULD SEE WAS THAT YOU WERE YOUNGER AND MORE IMMATURE THAN THE OTHERS.
I THOUGHT THAT YOU WOULD DEFINITELY FALL IN LOVE WITH ME AS THOSE BEFORE YOU HAD.
BUT YOU ONLY SPENT TIME WITH THE OTHER KNIGHTS...
YOU DIDN'T CONCERN YOURSELF WITH ME AT ALL.

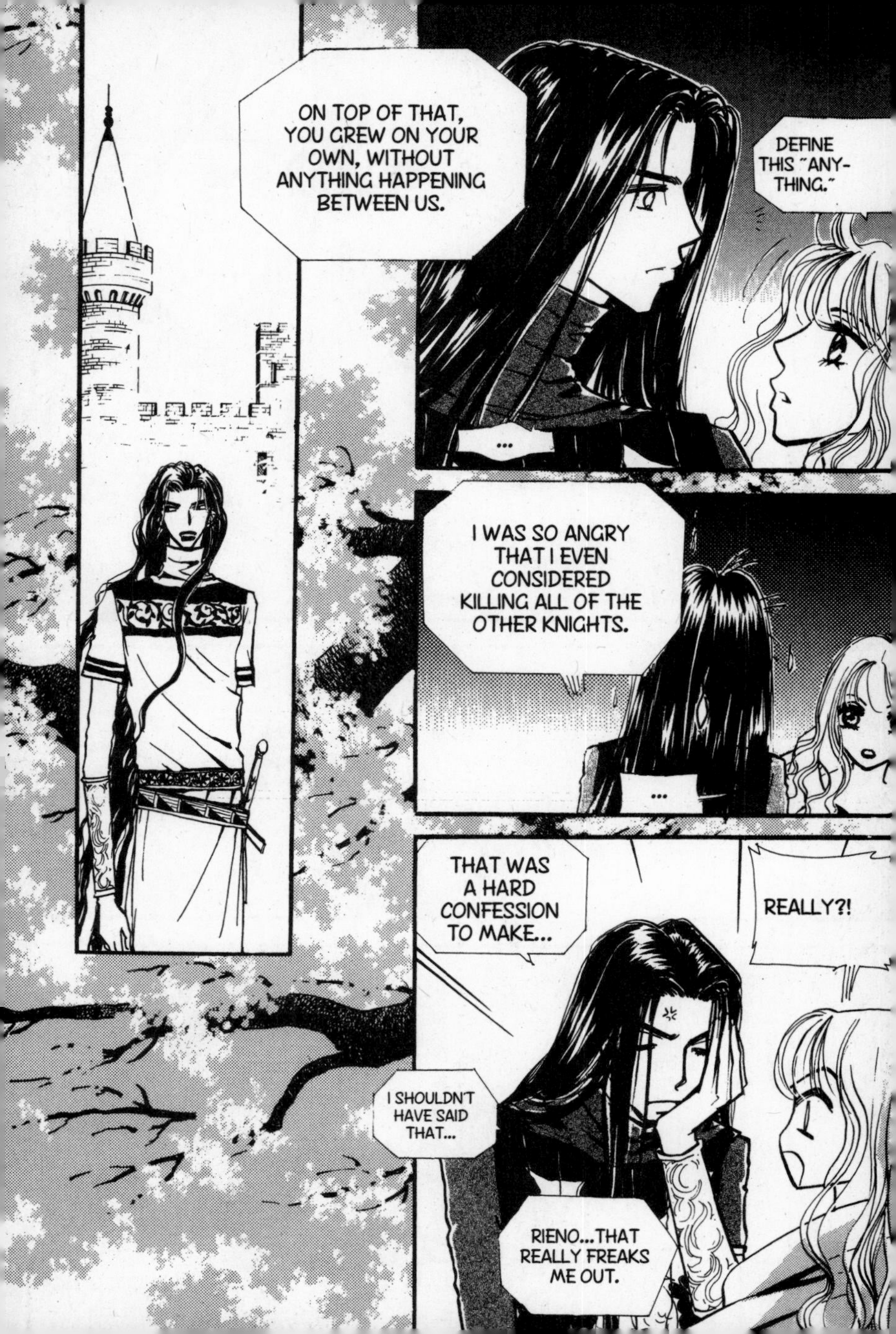
ON TOP OF THAT, YOU GREW ON YOUR OWN, WITHOUT ANYTHING HAPPENING BETWEEN US.
DEFINE THIS "ANY-THING."
...
I WAS SO ANGRY THAT I EVEN CONSIDERED KILLING ALL OF THE OTHER KNIGHTS.
...
THAT WAS A HARD CONFESSION TO MAKE...
REALLY?!
I SHOULDN'T HAVE SAID THAT...
RIENO...THAT REALLY FREAKS ME OUT.

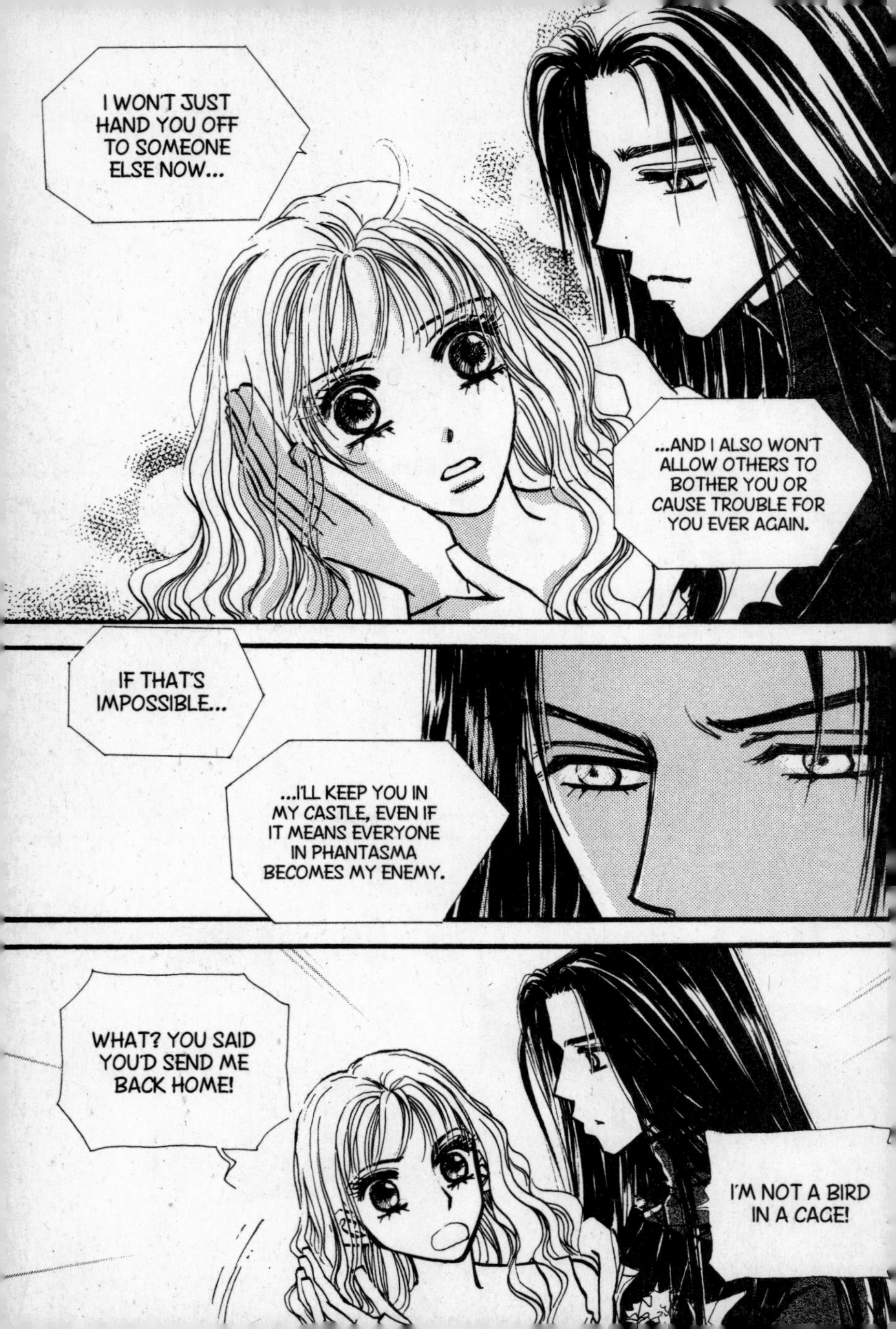
I WON'T JUST HAND YOU OFF TO SOMEONE ELSE NOW...
...AND I ALSO WON'T ALLOW OTHERS TO BOTHER YOU OR CAUSE TROUBLE FOR YOU EVER AGAIN.
IF THAT'S IMPOSSIBLE...
...I'LL KEEP YOU IN MY CASTLE, EVEN IF IT MEANS EVERYONE IN PHANTASMA BECOMES MY ENEMY.
WHAT? YOU SAID YOU'D SEND ME BACK HOME!
I'M NOT A BIRD IN A CAGE!

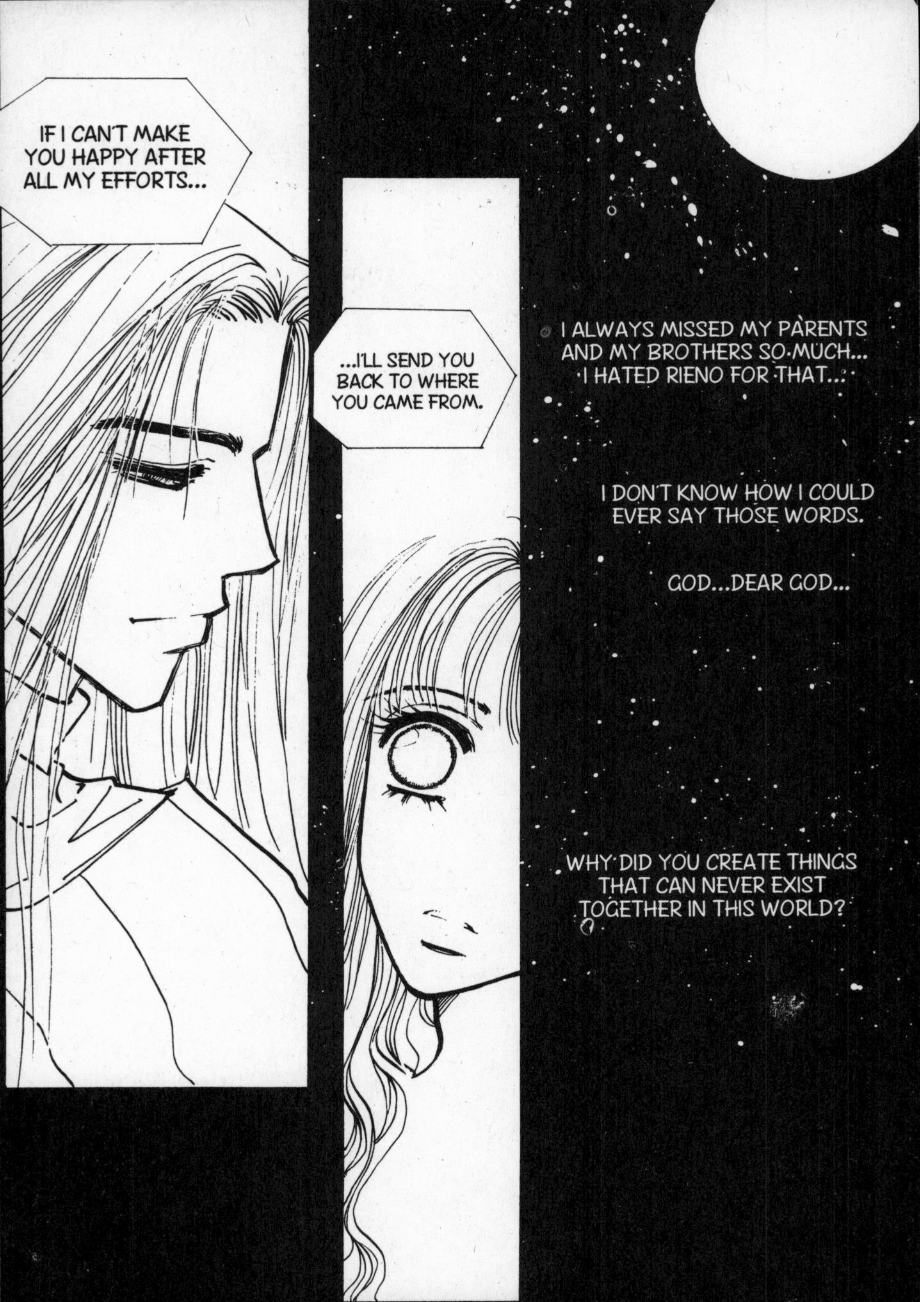
IF I CAN'T MAKE YOU HAPPY AFTER ALL MY EFFORTS...
...I'LL SEND YOU BACK TO WHERE YOU CAME FROM.
I ALWAYS MISSED MY PARENTS AND MY BROTHERS SO MUCH... I HATED RIENO FOR THAT...
I DON'T KNOW HOW I COULD EVER SAY THOSE WORDS.
GOD...DEAR GOD...
WHY DID YOU CREATE THINGS THAT CAN NEVER EXIST TOGETHER IN THIS WORLD?

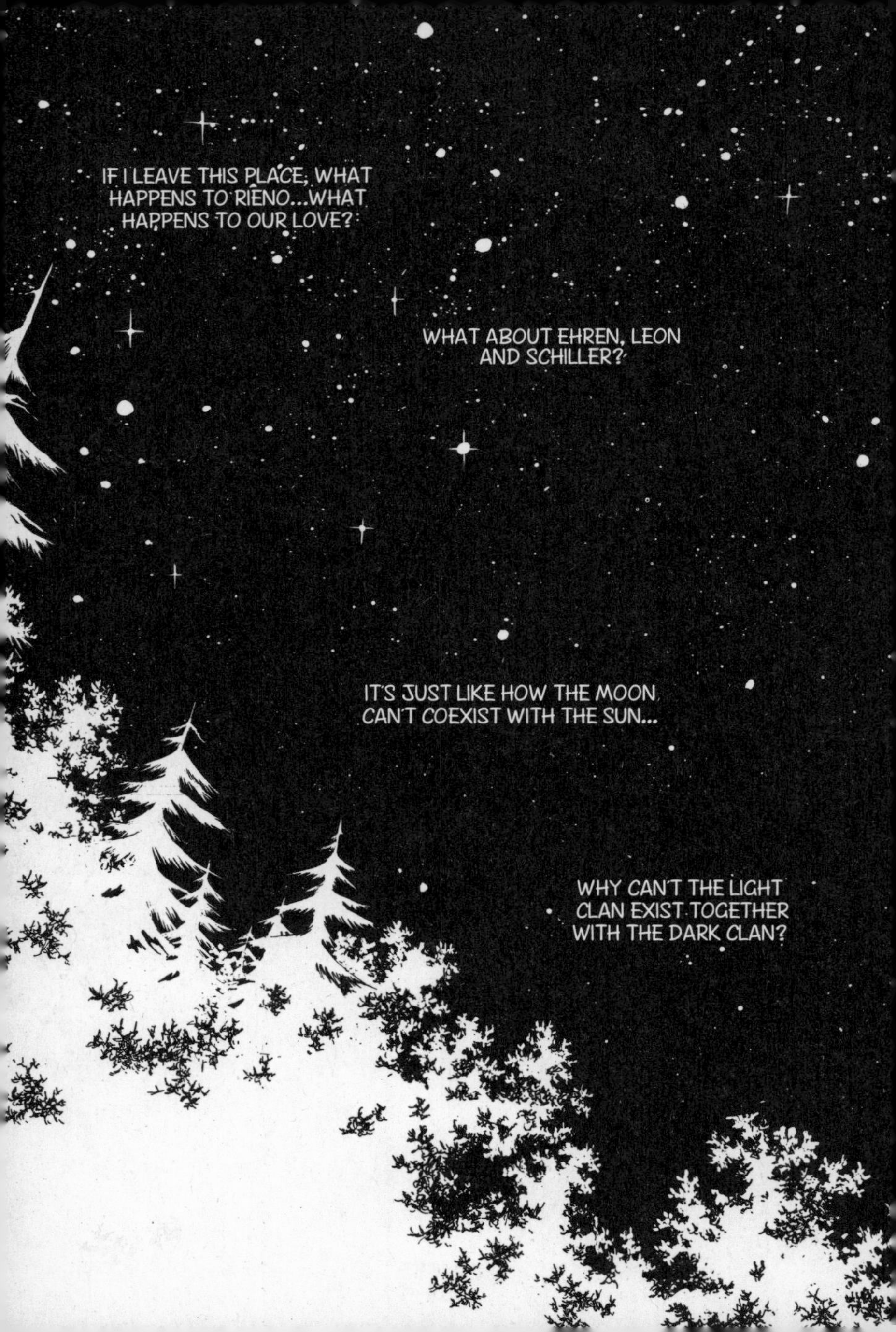
IF I LEAVE THIS PLACE, WHAT HAPPENS TO RIENO...WHAT HAPPENS TO OUR LOVE?
WHAT ABOUT EHREN, LEON AND SCHILLER?
IT'S JUST LIKE HOW THE MOON CAN'T COEXIST WITH THE SUN...
WHY CAN'T THE LIGHT CLAN EXIST TOGETHER WITH THE DARK CLAN?

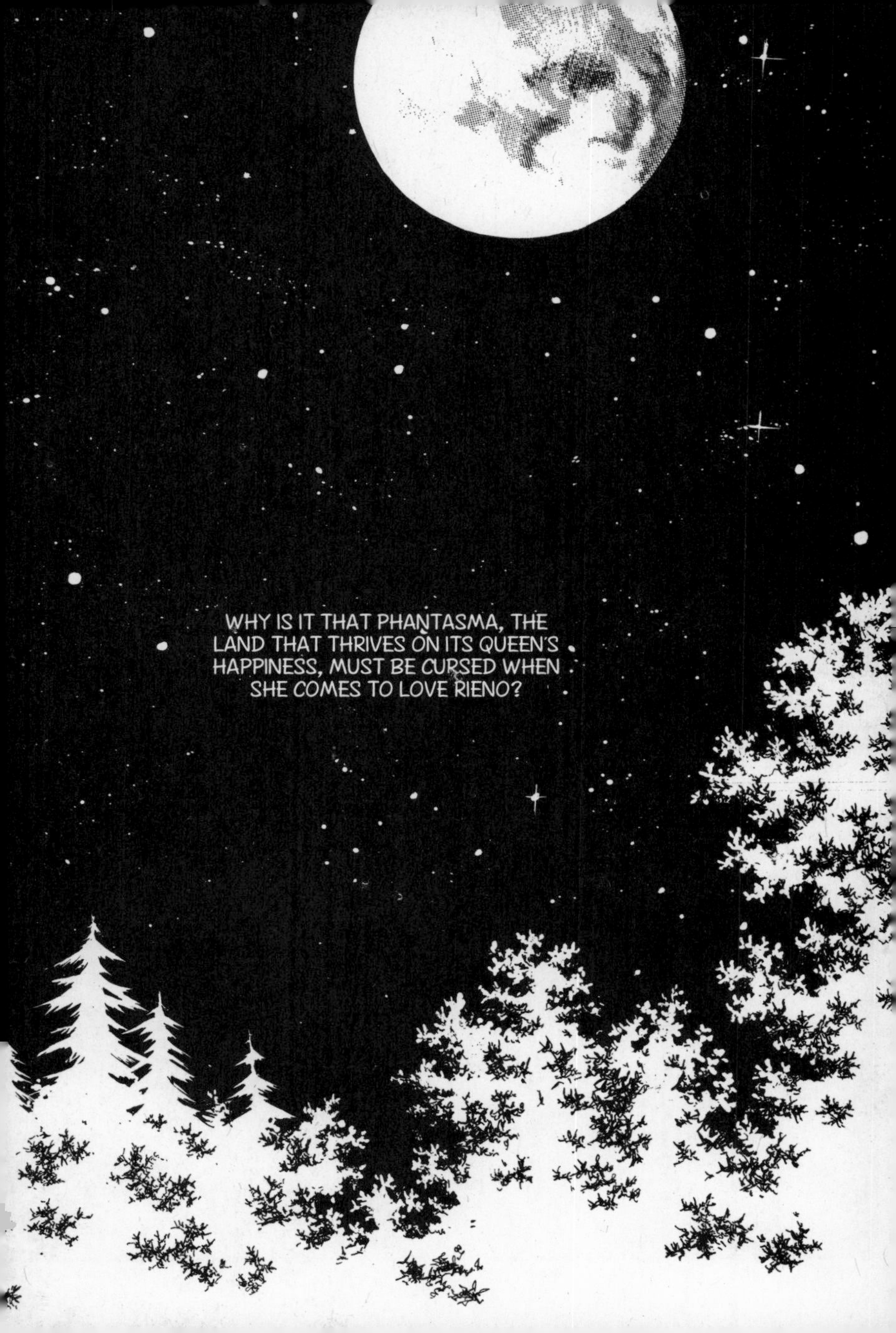
WHY IS IT THAT PHANTASMA, THE LAND THAT THRIVES ON ITS QUEEN'S HAPPINESS, MUST BE CURSED WHEN SHE COMES TO LOVE RIENO?

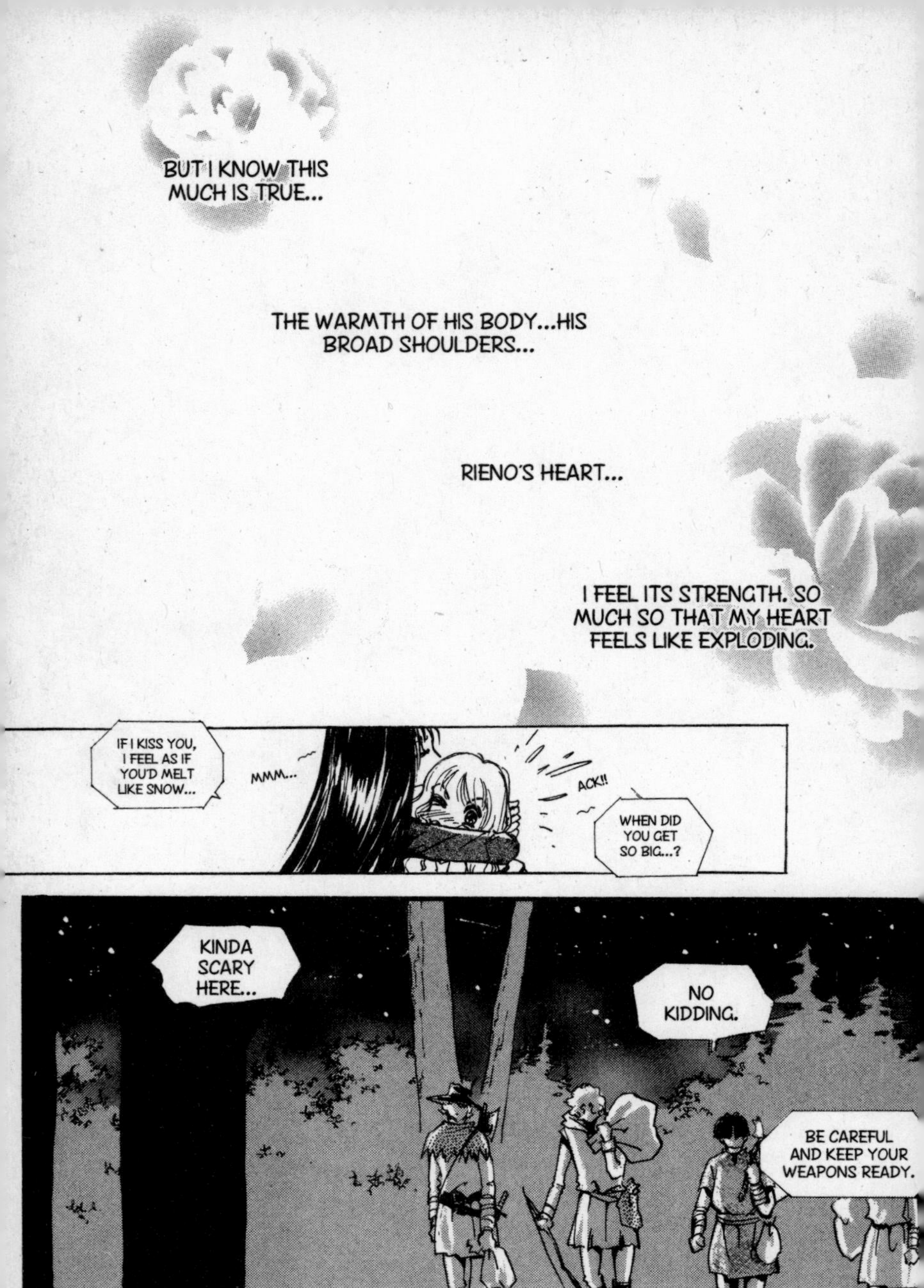
BUT I KNOW THIS MUCH IS TRUE...
THE WARMTH OF HIS BODY...HIS BROAD SHOULDERS...
RIENO'S HEART...
I FEEL ITS STRENGTH. SO MUCH SO THAT MY HEART FEELS LIKE EXPLODING.
IF I KISS YOU, I FEEL AS IF YOU'D MELT LIKE SNOW...
MMM...
ACK!!
WHEN DID YOU GET SO BIG...?
KINDA SCARY HERE...
NO KIDDING.
BE CAREFUL AND KEEP YOUR WEAPONS READY.

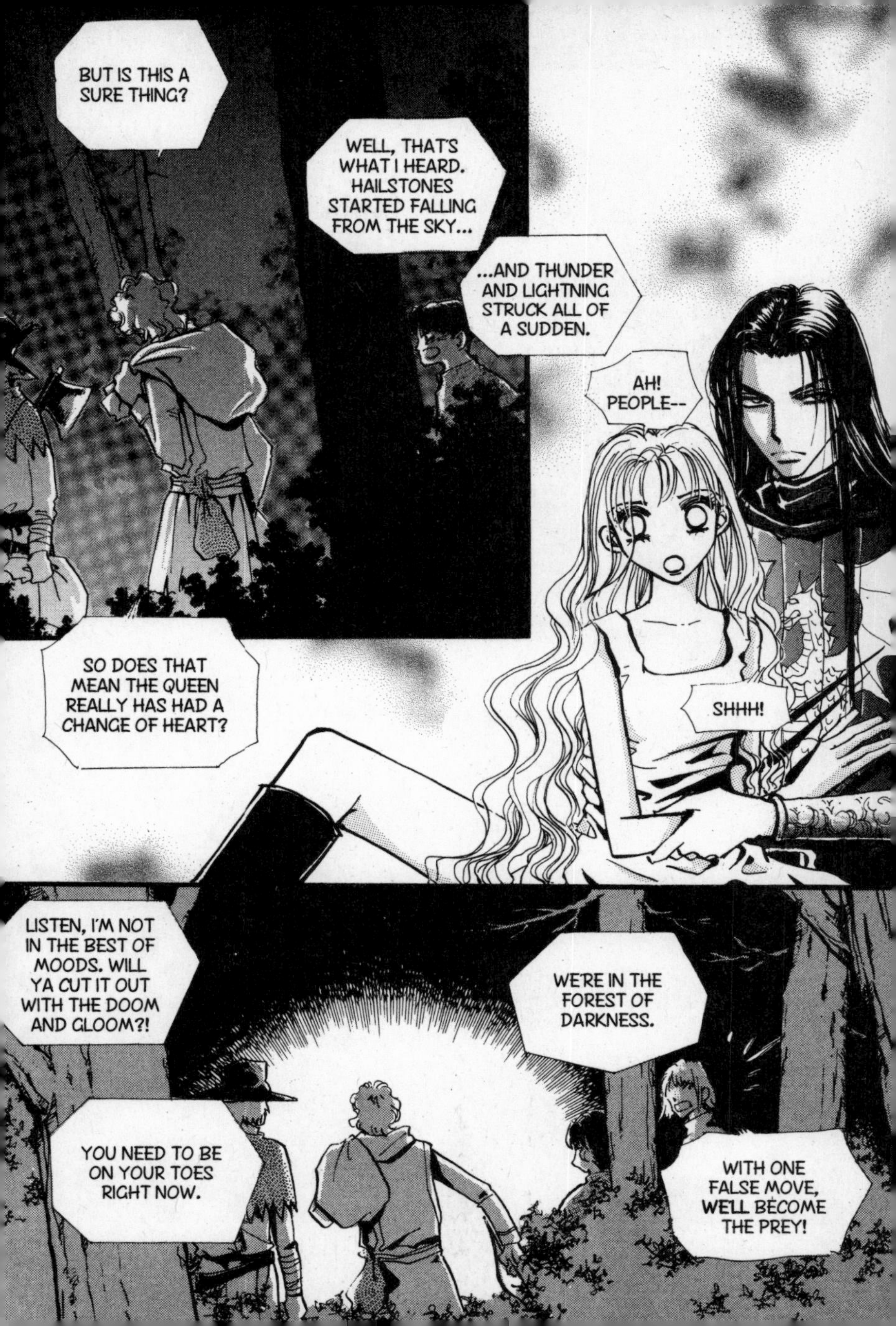
BUT IS THIS A SURE THING?
WELL, THAT'S WHAT I HEARD. HAILSTONES STARTED FALLING FROM THE SKY...
...AND THUNDER AND LIGHTNING STRUCK ALL OF A SUDDEN.
AH! PEOPLE--
SO DOES THAT MEAN THE QUEEN REALLY HAS HAD A CHANGE OF HEART?
SHHH!
LISTEN, I'M NOT IN THE BEST OF MOODS. WILL YA CUT IT OUT WITH THE DOOM AND GLOOM?!
YOU NEED TO BE ON YOUR TOES RIGHT NOW.
WE'RE IN THE FOREST OF DARKNESS.
WITH ONE FALSE MOVE, WE'LL BECOME THE PREY!

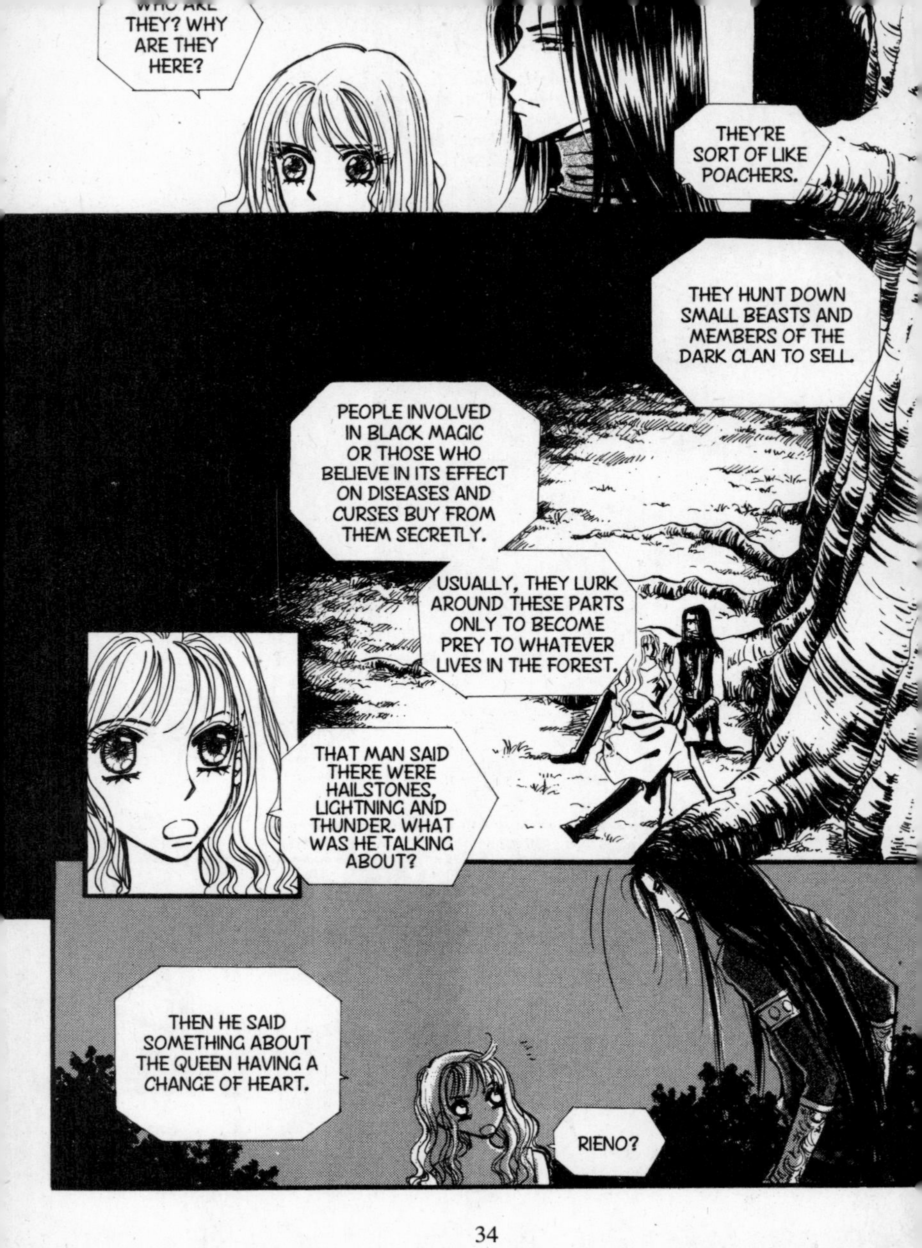
THEY? WHY ARE THEY HERE?
THEY'RE SORT OF LIKE POACHERS.
THEY HUNT DOWN SMALL BEASTS AND MEMBERS OF THE DARK CLAN TO SELL.
PEOPLE INVOLVED IN BLACK MAGIC OR THOSE WHO BELIEVE IN ITS EFFECT ON DISEASES AND CURSES BUY FROM THEM SECRETLY.
USUALLY, THEY LURK AROUND THESE PARTS ONLY TO BECOME PREY TO WHATEVER LIVES IN THE FOREST.
THAT MAN SAID THERE WERE HAILSTONES, LIGHTNING AND THUNDER. WHAT WAS HE TALKING ABOUT?
THEN HE SAID SOMETHING ABOUT THE QUEEN HAVING A CHANGE OF HEART.
RIENO?

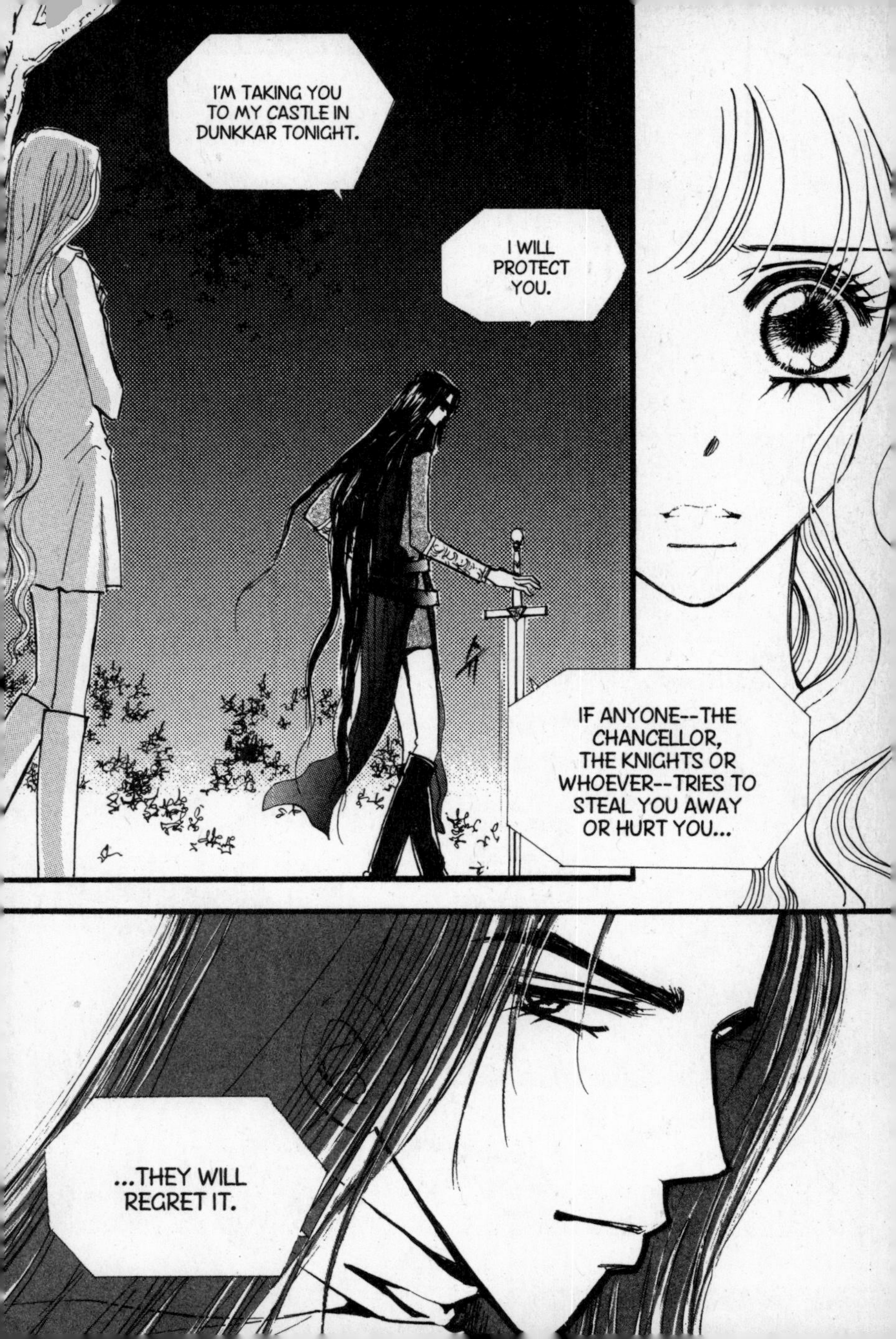
I'M TAKING YOU TO MY CASTLE IN DUNKKAR TONIGHT.
I WILL PROTECT YOU.
IF ANYONE--THE CHANCELLOR, THE KNIGHTS OR WHOEVER--TRIES TO STEAL YOU AWAY OR HURT YOU...
...THEY WILL REGRET IT.

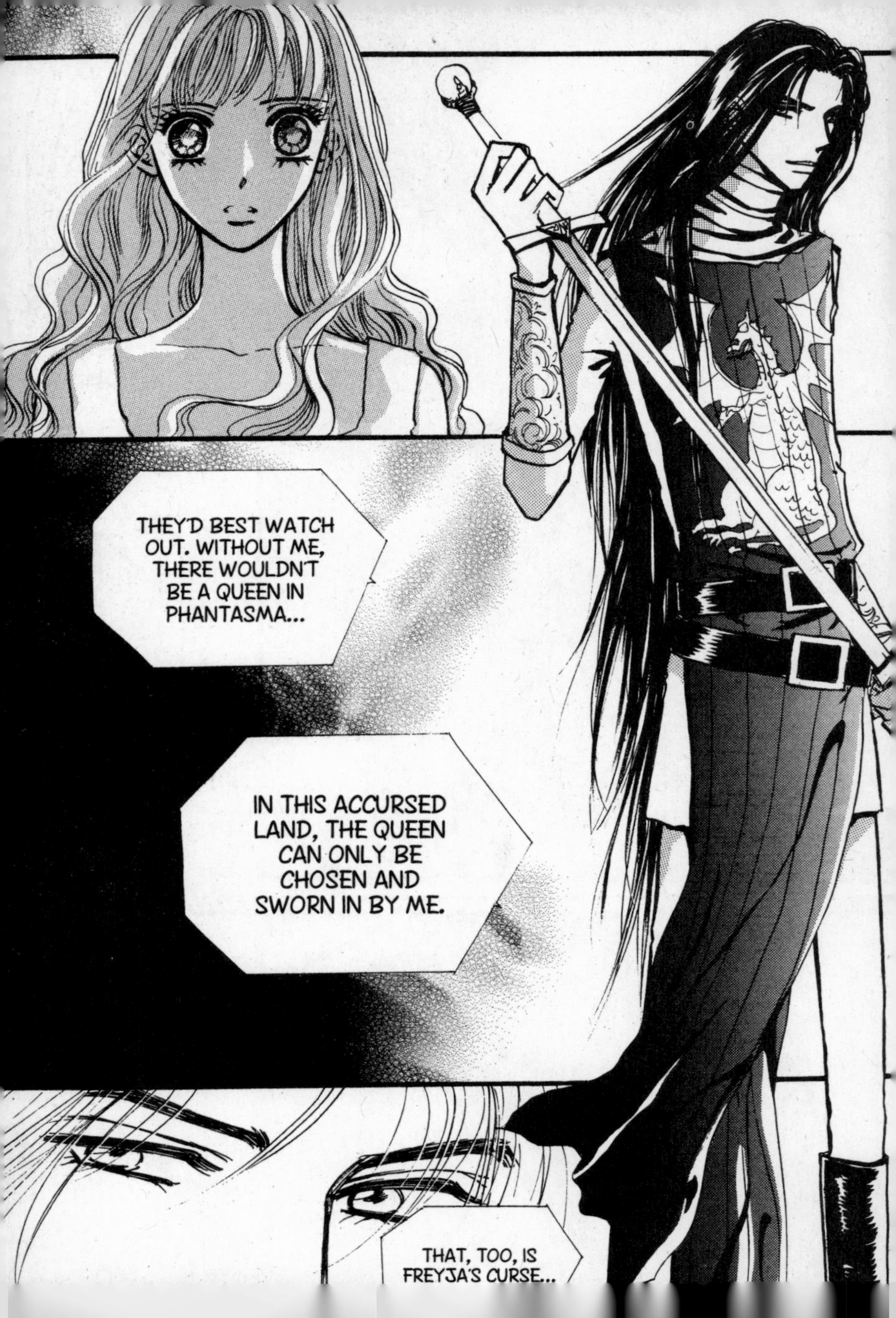
THEY'D BEST WATCH OUT. WITHOUT ME, THERE WOULDN'T BE A QUEEN IN PHANTASMA...
IN THIS ACCURSED LAND, THE QUEEN CAN ONLY BE CHOSEN AND SWORN IN BY ME.
THAT, TOO, IS FREYJA'S CURSE...

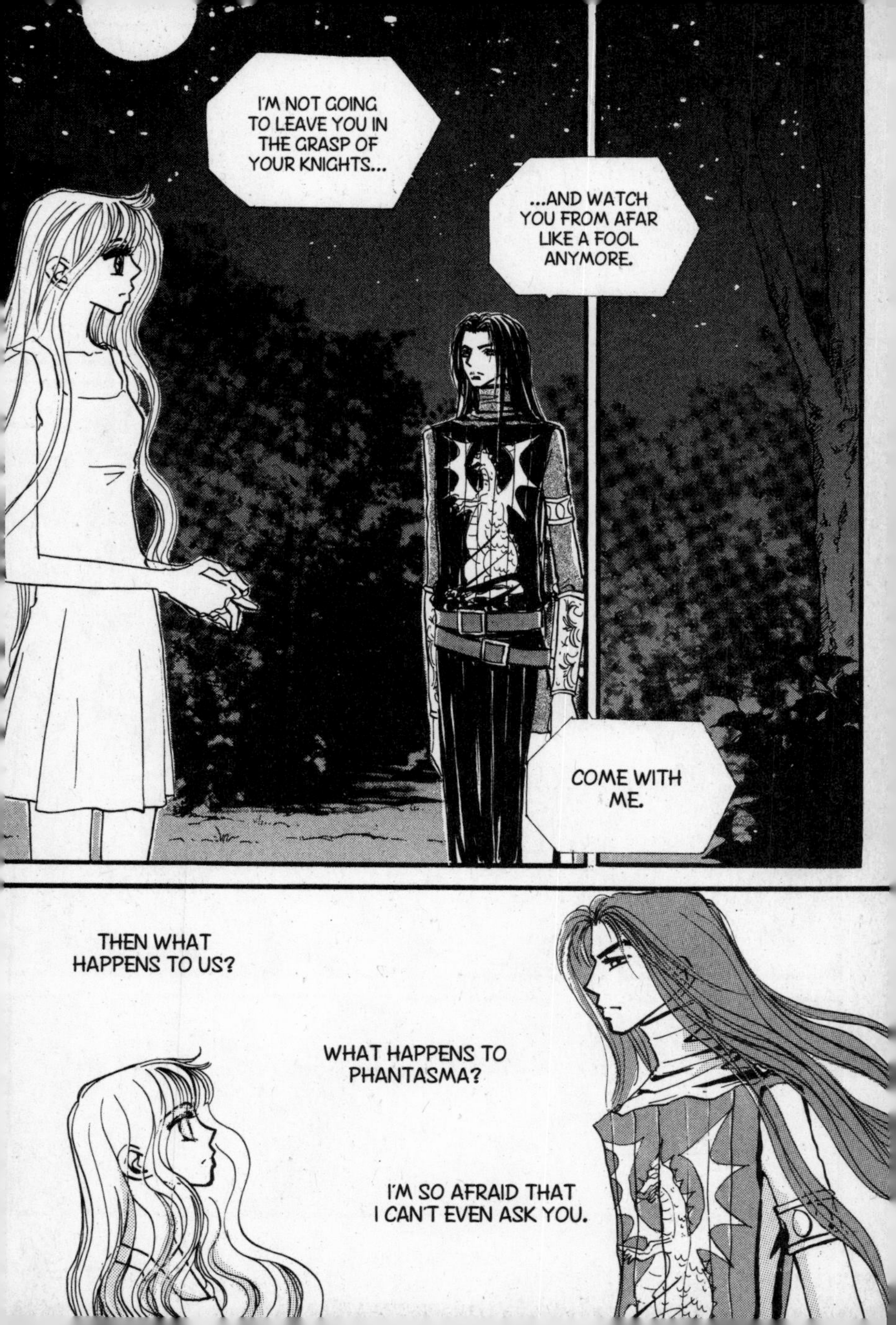
I'M NOT GOING TO LEAVE YOU IN THE GRASP OF YOUR KNIGHTS...
...AND WATCH YOU FROM AFAR LIKE A FOOL ANYMORE.
COME WITH ME.
THEN WHAT HAPPENS TO US?
WHAT HAPPENS TO PHANTASMA?
I'M SO AFRAID THAT I CAN'T EVEN ASK YOU.

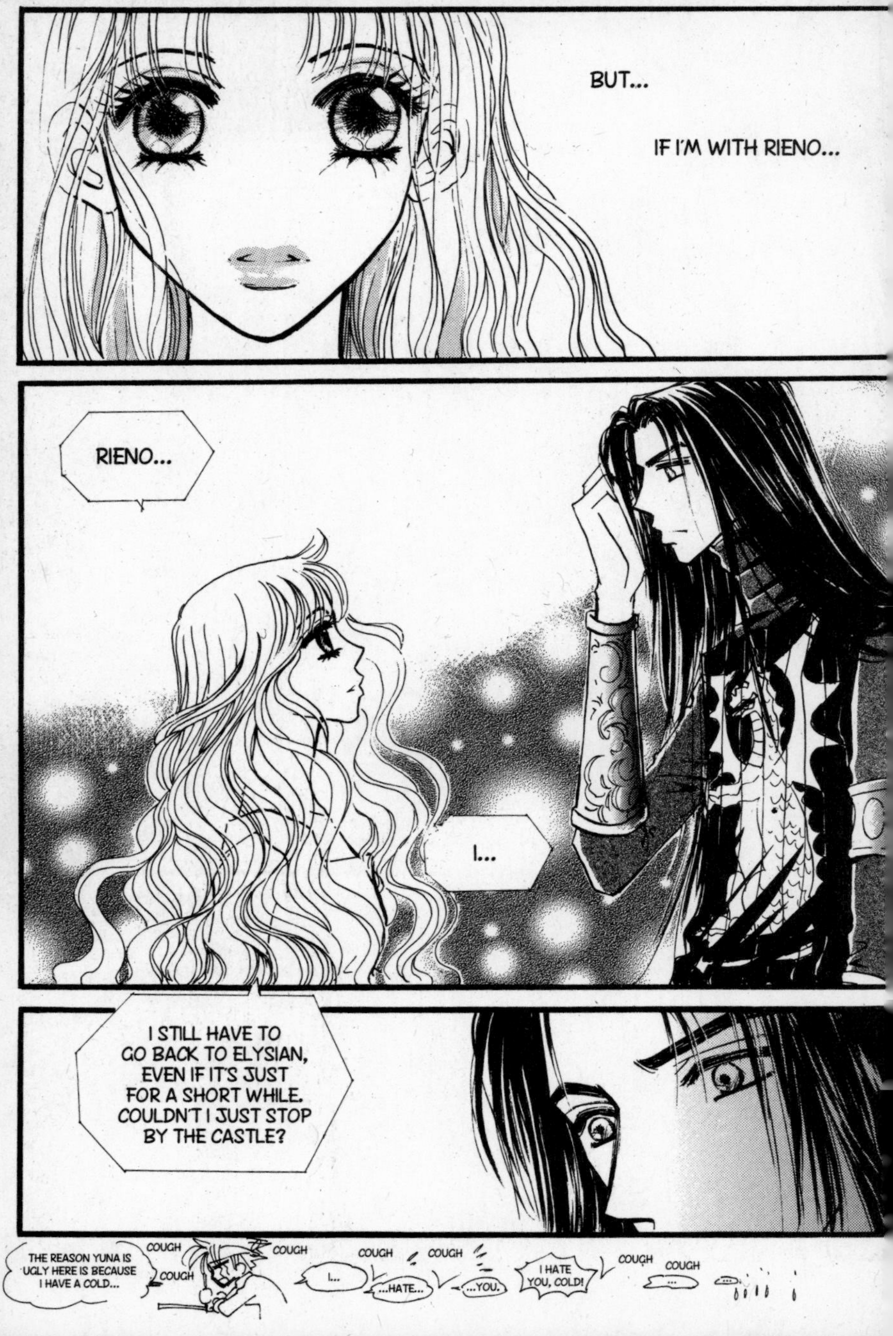
BUT...
IF I'M WITH RIENO...
RIENO...
I...
I STILL HAVE TO GO BACK TO ELYSIAN, EVEN IF IT'S JUST FOR A SHORT WHILE. COULDN'T I JUST STOP BY THE CASTLE?
THE REASON YUNA IS UGLY HERE IS BECAUSE I HAVE A COLD...
COUGH
COUGH
COUGH
COUGH
I...
COUGH
...HATE...
...YOU.
I HATE YOU, COLD!
COUGH
COUGH
...

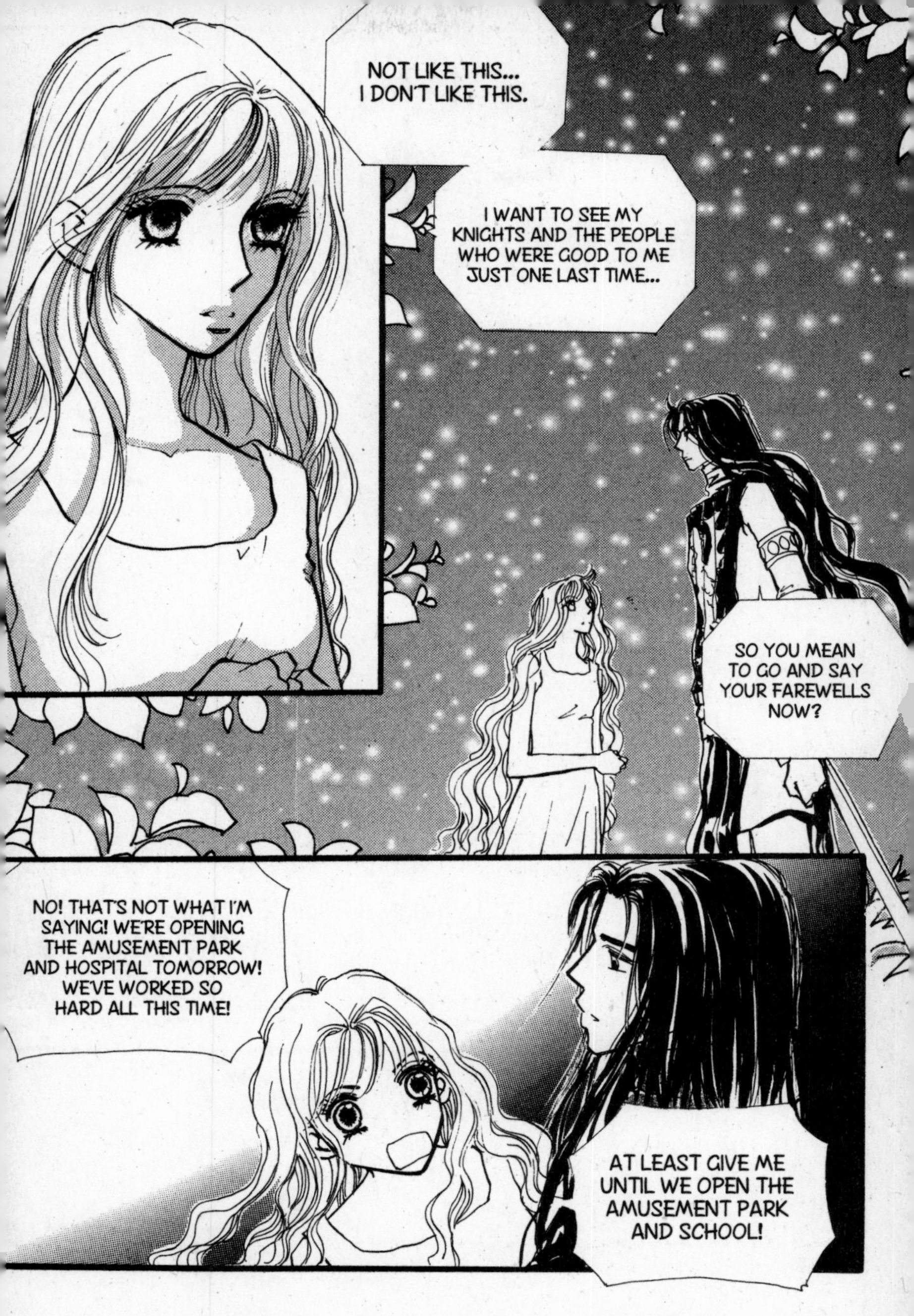
NOT LIKE THIS... I DON'T LIKE THIS.
I WANT TO SEE MY KNIGHTS AND THE PEOPLE WHO WERE GOOD TO ME JUST ONE LAST TIME...
SO YOU MEAN TO GO AND SAY YOUR FAREWELLS NOW?
NO! THAT'S NOT WHAT I'M SAYING! WE'RE OPENING THE AMUSEMENT PARK AND HOSPITAL TOMORROW! WE'VE WORKED SO HARD ALL THIS TIME!
AT LEAST GIVE ME UNTIL WE OPEN THE AMUSEMENT PARK AND SCHOOL!

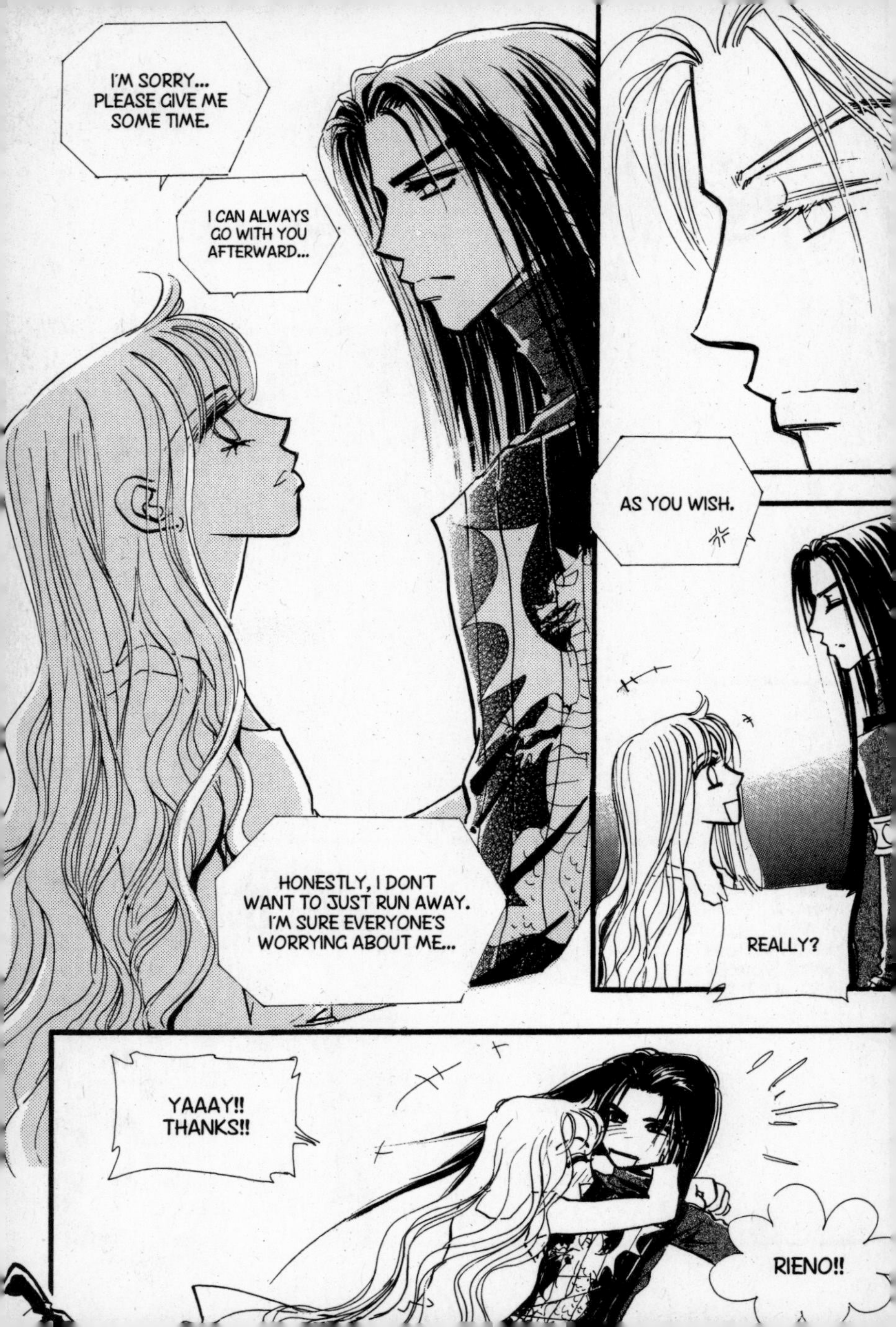
I'M SORRY... PLEASE GIVE ME SOME TIME.
I CAN ALWAYS GO WITH YOU AFTERWARD...
HONESTLY, I DON'T WANT TO JUST RUN AWAY. I'M SURE EVERYONE'S WORRYING ABOUT ME...
AS YOU WISH.
REALLY?
YAAAY!! THANKS!!
RIENO!!

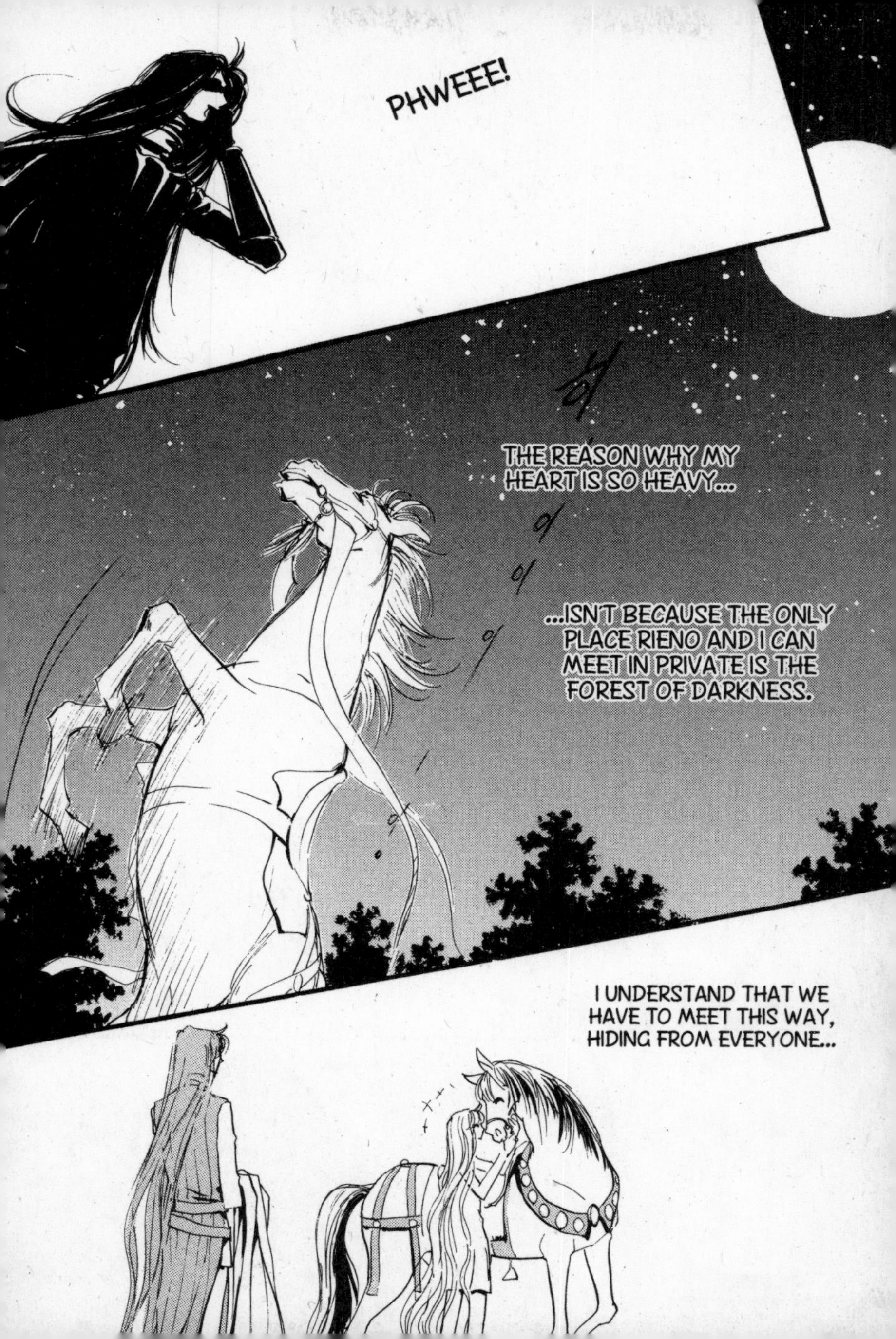
PHWEEE!
THE REASON WHY MY HEART IS SO HEAVY...
...ISN'T BECAUSE THE ONLY PLACE RIENO AND I CAN MEET IN PRIVATE IS THE FOREST OF DARKNESS.
I UNDERSTAND THAT WE HAVE TO MEET THIS WAY, HIDING FROM EVERYONE...

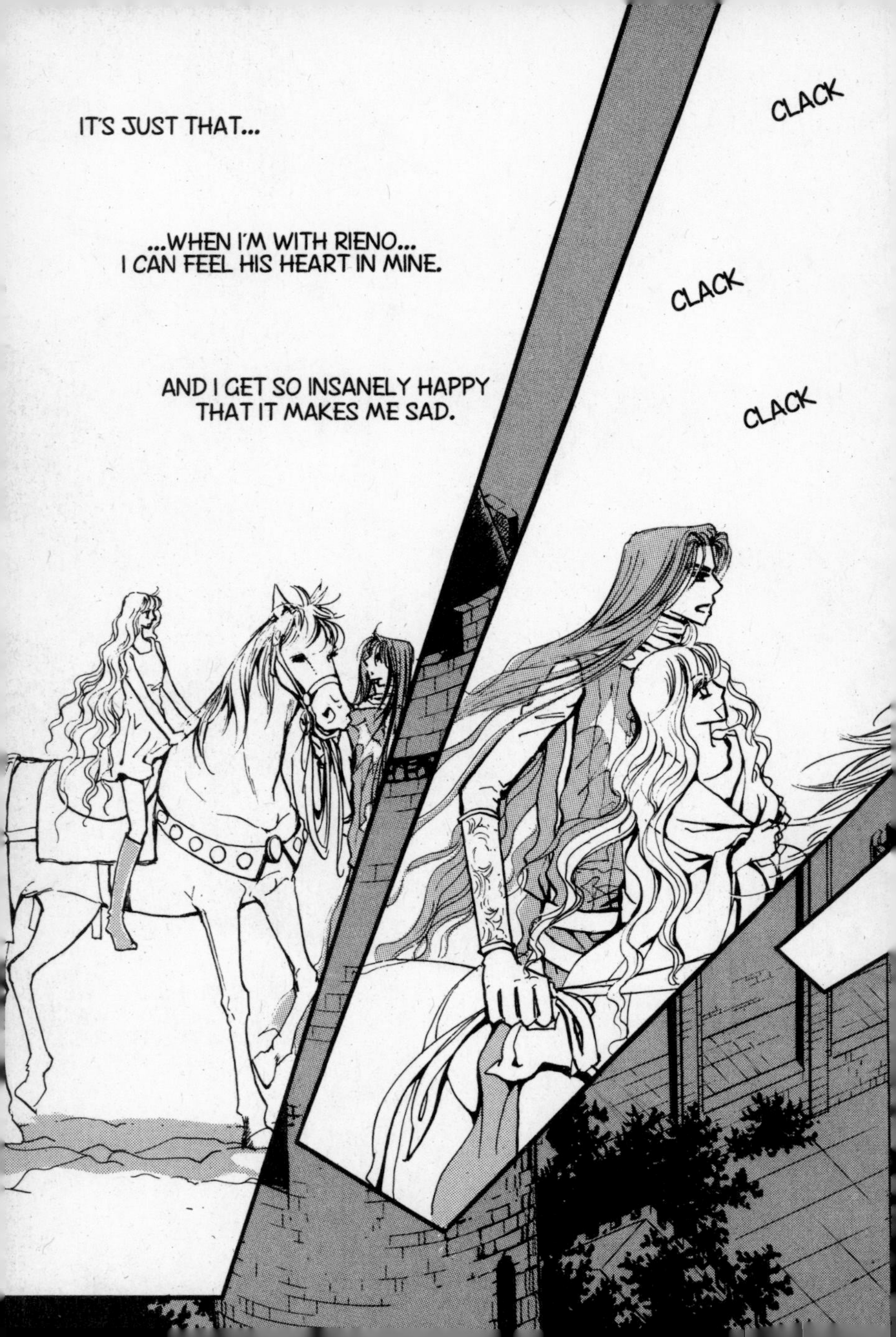
IT'S JUST THAT...
...WHEN I'M WITH RIENO...
I CAN FEEL HIS HEART IN MINE.
AND I GET SO INSANELY HAPPY
THAT IT MAKES ME SAD.
CLACK
CLACK
CLACK

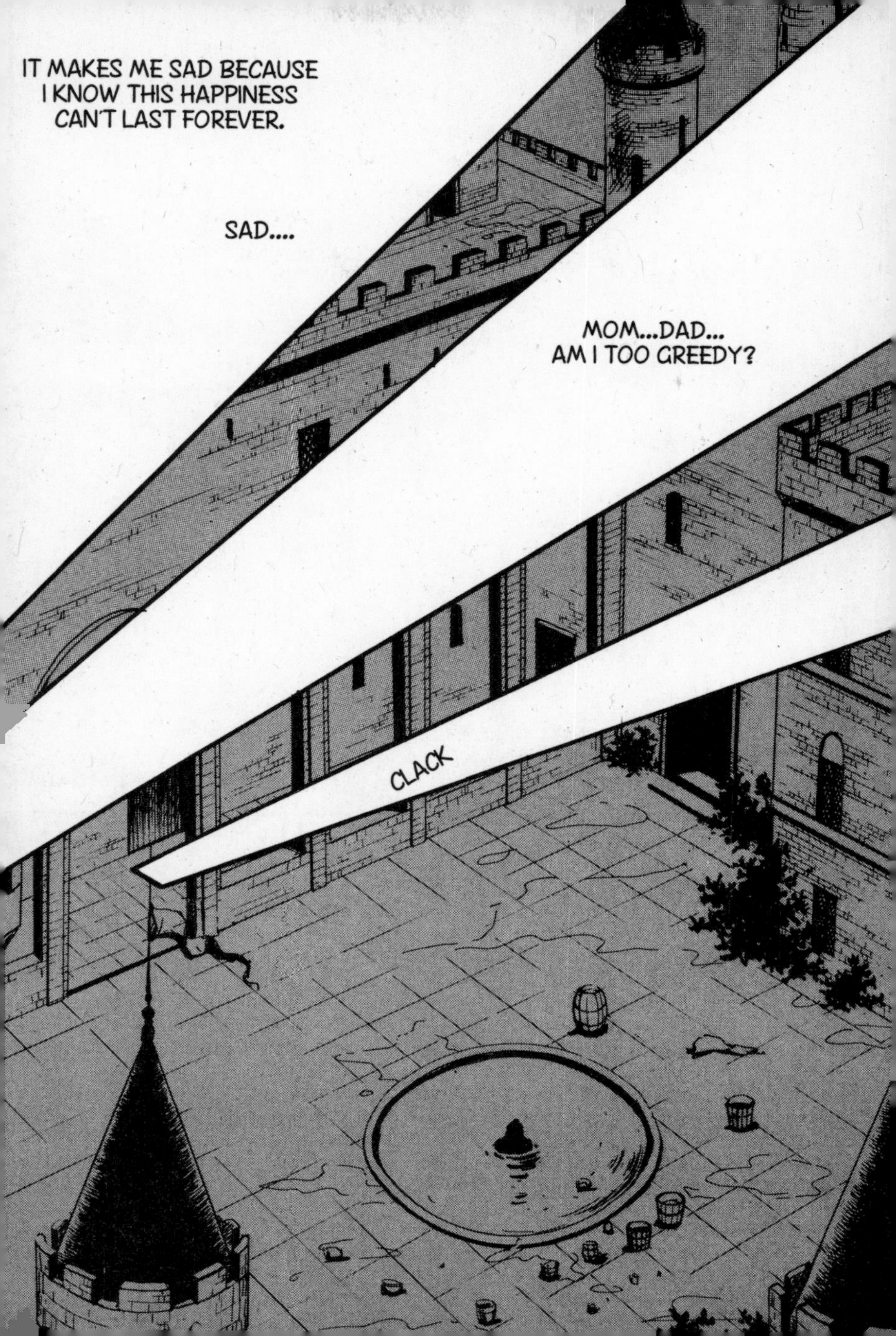
IT MAKES ME SAD BECAUSE I KNOW THIS HAPPINESS CAN'T LAST FOREVER.
SAD....
MOM...DAD... AM I TOO GREEDY?
CLACK

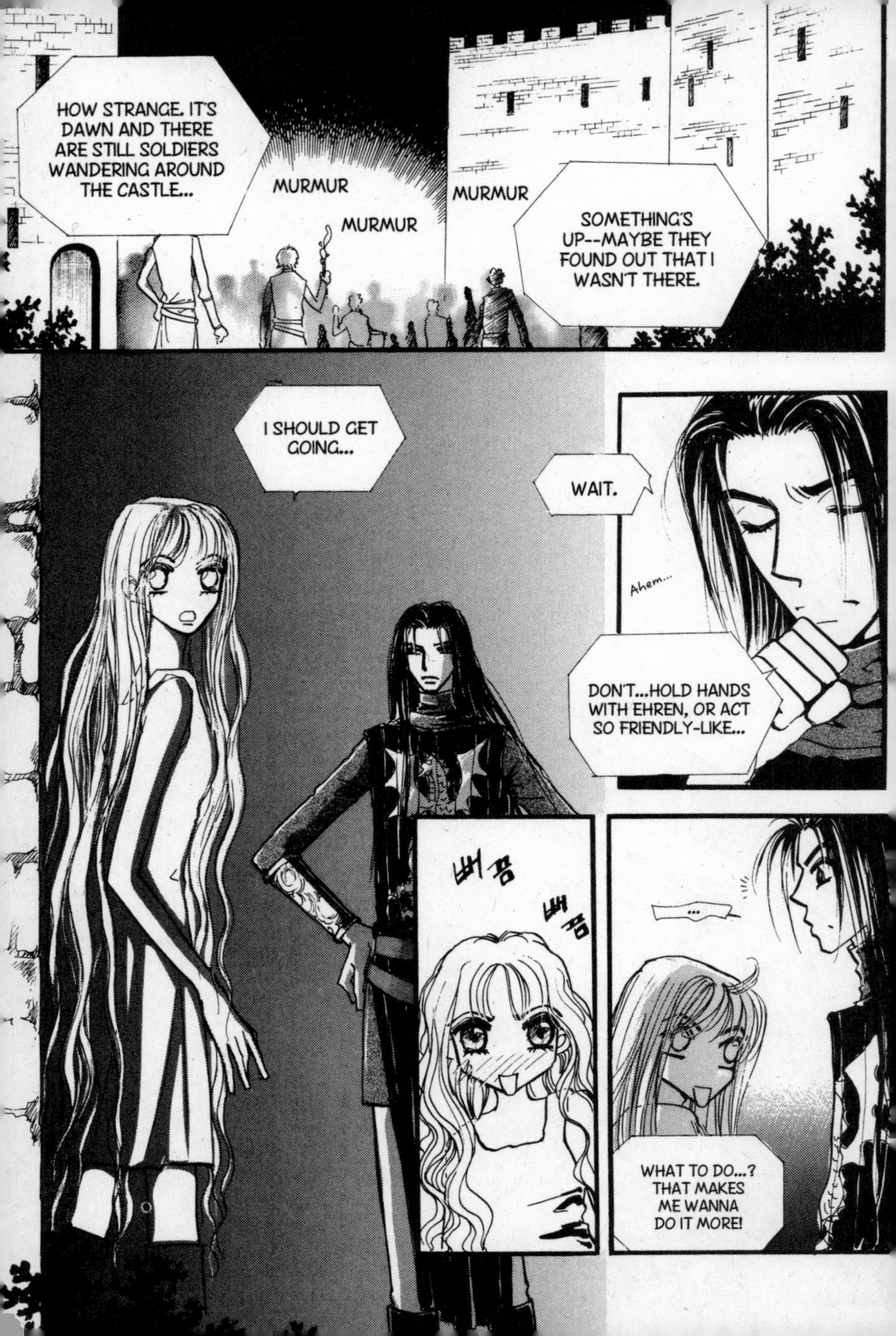
HOW STRANGE. IT'S DAWN AND THERE ARE STILL SOLDIERS WANDERING AROUND THE CASTLE...
MURMUR
MURMUR
MURMUR
SOMETHING'S UP--MAYBE THEY FOUND OUT THAT I WASN'T THERE.
I SHOULD GET GOING...
WAIT.
Ahem...
DON'T...HOLD HANDS WITH EHREN, OR ACT SO FRIENDLY-LIKE...
삐끔
삐끔
...
WHAT TO DO...? THAT MAKES ME WANNA DO IT MORE!

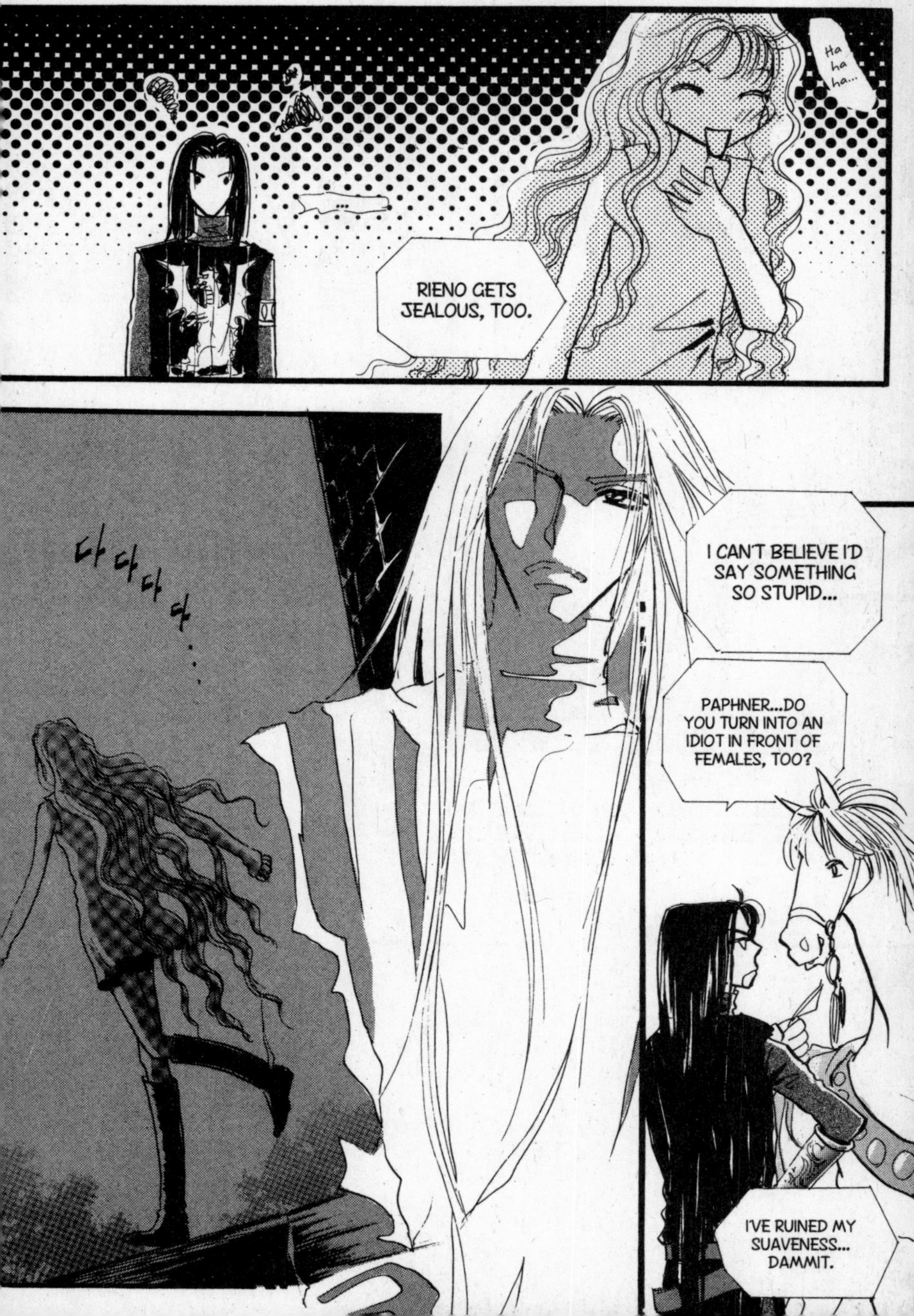
...
Ha ha ha...
RIENO GETS JEALOUS, TOO.
다다다다...
I CAN'T BELIEVE I'D SAY SOMETHING SO STUPID...
PAPHNER...DO YOU TURN INTO AN IDIOT IN FRONT OF FEMALES, TOO?
I'VE RUINED MY SUAVENESS... DAMMIT.

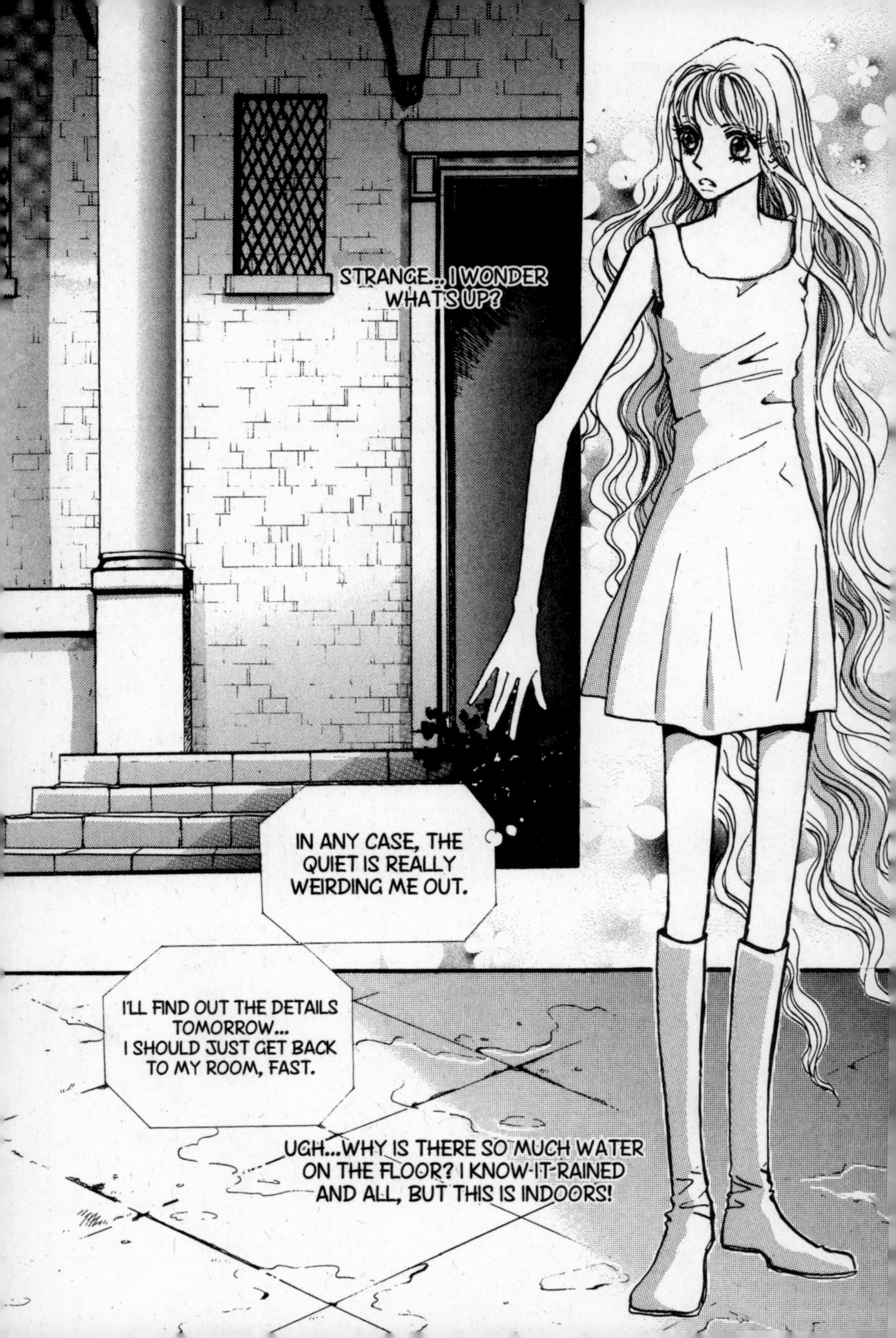
STRANGE... I WONDER WHAT'S UP?
IN ANY CASE, THE QUIET IS REALLY WEIRDING ME OUT.
I'LL FIND OUT THE DETAILS TOMORROW... I SHOULD JUST GET BACK TO MY ROOM, FAST.
UGH...WHY IS THERE SO MUCH WATER ON THE FLOOR? I KNOW IT RAINED AND ALL, BUT THIS IS INDOORS!

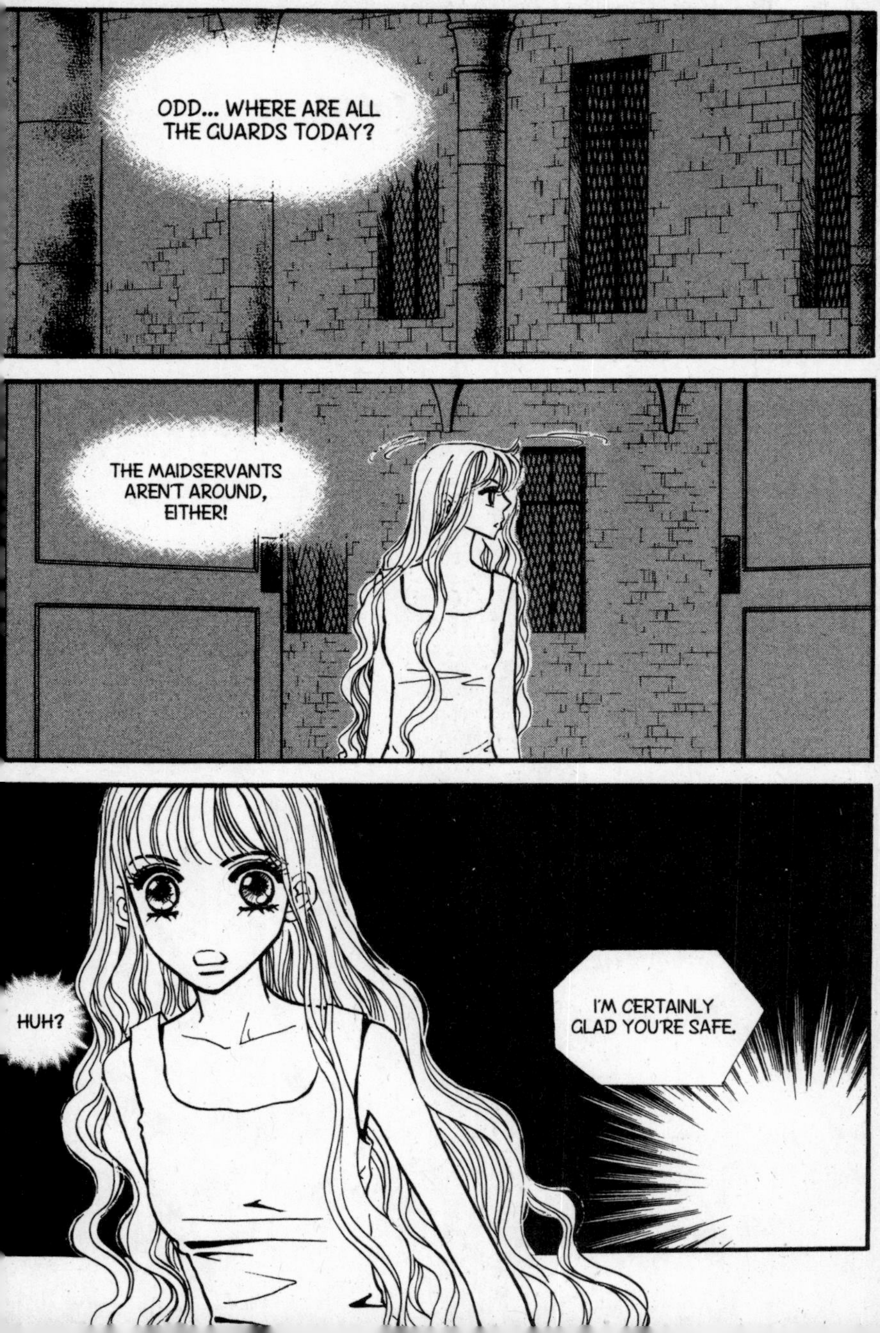
ODD... WHERE ARE ALL THE GUARDS TODAY?
THE MAIDSERVANTS AREN'T AROUND, EITHER!
HUH?
I'M CERTAINLY GLAD YOU'RE SAFE.

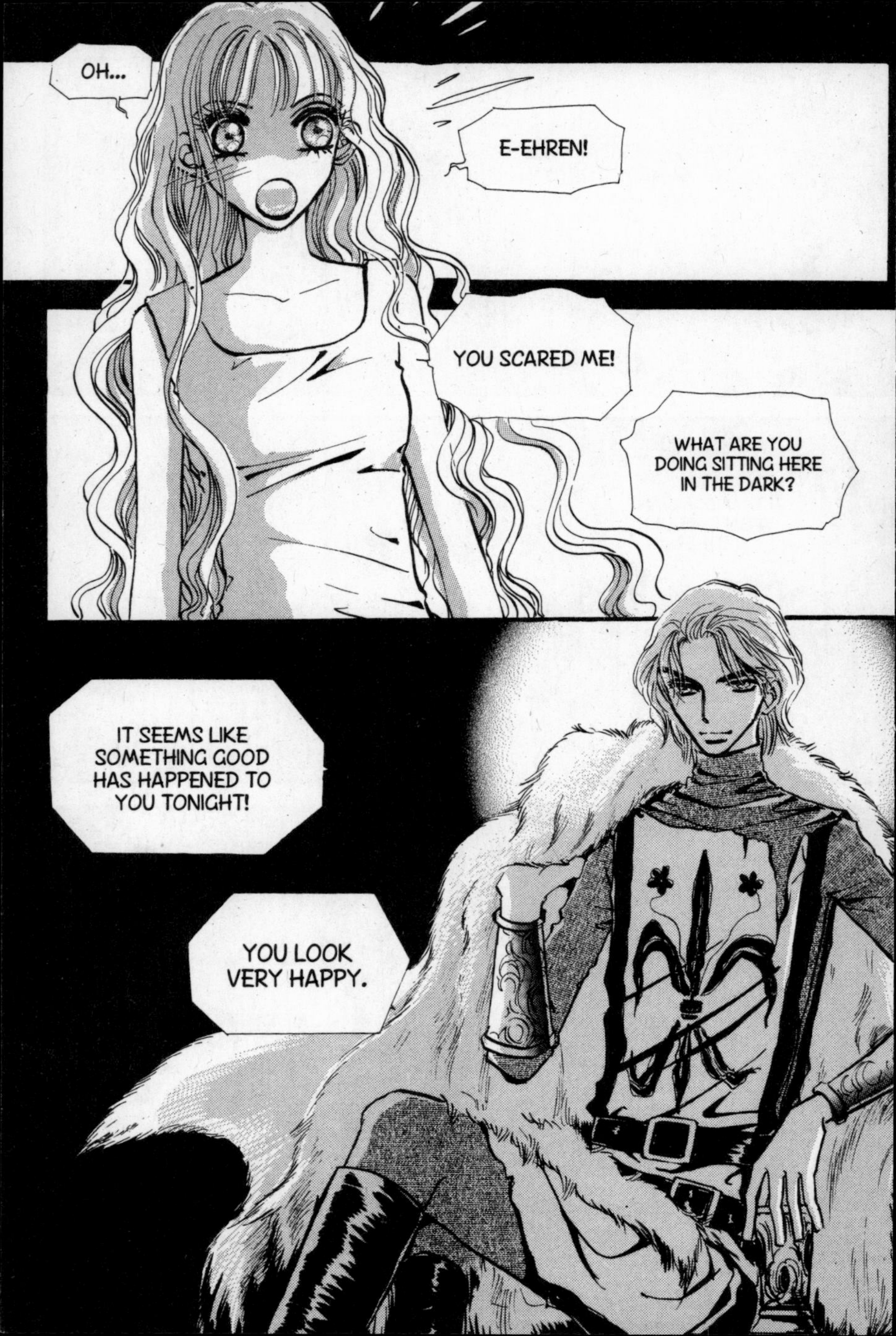
OH...
E-EHREN!
YOU SCARED ME!
WHAT ARE YOU DOING SITTING HERE IN THE DARK?
IT SEEMS LIKE SOMETHING GOOD HAS HAPPENED TO YOU TONIGHT!
YOU LOOK VERY HAPPY.

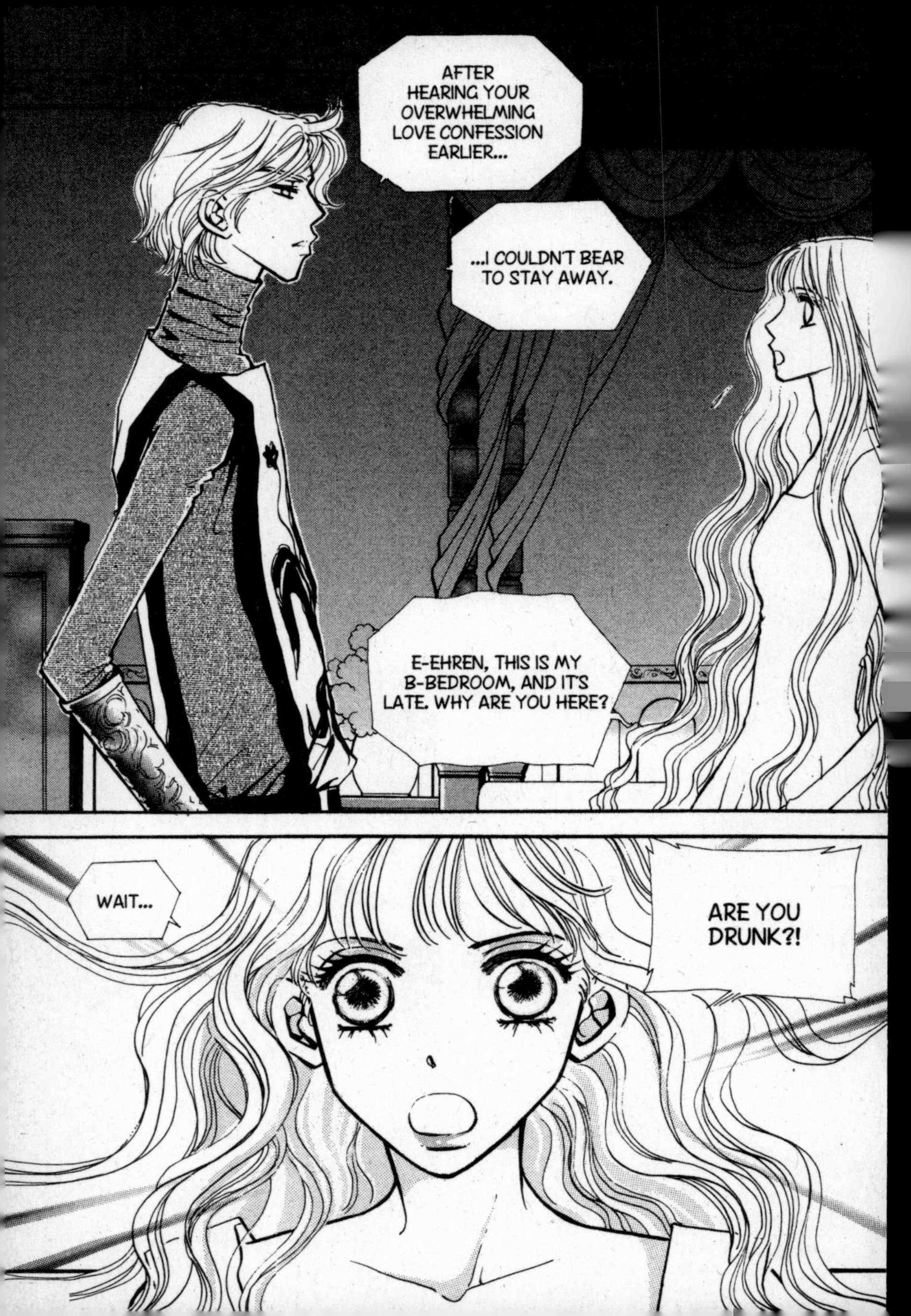
AFTER HEARING YOUR OVERWHELMING LOVE CONFESSION EARLIER...
...I COULDN'T BEAR TO STAY AWAY.
E-EHREN, THIS IS MY B-BEDROOM, AND IT'S LATE. WHY ARE YOU HERE?
WAIT...
ARE YOU DRUNK?!

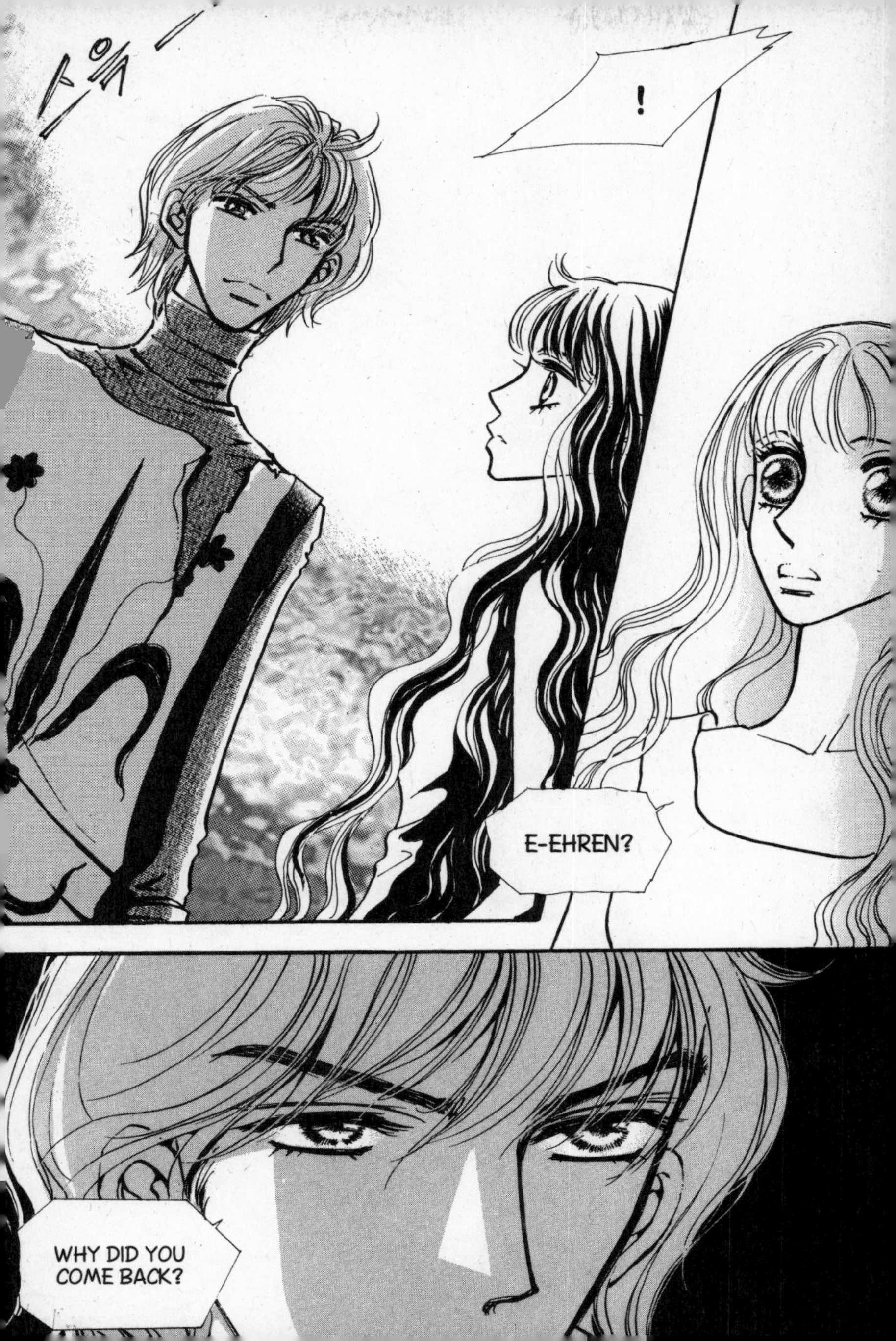
!
E-EHREN?
WHY DID YOU COME BACK?

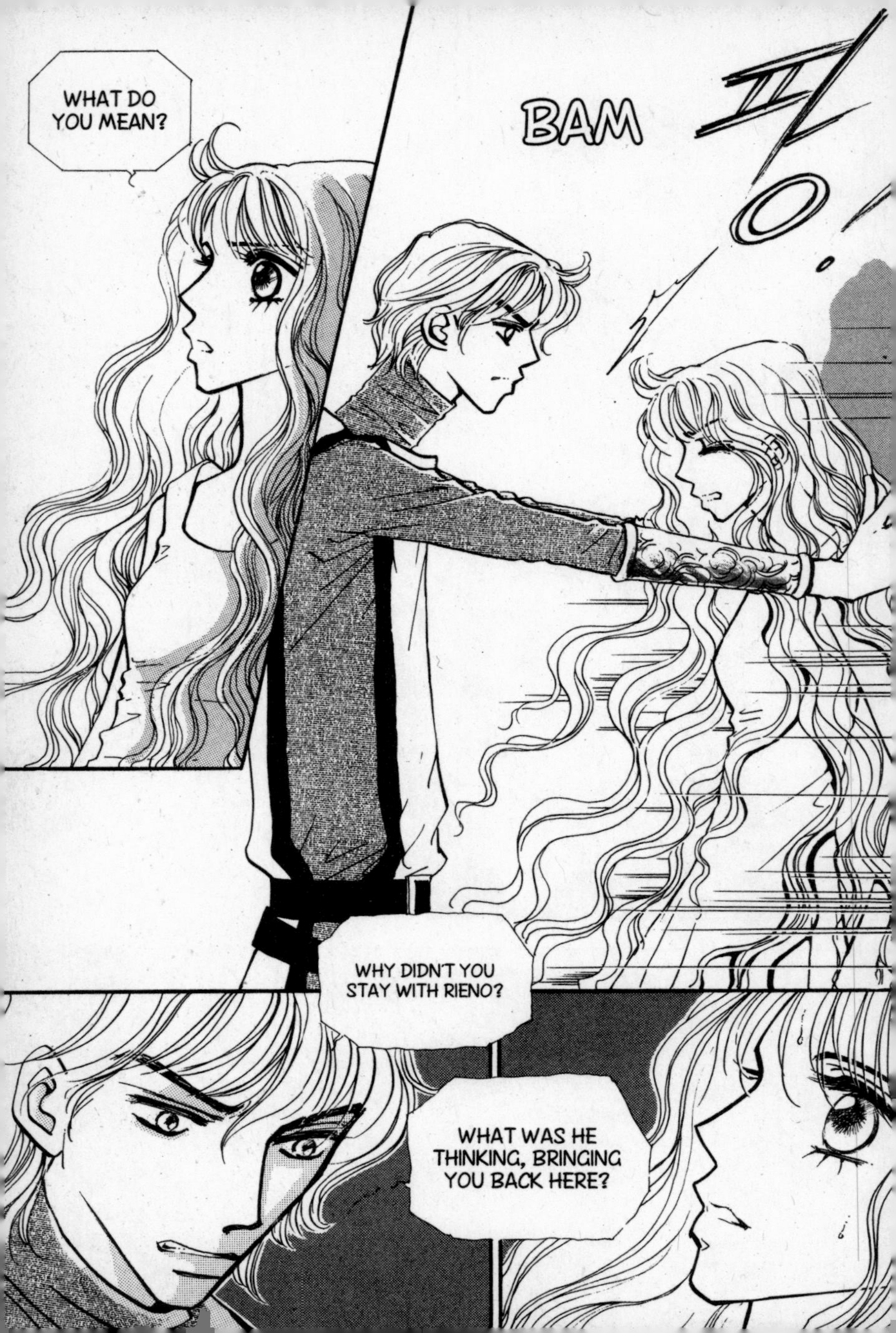
WHAT DO YOU MEAN?
BAM
WHY DIDN'T YOU STAY WITH RIENO?
WHAT WAS HE THINKING, BRINGING YOU BACK HERE?

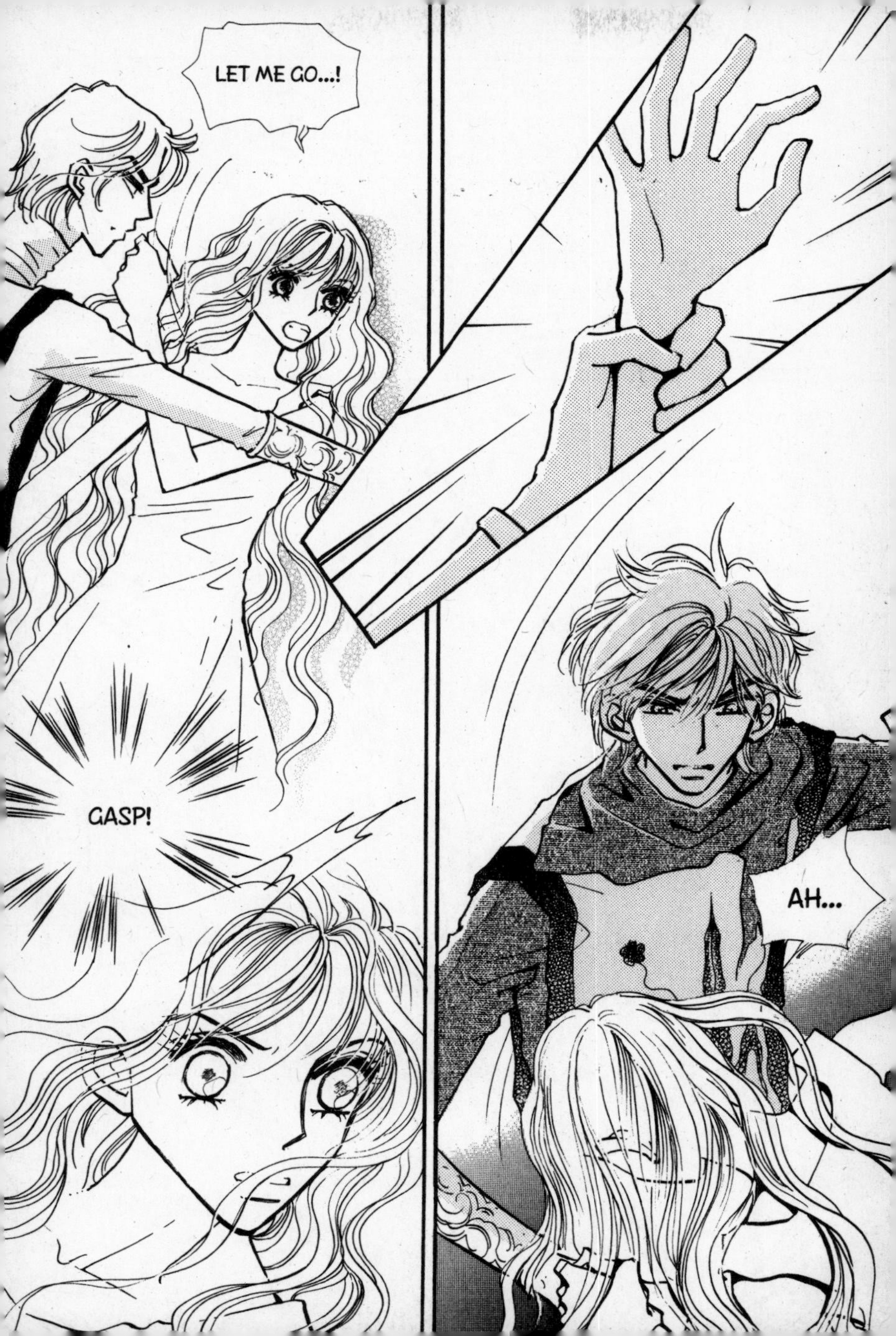
LET ME GO...!
GASP!
AH...

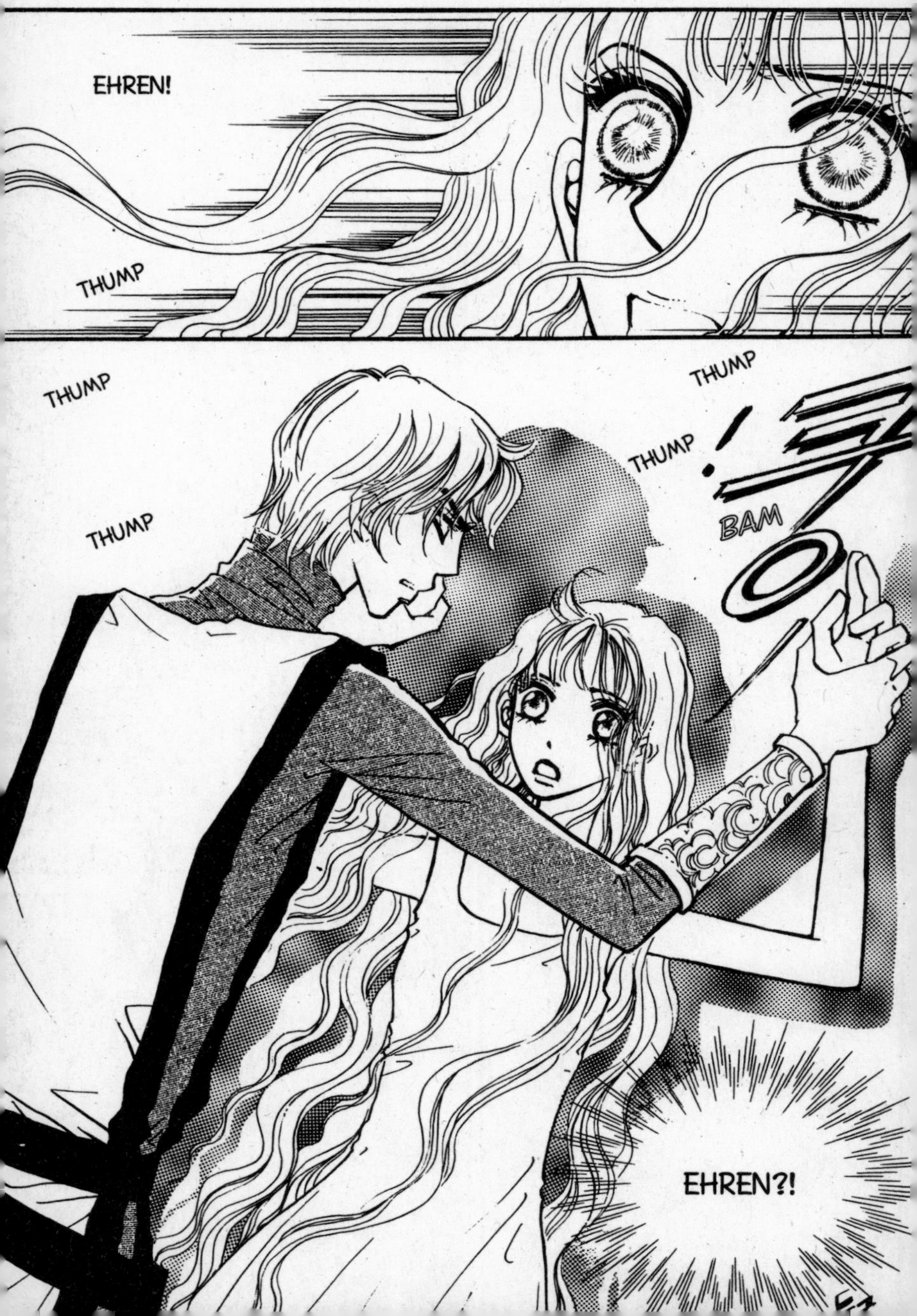
EHREN!
THUMP
THUMP
THUMP
THUMP
THUMP
BAM
EHREN?!

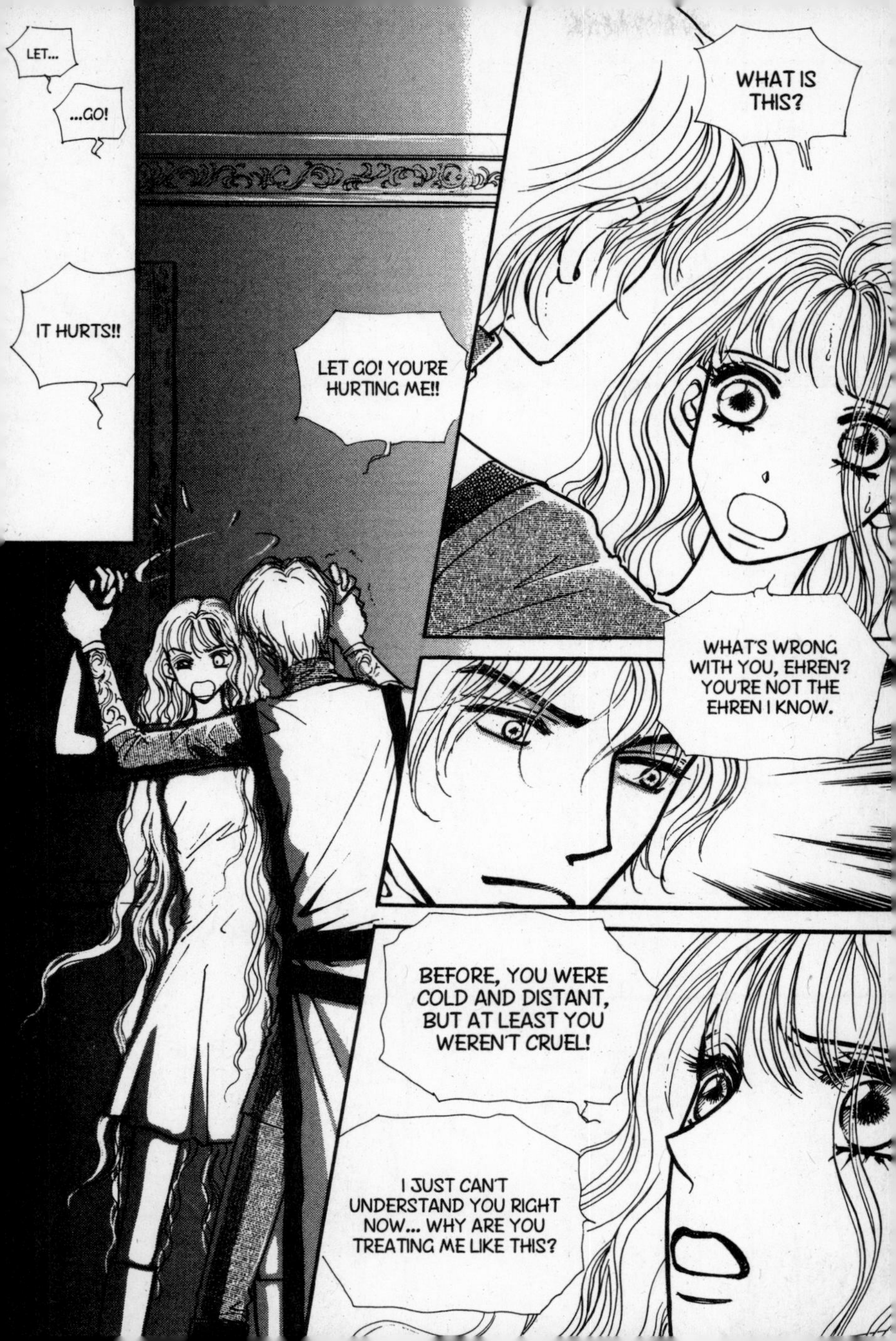
LET...
...GO!
IT HURTS!!
LET GO! YOU'RE HURTING ME!!
WHAT IS THIS?
WHAT'S WRONG WITH YOU, EHREN? YOU'RE NOT THE EHREN I KNOW.
BEFORE, YOU WERE COLD AND DISTANT, BUT AT LEAST YOU WEREN'T CRUEL!
I JUST CAN'T UNDERSTAND YOU RIGHT NOW... WHY ARE YOU TREATING ME LIKE THIS?

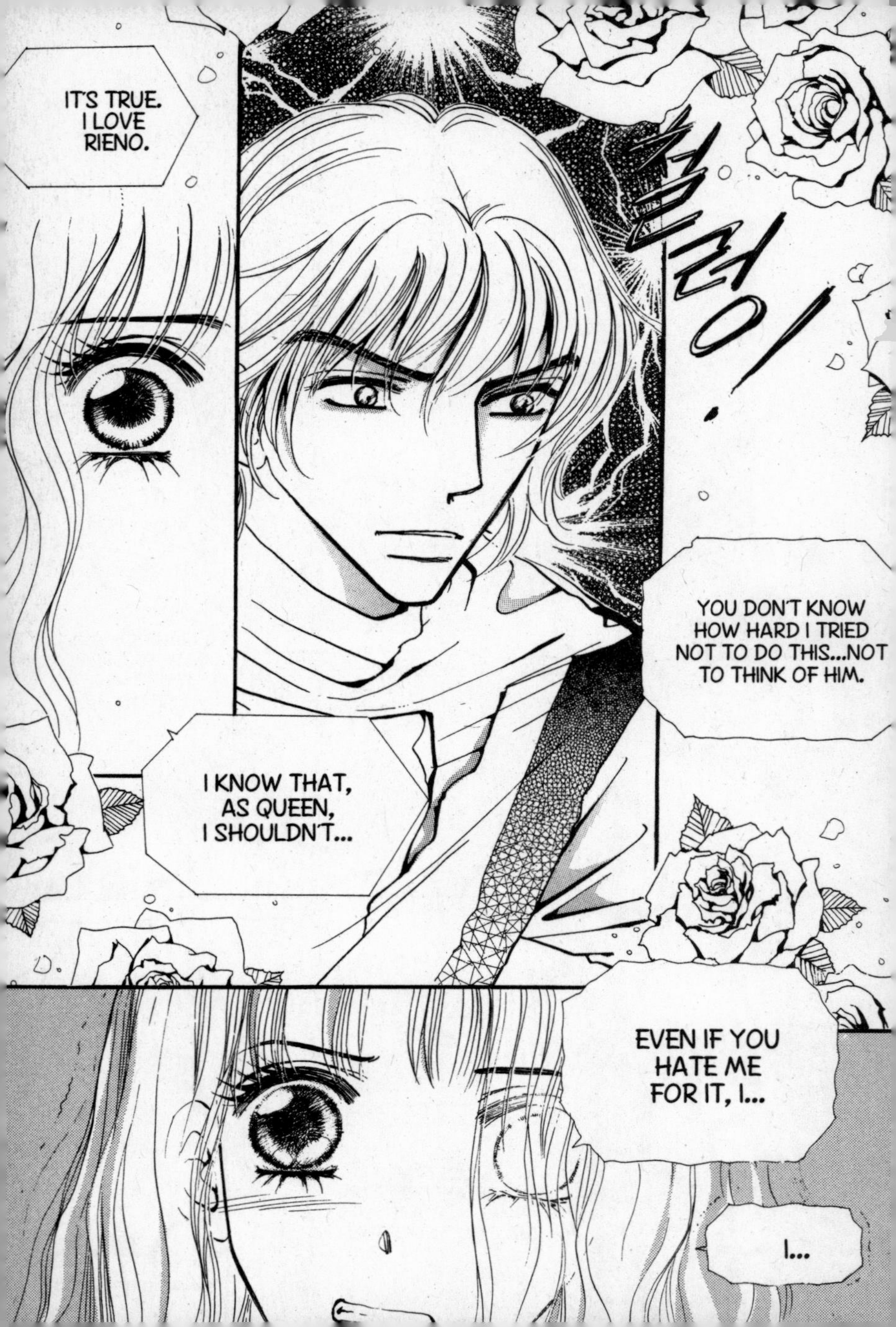
IT'S TRUE. I LOVE RIENO.
철런이!
YOU DON'T KNOW HOW HARD I TRIED NOT TO DO THIS...NOT TO THINK OF HIM.
I KNOW THAT, AS QUEEN, I SHOULDN'T...
EVEN IF YOU HATE ME FOR IT, I...
I...

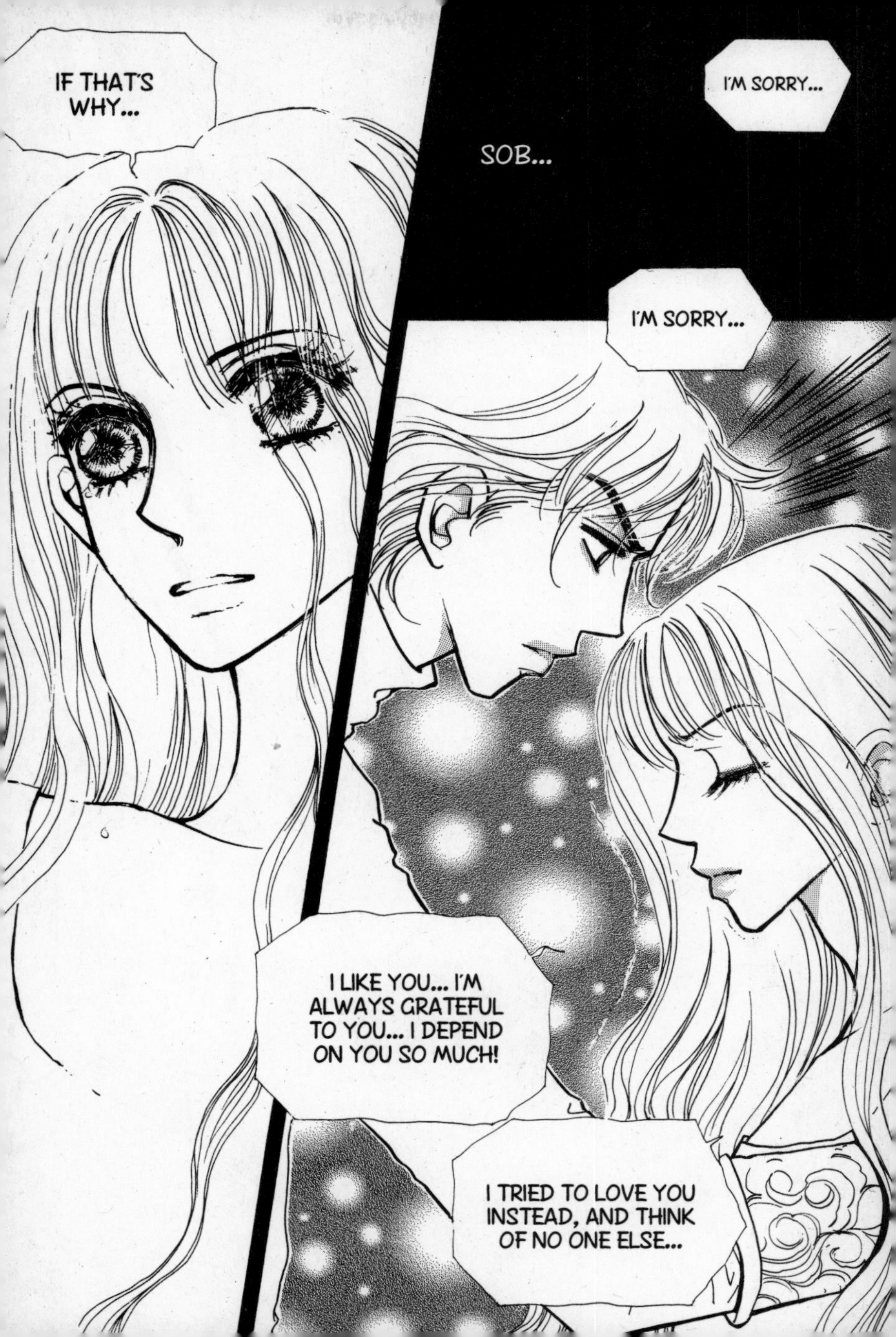
IF THAT'S WHY...
I'M SORRY...
SOB...
I'M SORRY...
I LIKE YOU... I'M ALWAYS GRATEFUL TO YOU... I DEPEND ON YOU SO MUCH!
I TRIED TO LOVE YOU INSTEAD, AND THINK OF NO ONE ELSE...

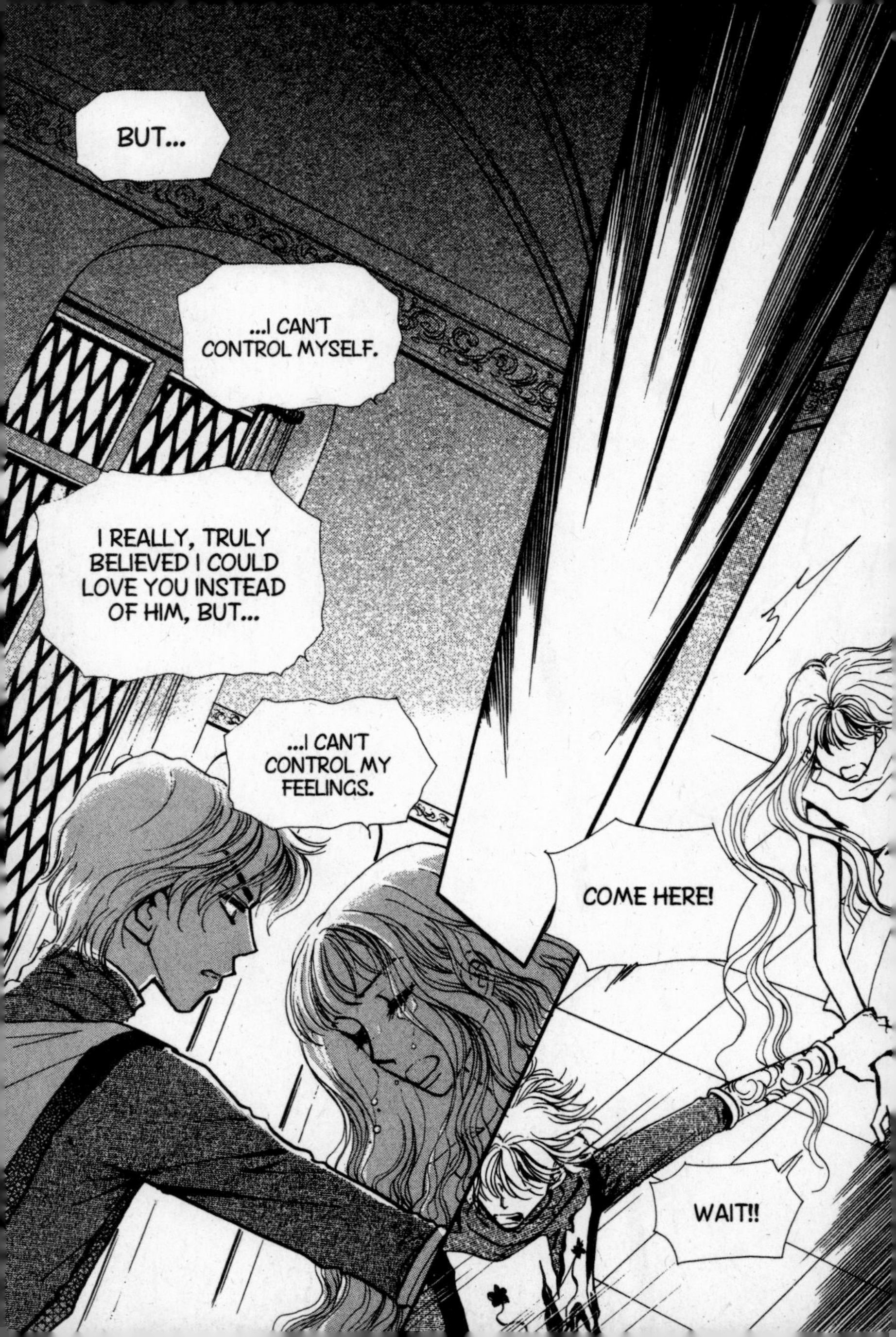
BUT...
...I CAN'T CONTROL MYSELF.
I REALLY, TRULY BELIEVED I COULD LOVE YOU INSTEAD OF HIM, BUT...
...I CAN'T CONTROL MY FEELINGS.
COME HERE!
WAIT!!

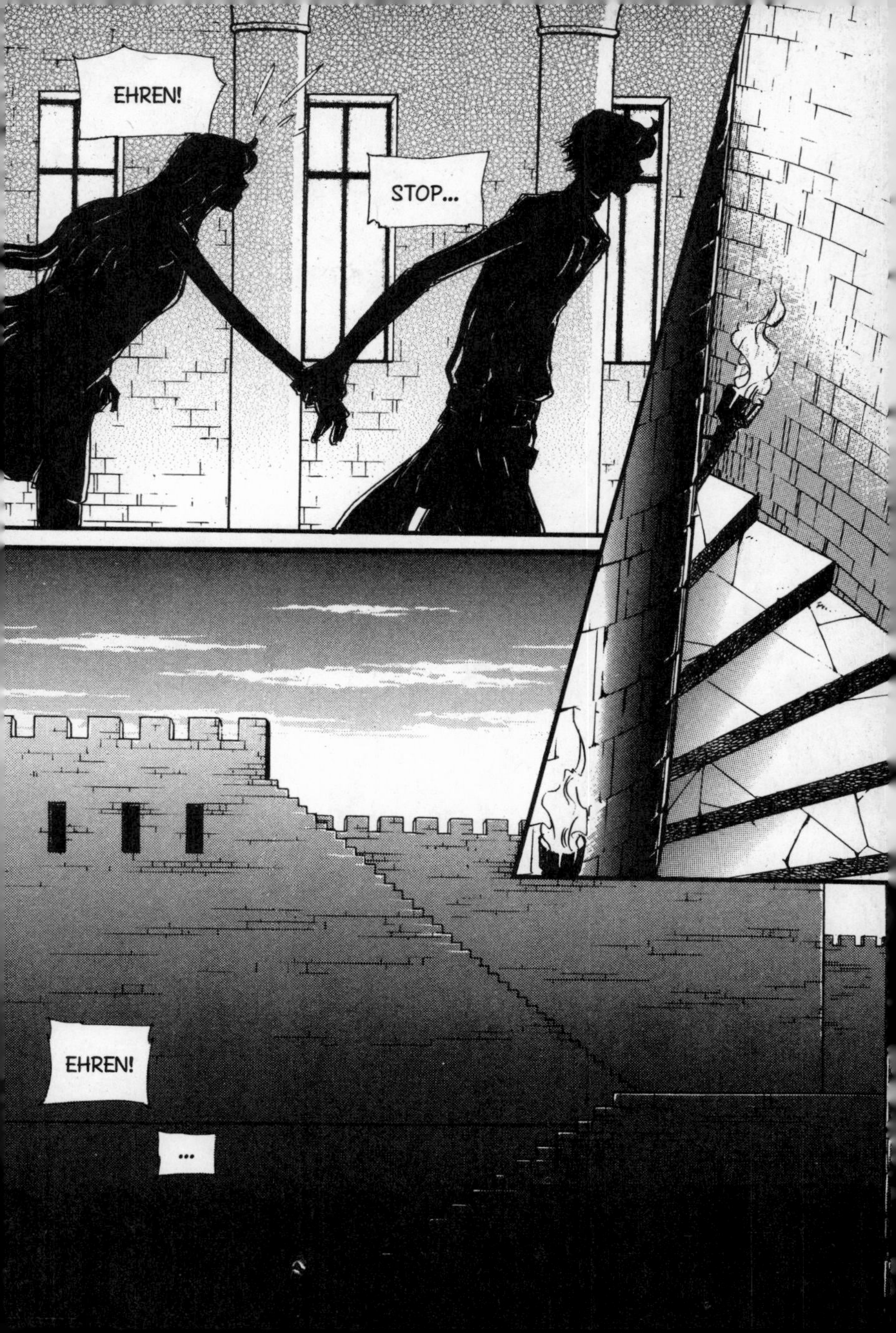
EHREN!
STOP...
EHREN!
...

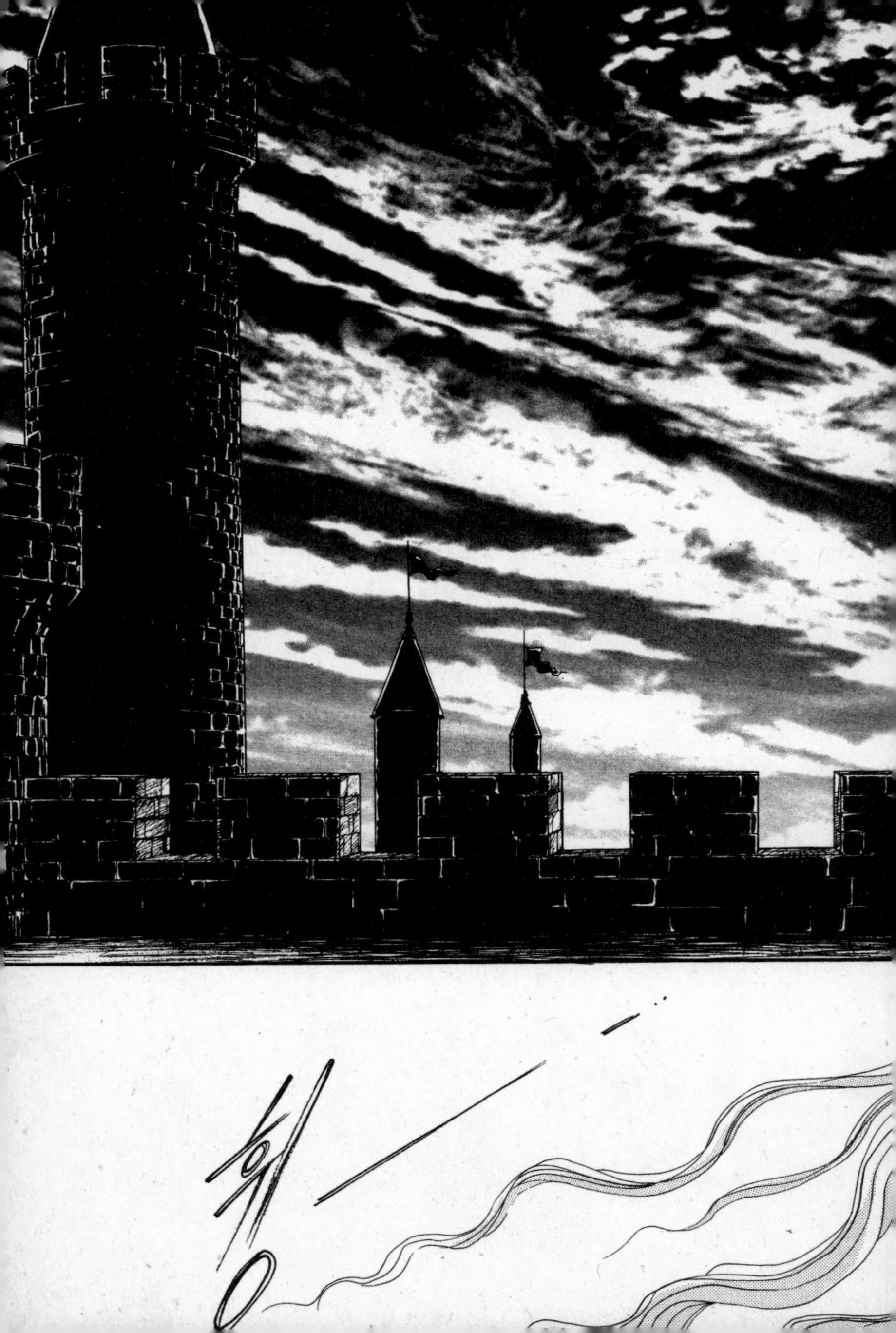

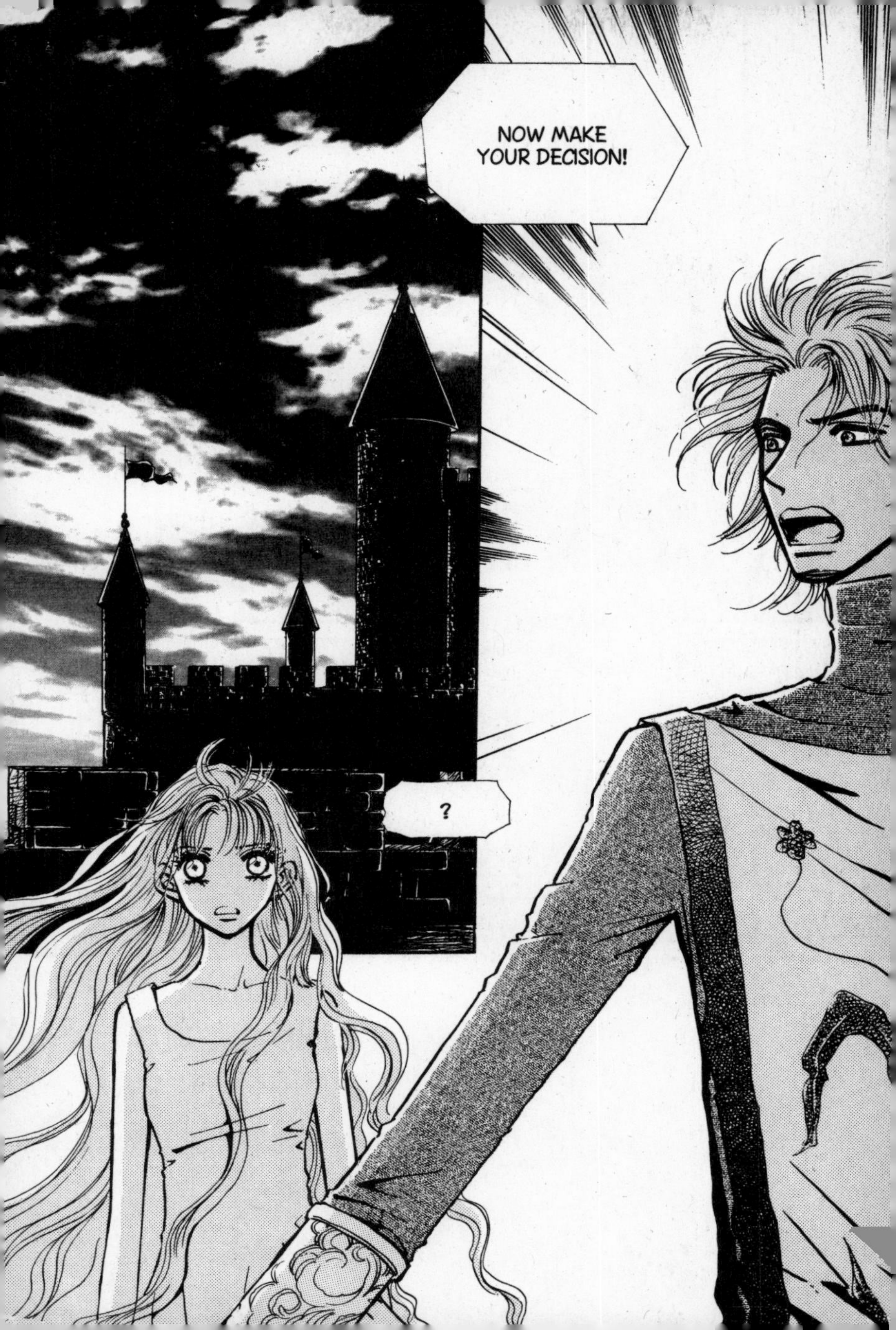
NOW MAKE
YOUR DECISION!
?

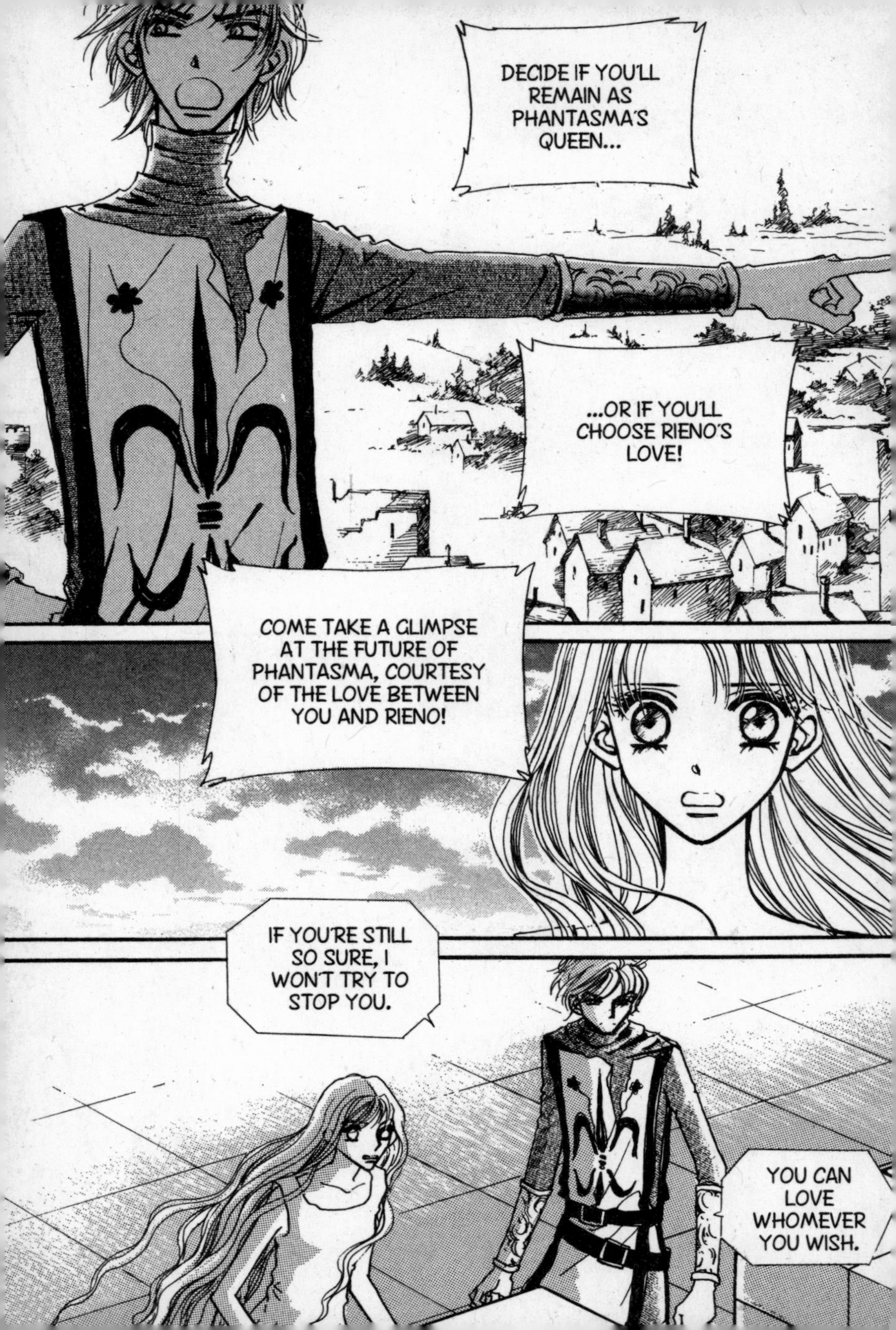
DECIDE IF YOU'LL REMAIN AS PHANTASMA'S QUEEN...
...OR IF YOU'LL CHOOSE RIENO'S LOVE!
COME TAKE A GLIMPSE AT THE FUTURE OF PHANTASMA, COURTESY OF THE LOVE BETWEEN YOU AND RIENO!
IF YOU'RE STILL SO SURE, I WON'T TRY TO STOP YOU.
YOU CAN LOVE WHOMEVER YOU WISH.

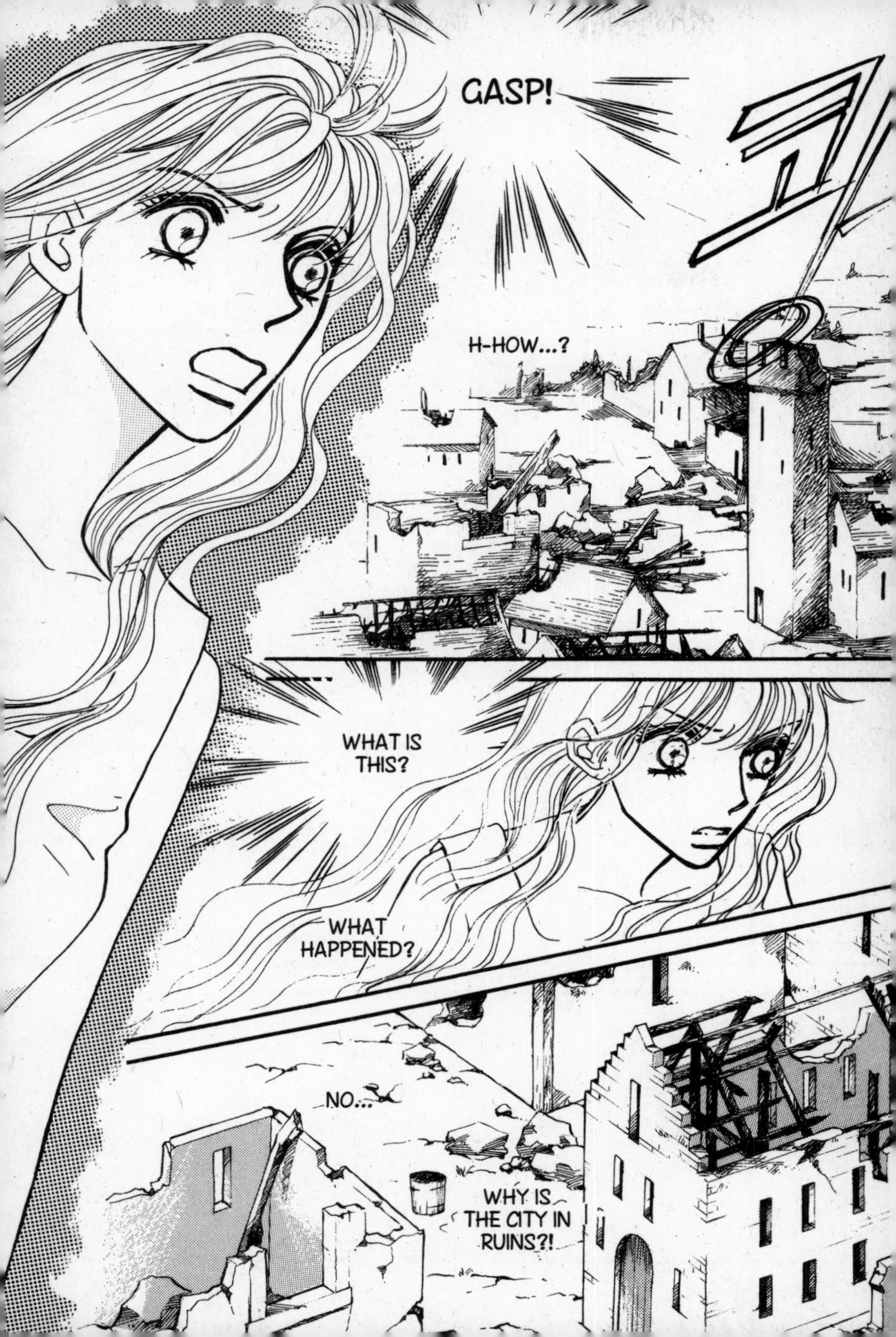
GASP!
H-HOW...?
WHAT IS THIS?
WHAT HAPPENED?
NO...
WHY IS THE CITY IN RUINS?!

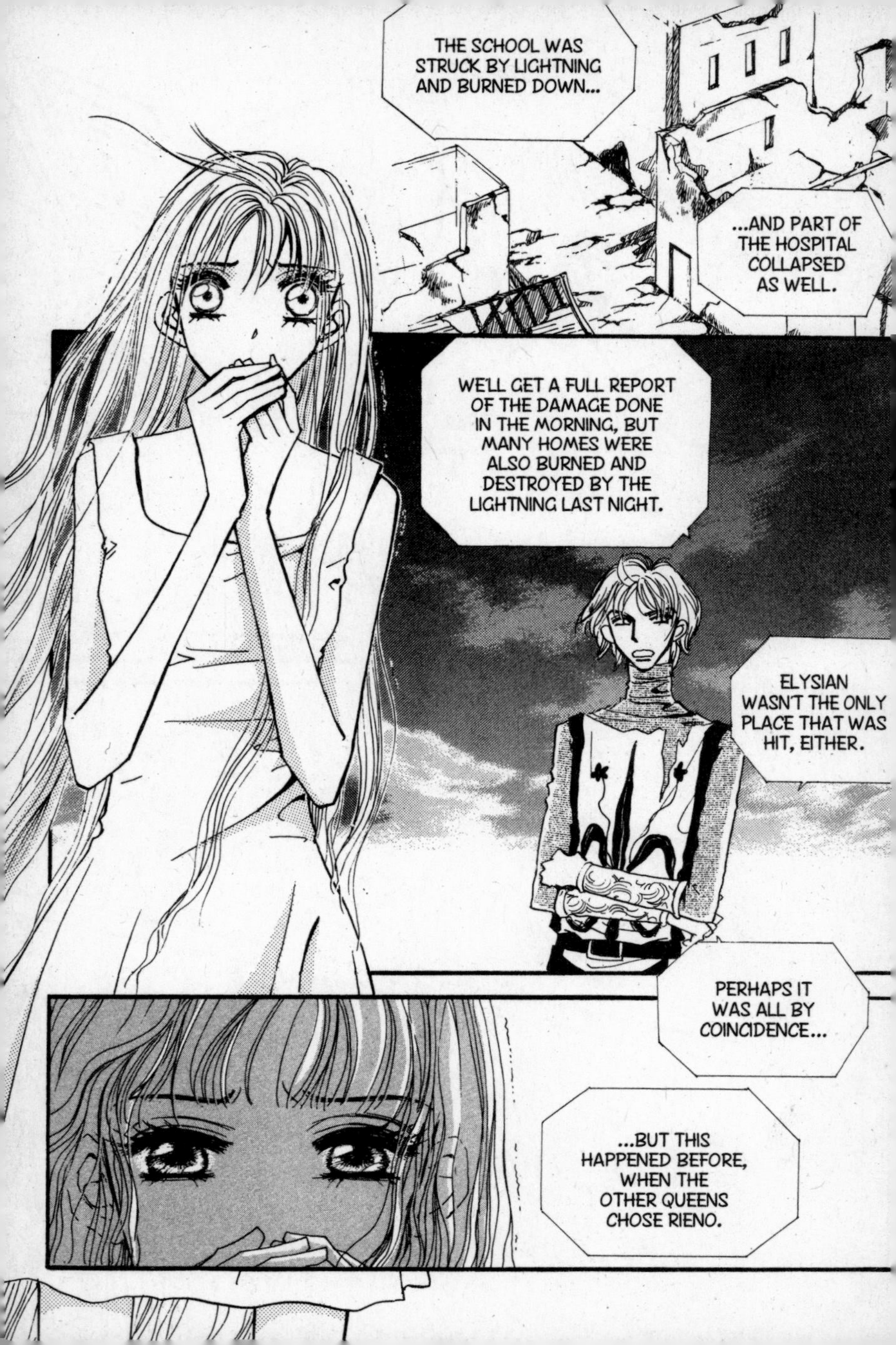
THE SCHOOL WAS STRUCK BY LIGHTNING AND BURNED DOWN...
...AND PART OF THE HOSPITAL COLLAPSED AS WELL.
WE'LL GET A FULL REPORT OF THE DAMAGE DONE IN THE MORNING, BUT MANY HOMES WERE ALSO BURNED AND DESTROYED BY THE LIGHTNING LAST NIGHT.
ELYSIAN WASN'T THE ONLY PLACE THAT WAS HIT, EITHER.
PERHAPS IT WAS ALL BY COINCIDENCE...
...BUT THIS HAPPENED BEFORE, WHEN THE OTHER QUEENS CHOSE RIENO.

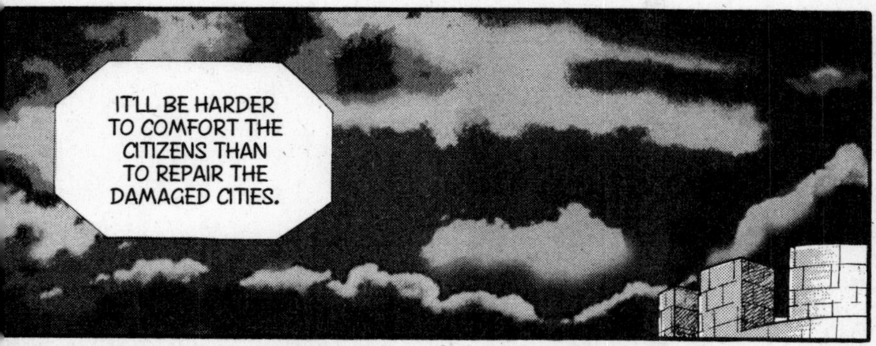
IT'LL BE HARDER TO COMFORT THE CITIZENS THAN TO REPAIR THE DAMAGED CITIES.

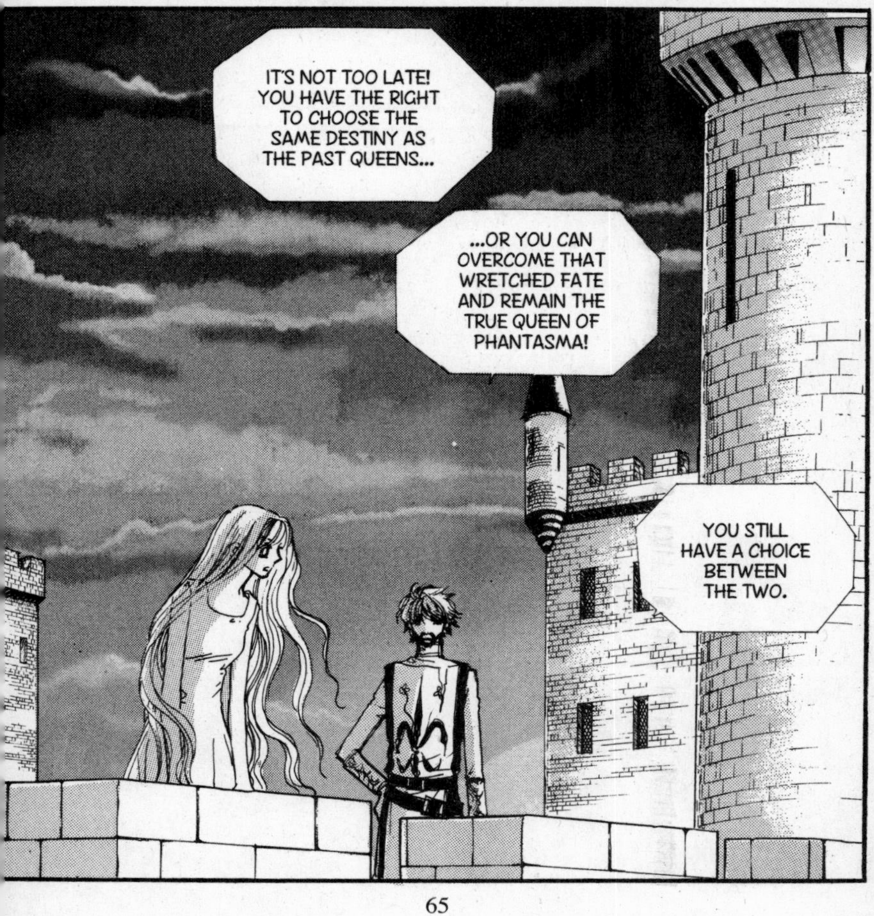
IT'S NOT TOO LATE! YOU HAVE THE RIGHT TO CHOOSE THE SAME DESTINY AS THE PAST QUEENS...
...OR YOU CAN OVERCOME THAT WRETCHED FATE AND REMAIN THE TRUE QUEEN OF PHANTASMA!
YOU STILL HAVE A CHOICE BETWEEN THE TWO.

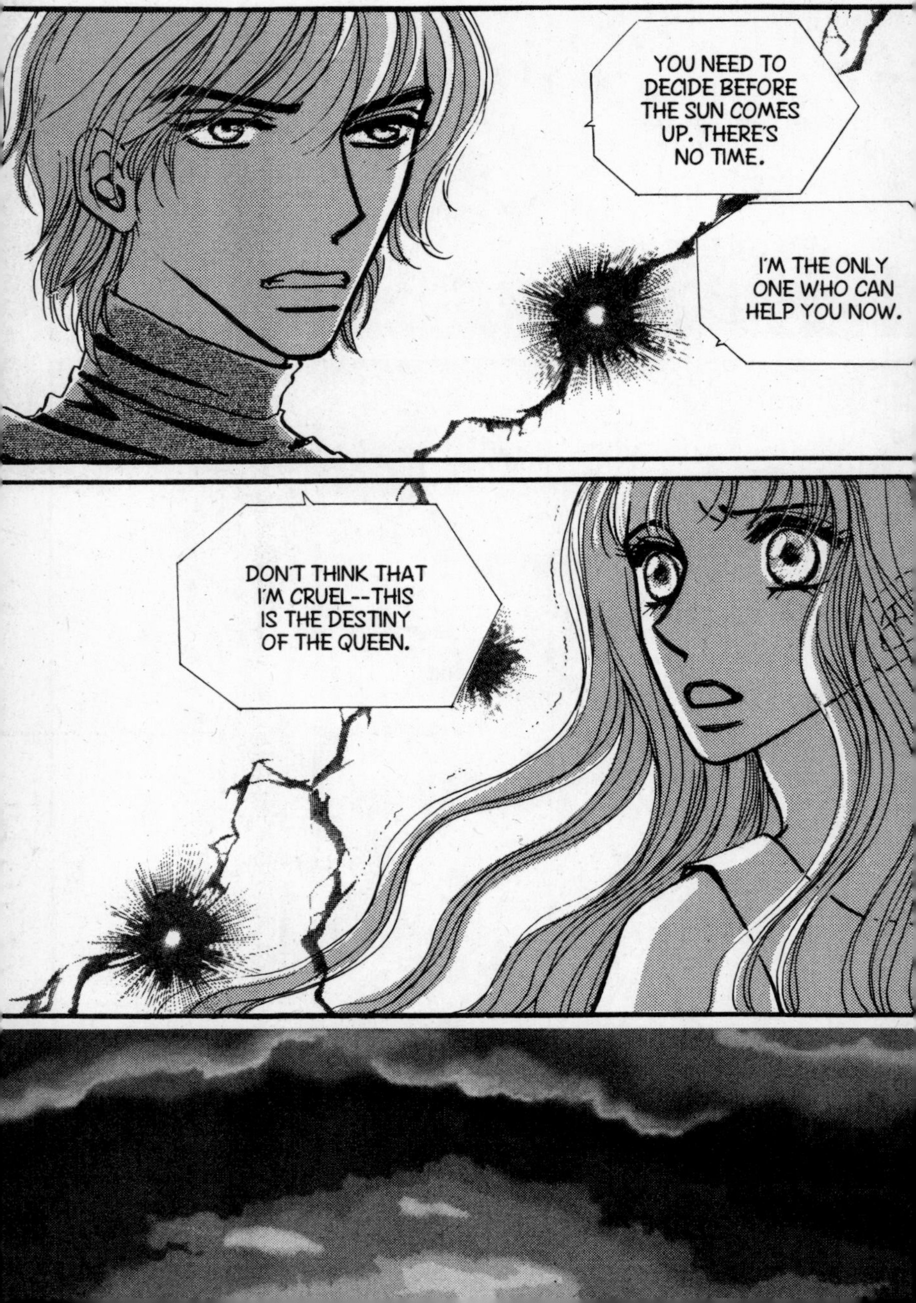
YOU NEED TO DECIDE BEFORE THE SUN COMES UP. THERE'S NO TIME.
I'M THE ONLY ONE WHO CAN HELP YOU NOW.
DON'T THINK THAT I'M CRUEL--THIS IS THE DESTINY OF THE QUEEN.

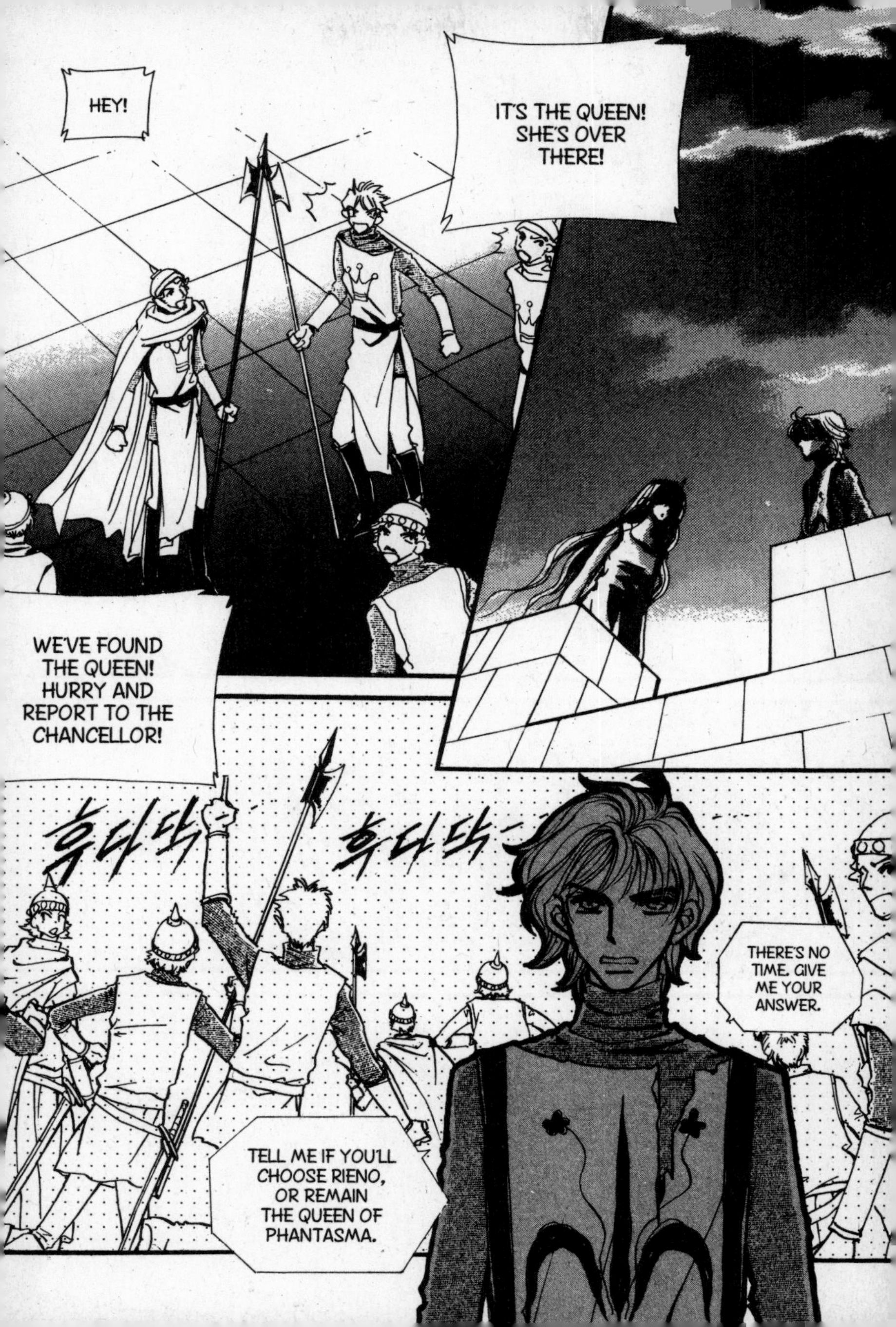
HEY!
IT'S THE QUEEN! SHE'S OVER THERE!
WE'VE FOUND THE QUEEN! HURRY AND REPORT TO THE CHANCELLOR!
후다닥
후다닥
THERE'S NO TIME. GIVE ME YOUR ANSWER.
TELL ME IF YOU'LL CHOOSE RIENO, OR REMAIN THE QUEEN OF PHANTASMA.

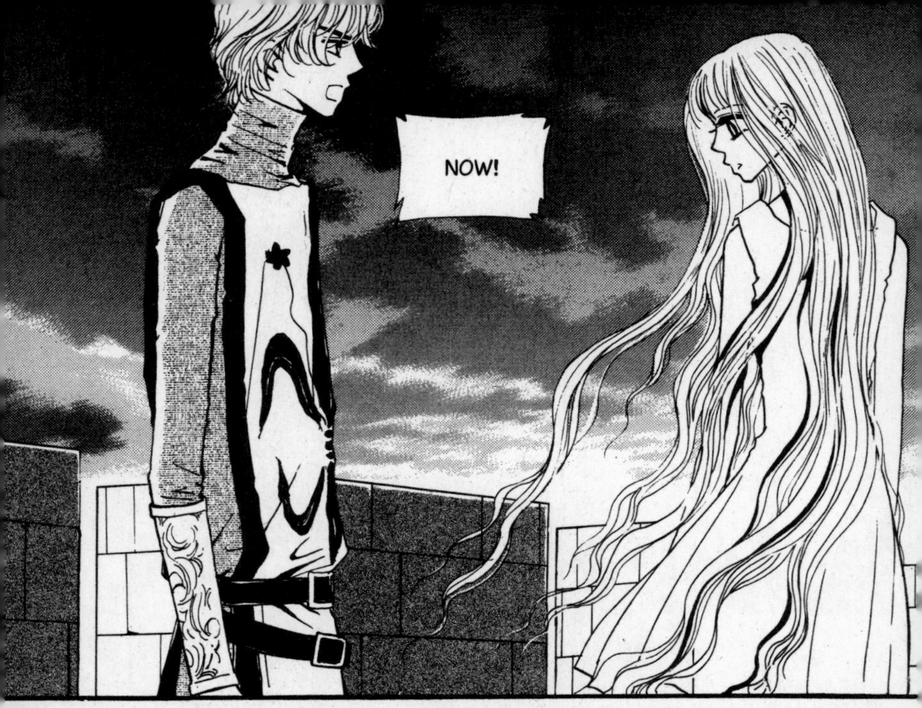
NOW!
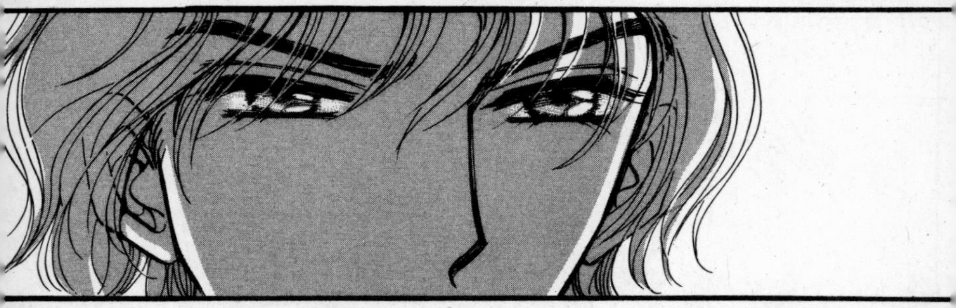
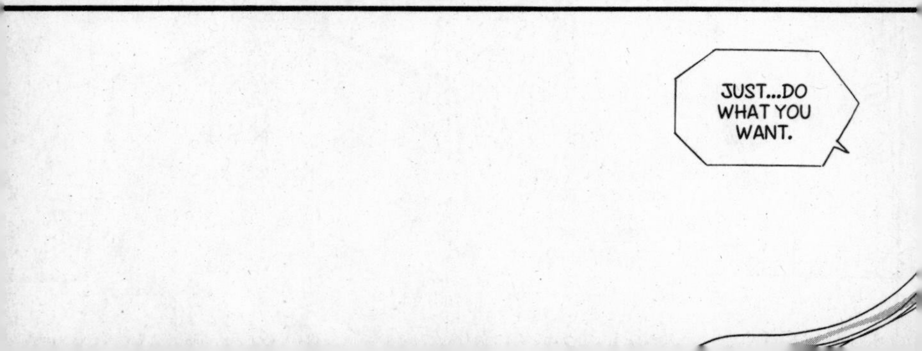
JUST...DO
WHAT YOU
WANT.

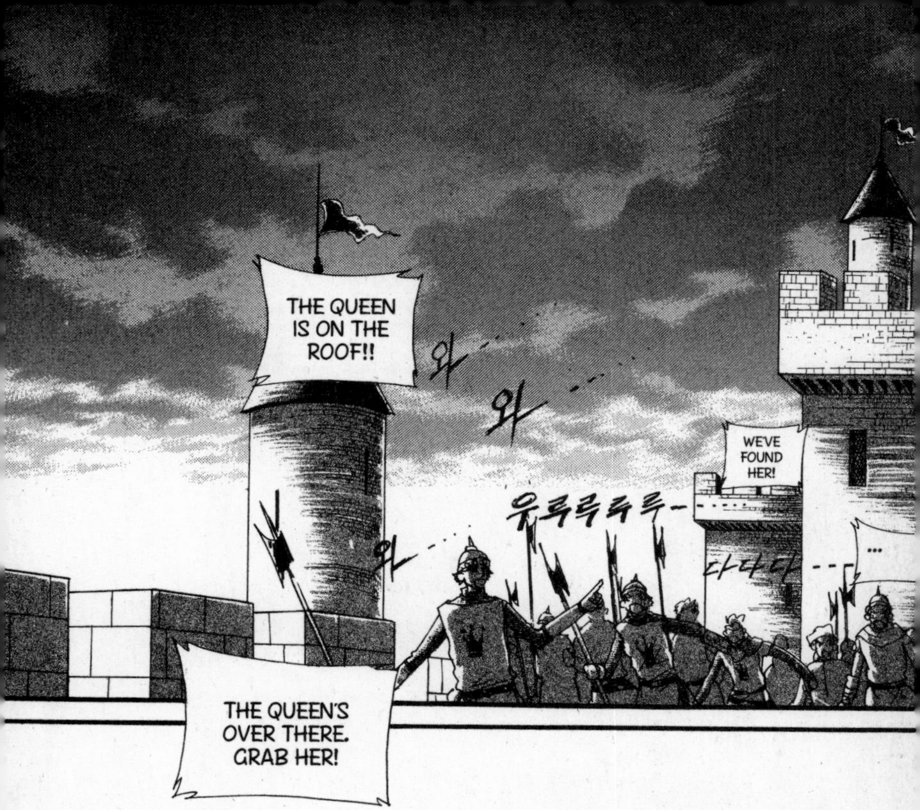
THE QUEEN IS ON THE ROOF!!
와-...
와-...
WE'VE FOUND HER!
우루루루루-
와-...
다다다---
...
THE QUEEN'S OVER THERE. GRAB HER!
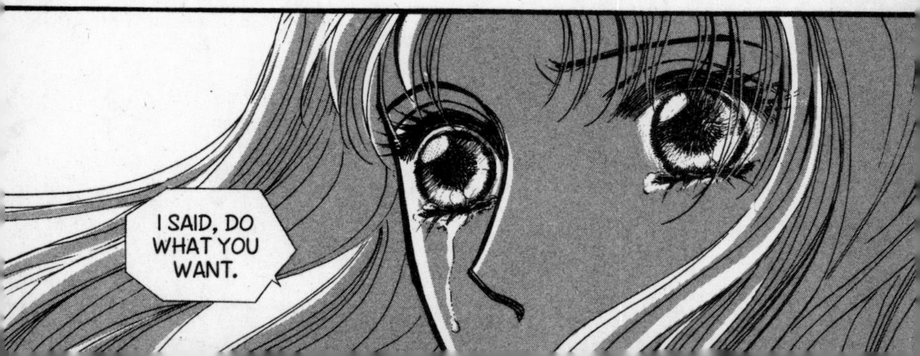
I SAID, DO WHAT YOU WANT.

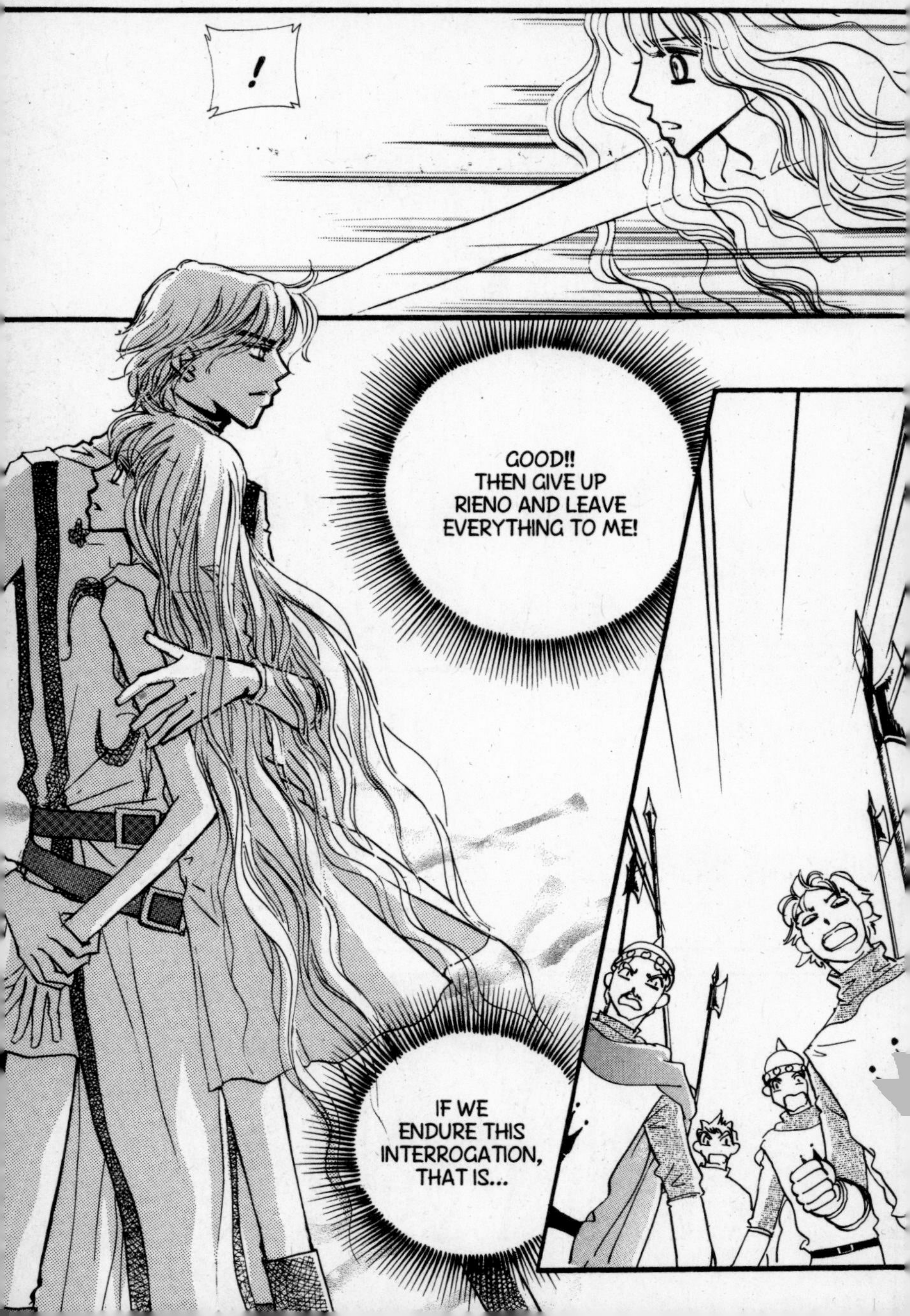
!
GOOD!! THEN GIVE UP RIENO AND LEAVE EVERYTHING TO ME!
IF WE ENDURE THIS INTERROGATION, THAT IS...

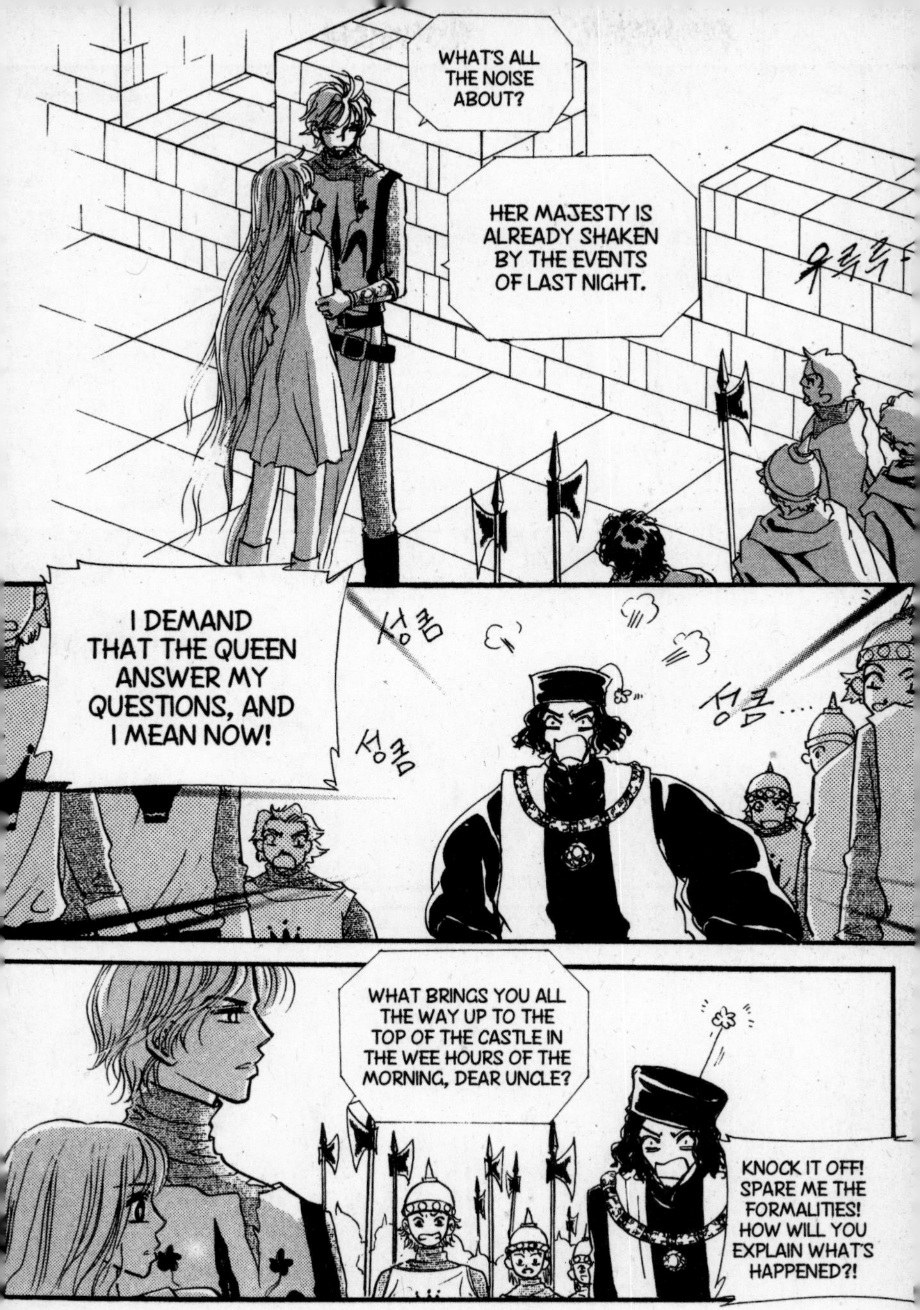
WHAT'S ALL THE NOISE ABOUT?
HER MAJESTY IS ALREADY SHAKEN BY THE EVENTS OF LAST NIGHT.
I DEMAND THAT THE QUEEN ANSWER MY QUESTIONS, AND I MEAN NOW!
성큼
성큼
성큼...
WHAT BRINGS YOU ALL THE WAY UP TO THE TOP OF THE CASTLE IN THE WEE HOURS OF THE MORNING, DEAR UNCLE?
KNOCK IT OFF! SPARE ME THE FORMALITIES! HOW WILL YOU EXPLAIN WHAT'S HAPPENED?!

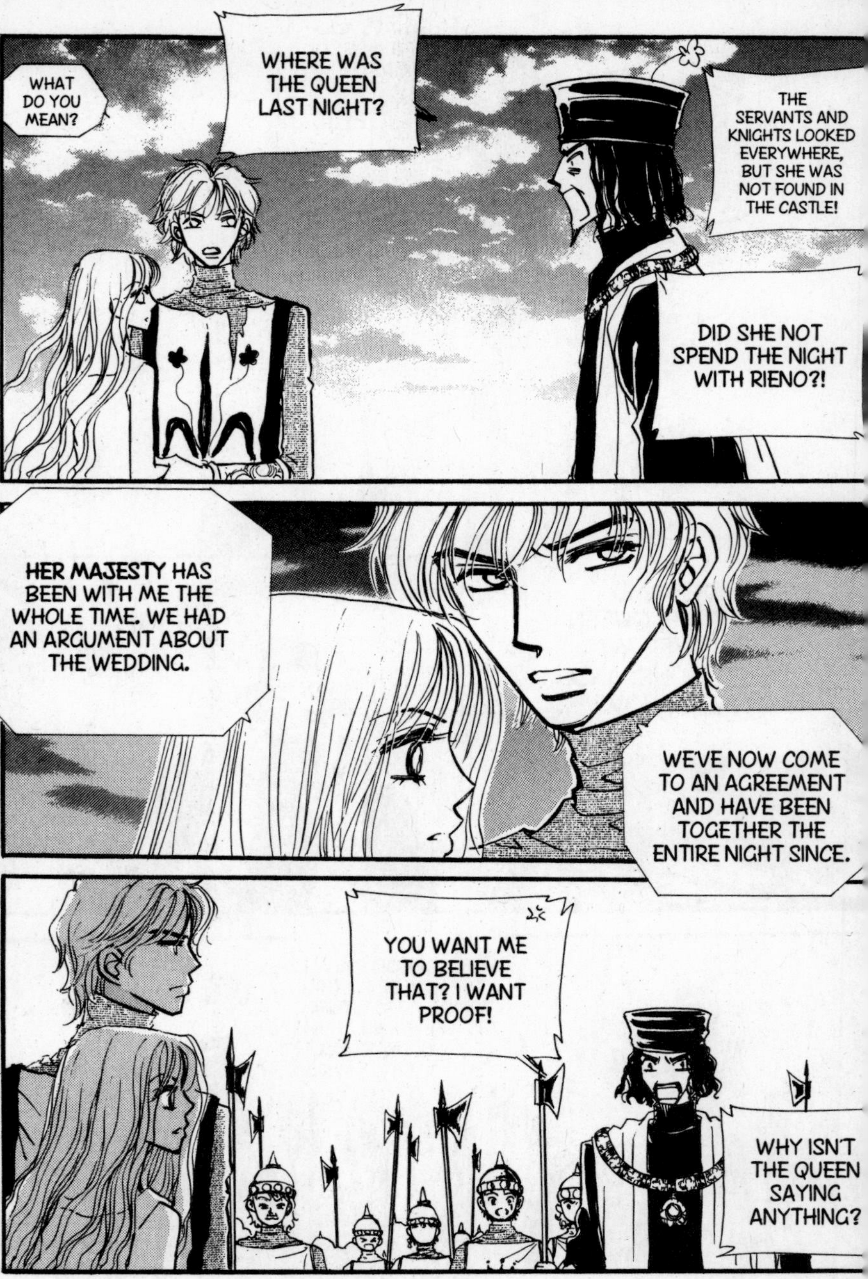
WHAT DO YOU MEAN?
WHERE WAS THE QUEEN LAST NIGHT?
THE SERVANTS AND KNIGHTS LOOKED EVERYWHERE, BUT SHE WAS NOT FOUND IN THE CASTLE!
DID SHE NOT SPEND THE NIGHT WITH RIENO?!
HER MAJESTY HAS BEEN WITH ME THE WHOLE TIME. WE HAD AN ARGUMENT ABOUT THE WEDDING.
WE'VE NOW COME TO AN AGREEMENT AND HAVE BEEN TOGETHER THE ENTIRE NIGHT SINCE.
YOU WANT ME TO BELIEVE THAT? I WANT PROOF!
WHY ISN'T THE QUEEN SAYING ANYTHING?

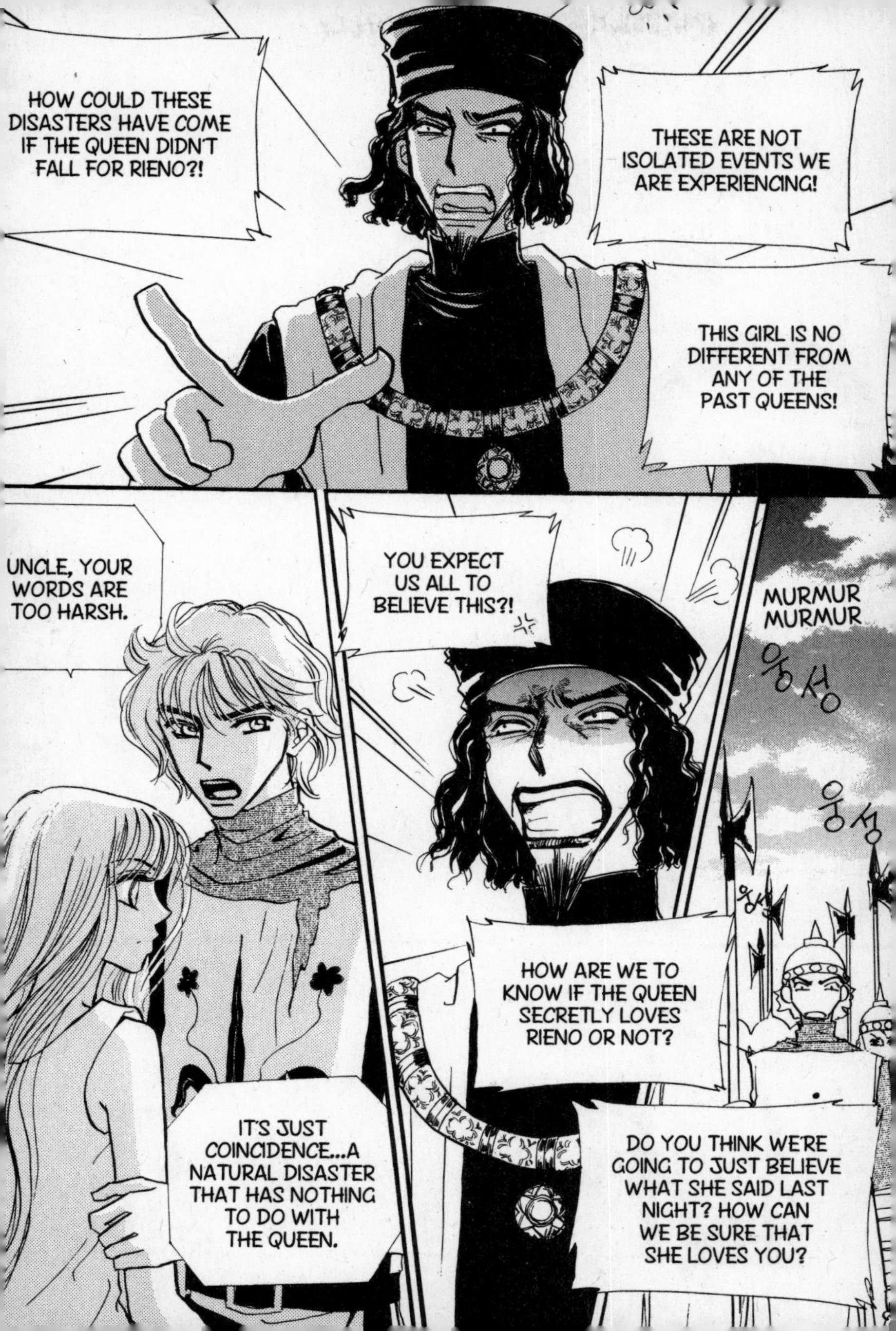

HOW COULD THESE DISASTERS HAVE COME IF THE QUEEN DIDN'T FALL FOR RIENO?!
THESE ARE NOT ISOLATED EVENTS WE ARE EXPERIENCING!
THIS GIRL IS NO DIFFERENT FROM ANY OF THE PAST QUEENS!
UNCLE, YOUR WORDS ARE TOO HARSH.
IT'S JUST COINCIDENCE...A NATURAL DISASTER THAT HAS NOTHING TO DO WITH THE QUEEN.
YOU EXPECT US ALL TO BELIEVE THIS?!
HOW ARE WE TO KNOW IF THE QUEEN SECRETLY LOVES RIENO OR NOT?
DO YOU THINK WE'RE GOING TO JUST BELIEVE WHAT SHE SAID LAST NIGHT? HOW CAN WE BE SURE THAT SHE LOVES YOU?
MURMUR MURMUR

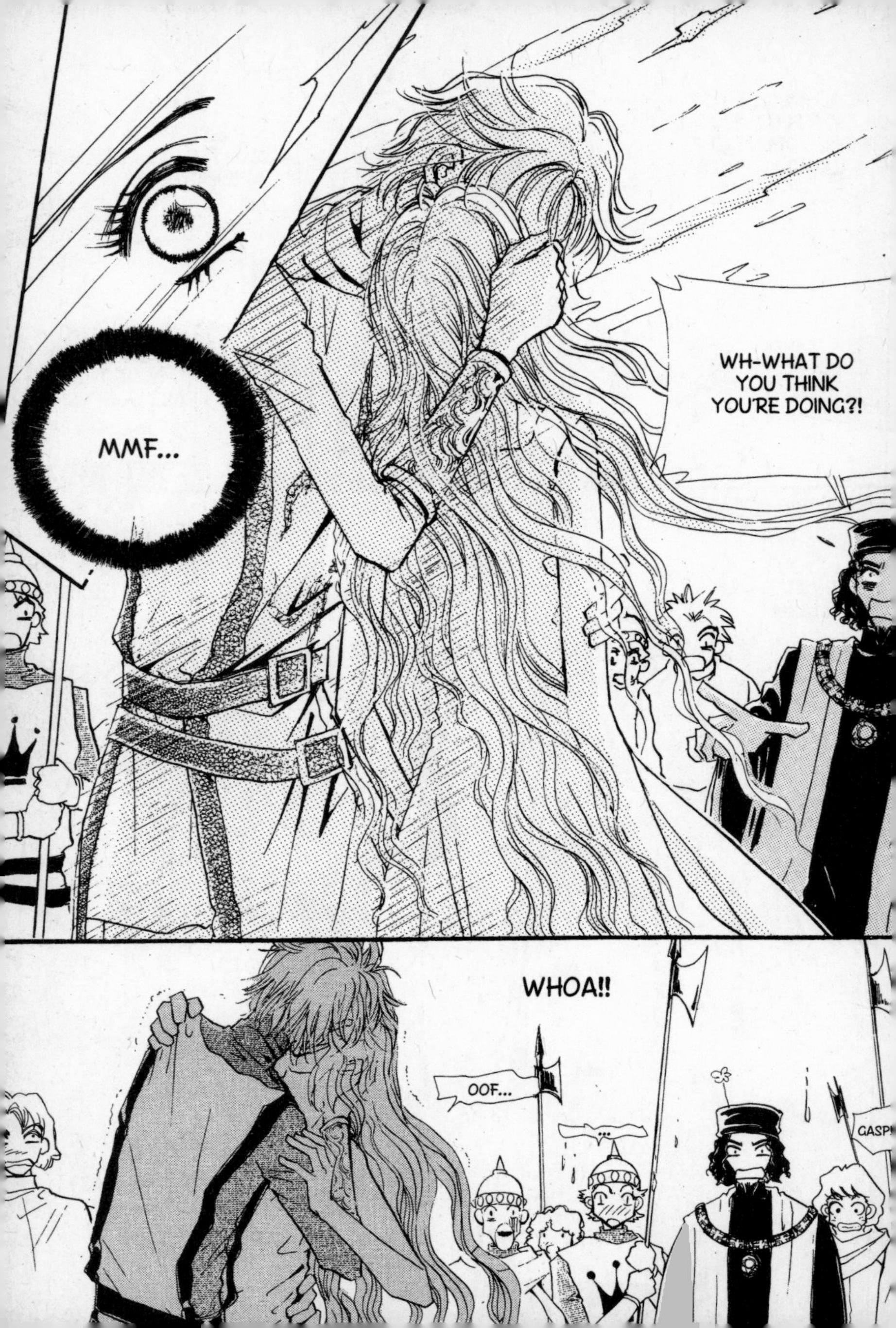
MMF...
WH-WHAT DO YOU THINK YOU'RE DOING?!
WHOA!!
OOF...
...
GASP!

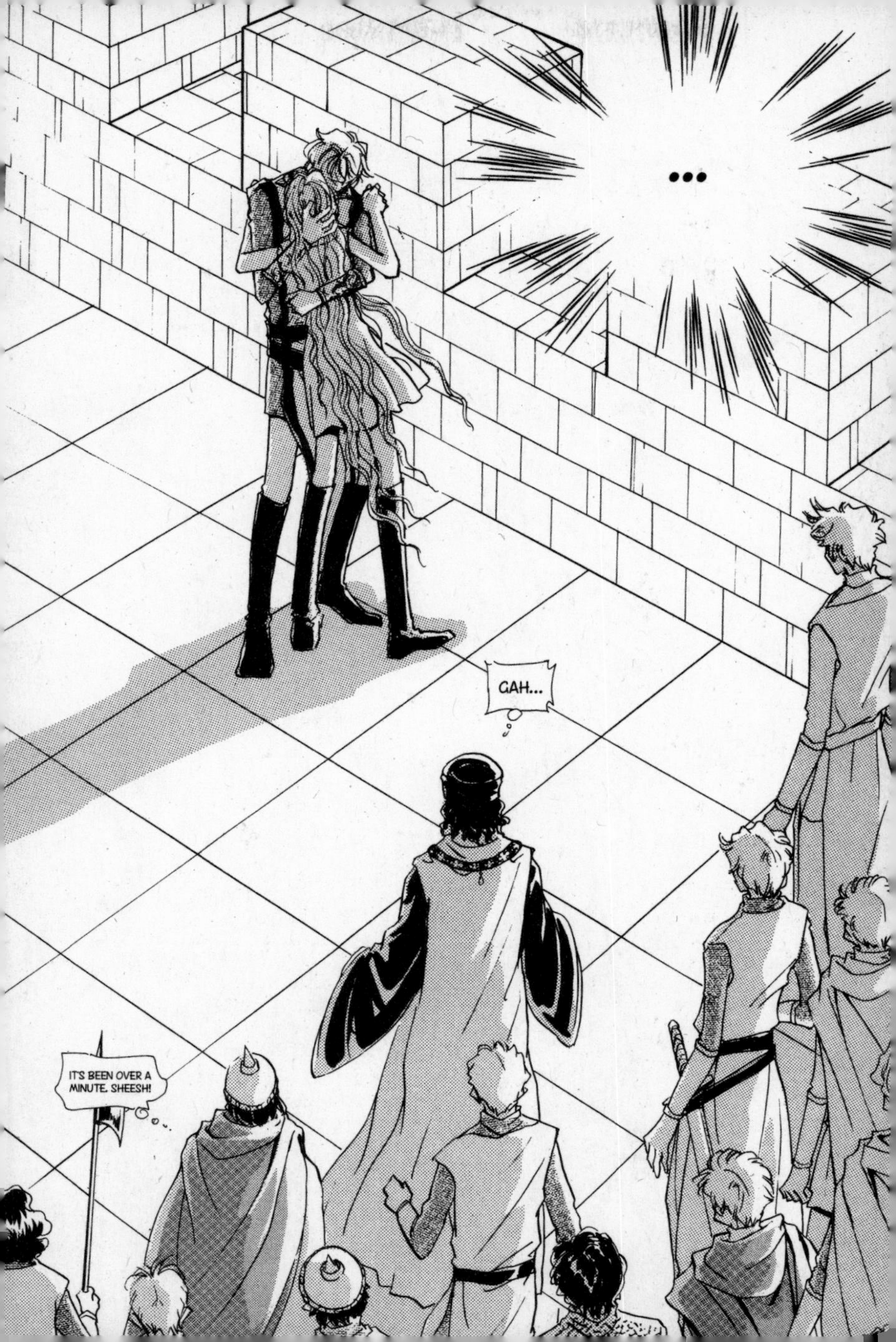
...
GAH...
IT'S BEEN OVER A MINUTE. SHEESH!

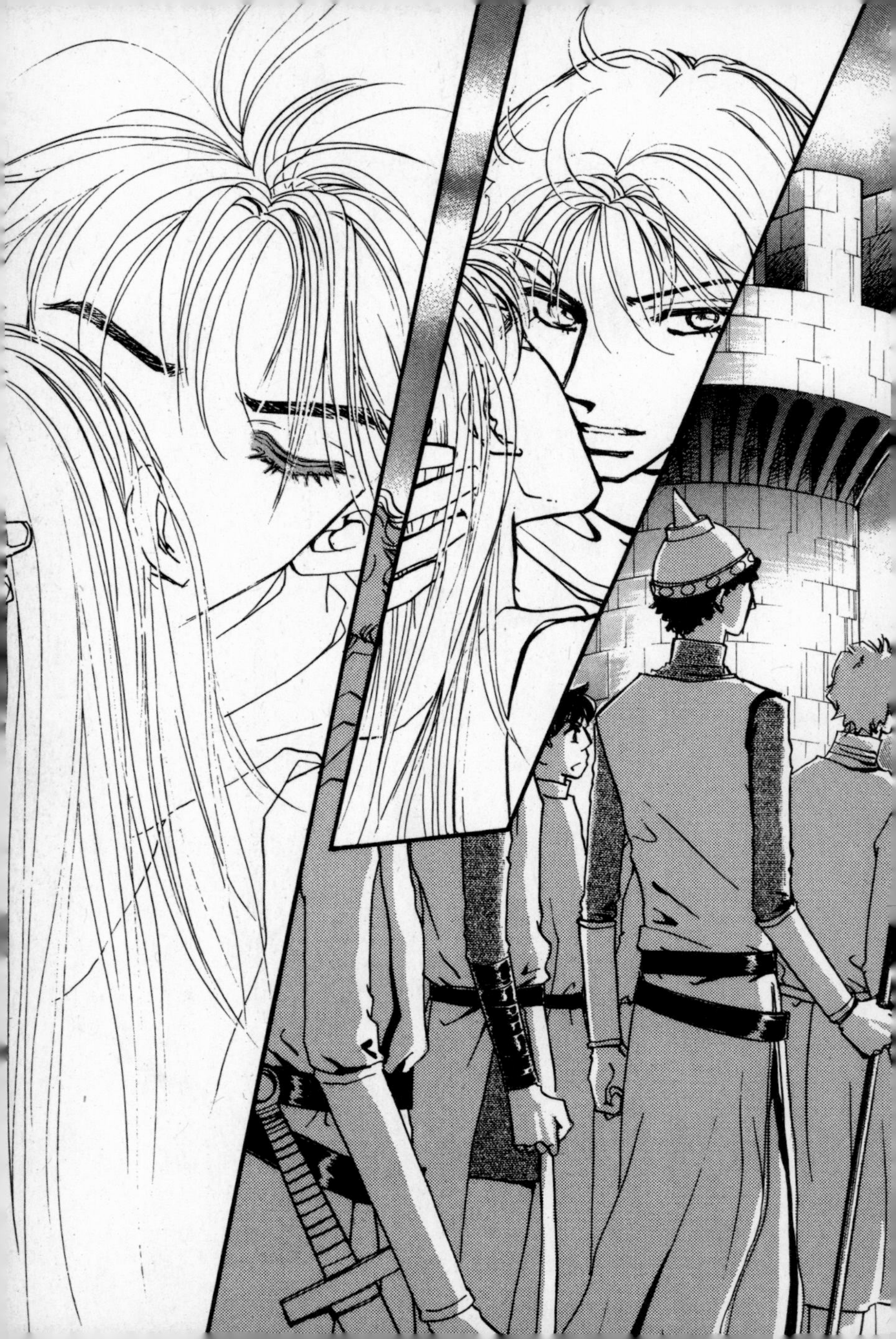

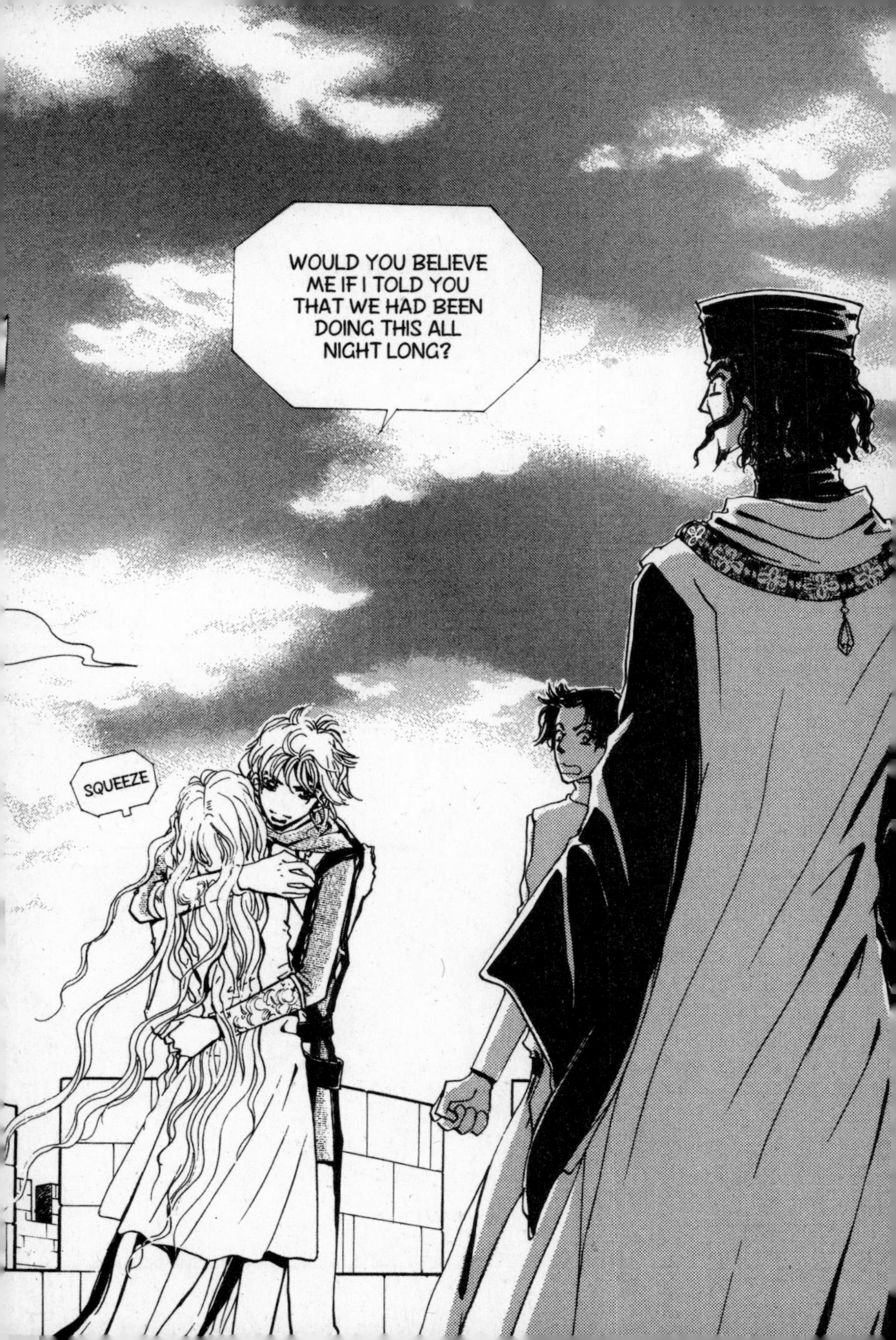
WOULD YOU BELIEVE ME IF I TOLD YOU THAT WE HAD BEEN DOING THIS ALL NIGHT LONG?
SQUEEZE

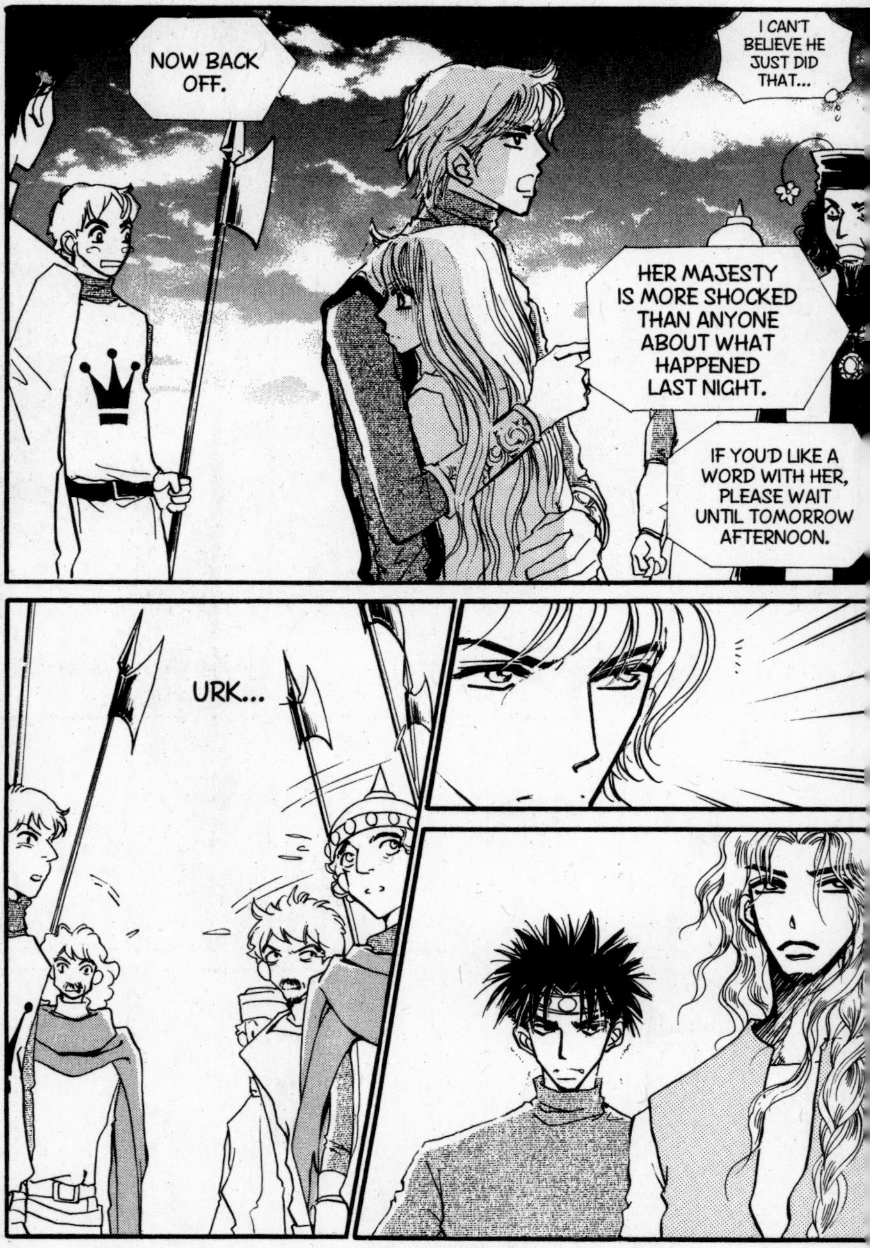
NOW BACK OFF.
I CAN'T BELIEVE HE JUST DID THAT...
HER MAJESTY IS MORE SHOCKED THAN ANYONE ABOUT WHAT HAPPENED LAST NIGHT.
IF YOU'D LIKE A WORD WITH HER, PLEASE WAIT UNTIL TOMORROW AFTERNOON.
URK...

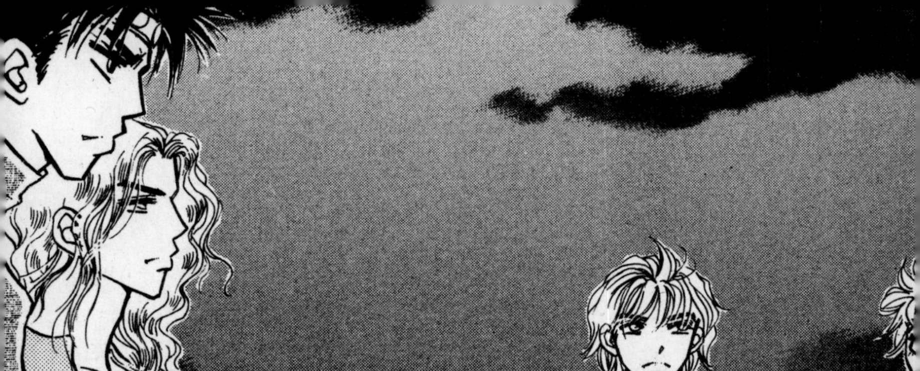
BAH!

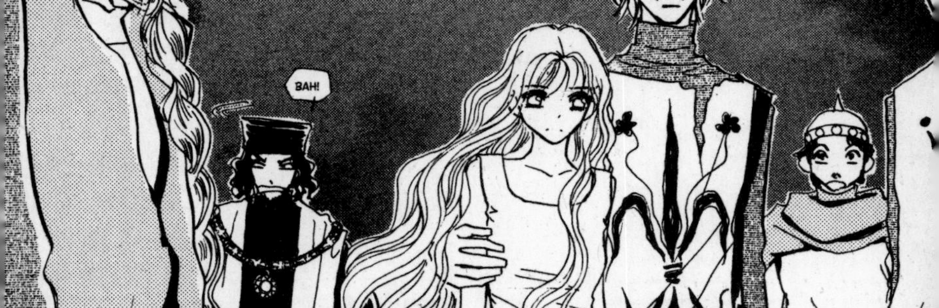

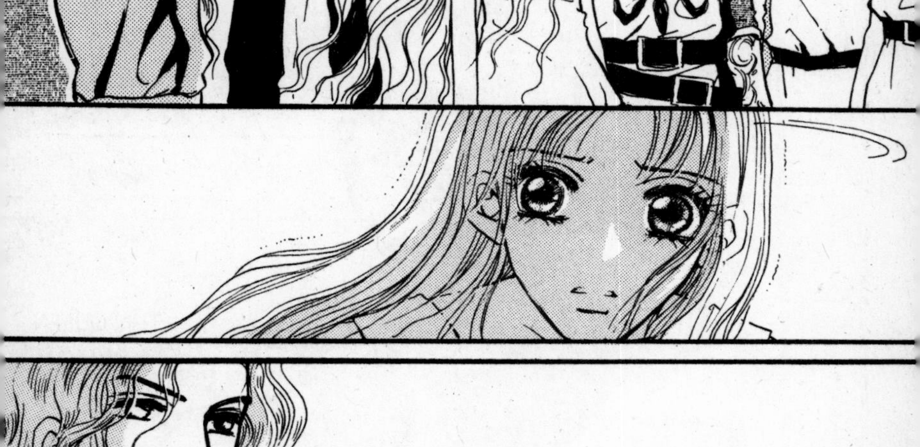

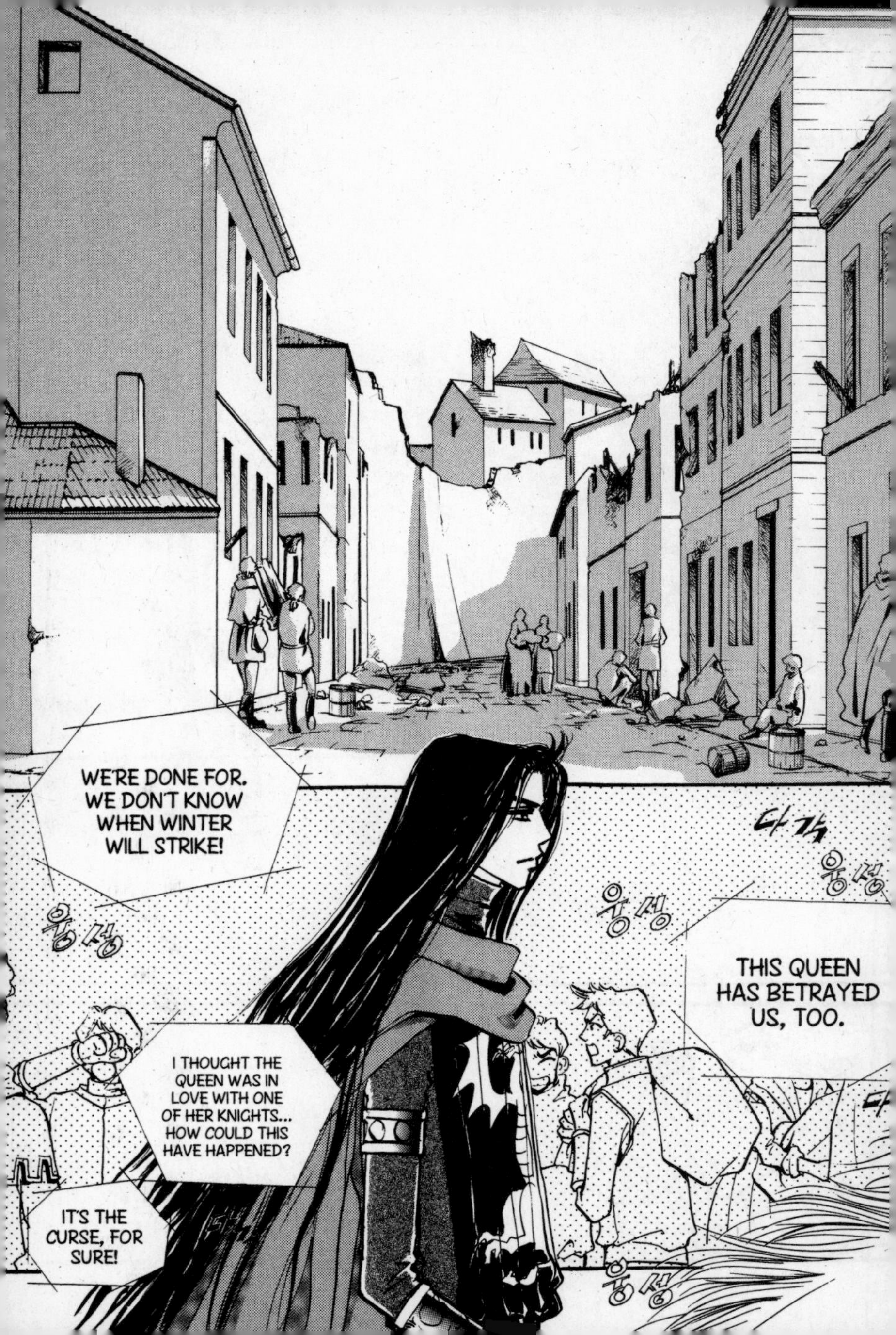
WE'RE DONE FOR. WE DON'T KNOW WHEN WINTER WILL STRIKE!
다각
웅성
웅성
웅성
THIS QUEEN HAS BETRAYED US, TOO.
I THOUGHT THE QUEEN WAS IN LOVE WITH ONE OF HER KNIGHTS... HOW COULD THIS HAVE HAPPENED?
IT'S THE CURSE, FOR SURE!
웅성

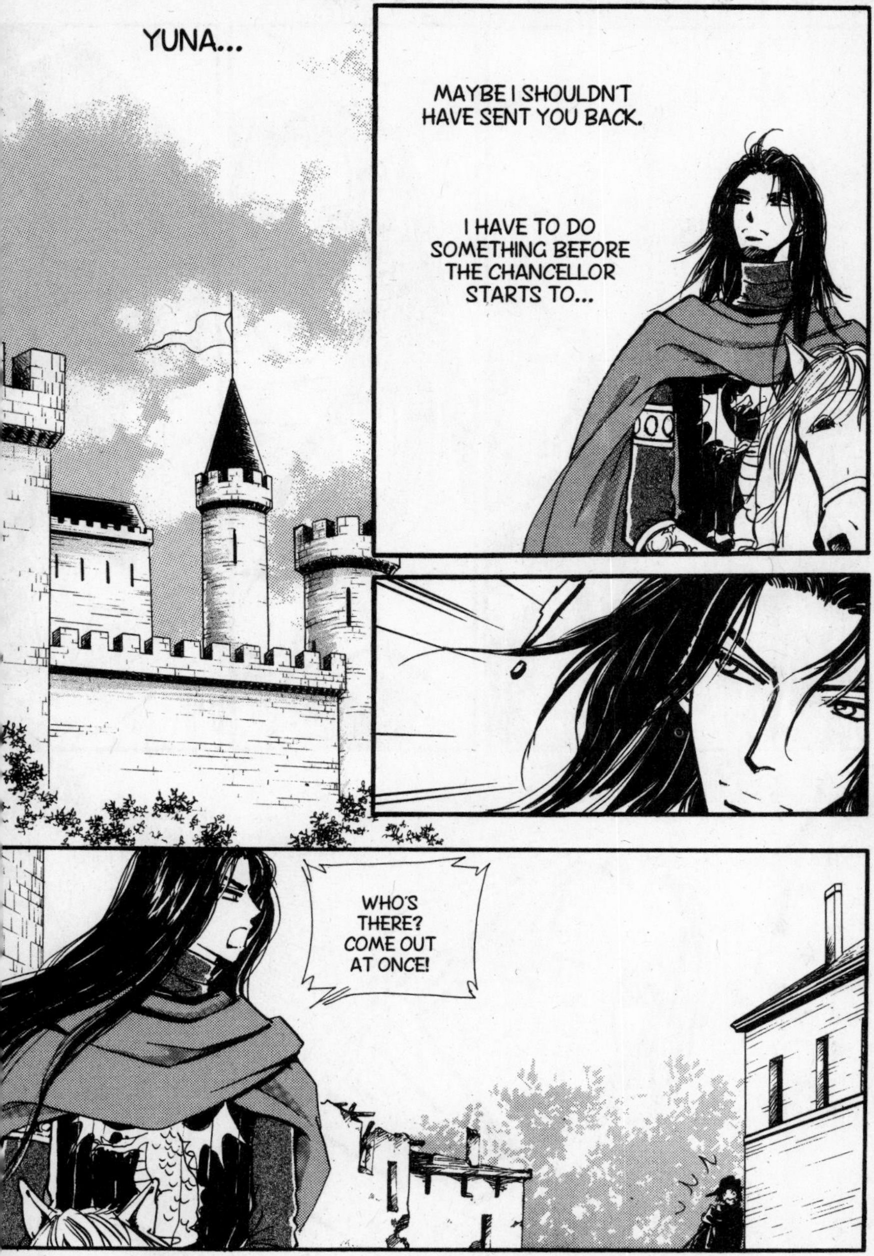
YUNA...
MAYBE I SHOULDN'T HAVE SENT YOU BACK.
I HAVE TO DO SOMETHING BEFORE THE CHANCELLOR STARTS TO...
WHO'S THERE? COME OUT AT ONCE!

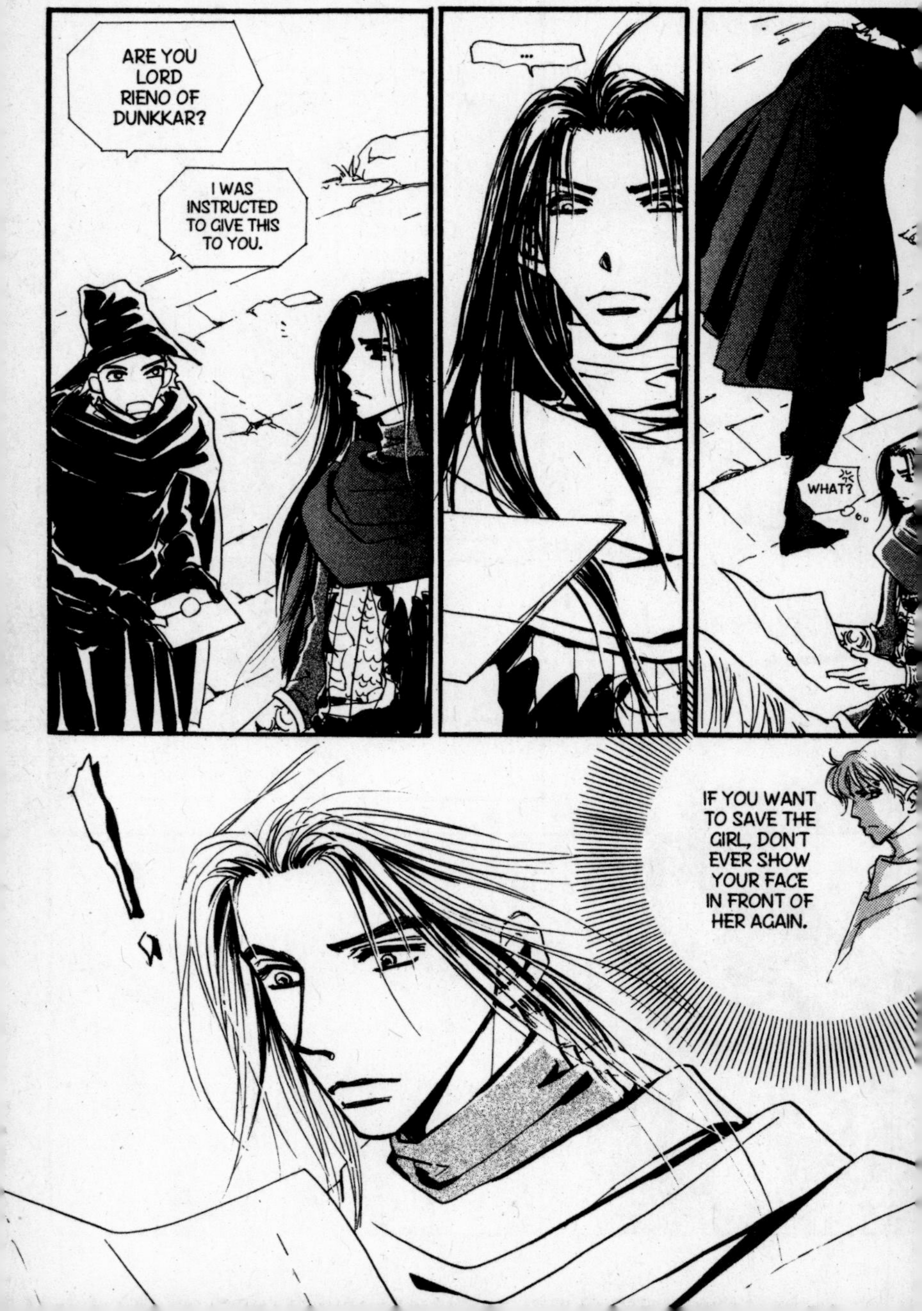
ARE YOU LORD RIENO OF DUNKKAR?
I WAS INSTRUCTED TO GIVE THIS TO YOU.
...
WHAT?
!
IF YOU WANT TO SAVE THE GIRL, DON'T EVER SHOW YOUR FACE IN FRONT OF HER AGAIN.

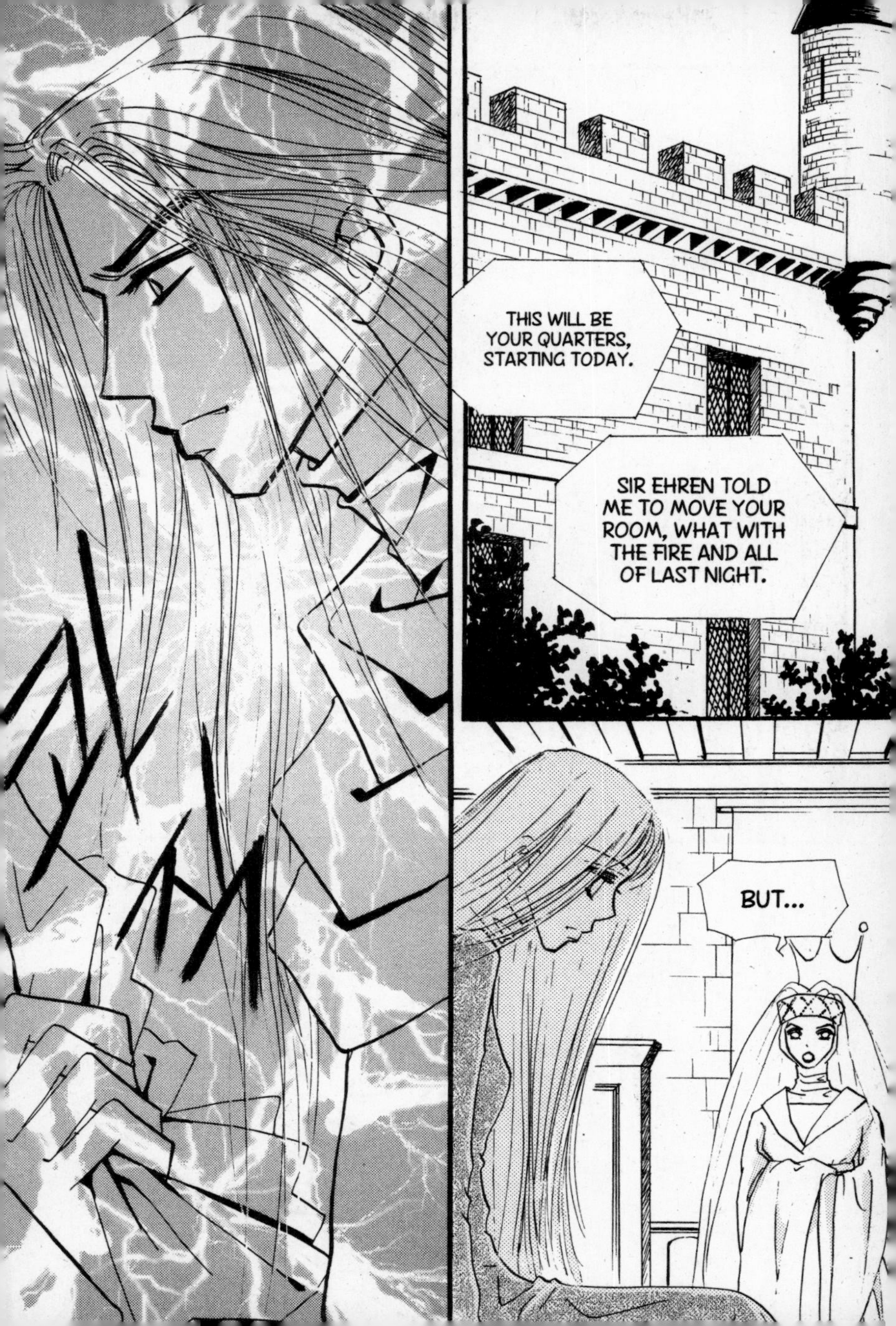
THIS WILL BE YOUR QUARTERS, STARTING TODAY.
SIR EHREN TOLD ME TO MOVE YOUR ROOM, WHAT WITH THE FIRE AND ALL OF LAST NIGHT.
BUT...

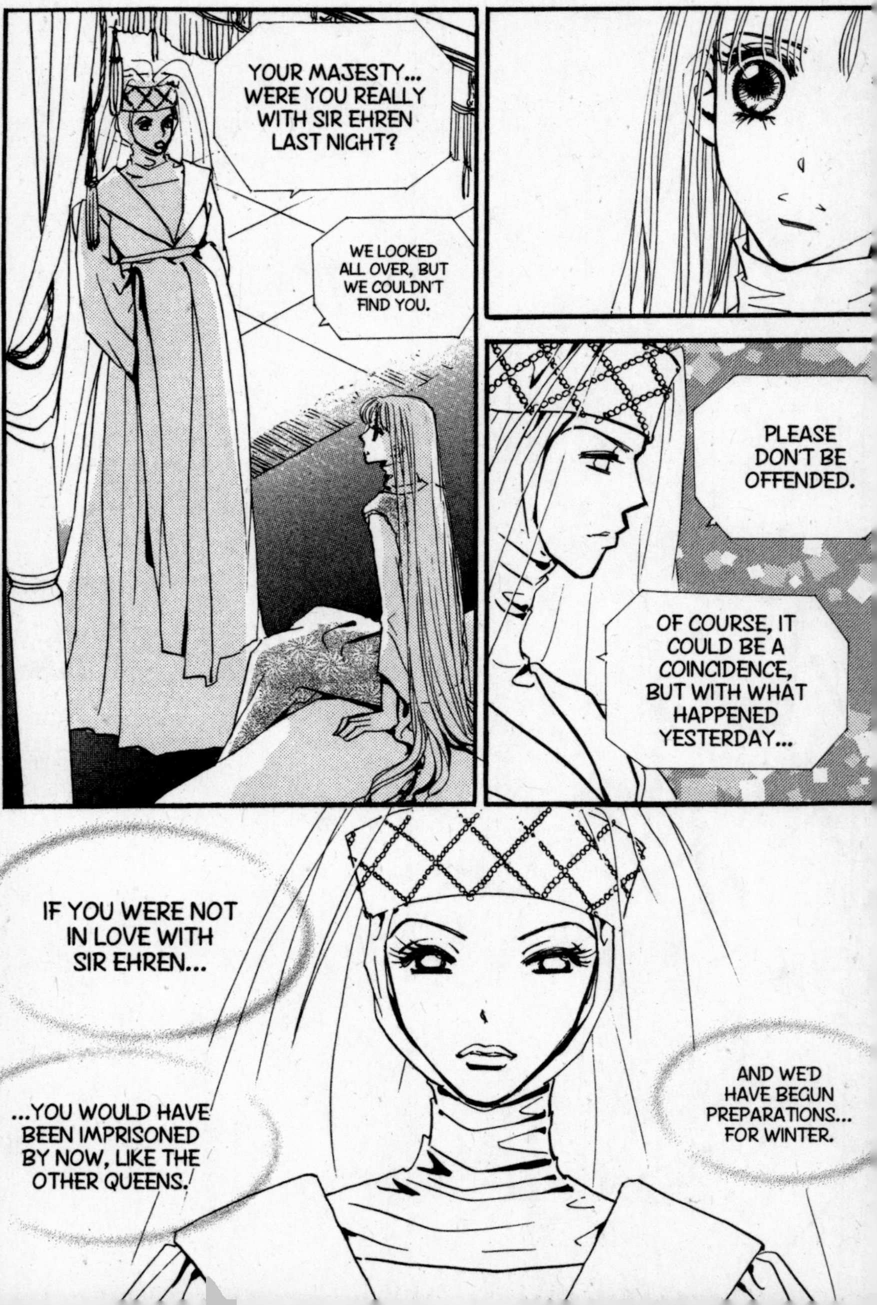
YOUR MAJESTY... WERE YOU REALLY WITH SIR EHREN LAST NIGHT?
WE LOOKED ALL OVER, BUT WE COULDN'T FIND YOU.
PLEASE DON'T BE OFFENDED.
OF COURSE, IT COULD BE A COINCIDENCE, BUT WITH WHAT HAPPENED YESTERDAY...
IF YOU WERE NOT IN LOVE WITH SIR EHREN...
...YOU WOULD HAVE BEEN IMPRISONED BY NOW, LIKE THE OTHER QUEENS.
AND WE'D HAVE BEGUN PREPARATIONS... FOR WINTER.

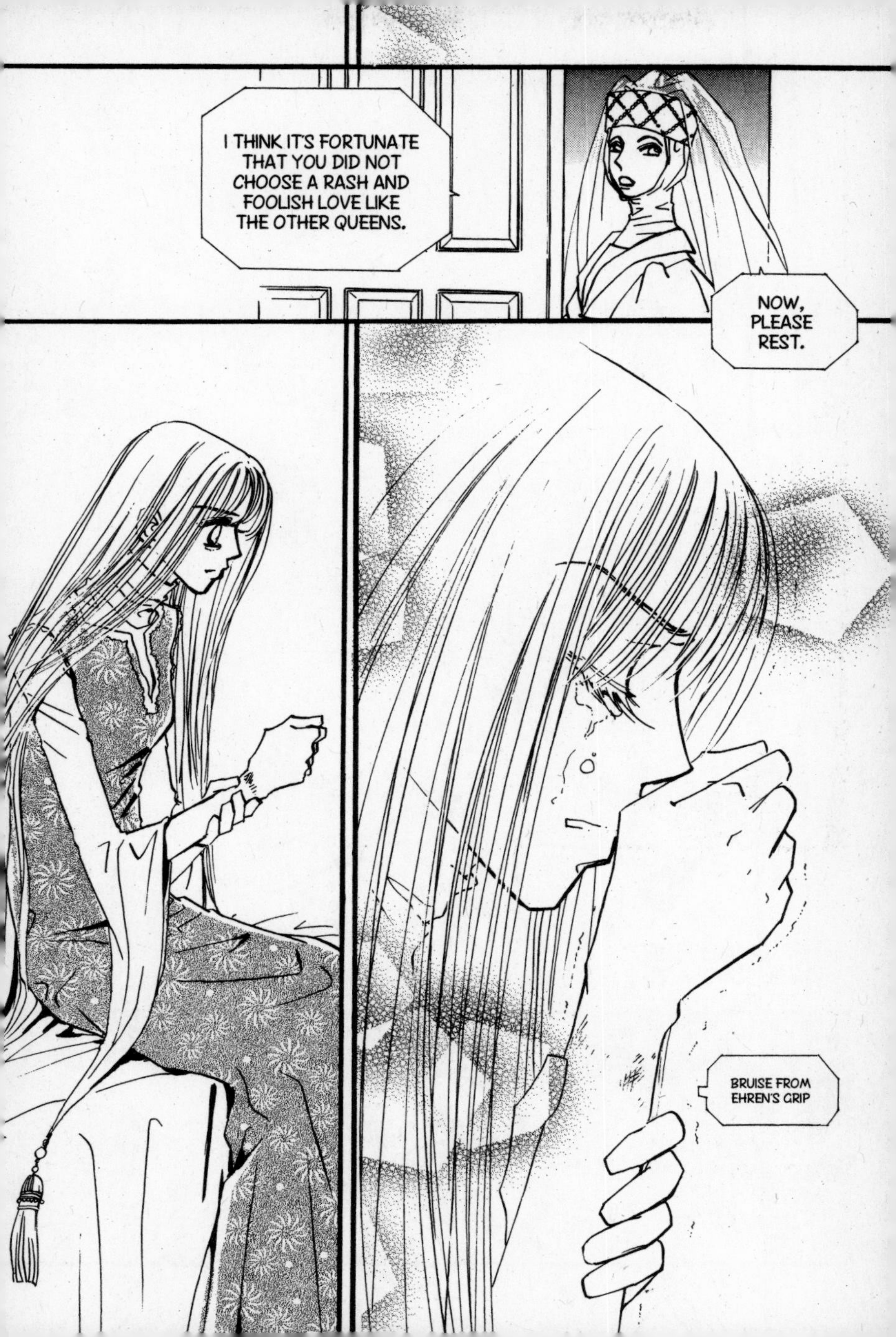
I THINK IT'S FORTUNATE THAT YOU DID NOT CHOOSE A RASH AND FOOLISH LOVE LIKE THE OTHER QUEENS.
NOW, PLEASE REST.
BRUISE FROM EHREN'S GRIP

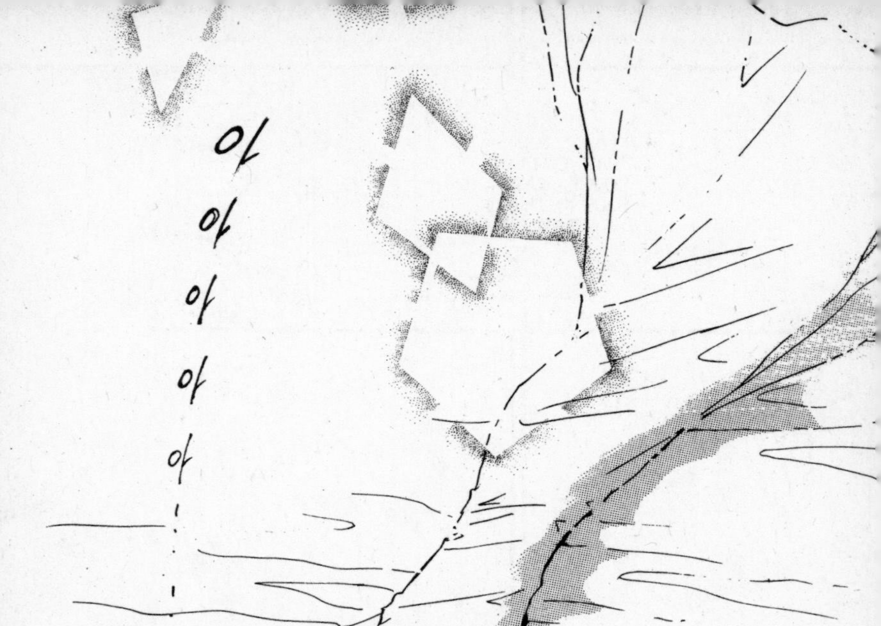
아아아아아
WEEP...

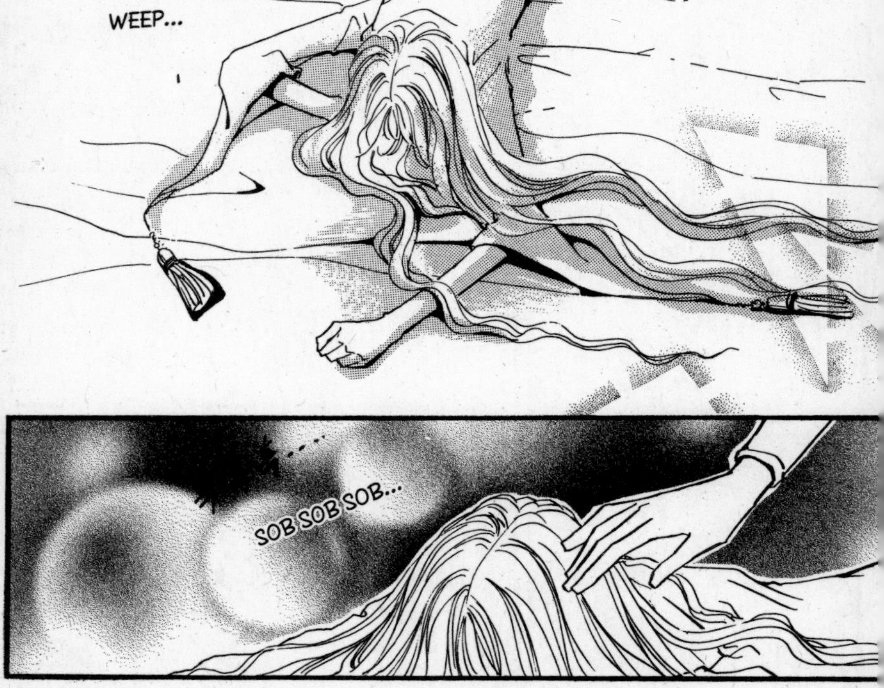
SOB SOB SOB...

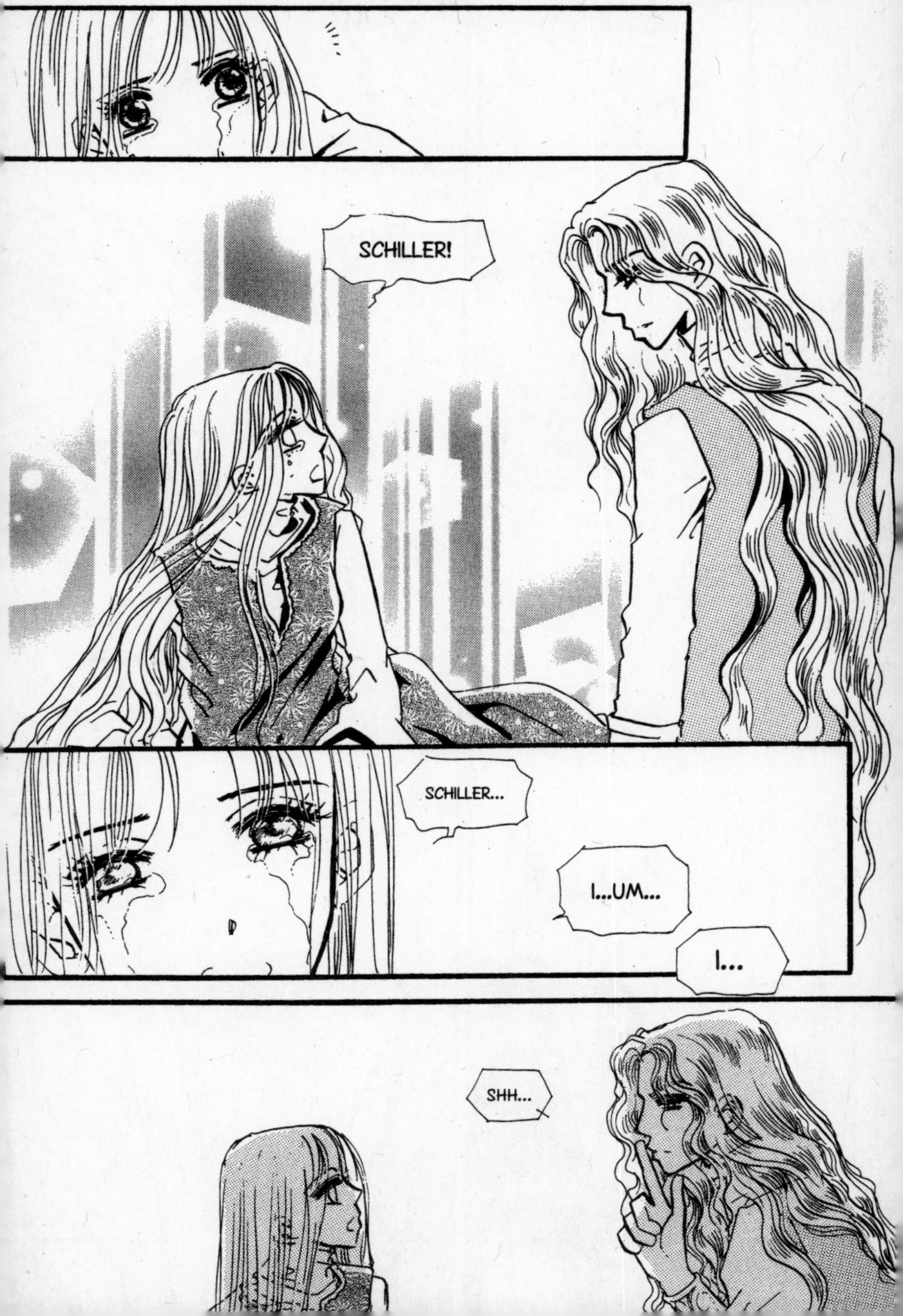
SCHILLER!
SCHILLER...
I...UM...
I...
SHH...

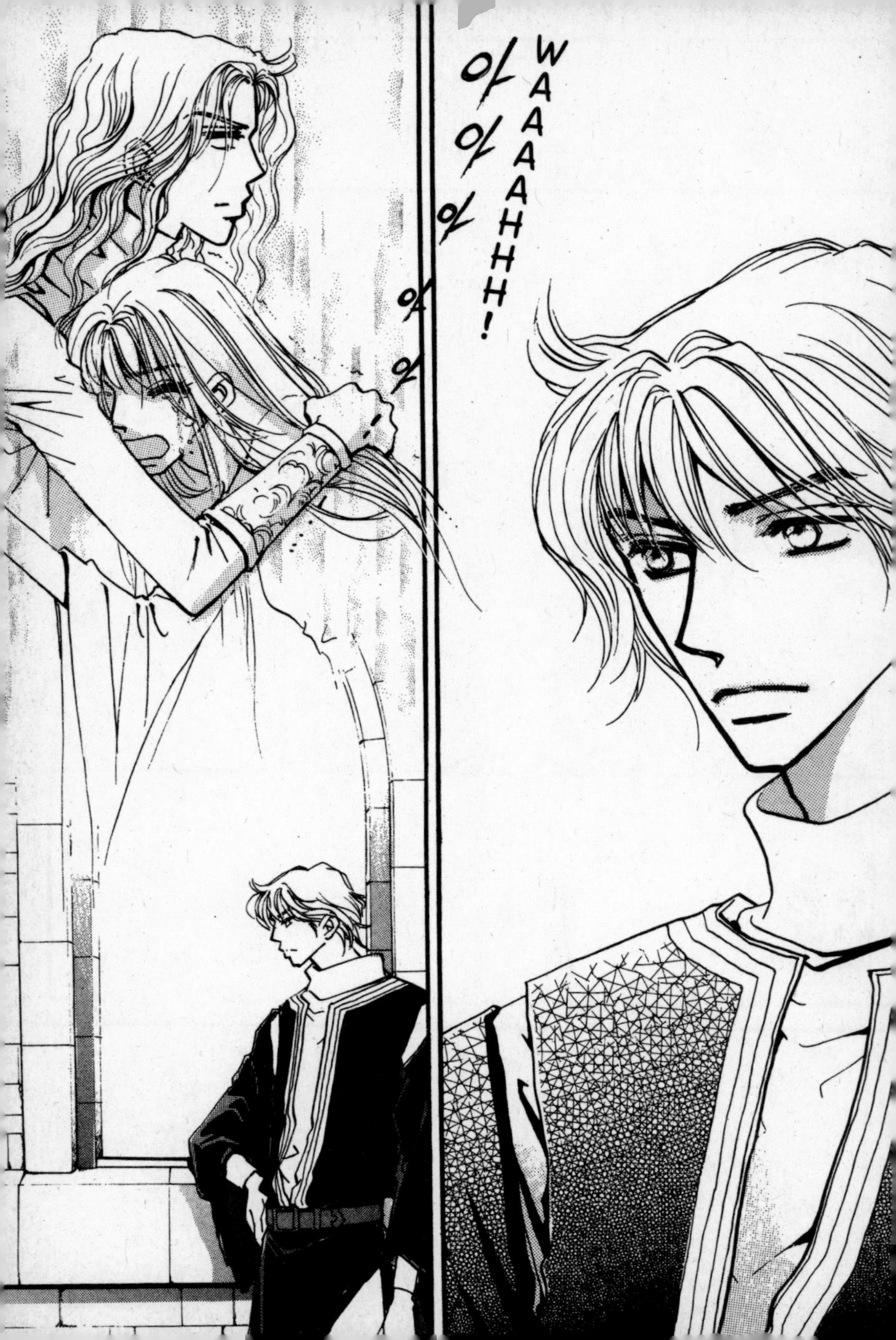
아아아아아
WAAAAHHH!

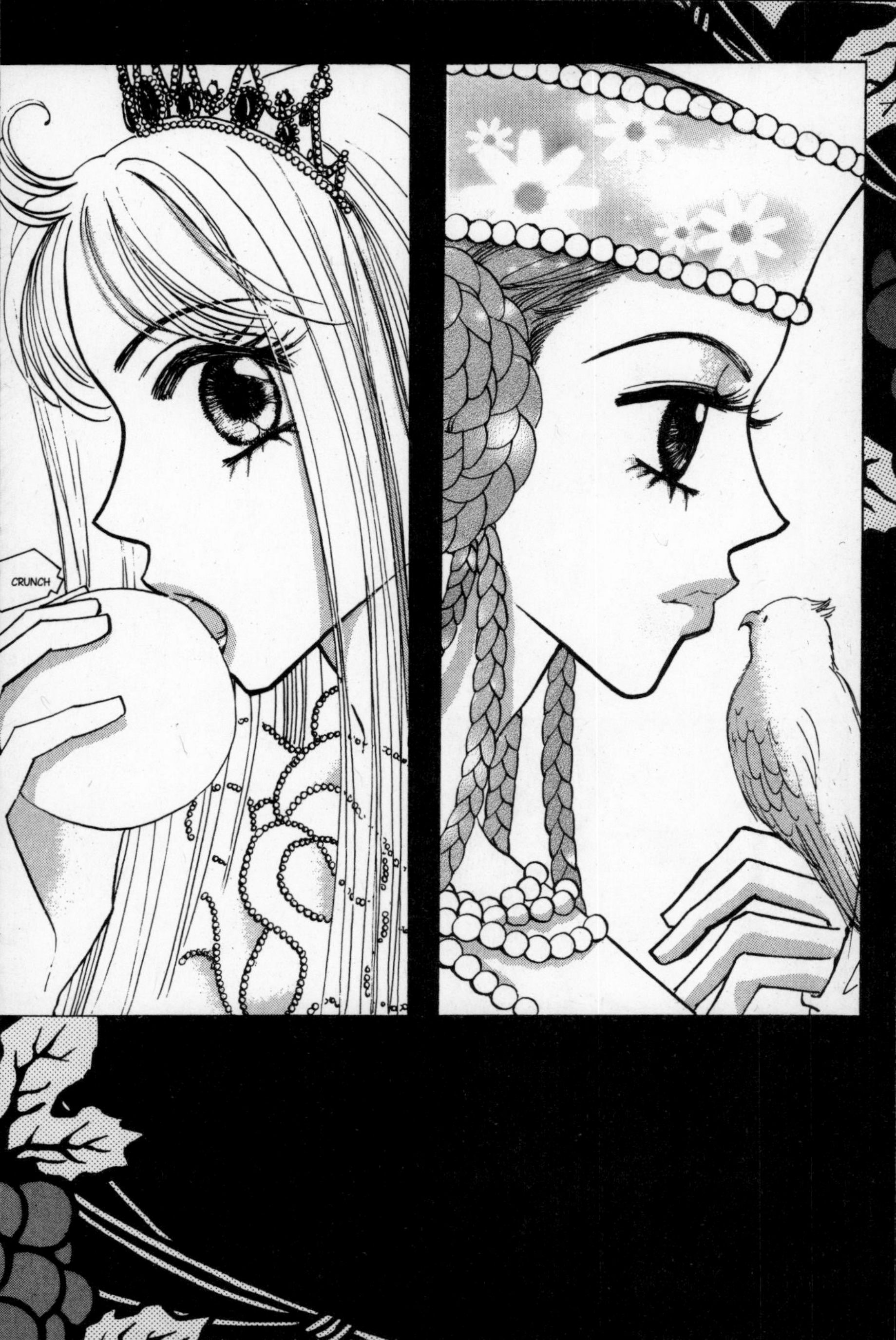
CRUNCH

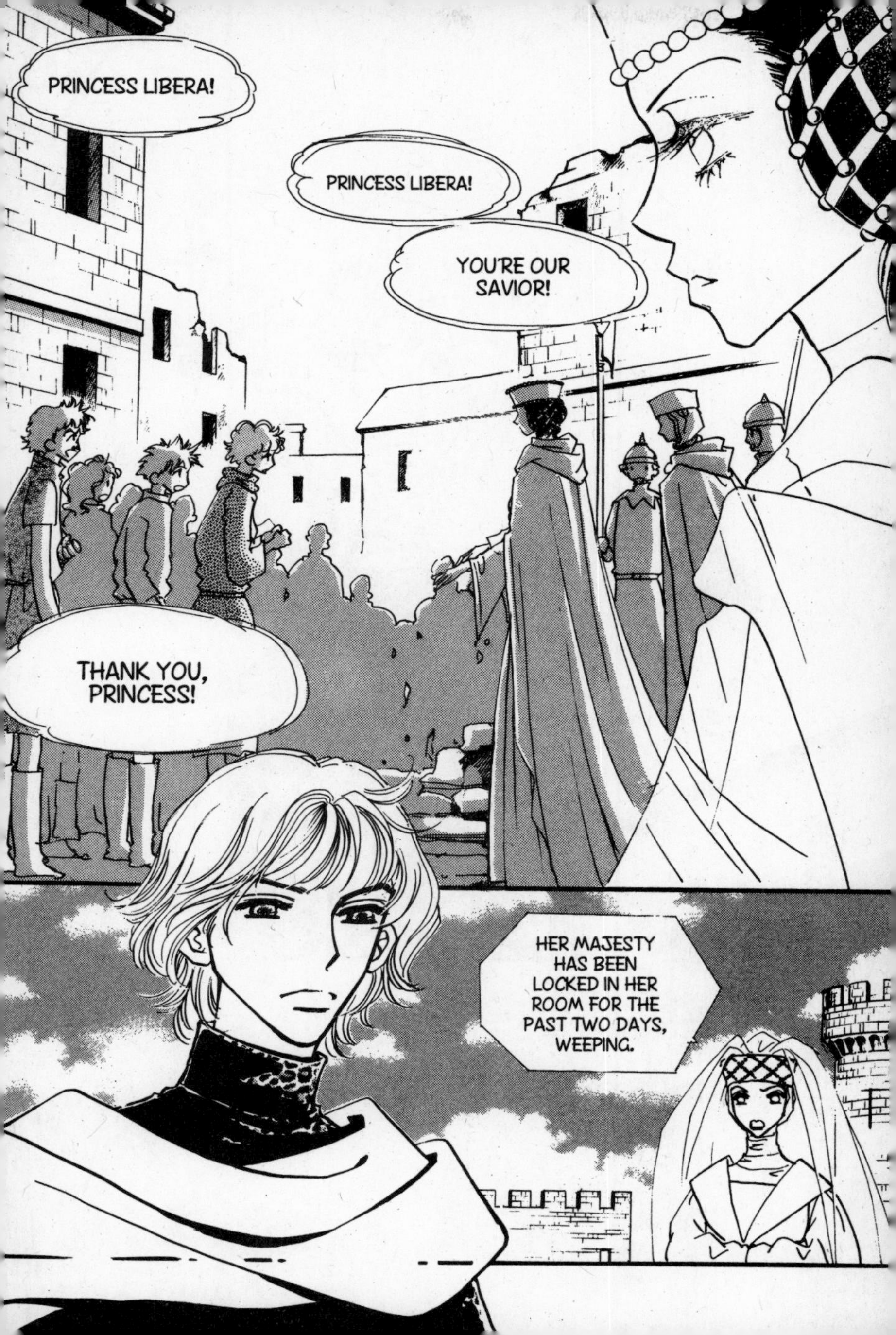
PRINCESS LIBERA!
PRINCESS LIBERA!
YOU'RE OUR SAVIOR!
THANK YOU, PRINCESS!
HER MAJESTY HAS BEEN LOCKED IN HER ROOM FOR THE PAST TWO DAYS, WEEPING.

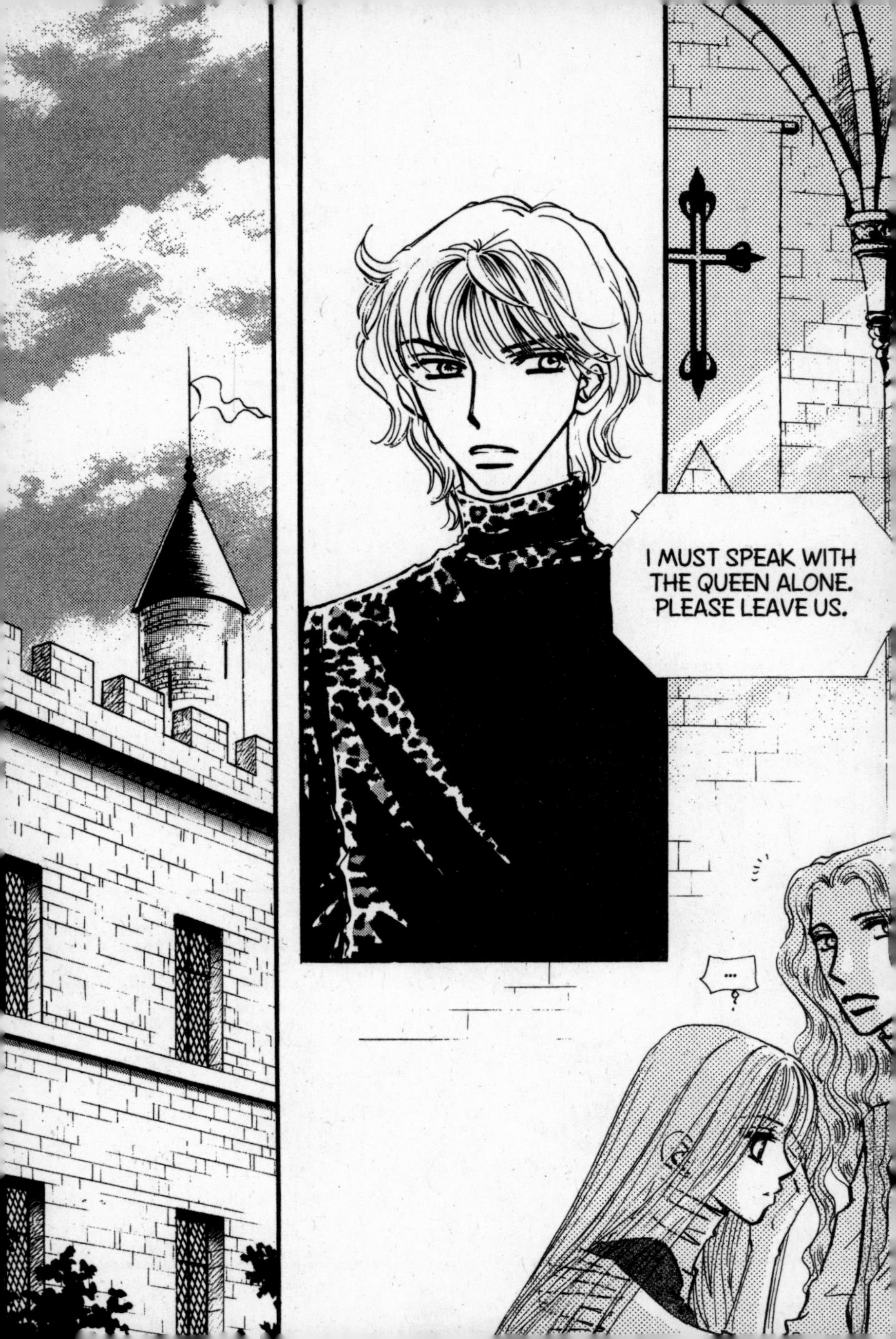
I MUST SPEAK WITH THE QUEEN ALONE. PLEASE LEAVE US.
...?

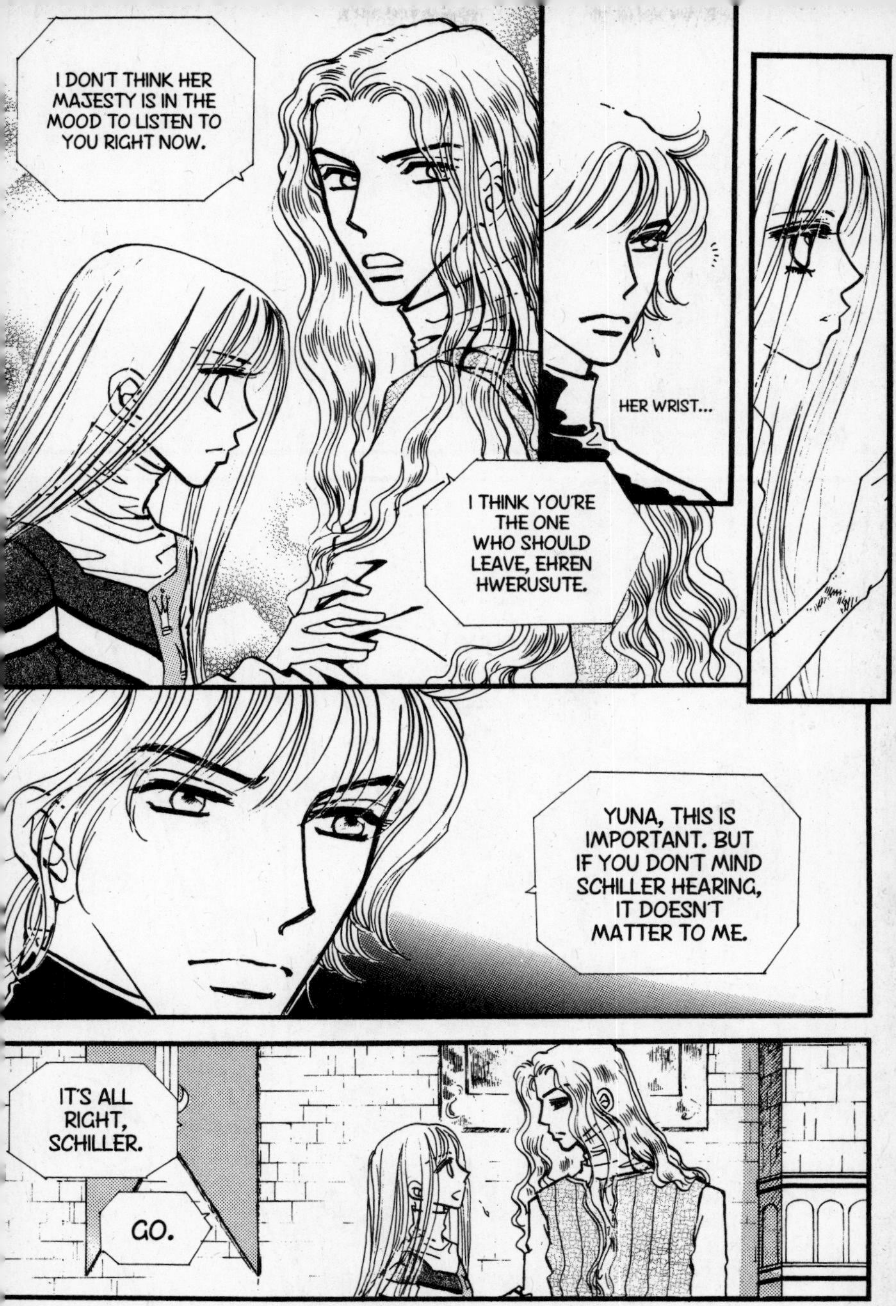
I DON'T THINK HER MAJESTY IS IN THE MOOD TO LISTEN TO YOU RIGHT NOW.
I THINK YOU'RE THE ONE WHO SHOULD LEAVE, EHREN HWERUSUTE.
HER WRIST...
YUNA, THIS IS IMPORTANT. BUT IF YOU DON'T MIND SCHILLER HEARING, IT DOESN'T MATTER TO ME.
IT'S ALL RIGHT, SCHILLER.
GO.

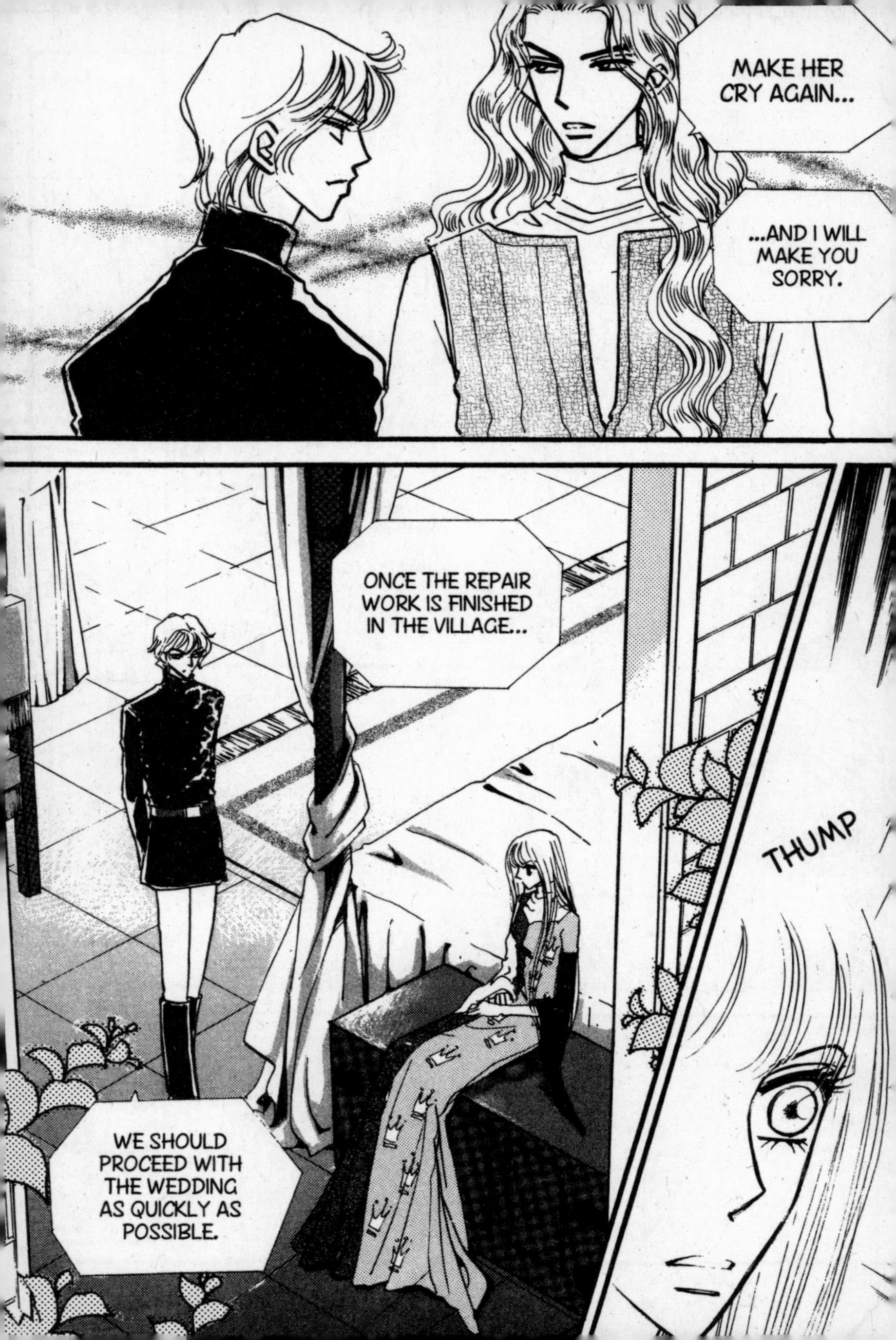
MAKE HER CRY AGAIN...
...AND I WILL MAKE YOU SORRY.
ONCE THE REPAIR WORK IS FINISHED IN THE VILLAGE...
WE SHOULD PROCEED WITH THE WEDDING AS QUICKLY AS POSSIBLE.
THUMP

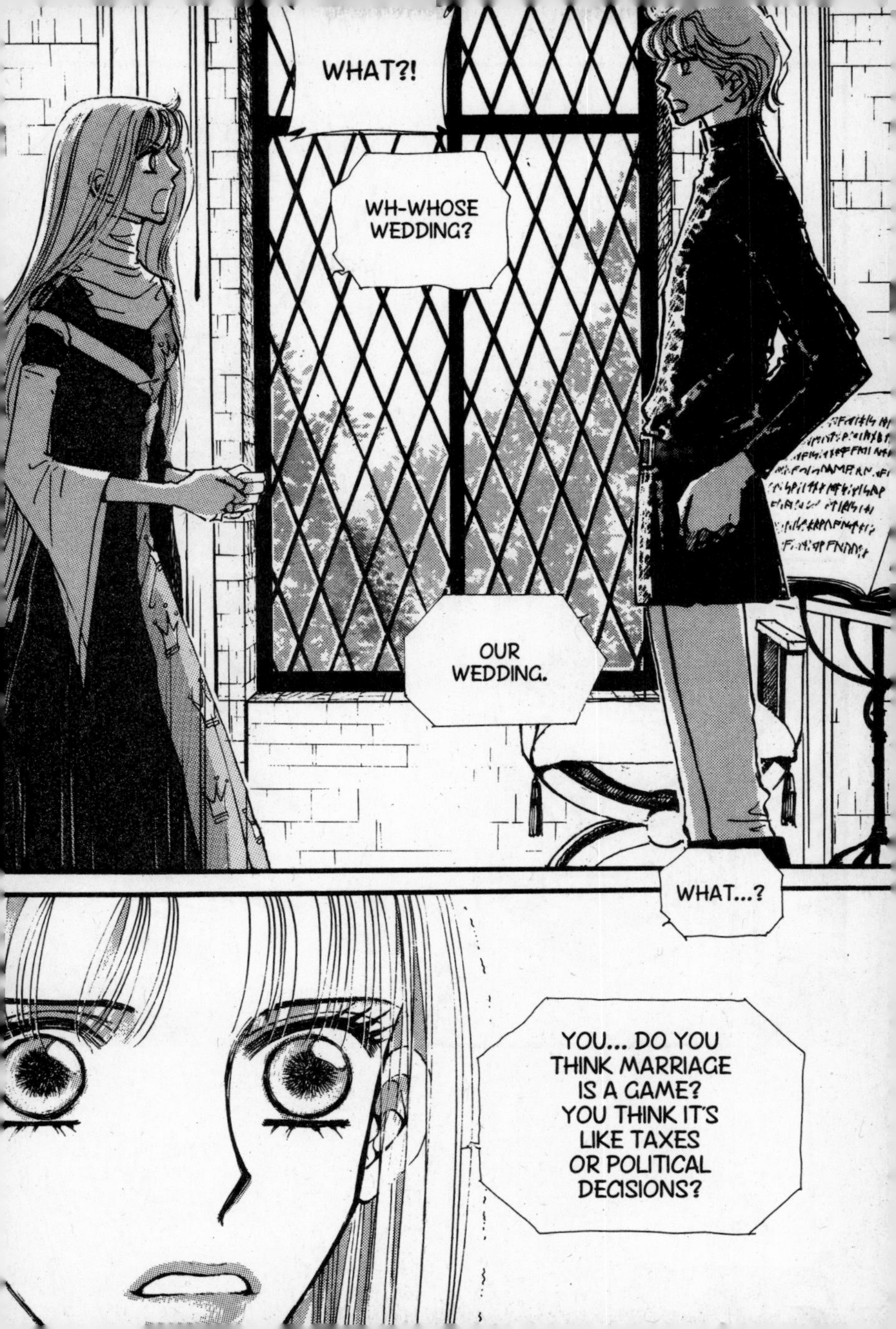
WHAT?!
WH-WHOSE WEDDING?
OUR WEDDING.
WHAT...?
YOU... DO YOU THINK MARRIAGE IS A GAME? YOU THINK IT'S LIKE TAXES OR POLITICAL DECISIONS?

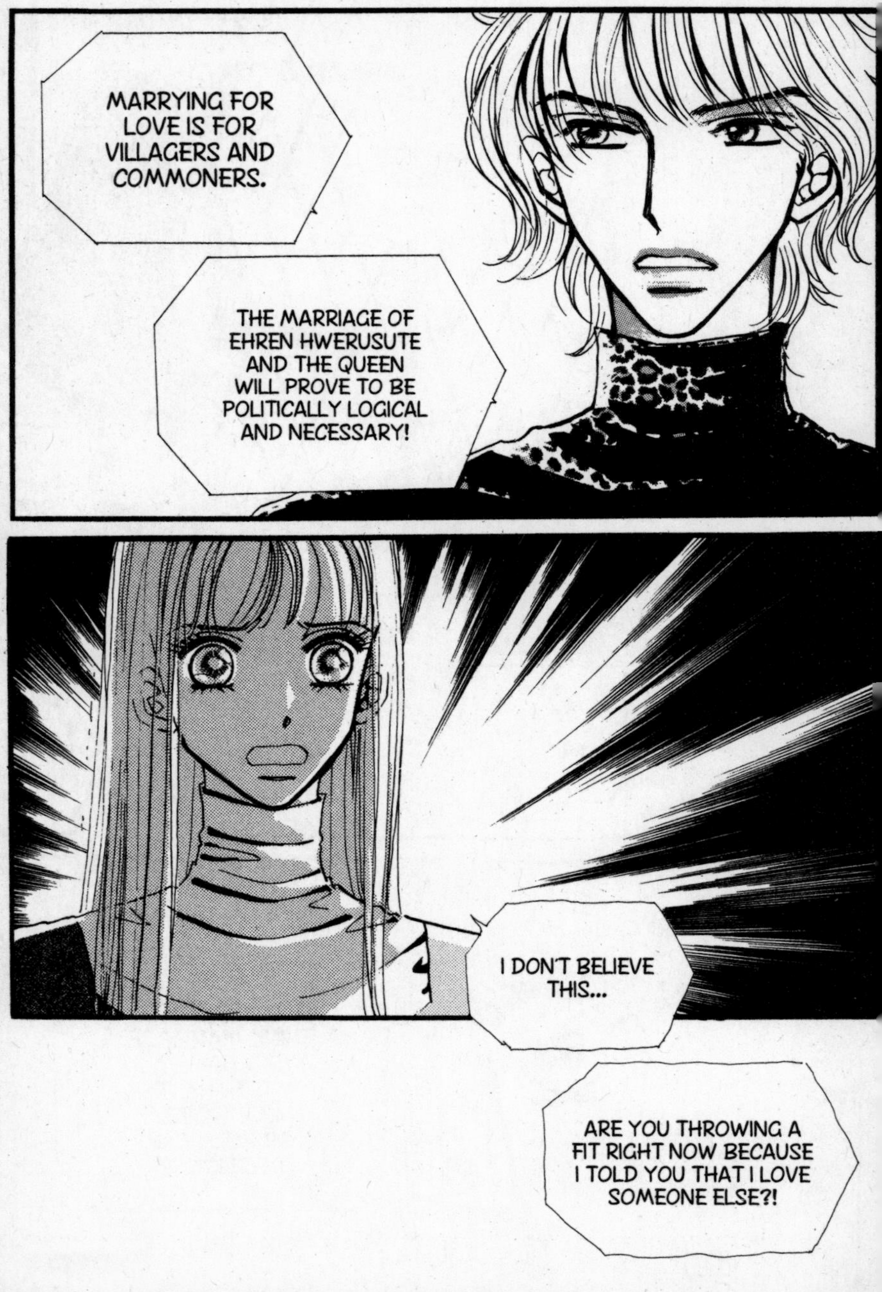
MARRYING FOR LOVE IS FOR VILLAGERS AND COMMONERS.
THE MARRIAGE OF EHREN HWERUSUTE AND THE QUEEN WILL PROVE TO BE POLITICALLY LOGICAL AND NECESSARY!
I DON'T BELIEVE THIS...
ARE YOU THROWING A FIT RIGHT NOW BECAUSE I TOLD YOU THAT I LOVE SOMEONE ELSE?!

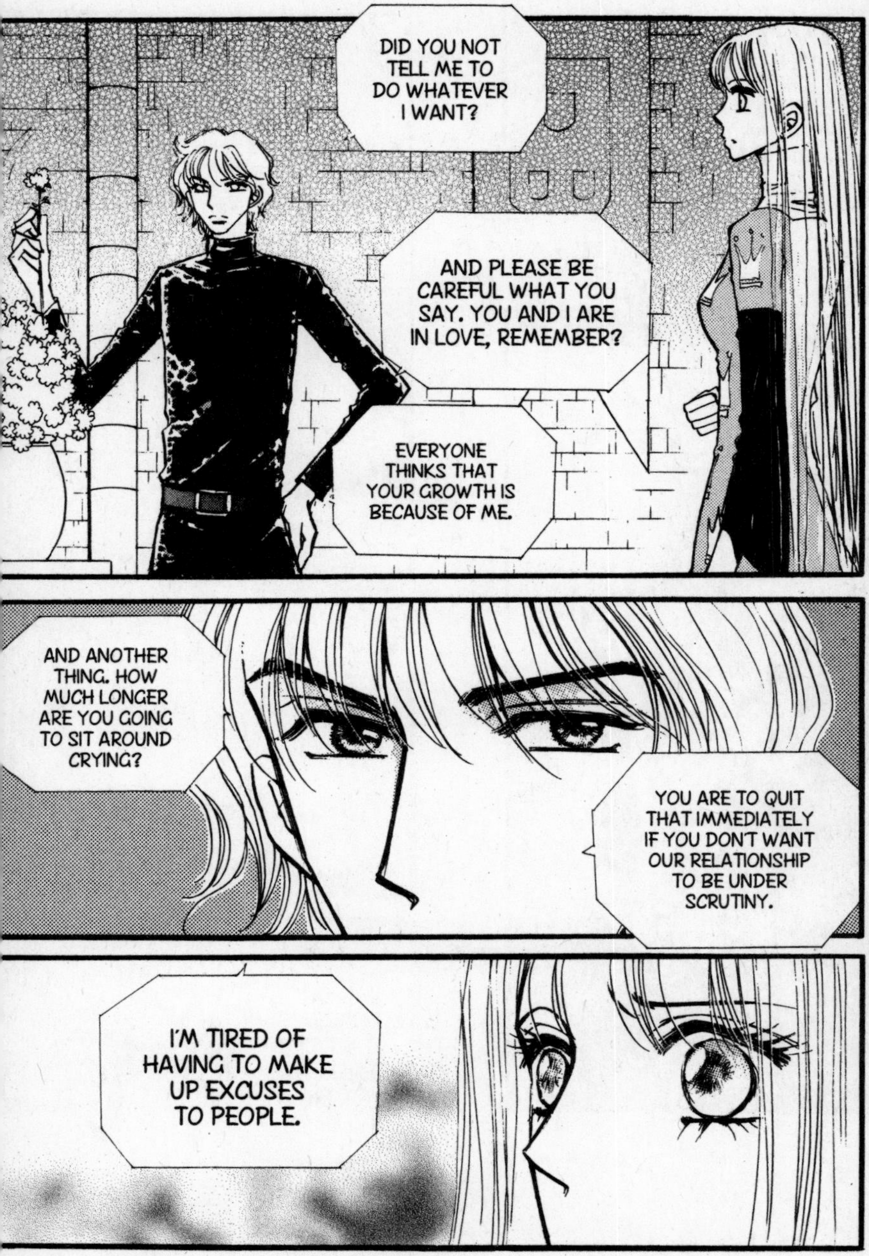
DID YOU NOT TELL ME TO DO WHATEVER I WANT?
AND PLEASE BE CAREFUL WHAT YOU SAY. YOU AND I ARE IN LOVE, REMEMBER?
EVERYONE THINKS THAT YOUR GROWTH IS BECAUSE OF ME.
AND ANOTHER THING. HOW MUCH LONGER ARE YOU GOING TO SIT AROUND CRYING?
YOU ARE TO QUIT THAT IMMEDIATELY IF YOU DON'T WANT OUR RELATIONSHIP TO BE UNDER SCRUTINY.
I'M TIRED OF HAVING TO MAKE UP EXCUSES TO PEOPLE.

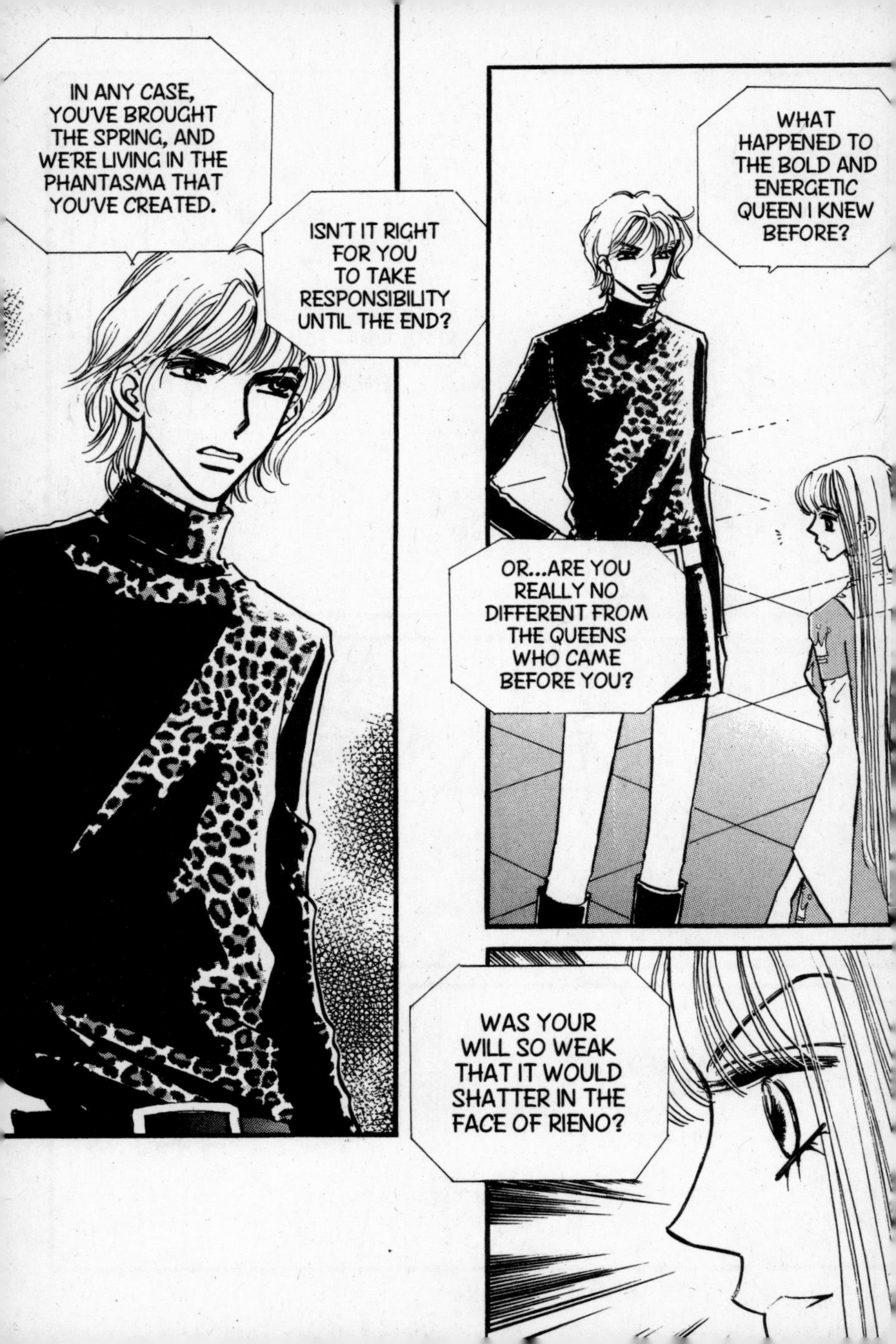
IN ANY CASE, YOU'VE BROUGHT THE SPRING, AND WE'RE LIVING IN THE PHANTASMA THAT YOU'VE CREATED.
ISN'T IT RIGHT FOR YOU TO TAKE RESPONSIBILITY UNTIL THE END?
WHAT HAPPENED TO THE BOLD AND ENERGETIC QUEEN I KNEW BEFORE?
OR...ARE YOU REALLY NO DIFFERENT FROM THE QUEENS WHO CAME BEFORE YOU?
WAS YOUR WILL SO WEAK THAT IT WOULD SHATTER IN THE FACE OF RIENO?

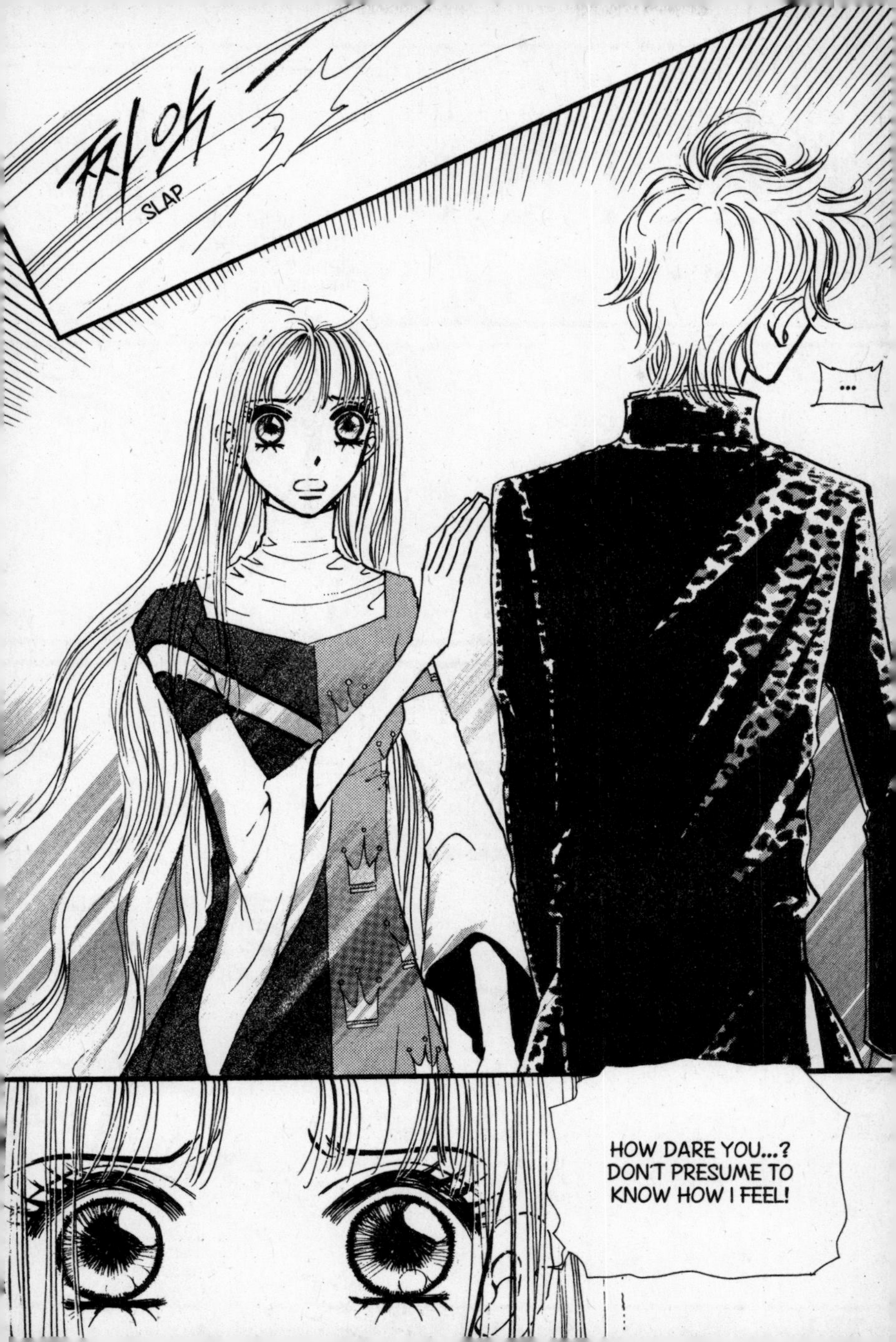

짜악
SLAP
...
HOW DARE YOU...? DON'T PRESUME TO KNOW HOW I FEEL!

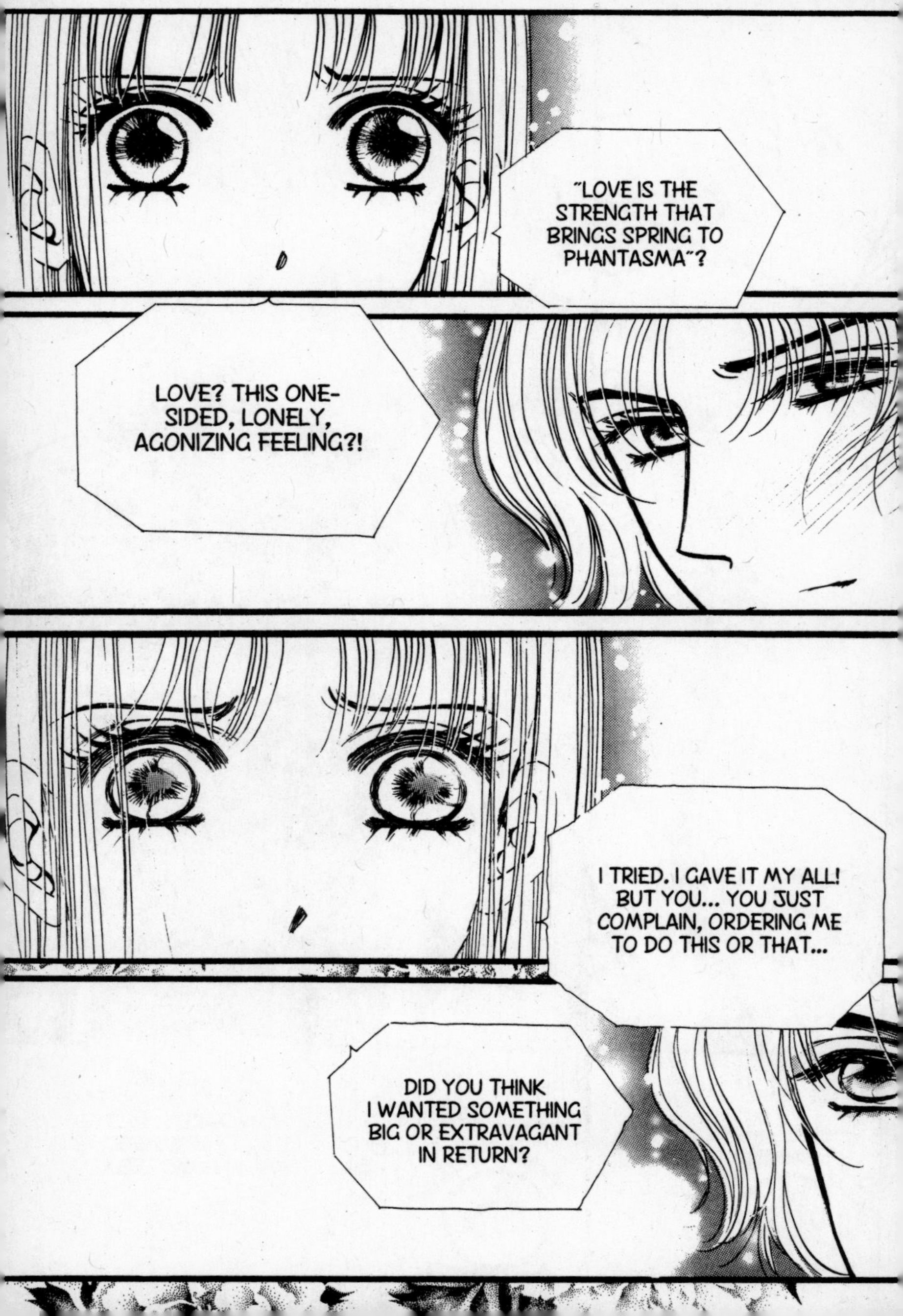
"LOVE IS THE STRENGTH THAT BRINGS SPRING TO PHANTASMA"?
LOVE? THIS ONE-SIDED, LONELY, AGONIZING FEELING?!
I TRIED. I GAVE IT MY ALL! BUT YOU... YOU JUST COMPLAIN, ORDERING ME TO DO THIS OR THAT...
DID YOU THINK I WANTED SOMETHING BIG OR EXTRAVAGANT IN RETURN?

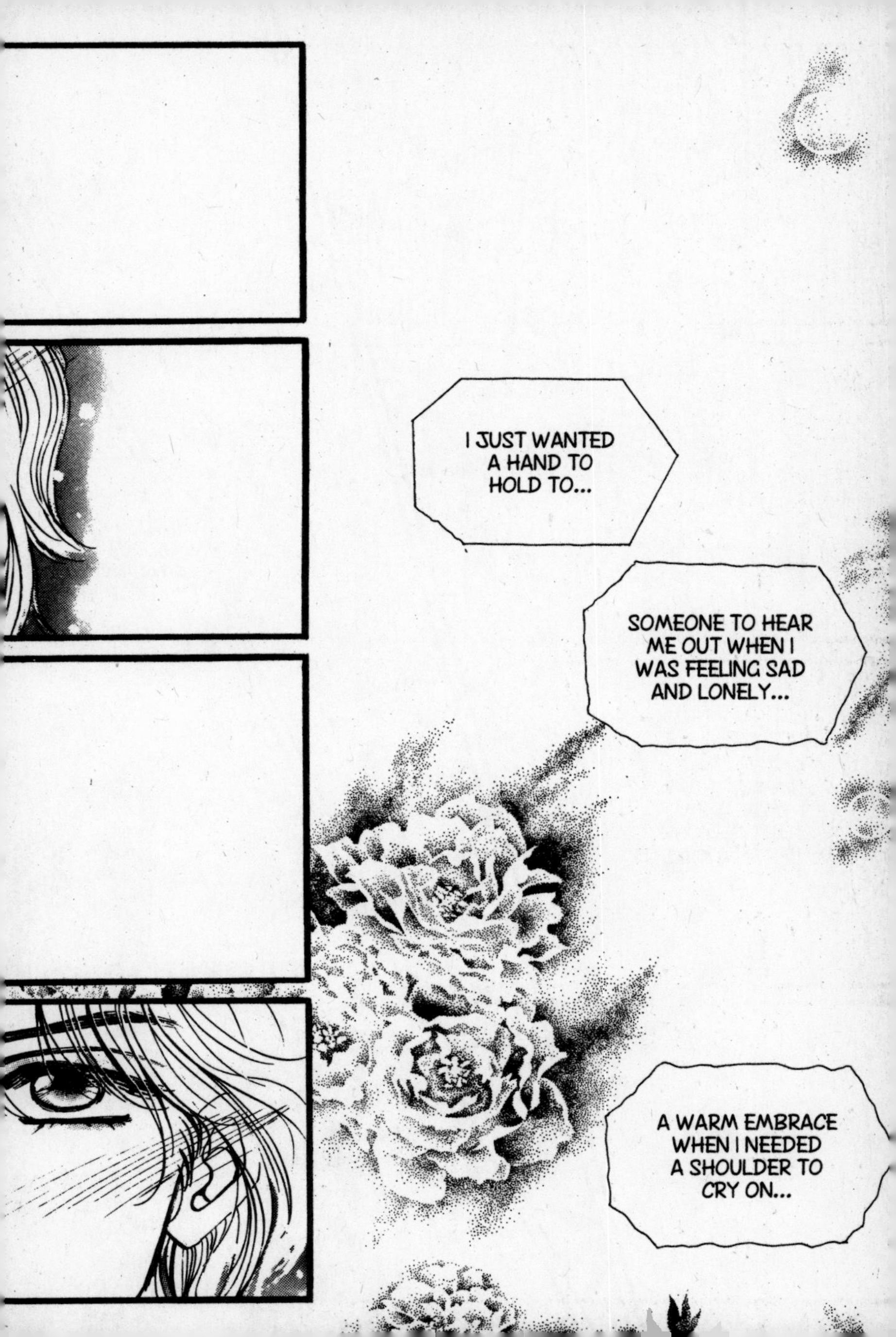
I JUST WANTED A HAND TO HOLD TO...
SOMEONE TO HEAR ME OUT WHEN I WAS FEELING SAD AND LONELY...
A WARM EMBRACE WHEN I NEEDED A SHOULDER TO CRY ON...

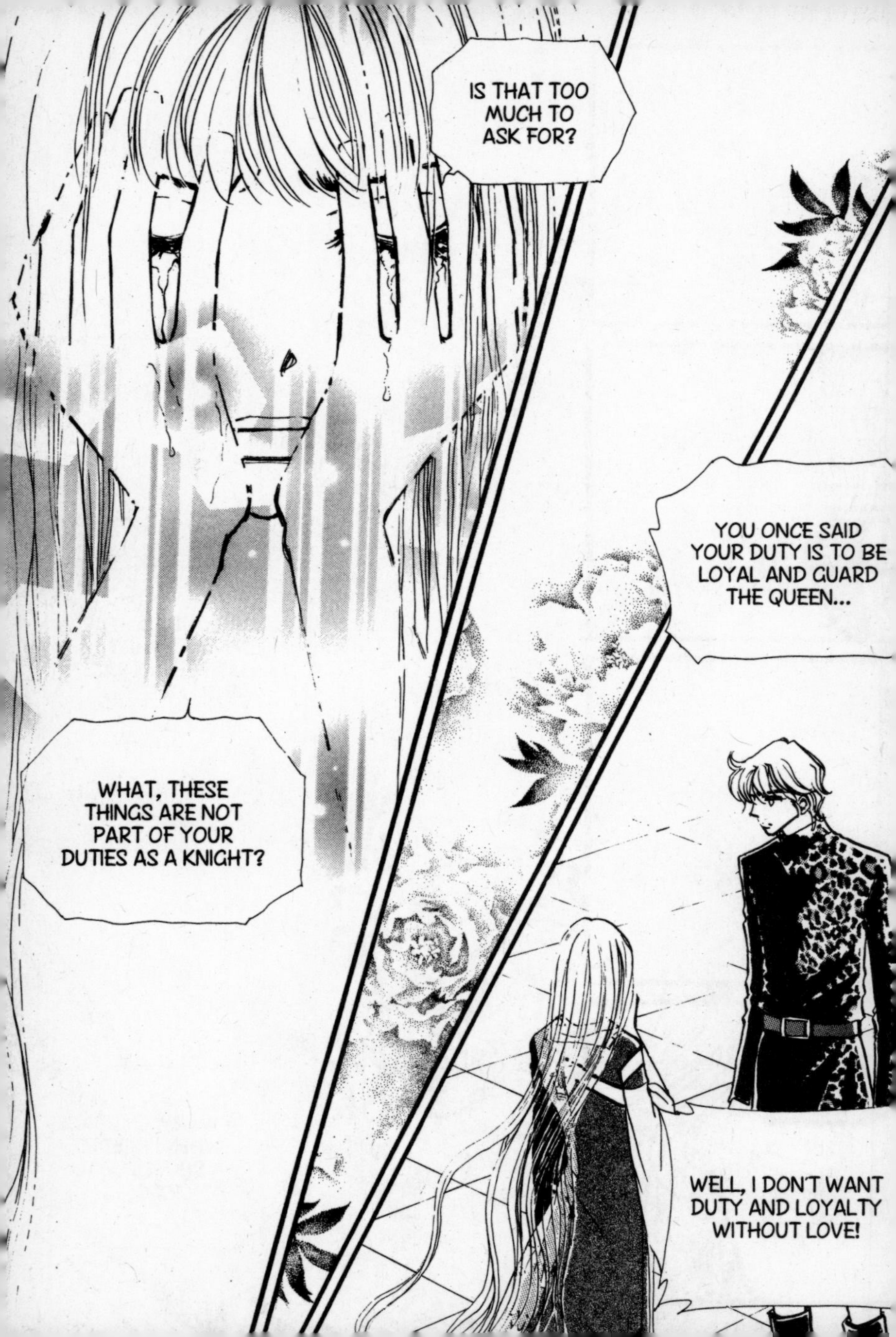

IS THAT TOO MUCH TO ASK FOR?
WHAT, THESE THINGS ARE NOT PART OF YOUR DUTIES AS A KNIGHT?
YOU ONCE SAID YOUR DUTY IS TO BE LOYAL AND GUARD THE QUEEN...
WELL, I DON'T WANT DUTY AND LOYALTY WITHOUT LOVE!

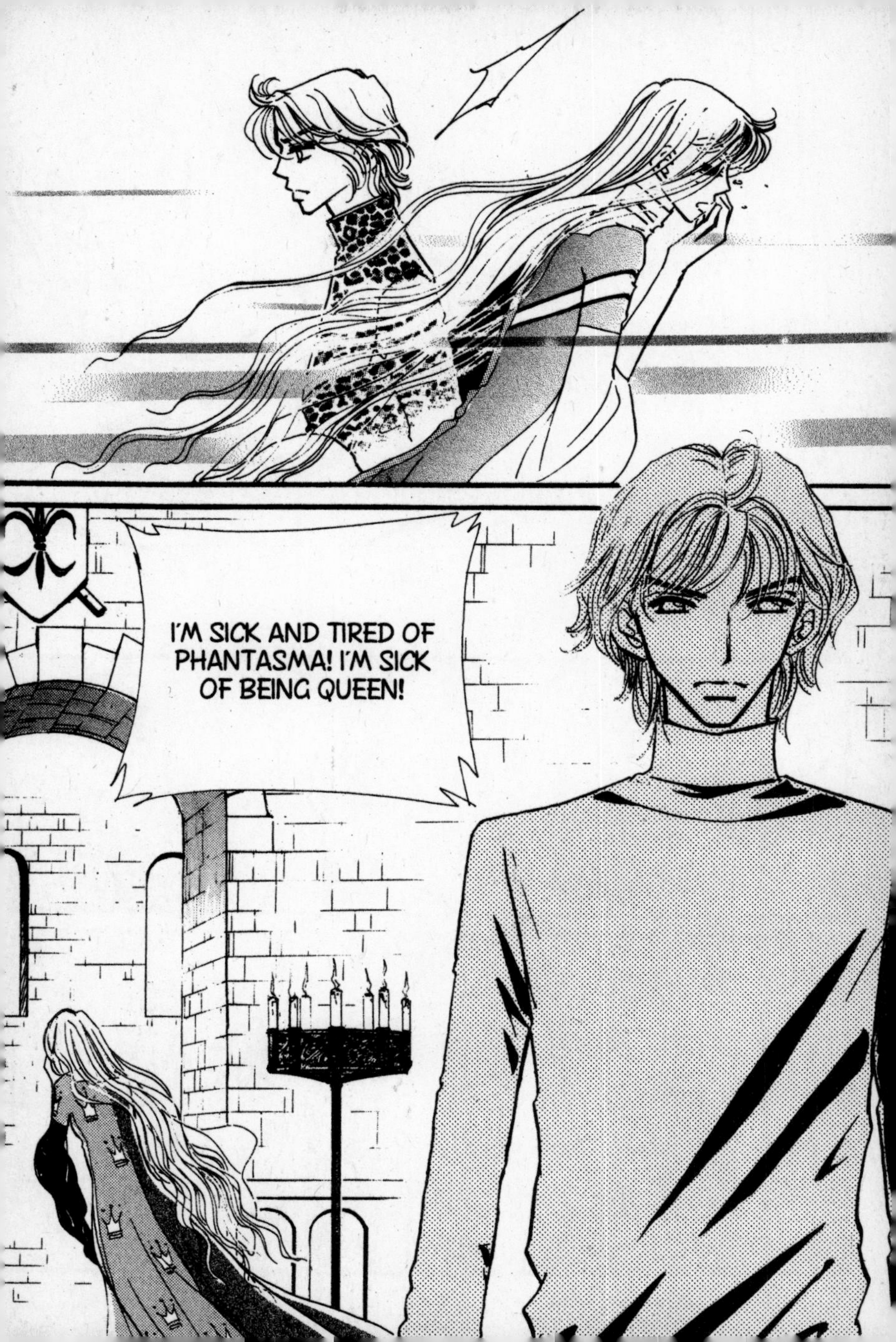
I'M SICK AND TIRED OF PHANTASMA! I'M SICK OF BEING QUEEN!

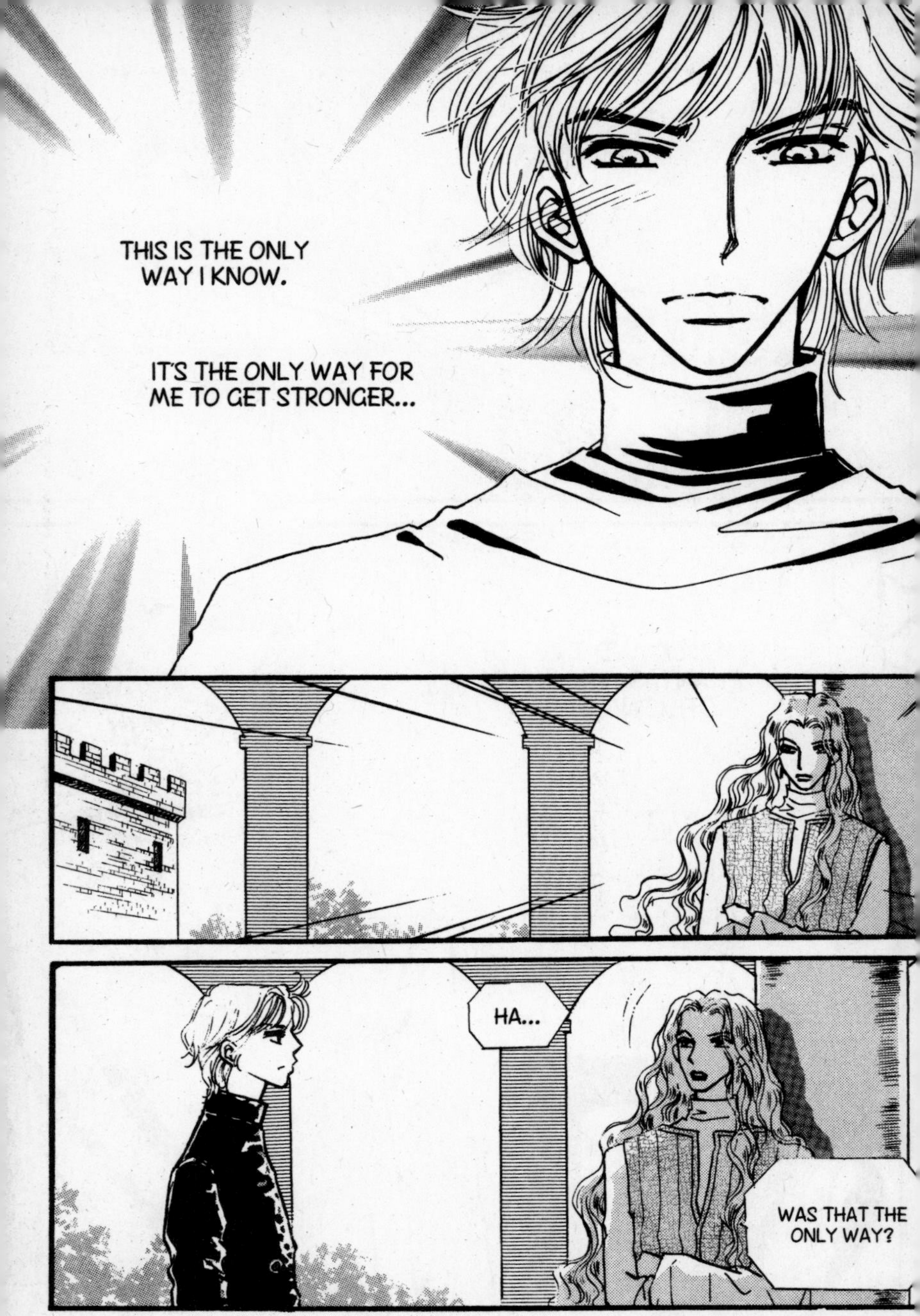
THIS IS THE ONLY WAY I KNOW.
IT'S THE ONLY WAY FOR ME TO GET STRONGER...
HA...
WAS THAT THE ONLY WAY?

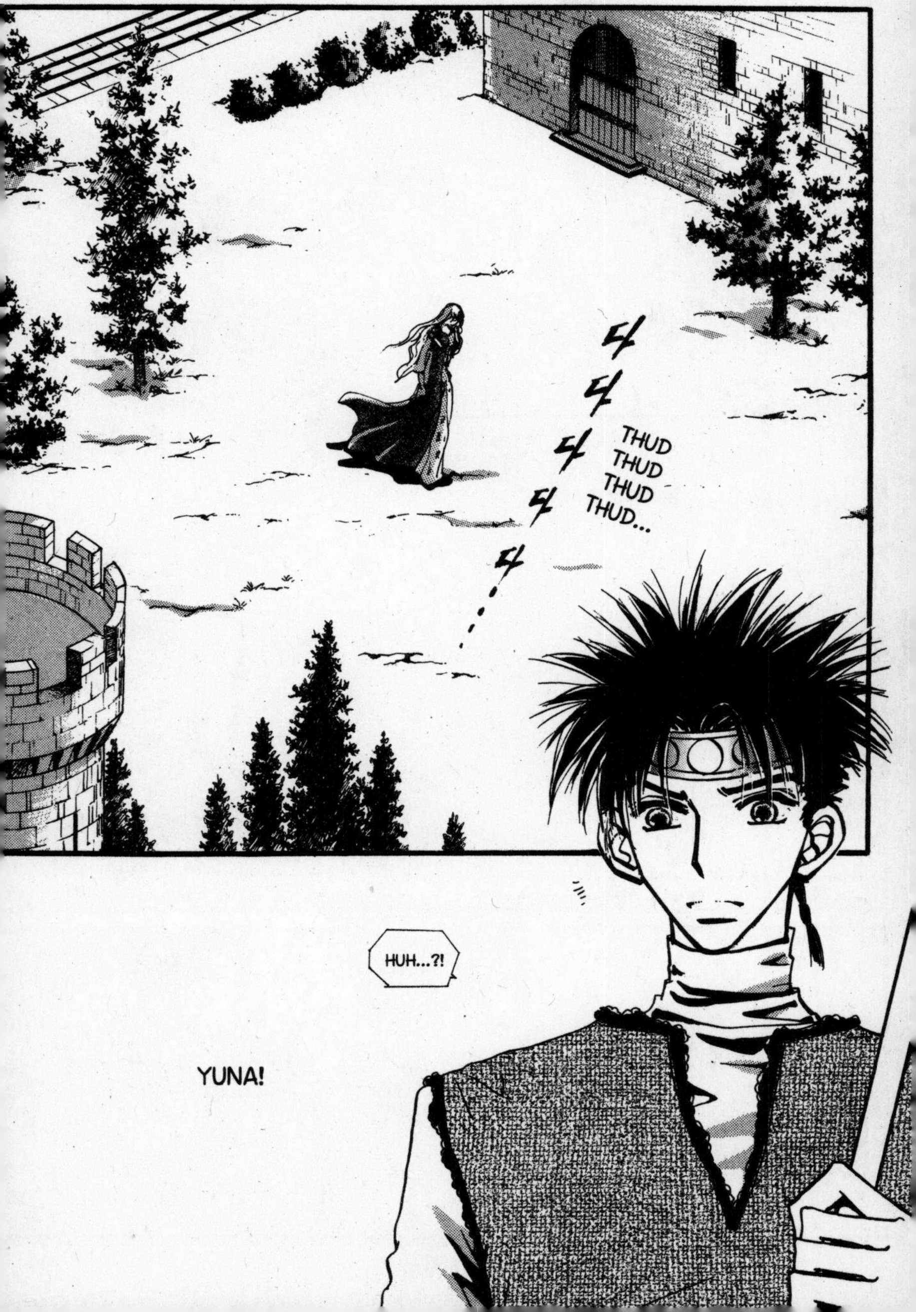
다
다
다
다
다...
THUD
THUD
THUD
THUD...
HUH...?!
YUNA!

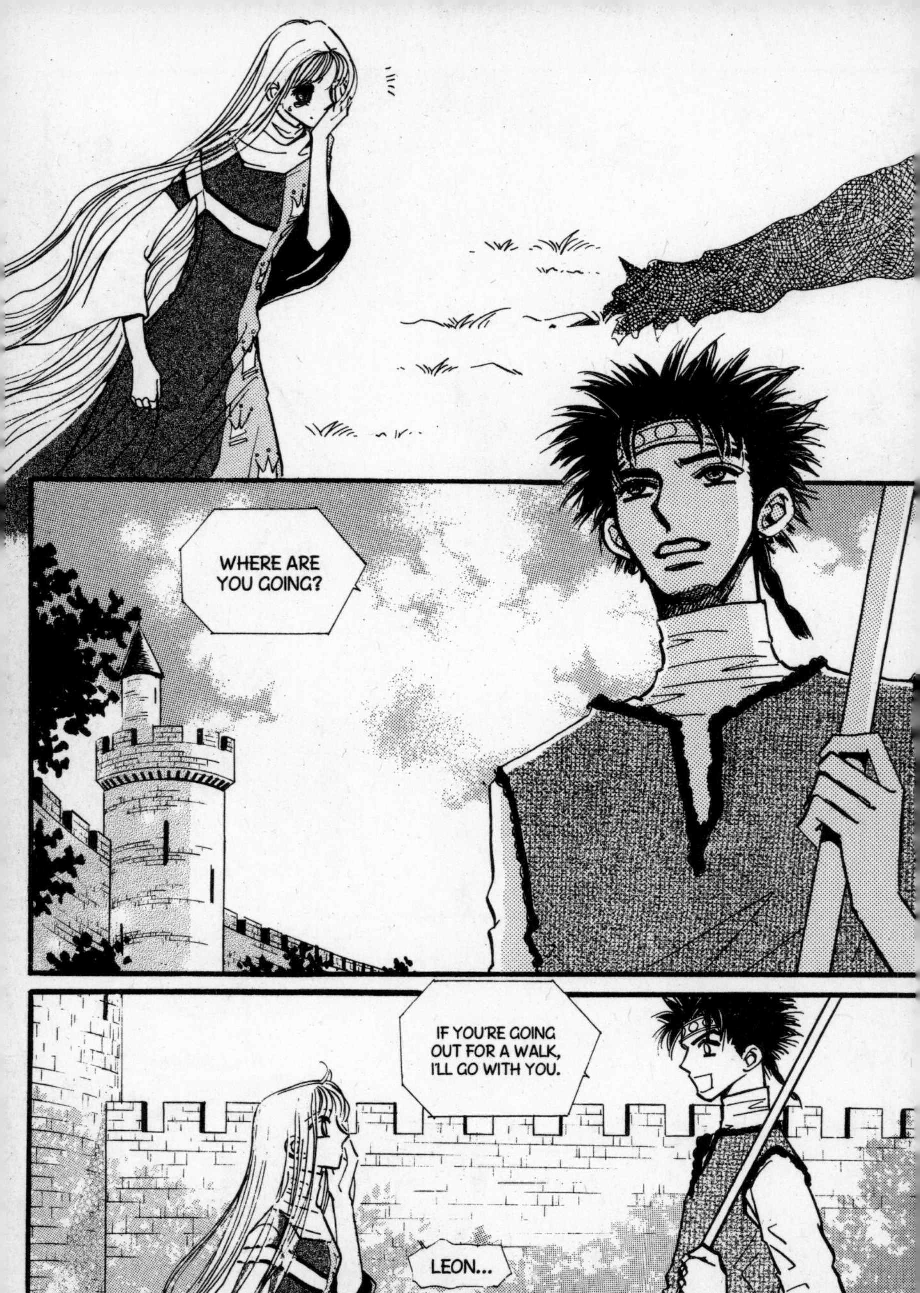
WHERE ARE YOU GOING?
IF YOU'RE GOING OUT FOR A WALK, I'LL GO WITH YOU.
LEON...

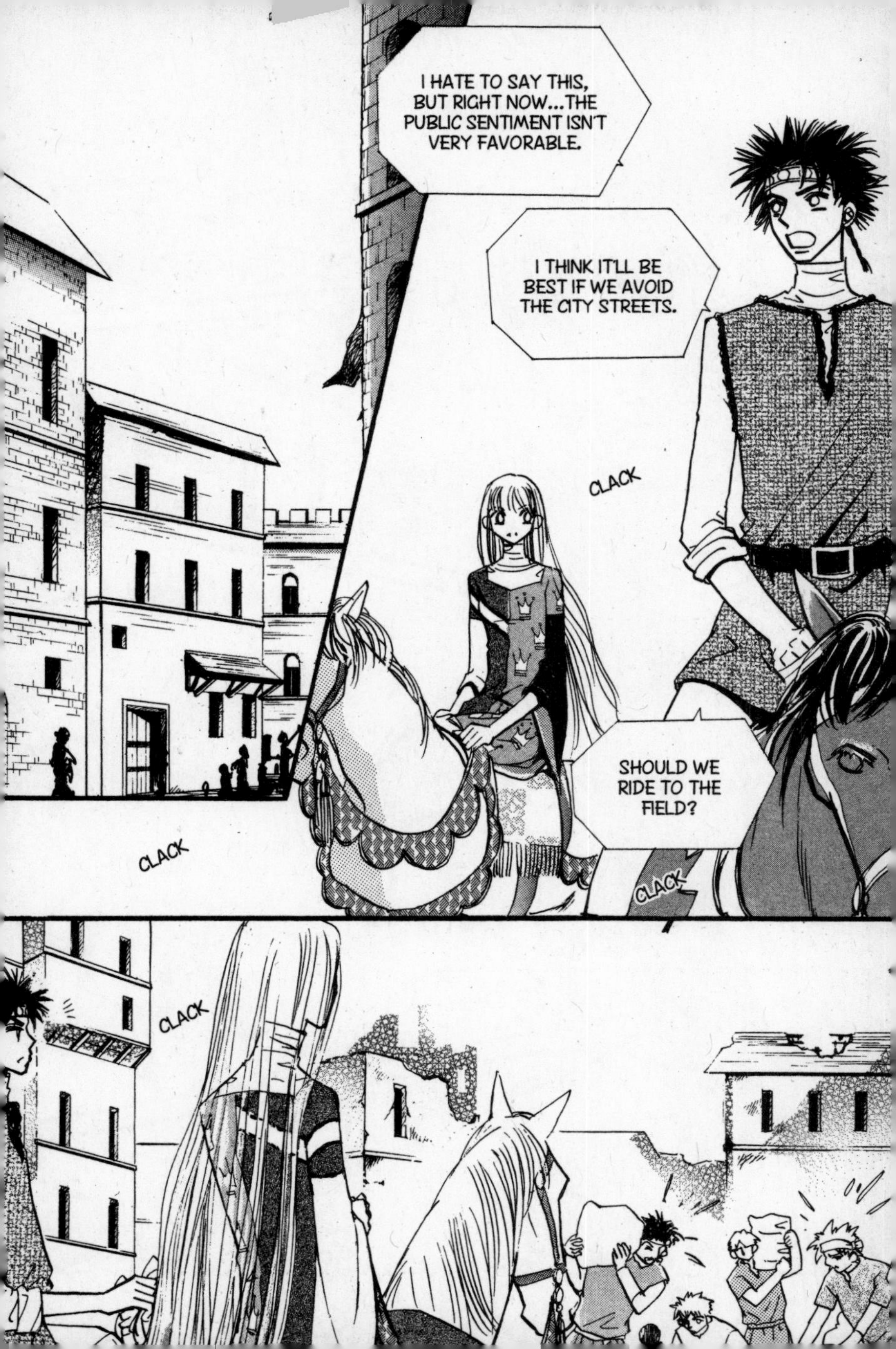
I HATE TO SAY THIS, BUT RIGHT NOW...THE PUBLIC SENTIMENT ISN'T VERY FAVORABLE.
I THINK IT'LL BE BEST IF WE AVOID THE CITY STREETS.
CLACK
CLACK
SHOULD WE RIDE TO THE FIELD?
CLACK
CLACK

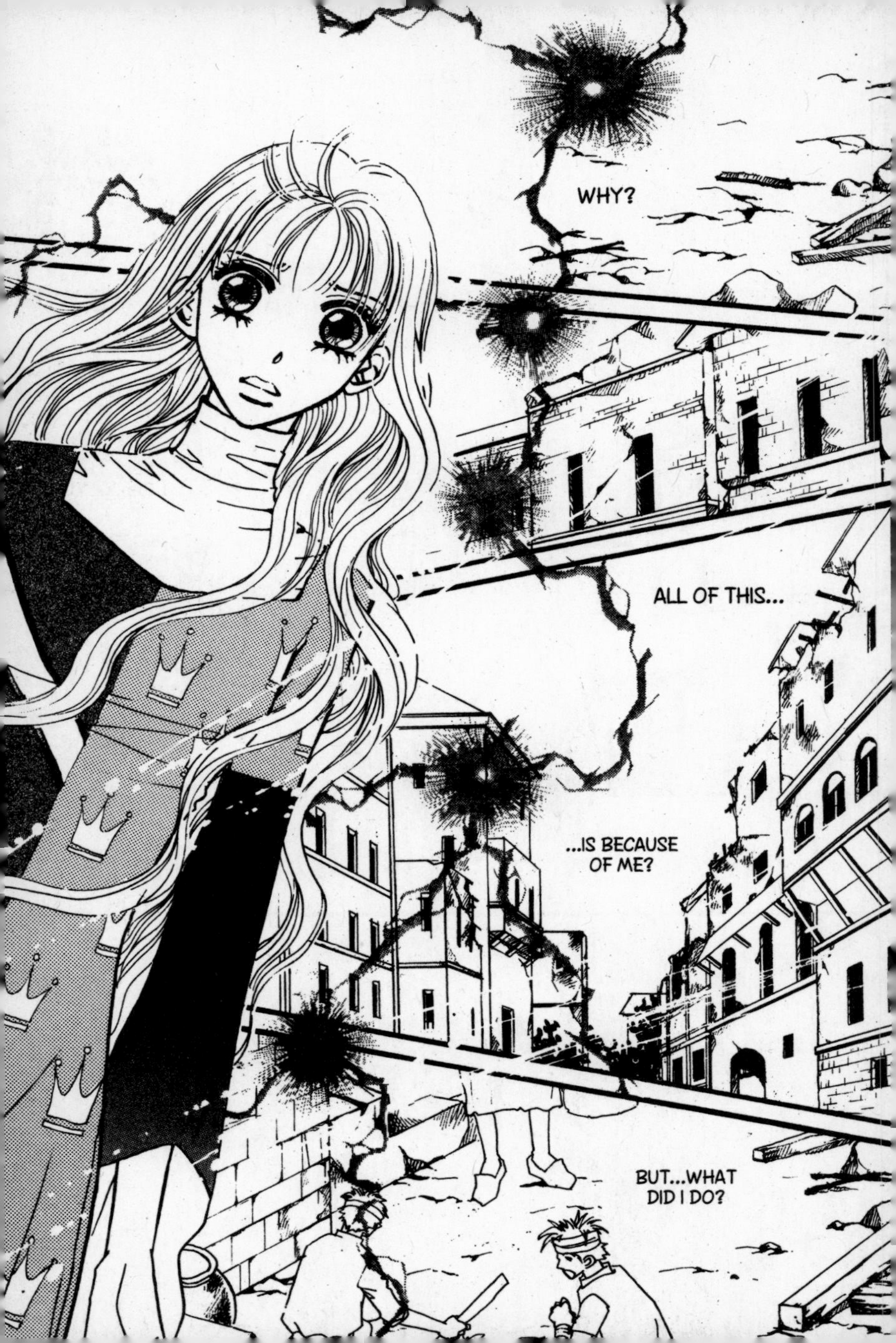
WHY?
ALL OF THIS...
...IS BECAUSE OF ME?
BUT...WHAT DID I DO?

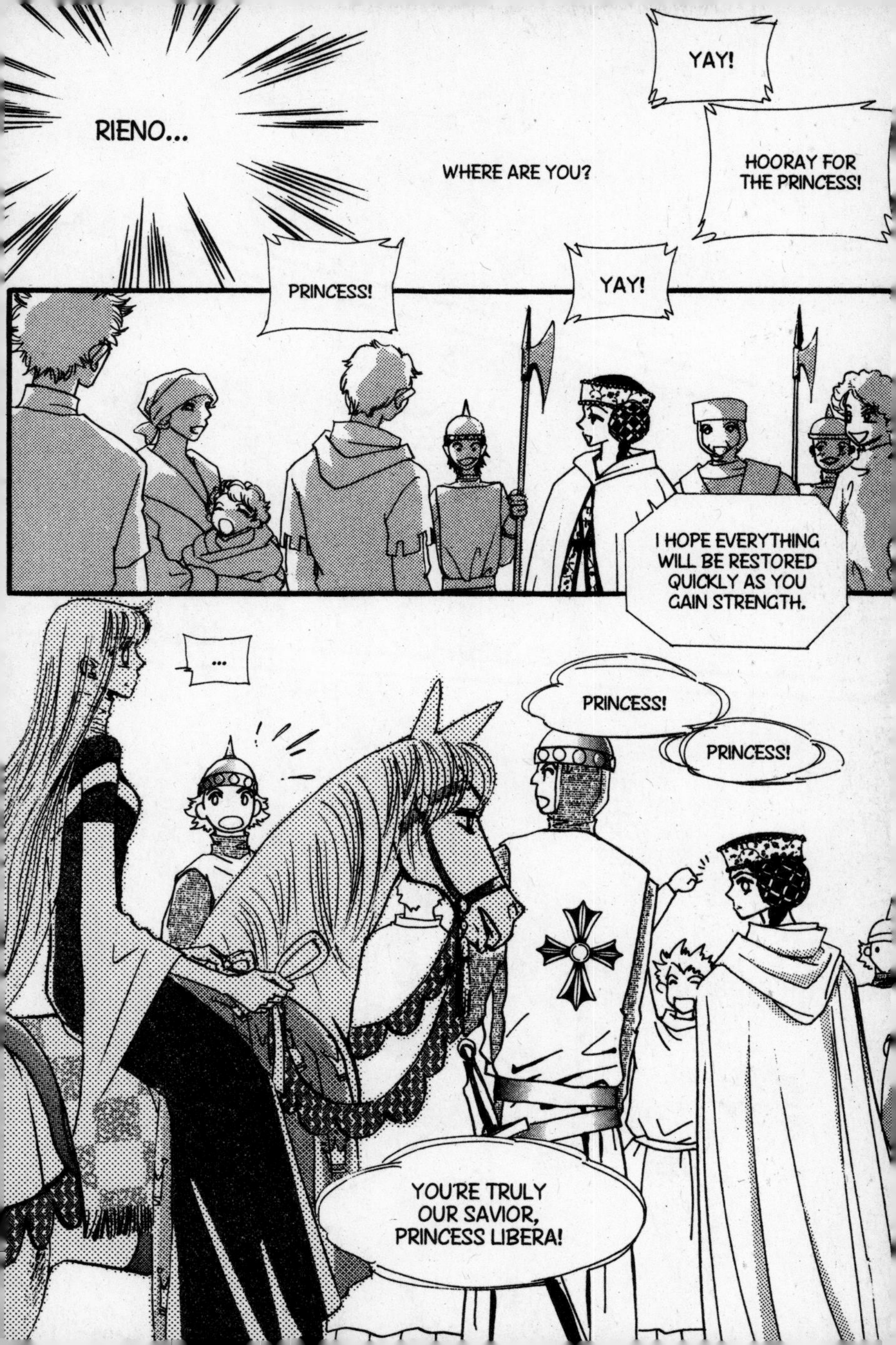
RIENO...
WHERE ARE YOU?
YAY!
HOORAY FOR THE PRINCESS!
PRINCESS!
YAY!
I HOPE EVERYTHING WILL BE RESTORED QUICKLY AS YOU GAIN STRENGTH.
...
PRINCESS!
PRINCESS!
YOU'RE TRULY OUR SAVIOR, PRINCESS LIBERA!

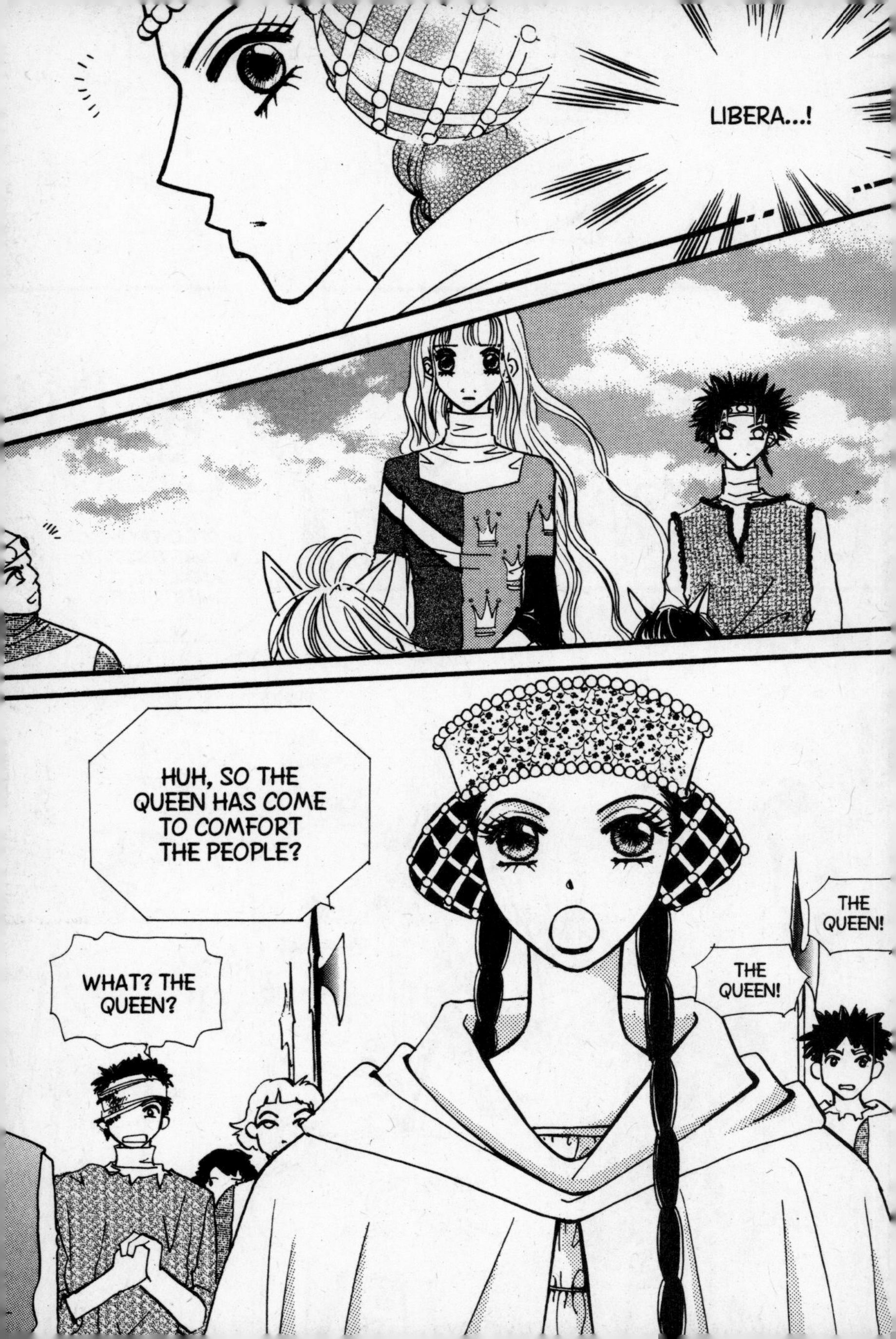
LIBERA...!
HUH, SO THE QUEEN HAS COME TO COMFORT THE PEOPLE?
WHAT? THE QUEEN?
THE QUEEN!
THE QUEEN!

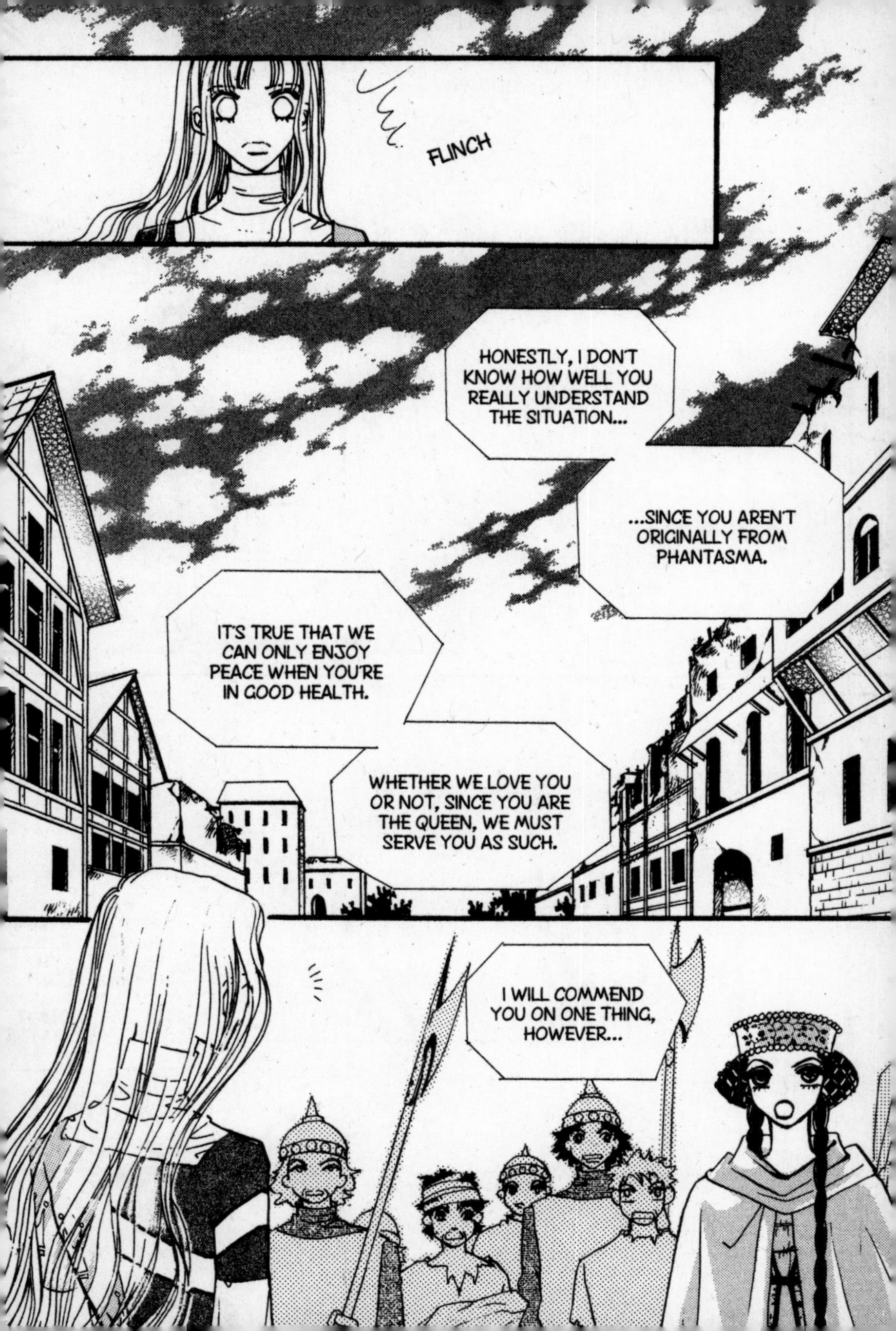
FLINCH
HONESTLY, I DON'T KNOW HOW WELL YOU REALLY UNDERSTAND THE SITUATION...
...SINCE YOU AREN'T ORIGINALLY FROM PHANTASMA.
IT'S TRUE THAT WE CAN ONLY ENJOY PEACE WHEN YOU'RE IN GOOD HEALTH.
WHETHER WE LOVE YOU OR NOT, SINCE YOU ARE THE QUEEN, WE MUST SERVE YOU AS SUCH.
I WILL COMMEND YOU ON ONE THING, HOWEVER...

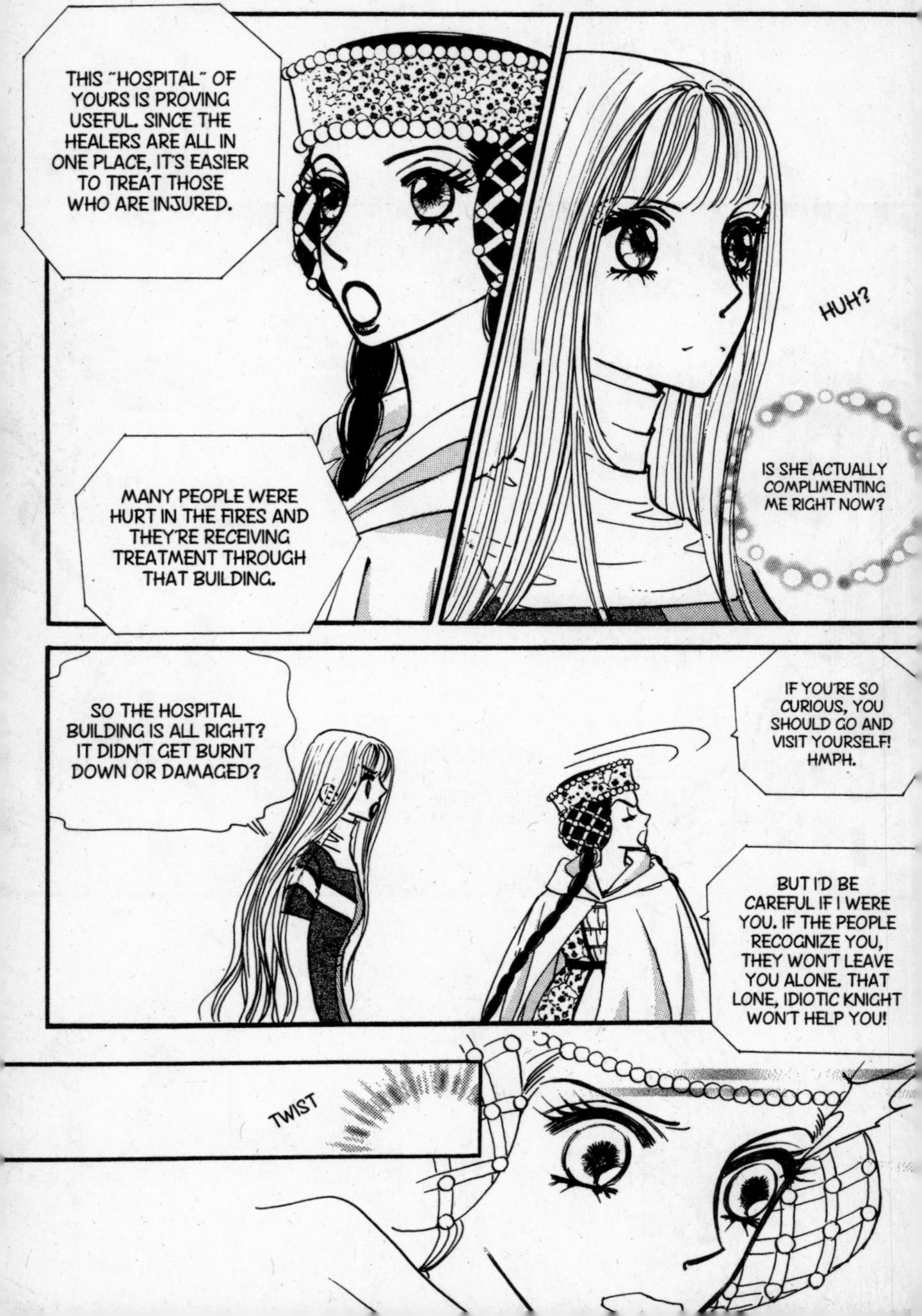
THIS "HOSPITAL" OF YOURS IS PROVING USEFUL. SINCE THE HEALERS ARE ALL IN ONE PLACE, IT'S EASIER TO TREAT THOSE WHO ARE INJURED.
MANY PEOPLE WERE HURT IN THE FIRES AND THEY'RE RECEIVING TREATMENT THROUGH THAT BUILDING.
HUH?
IS SHE ACTUALLY COMPLIMENTING ME RIGHT NOW?
SO THE HOSPITAL BUILDING IS ALL RIGHT? IT DIDN'T GET BURNT DOWN OR DAMAGED?
IF YOU'RE SO CURIOUS, YOU SHOULD GO AND VISIT YOURSELF! HMPH.
BUT I'D BE CAREFUL IF I WERE YOU. IF THE PEOPLE RECOGNIZE YOU, THEY WON'T LEAVE YOU ALONE. THAT LONE, IDIOTIC KNIGHT WON'T HELP YOU!
TWIST

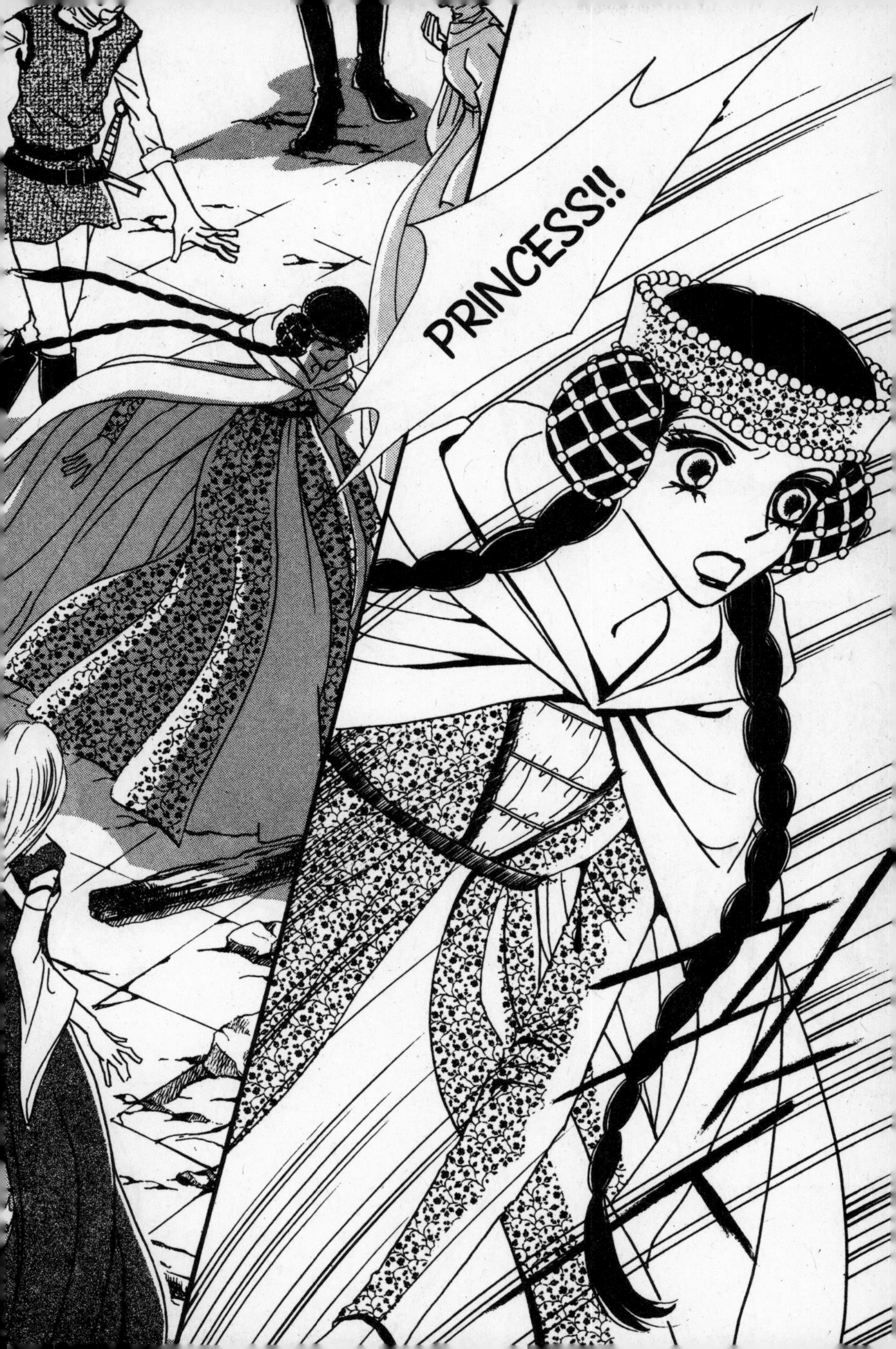
PRINCESS!!

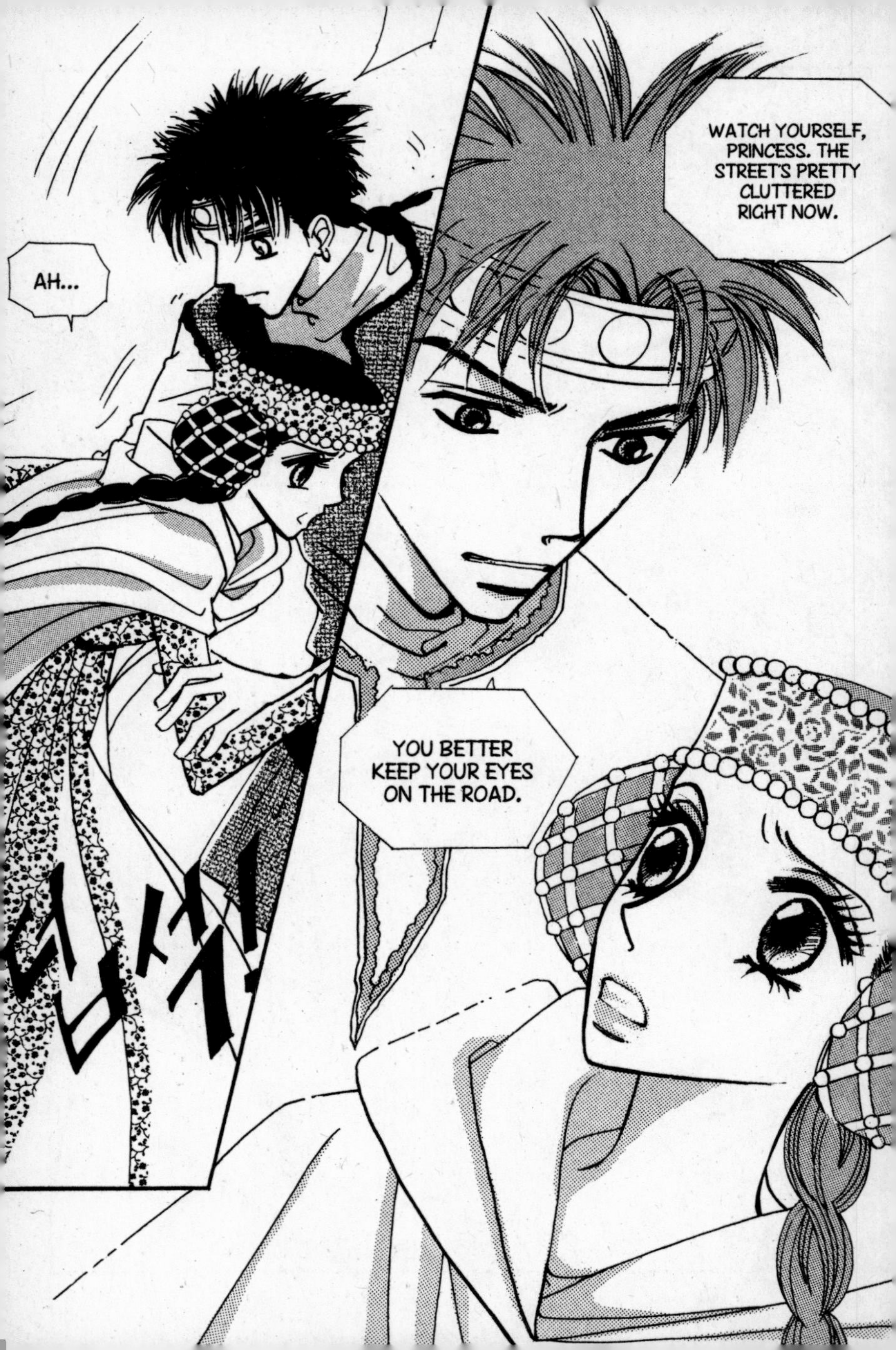
AH...
WATCH YOURSELF, PRINCESS. THE STREET'S PRETTY CLUTTERED RIGHT NOW.
YOU BETTER KEEP YOUR EYES ON THE ROAD.

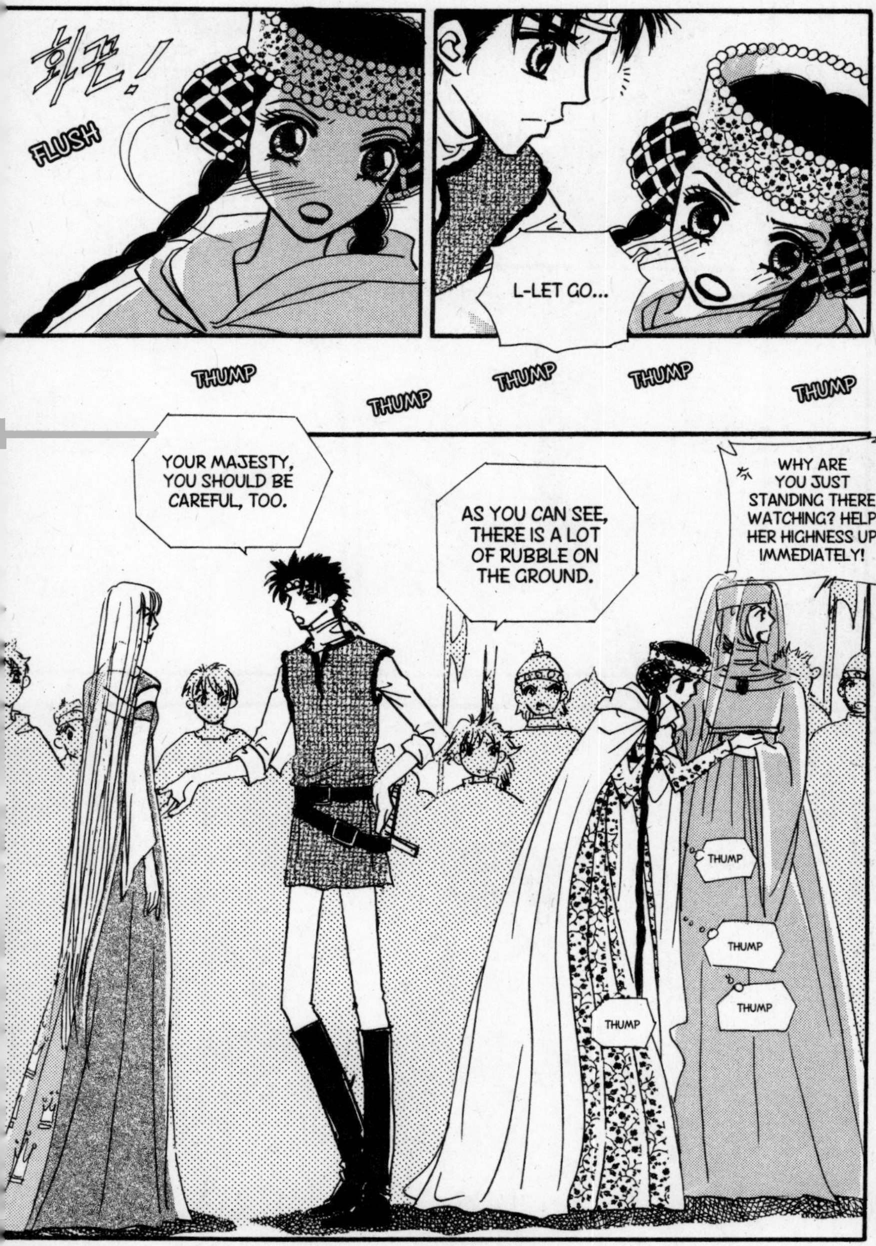
화끈!
FLUSH
L-LET GO...
THUMP
THUMP
THUMP
THUMP
THUMP
YOUR MAJESTY, YOU SHOULD BE CAREFUL, TOO.
AS YOU CAN SEE, THERE IS A LOT OF RUBBLE ON THE GROUND.
WHY ARE YOU JUST STANDING THERE WATCHING? HELP HER HIGHNESS UP IMMEDIATELY!
THUMP
THUMP
THUMP
THUMP

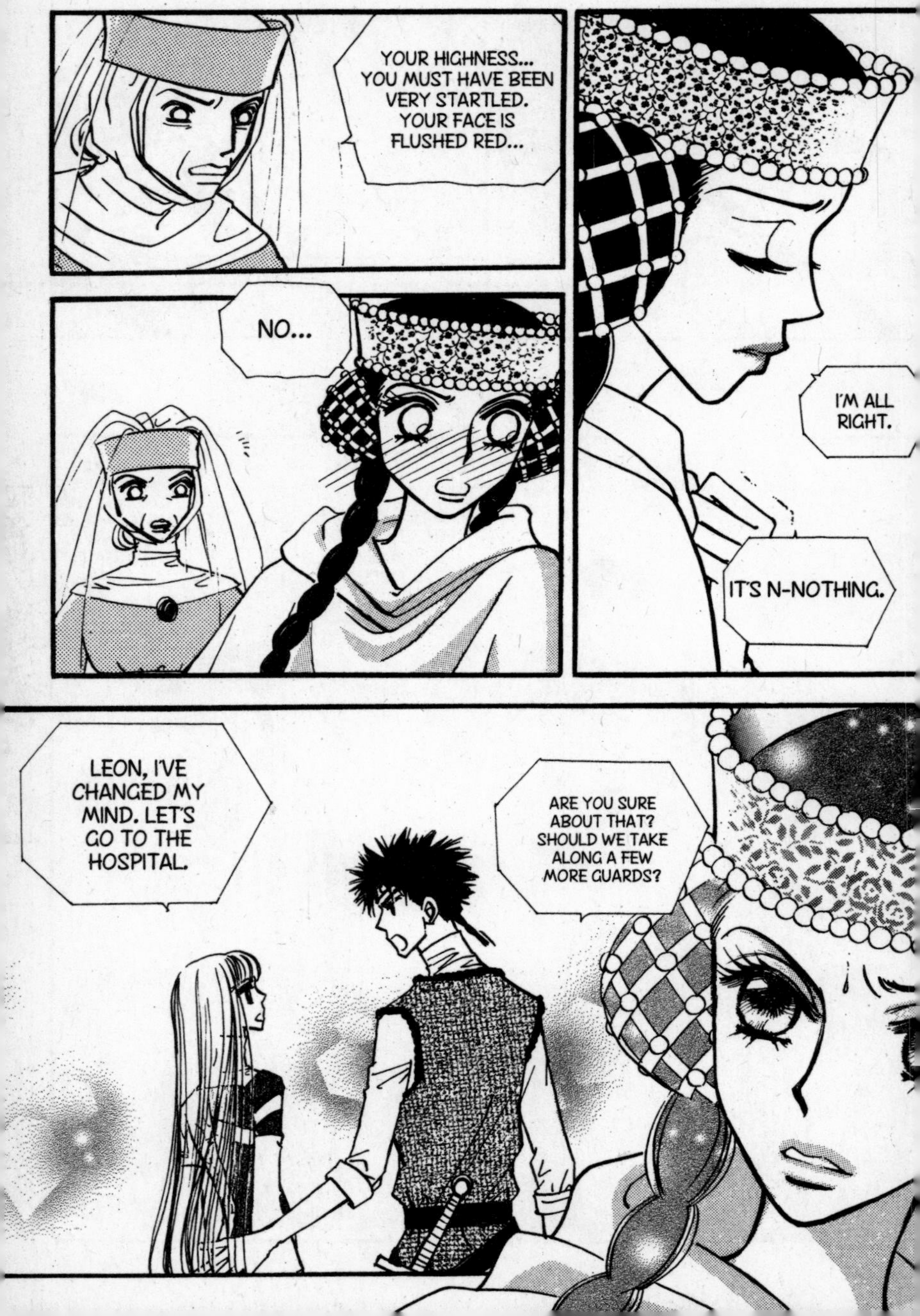
YOUR HIGHNESS... YOU MUST HAVE BEEN VERY STARTLED. YOUR FACE IS FLUSHED RED...
NO...
I'M ALL RIGHT.
IT'S N-NOTHING.
LEON, I'VE CHANGED MY MIND. LET'S GO TO THE HOSPITAL.
ARE YOU SURE ABOUT THAT? SHOULD WE TAKE ALONG A FEW MORE GUARDS?

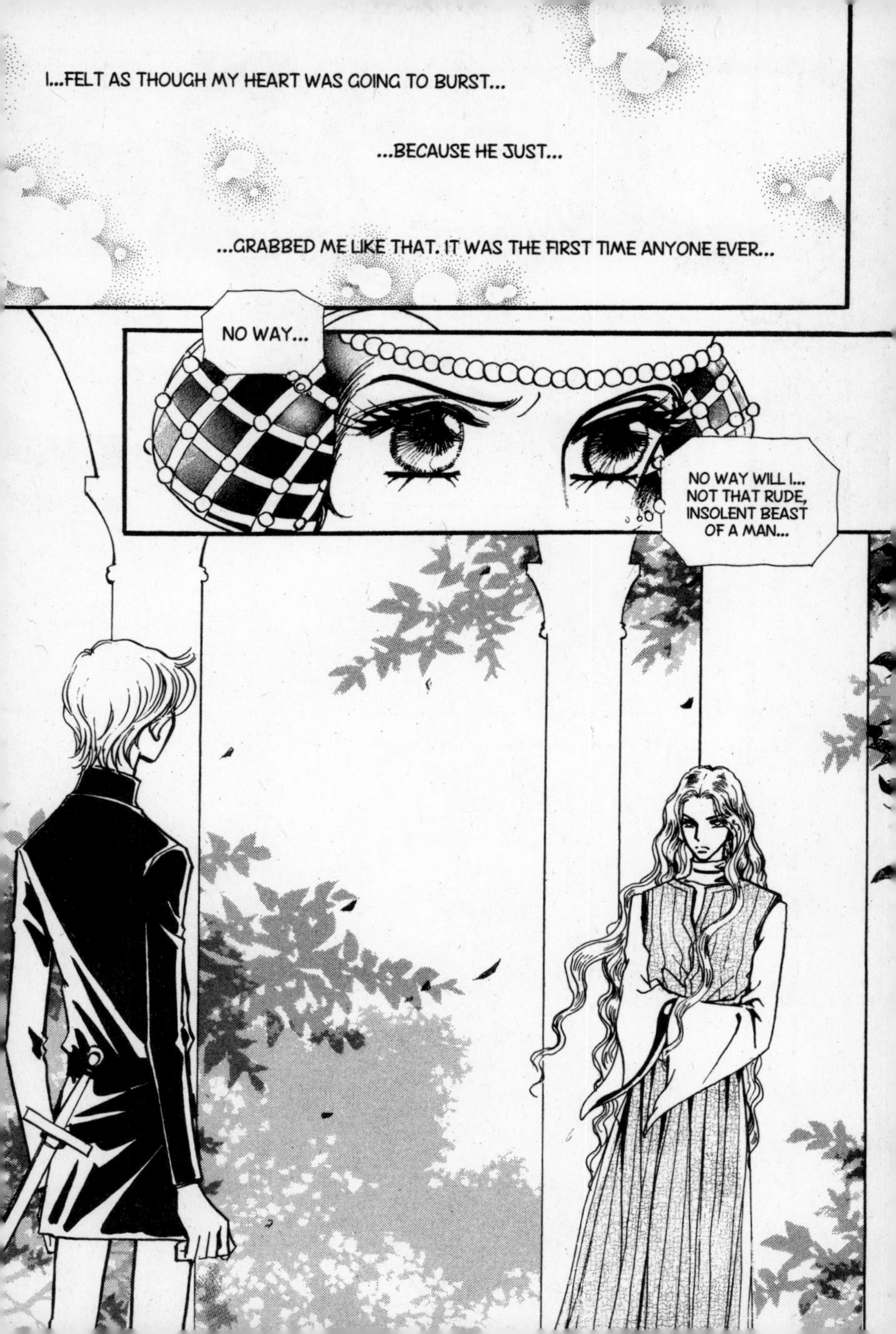
I...FELT AS THOUGH MY HEART WAS GOING TO BURST...
...BECAUSE HE JUST...
...GRABBED ME LIKE THAT. IT WAS THE FIRST TIME ANYONE EVER...
NO WAY...
NO WAY WILL I... NOT THAT RUDE, INSOLENT BEAST OF A MAN...

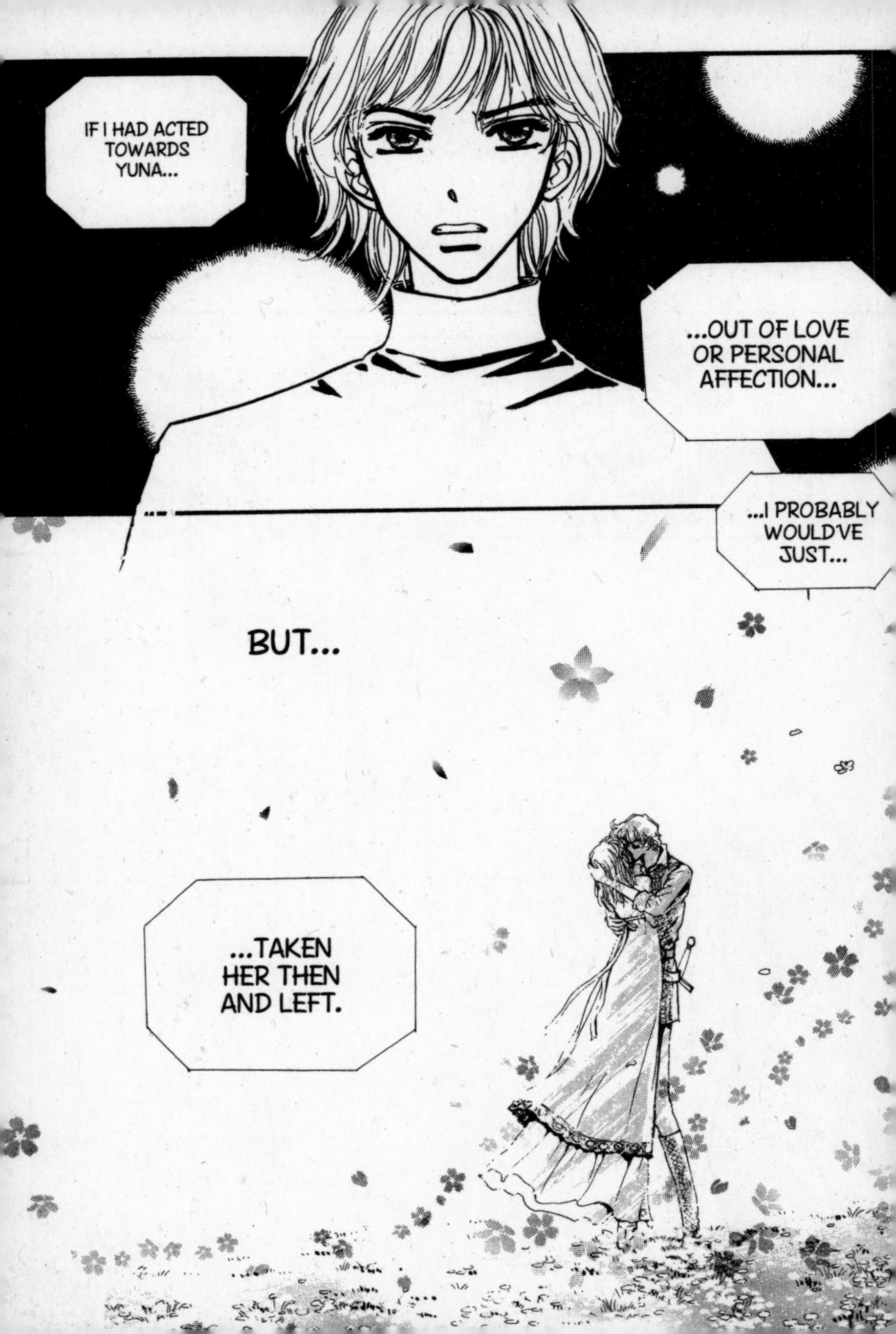
IF I HAD ACTED TOWARDS YUNA...
...OUT OF LOVE OR PERSONAL AFFECTION...
...I PROBABLY WOULD'VE JUST...
BUT...
...TAKEN HER THEN AND LEFT.

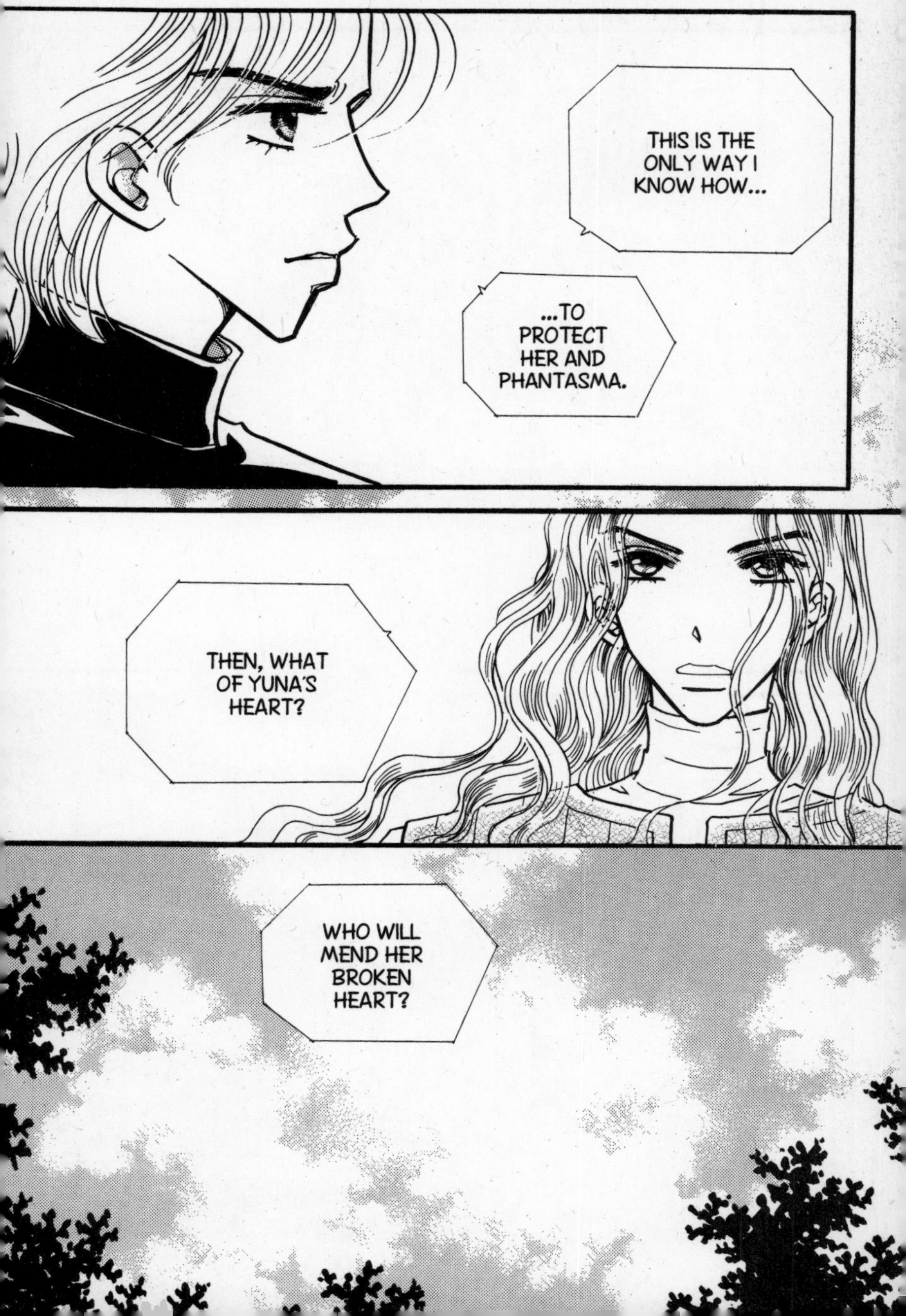
THIS IS THE ONLY WAY I KNOW HOW...
...TO PROTECT HER AND PHANTASMA.
THEN, WHAT OF YUNA'S HEART?
WHO WILL MEND HER BROKEN HEART?

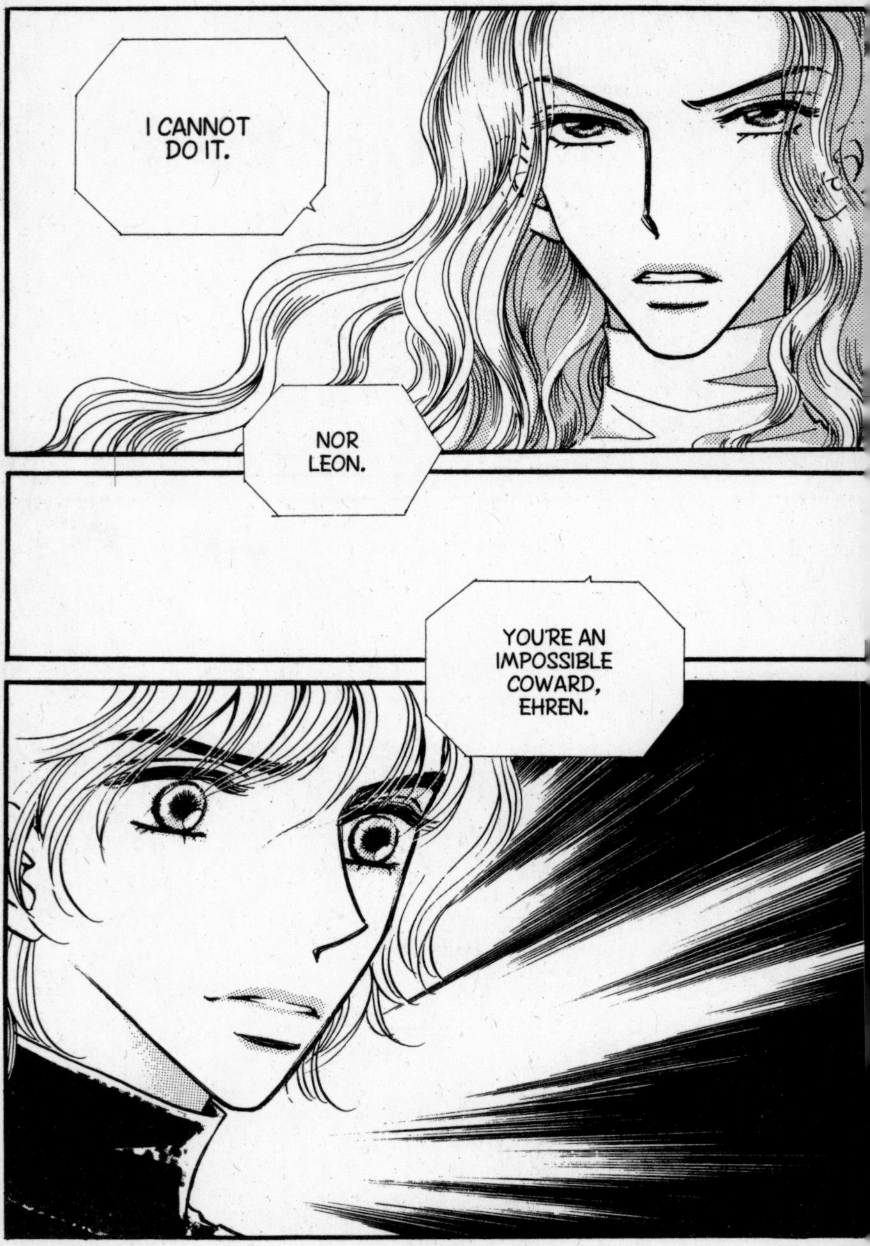
I CANNOT DO IT.
NOR LEON.
YOU'RE AN IMPOSSIBLE COWARD, EHREN.

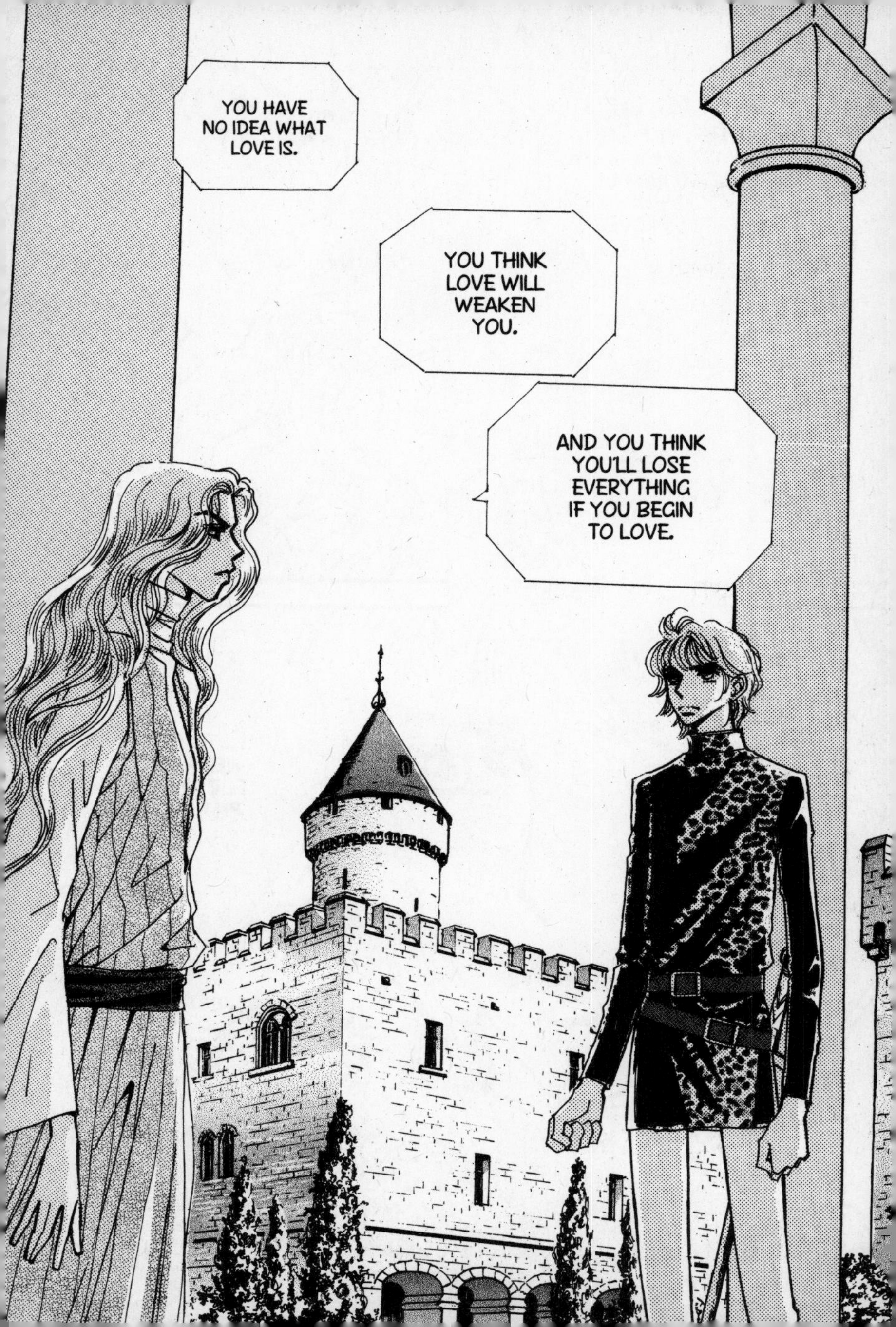
YOU HAVE NO IDEA WHAT LOVE IS.
YOU THINK LOVE WILL WEAKEN YOU.
AND YOU THINK YOU'LL LOSE EVERYTHING IF YOU BEGIN TO LOVE.

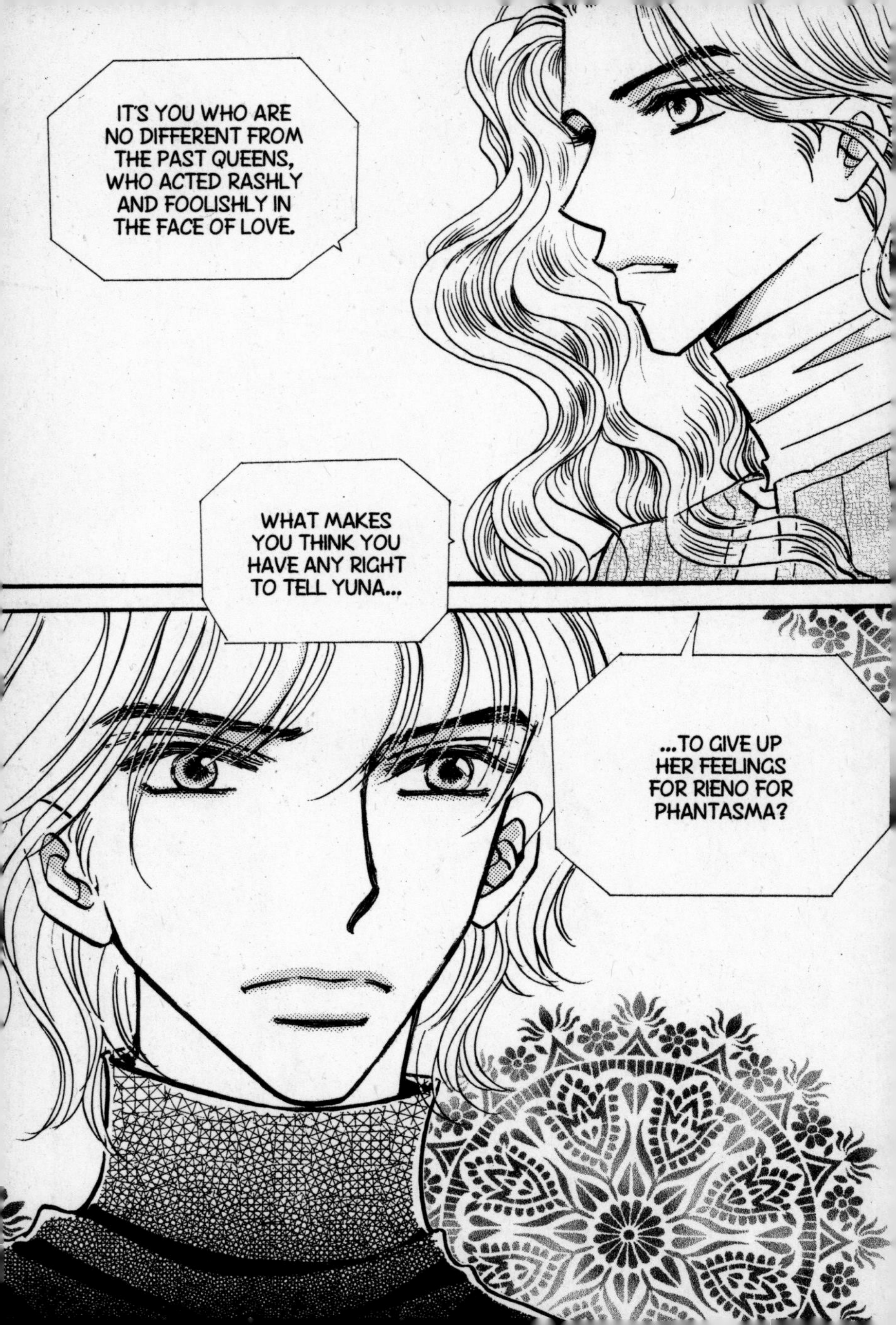
IT'S YOU WHO ARE NO DIFFERENT FROM THE PAST QUEENS, WHO ACTED RASHLY AND FOOLISHLY IN THE FACE OF LOVE.
WHAT MAKES YOU THINK YOU HAVE ANY RIGHT TO TELL YUNA...
...TO GIVE UP HER FEELINGS FOR RIENO FOR PHANTASMA?

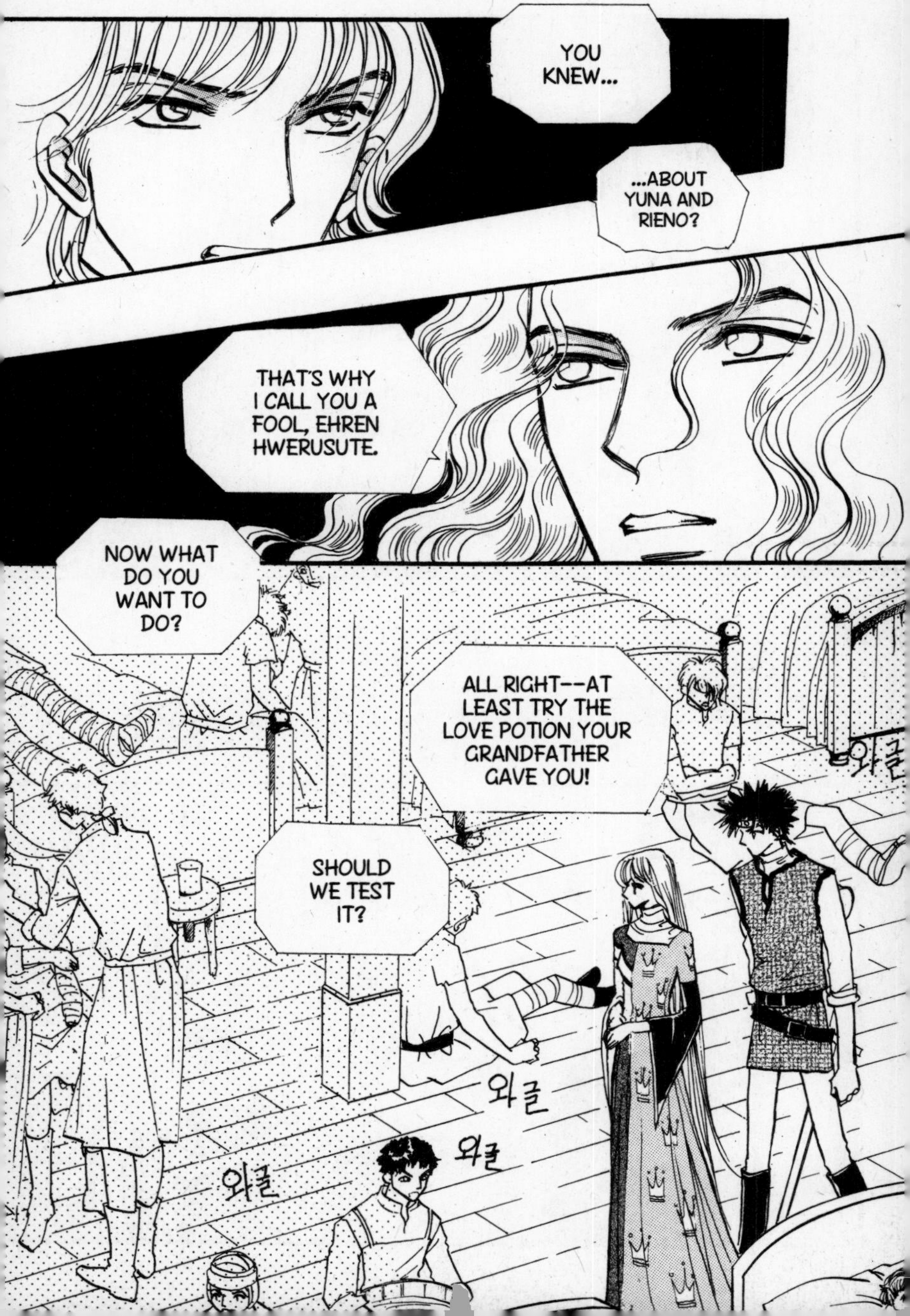
YOU KNEW...
...ABOUT YUNA AND RIENO?
THAT'S WHY I CALL YOU A FOOL, EHREN HWERUSUTE.
NOW WHAT DO YOU WANT TO DO?
ALL RIGHT--AT LEAST TRY THE LOVE POTION YOUR GRANDFATHER GAVE YOU!
와글
SHOULD WE TEST IT?
와글
와글
와글

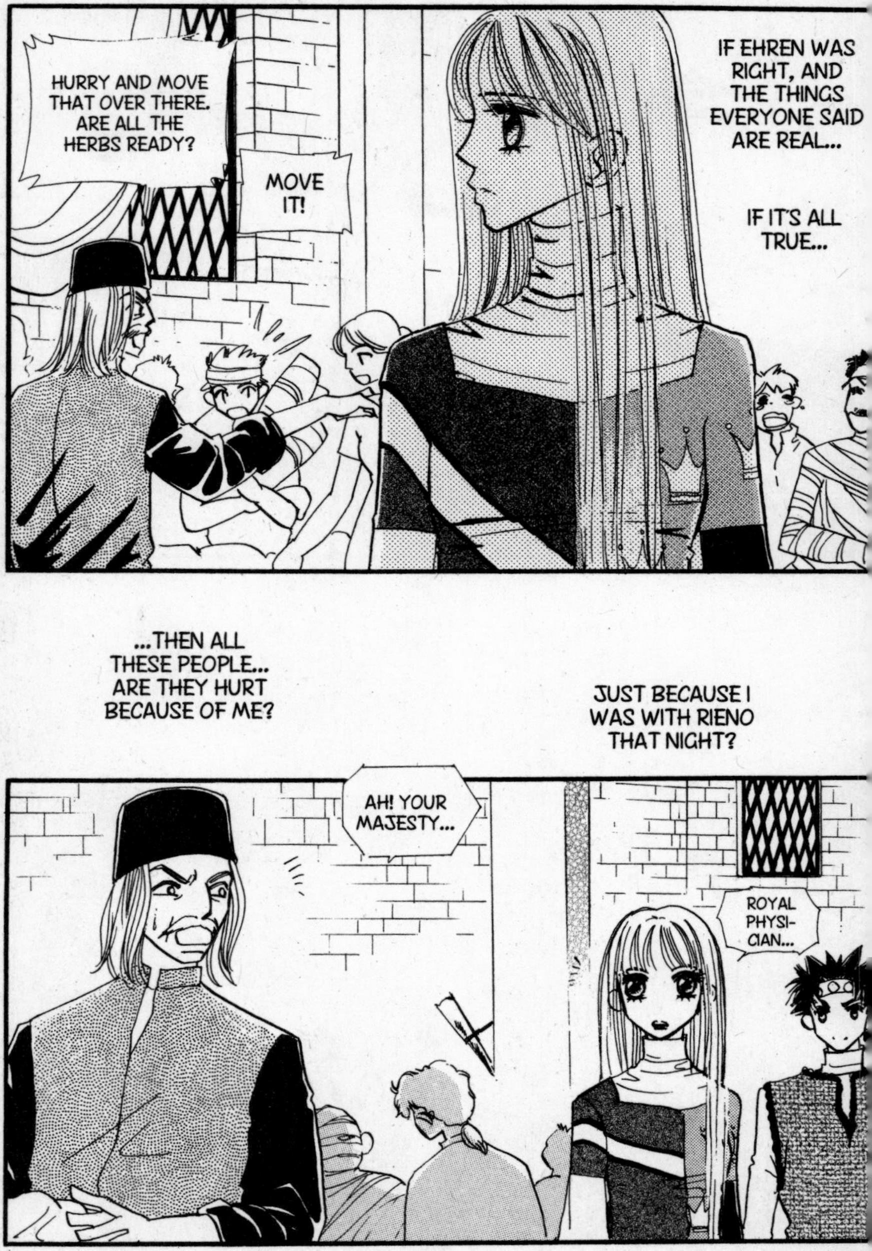
HURRY AND MOVE THAT OVER THERE. ARE ALL THE HERBS READY?
MOVE IT!
IF EHREN WAS RIGHT, AND THE THINGS EVERYONE SAID ARE REAL...
IF IT'S ALL TRUE...
...THEN ALL THESE PEOPLE... ARE THEY HURT BECAUSE OF ME?
JUST BECAUSE I WAS WITH RIENO THAT NIGHT?
AH! YOUR MAJESTY...
ROYAL PHYSI-CIAN...

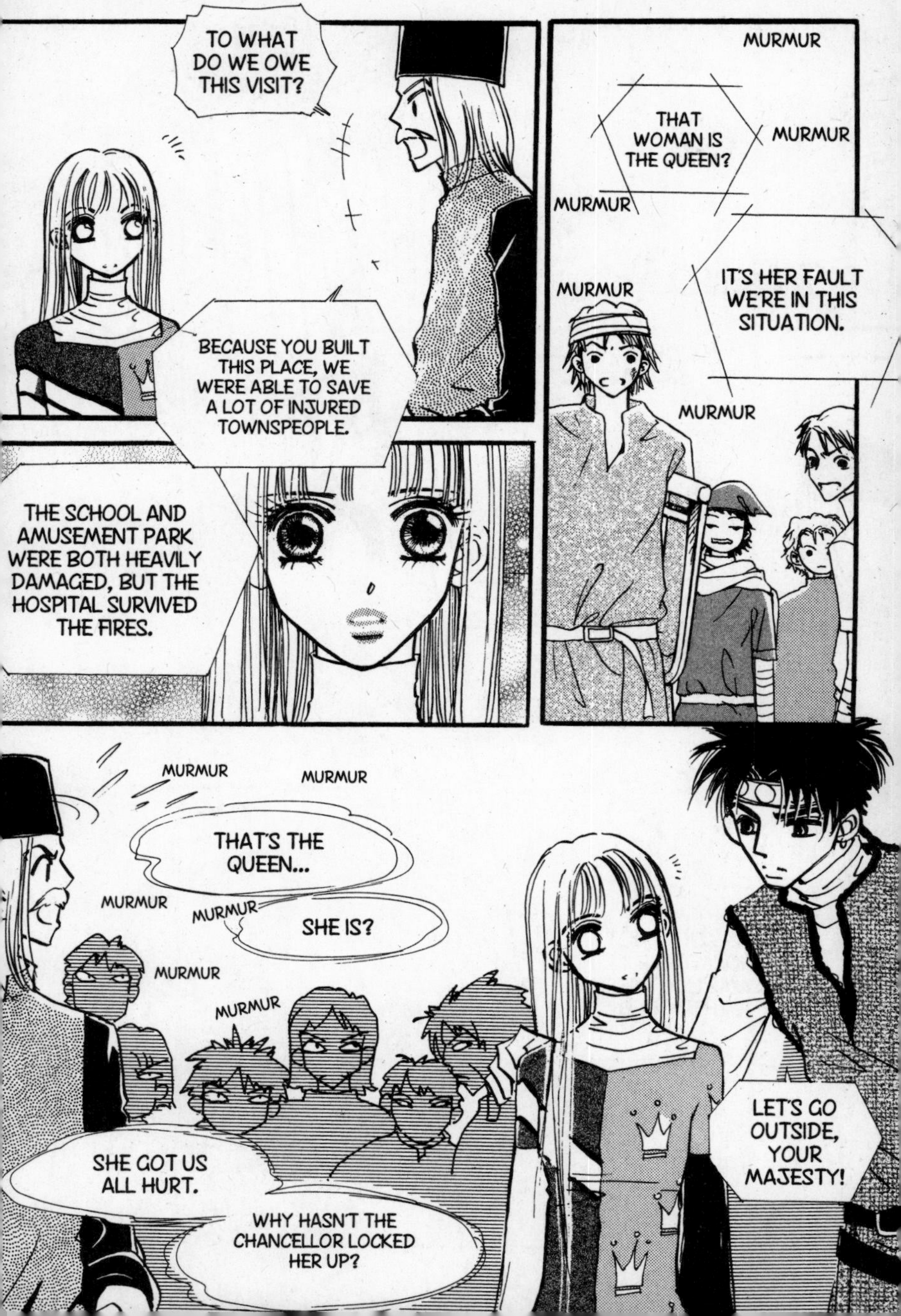
TO WHAT DO WE OWE THIS VISIT?
BECAUSE YOU BUILT THIS PLACE, WE WERE ABLE TO SAVE A LOT OF INJURED TOWNSPEOPLE.
THE SCHOOL AND AMUSEMENT PARK WERE BOTH HEAVILY DAMAGED, BUT THE HOSPITAL SURVIVED THE FIRES.
MURMUR
THAT WOMAN IS THE QUEEN?
MURMUR
MURMUR
MURMUR
IT'S HER FAULT WE'RE IN THIS SITUATION.
MURMUR
MURMUR
MURMUR
THAT'S THE QUEEN...
MURMUR
MURMUR
SHE IS?
MURMUR
MURMUR
SHE GOT US ALL HURT.
WHY HASN'T THE CHANCELLOR LOCKED HER UP?
LET'S GO OUTSIDE, YOUR MAJESTY!

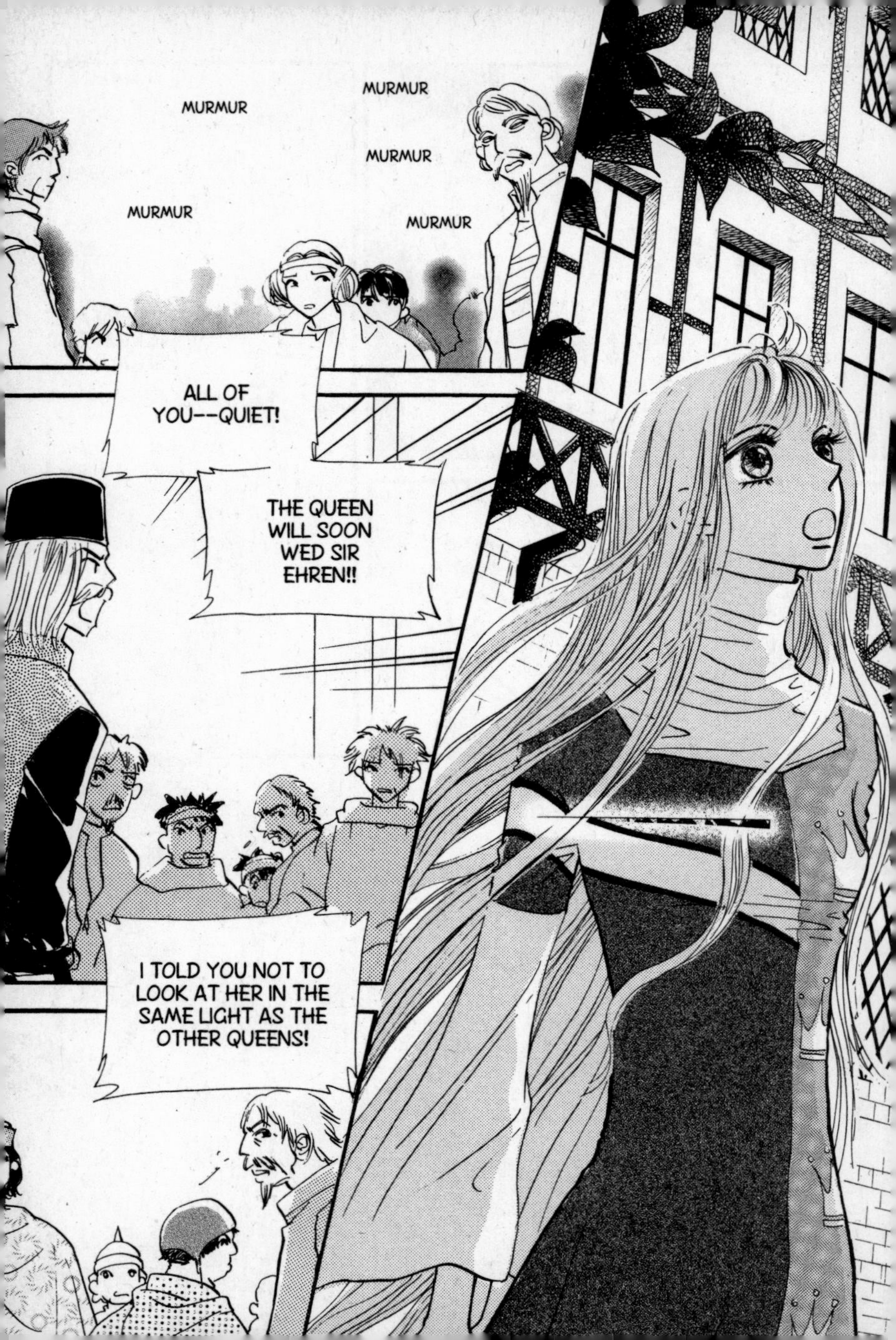
MURMUR
MURMUR
MURMUR
MURMUR
MURMUR
ALL OF YOU--QUIET!
THE QUEEN WILL SOON WED SIR EHREN!!
I TOLD YOU NOT TO LOOK AT HER IN THE SAME LIGHT AS THE OTHER QUEENS!

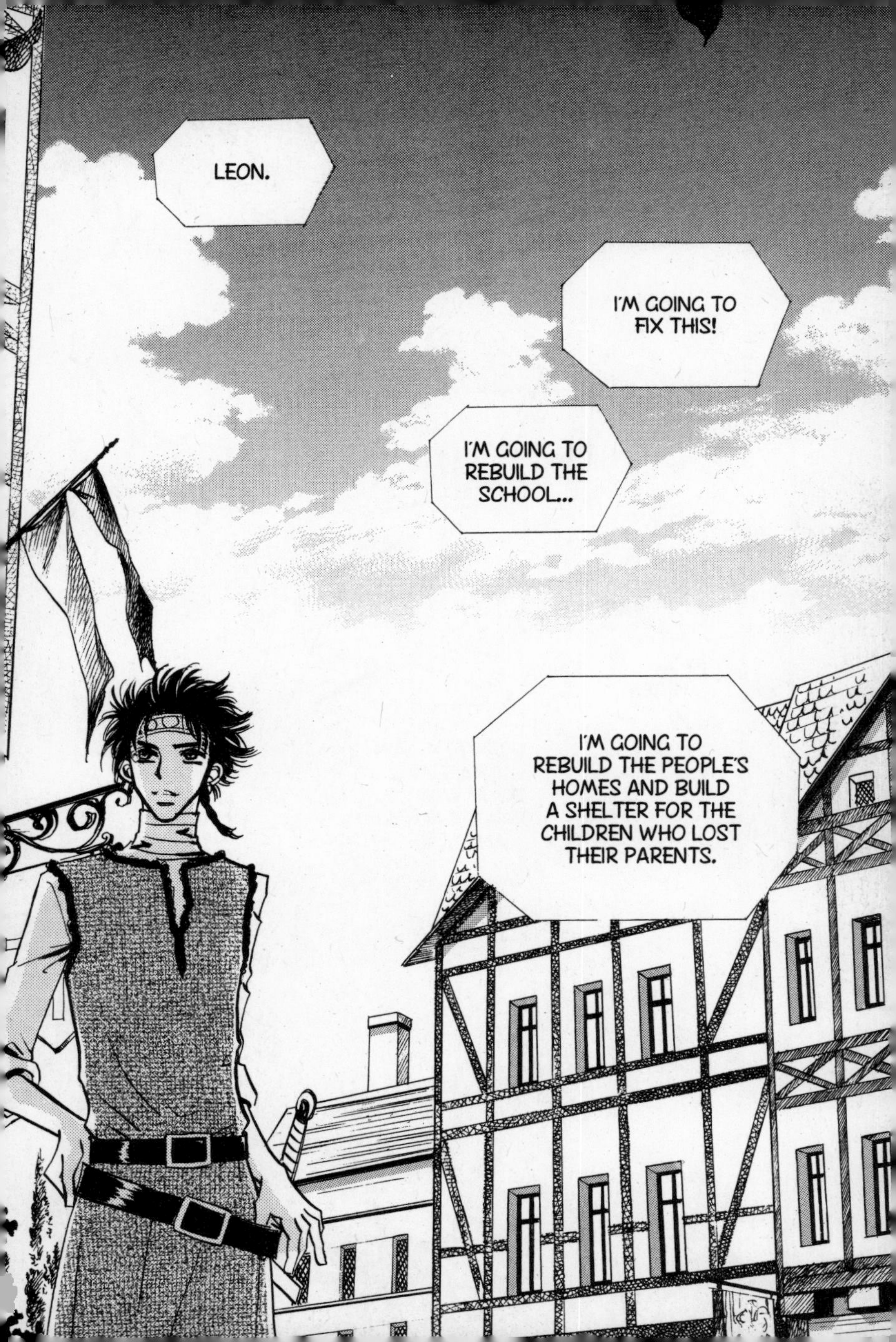
LEON.
I'M GOING TO FIX THIS!
I'M GOING TO REBUILD THE SCHOOL...
I'M GOING TO REBUILD THE PEOPLE'S HOMES AND BUILD A SHELTER FOR THE CHILDREN WHO LOST THEIR PARENTS.

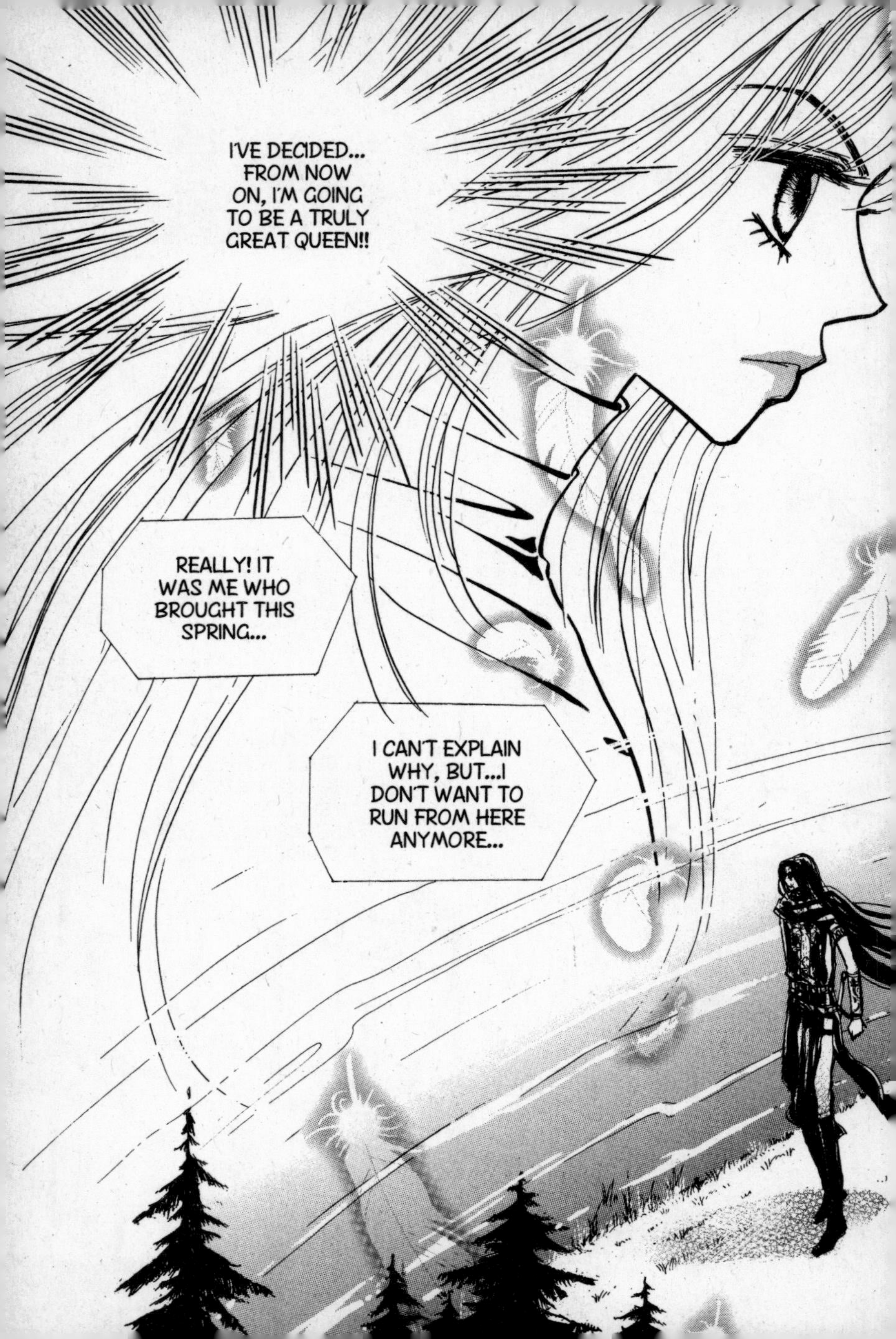
I'VE DECIDED... FROM NOW ON, I'M GOING TO BE A TRULY GREAT QUEEN!!
REALLY! IT WAS ME WHO BROUGHT THIS SPRING...
I CAN'T EXPLAIN WHY, BUT...I DON'T WANT TO RUN FROM HERE ANYMORE...

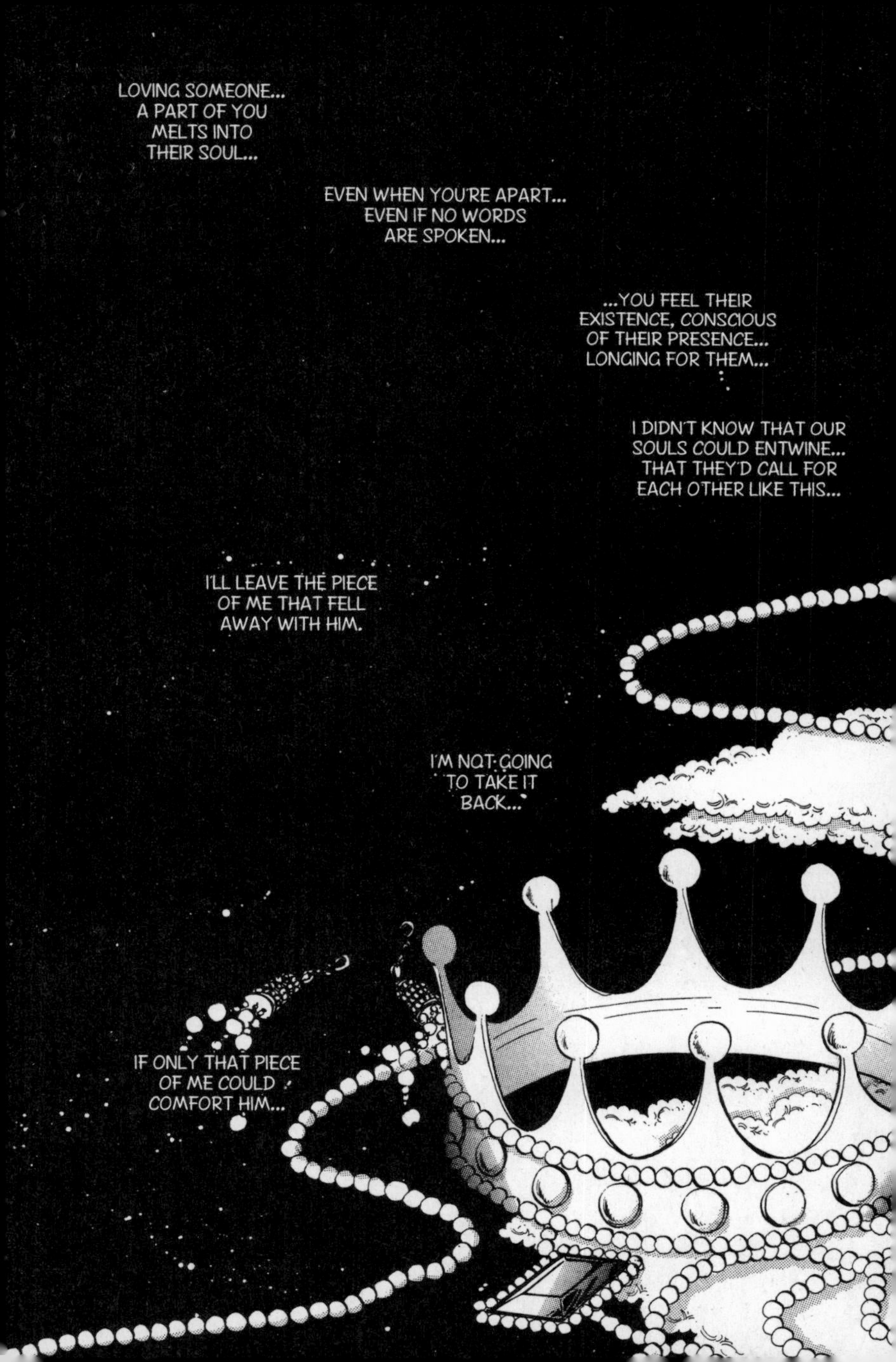
LOVING SOMEONE... A PART OF YOU MELTS INTO THEIR SOUL...
EVEN WHEN YOU'RE APART... EVEN IF NO WORDS ARE SPOKEN...
...YOU FEEL THEIR EXISTENCE, CONSCIOUS OF THEIR PRESENCE... LONGING FOR THEM...
I DIDN'T KNOW THAT OUR SOULS COULD ENTWINE... THAT THEY'D CALL FOR EACH OTHER LIKE THIS...
I'LL LEAVE THE PIECE OF ME THAT FELL AWAY WITH HIM.
I'M NOT GOING TO TAKE IT BACK...
IF ONLY THAT PIECE OF ME COULD COMFORT HIM...

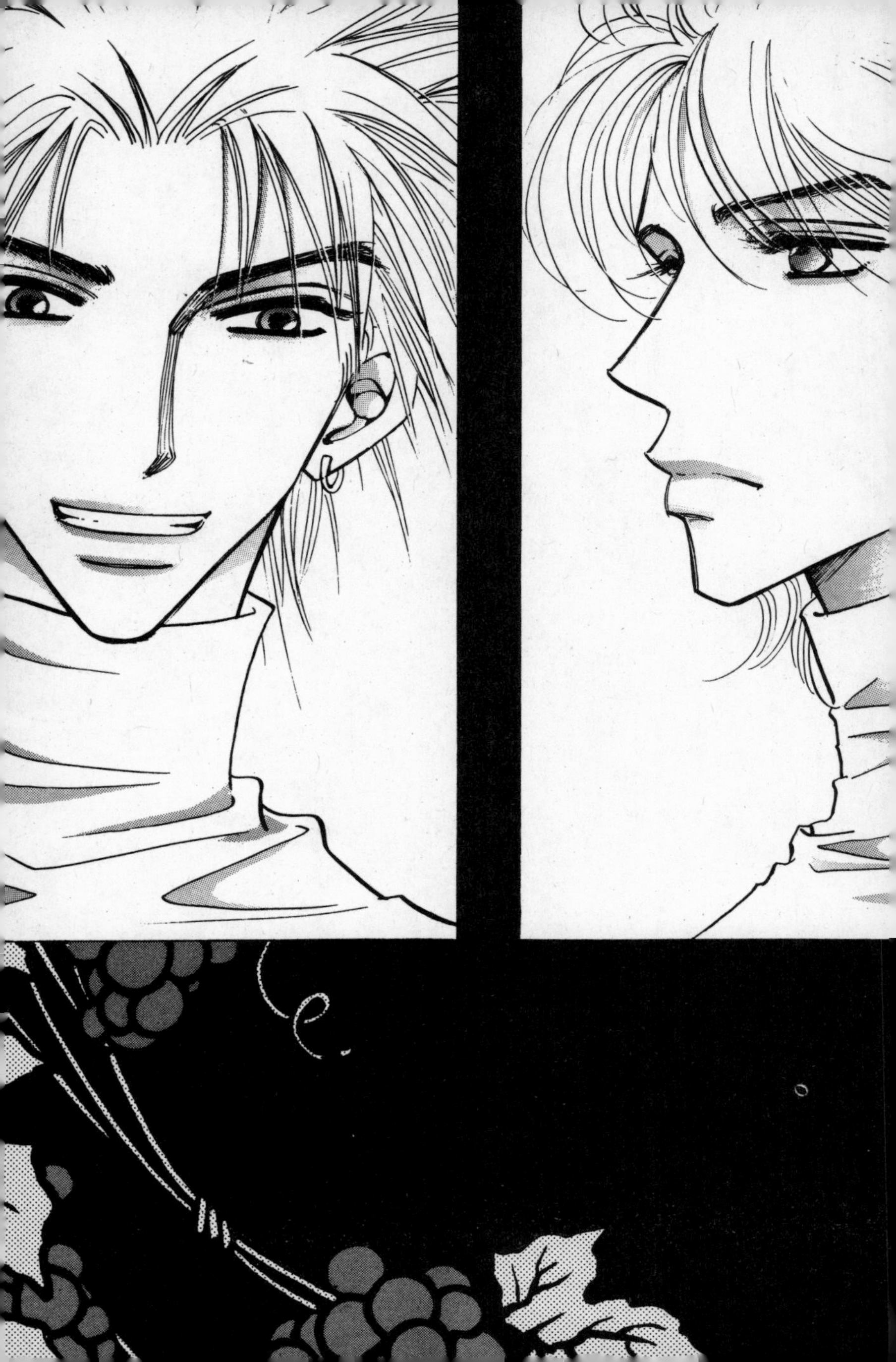

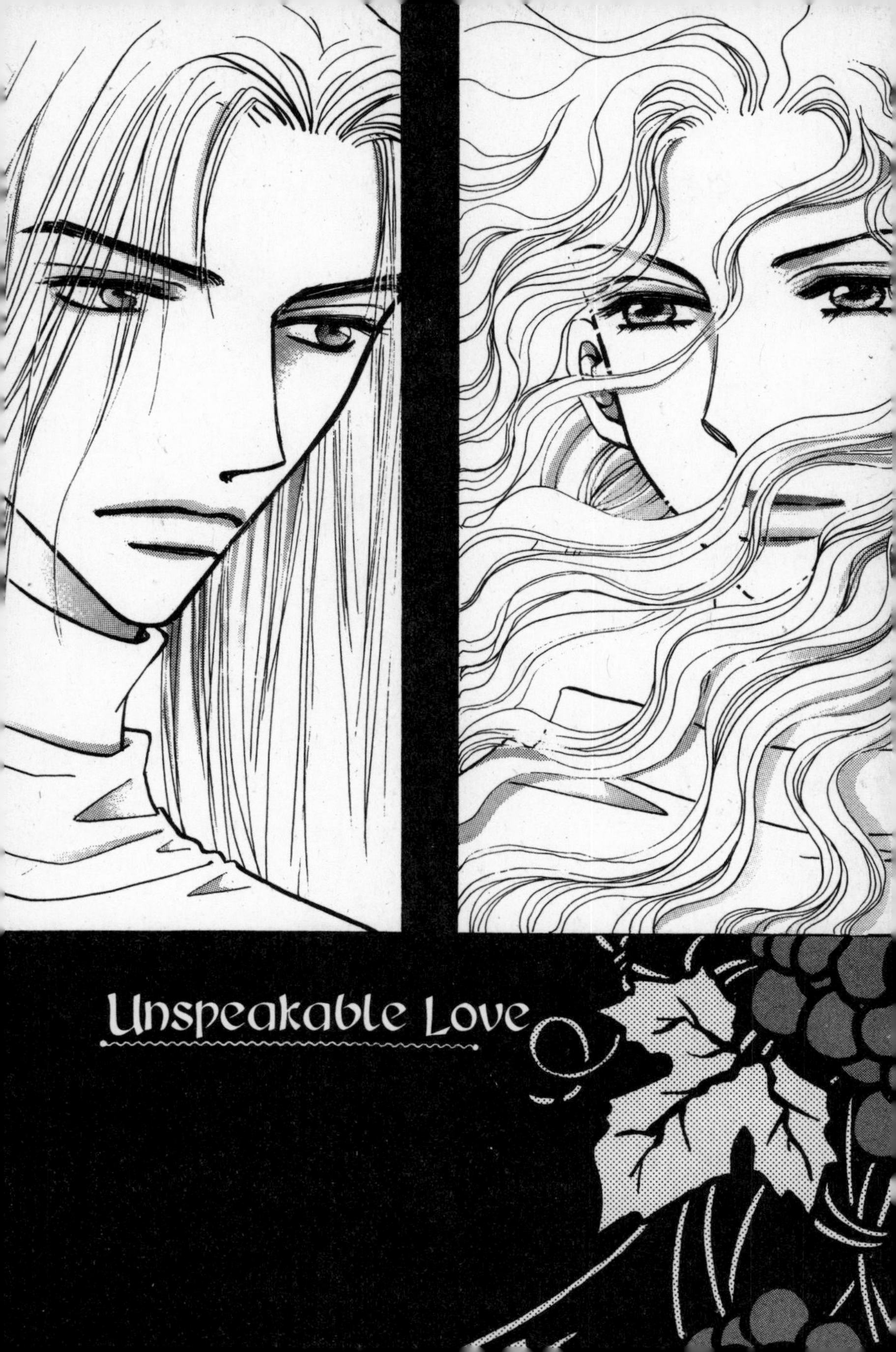
Unspeakable Love

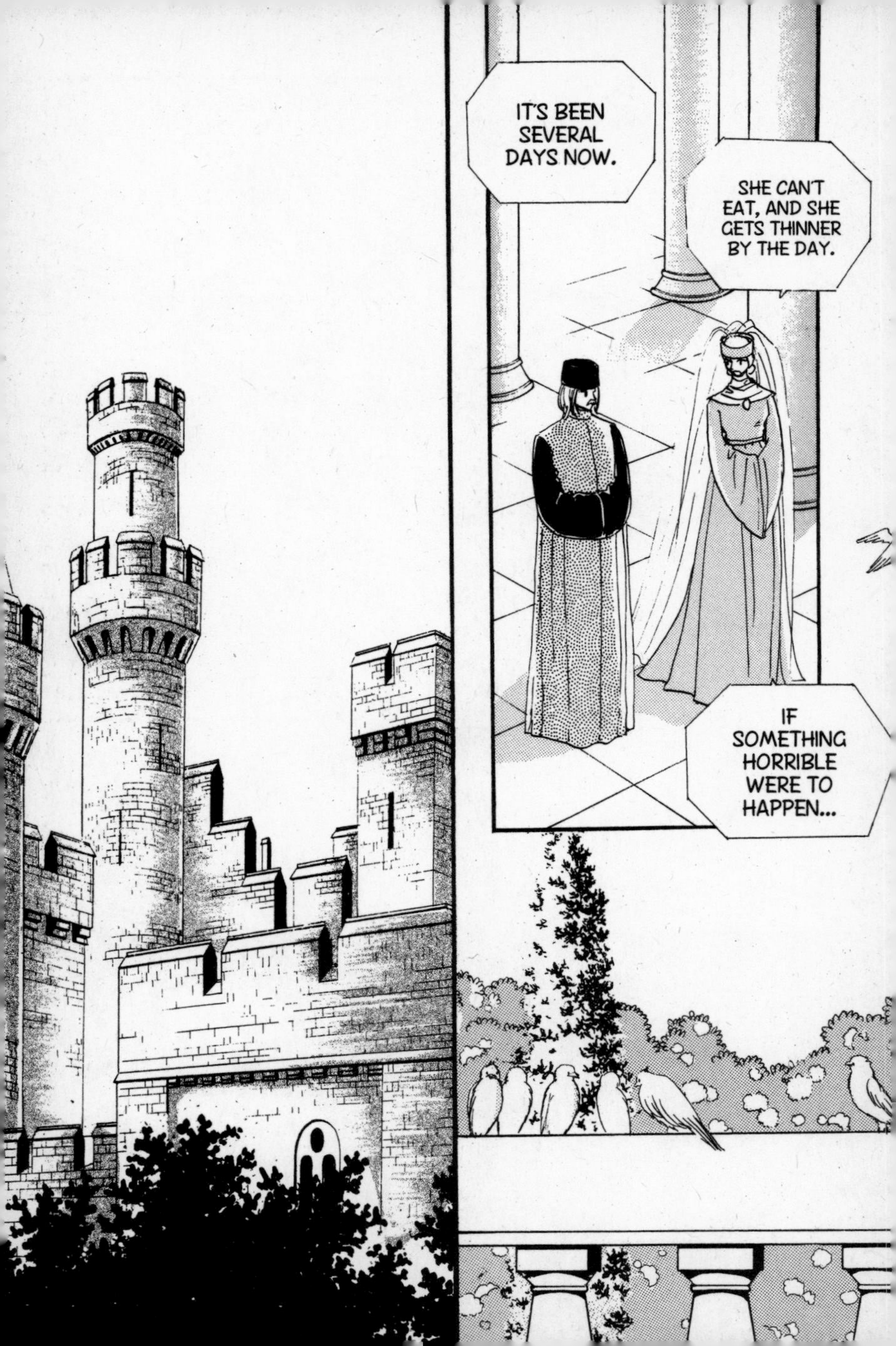
IT'S BEEN SEVERAL DAYS NOW.
SHE CAN'T EAT, AND SHE GETS THINNER BY THE DAY.
IF SOMETHING HORRIBLE WERE TO HAPPEN...

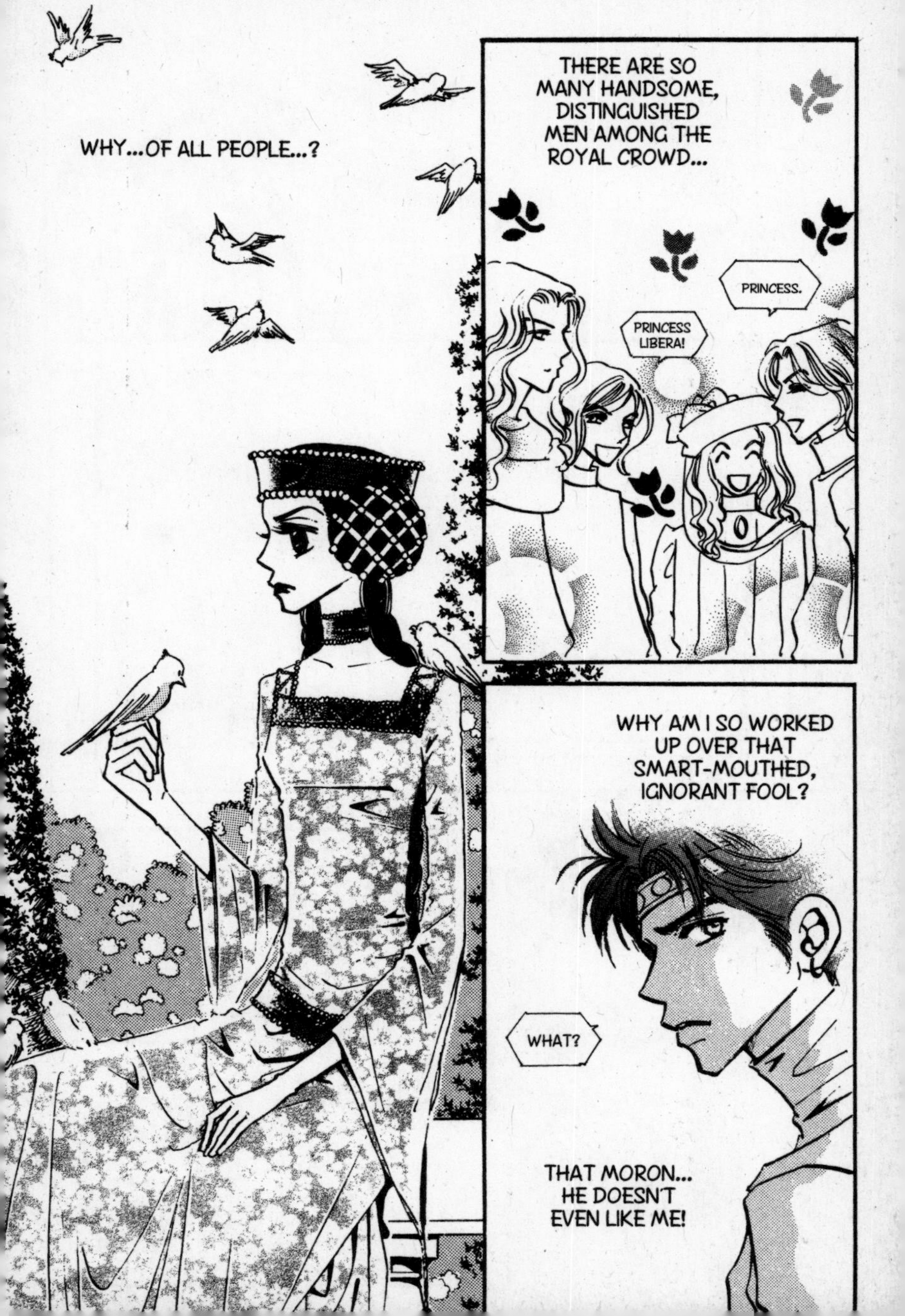
WHY...OF ALL PEOPLE...?
THERE ARE SO MANY HANDSOME, DISTINGUISHED MEN AMONG THE ROYAL CROWD...
PRINCESS LIBERA!
PRINCESS.
WHY AM I SO WORKED UP OVER THAT SMART-MOUTHED, IGNORANT FOOL?
WHAT?
THAT MORON... HE DOESN'T EVEN LIKE ME!

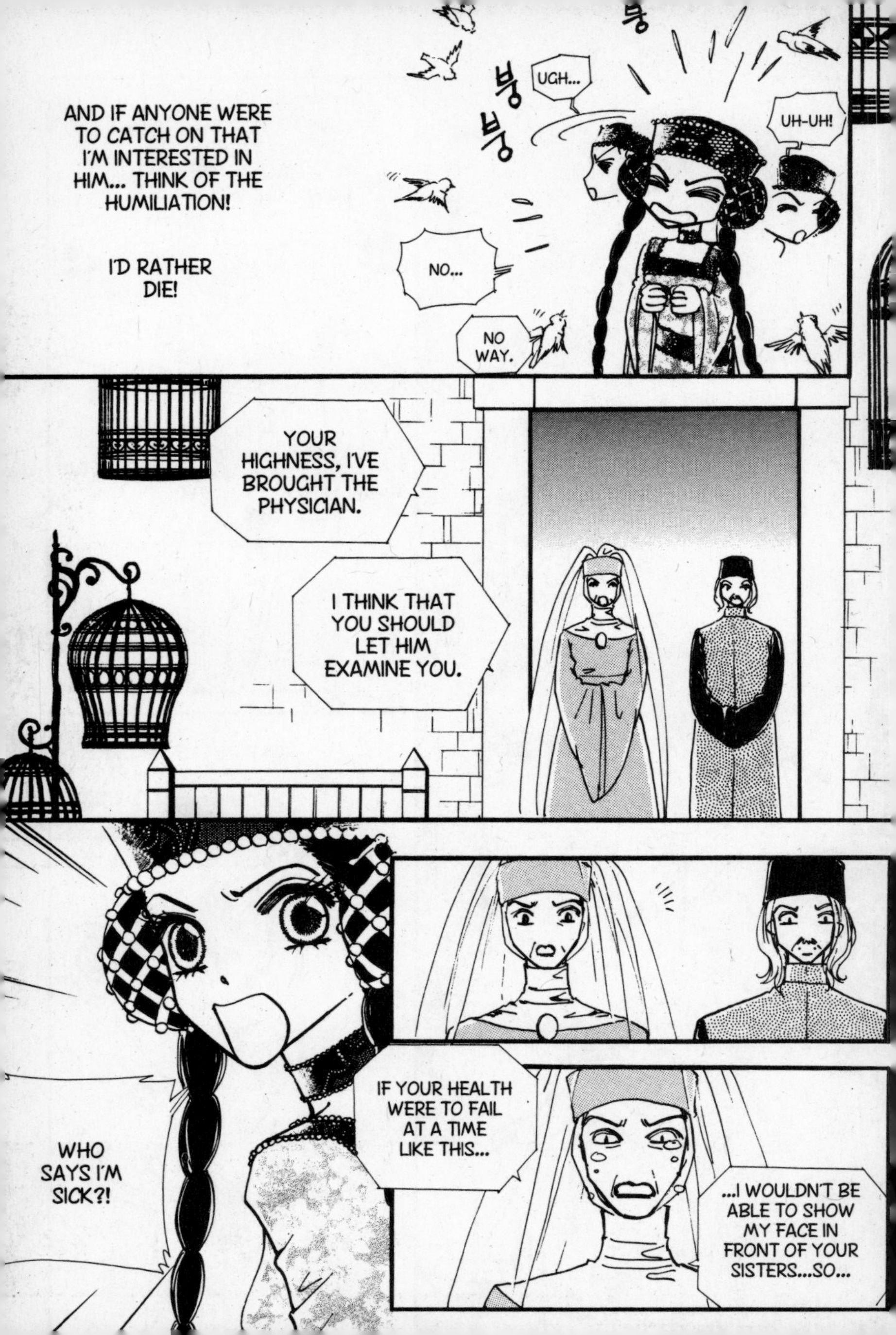
AND IF ANYONE WERE TO CATCH ON THAT I'M INTERESTED IN HIM... THINK OF THE HUMILIATION!
I'D RATHER DIE!
붕
붕
붕
UGH...
UH-UH!
NO...
NO WAY.
YOUR HIGHNESS, I'VE BROUGHT THE PHYSICIAN.
I THINK THAT YOU SHOULD LET HIM EXAMINE YOU.
WHO SAYS I'M SICK?!
IF YOUR HEALTH WERE TO FAIL AT A TIME LIKE THIS...
...I WOULDN'T BE ABLE TO SHOW MY FACE IN FRONT OF YOUR SISTERS...SO...

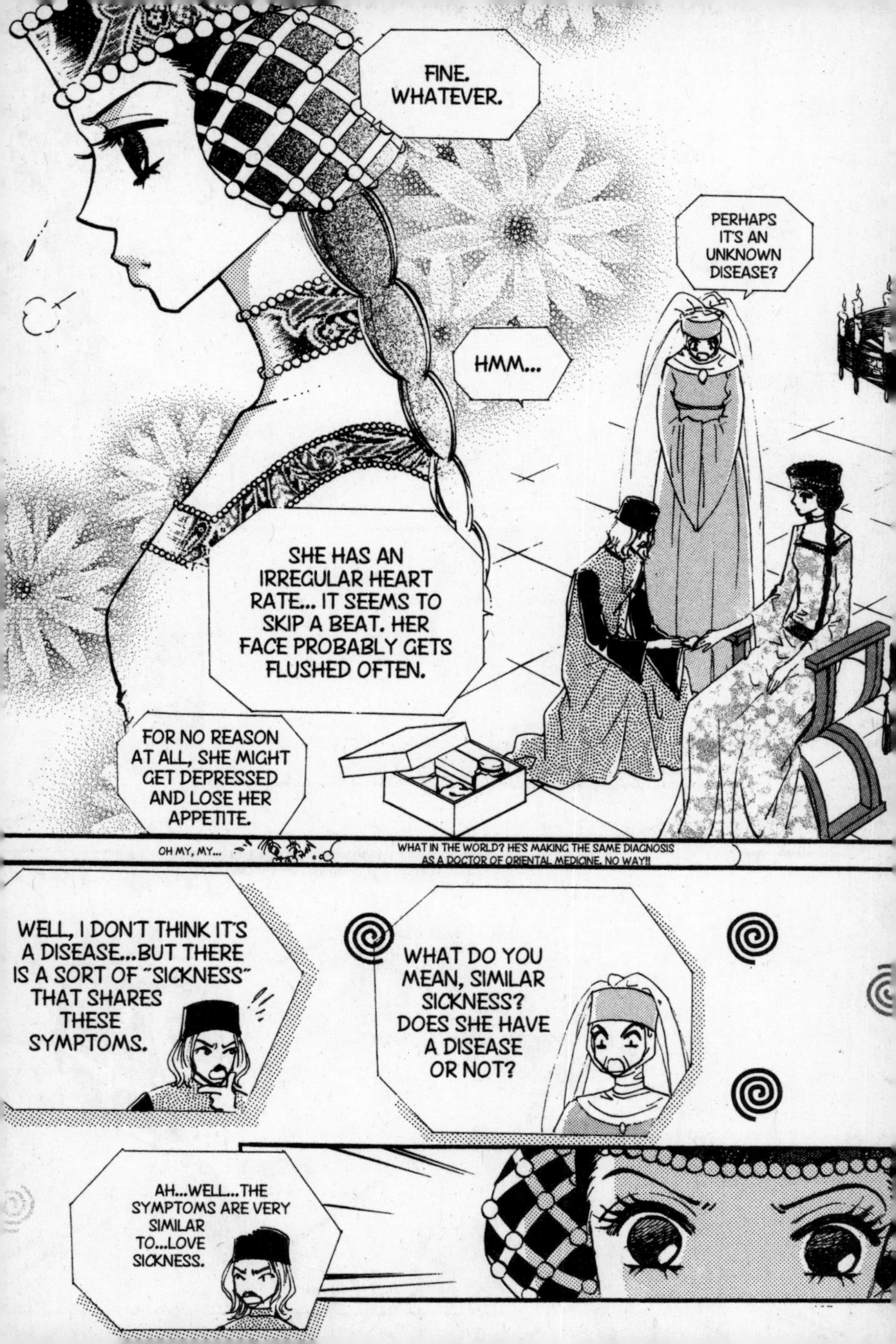
FINE. WHATEVER.
PERHAPS IT'S AN UNKNOWN DISEASE?
HMM...
SHE HAS AN IRREGULAR HEART RATE... IT SEEMS TO SKIP A BEAT. HER FACE PROBABLY GETS FLUSHED OFTEN.
FOR NO REASON AT ALL, SHE MIGHT GET DEPRESSED AND LOSE HER APPETITE.
OH MY, MY...
WHAT IN THE WORLD? HE'S MAKING THE SAME DIAGNOSIS AS A DOCTOR OF ORIENTAL MEDICINE. NO WAY!!
WELL, I DON'T THINK IT'S A DISEASE...BUT THERE IS A SORT OF "SICKNESS" THAT SHARES THESE SYMPTOMS.
WHAT DO YOU MEAN, SIMILAR SICKNESS? DOES SHE HAVE A DISEASE OR NOT?
AH...WELL...THE SYMPTOMS ARE VERY SIMILAR TO...LOVE SICKNESS.

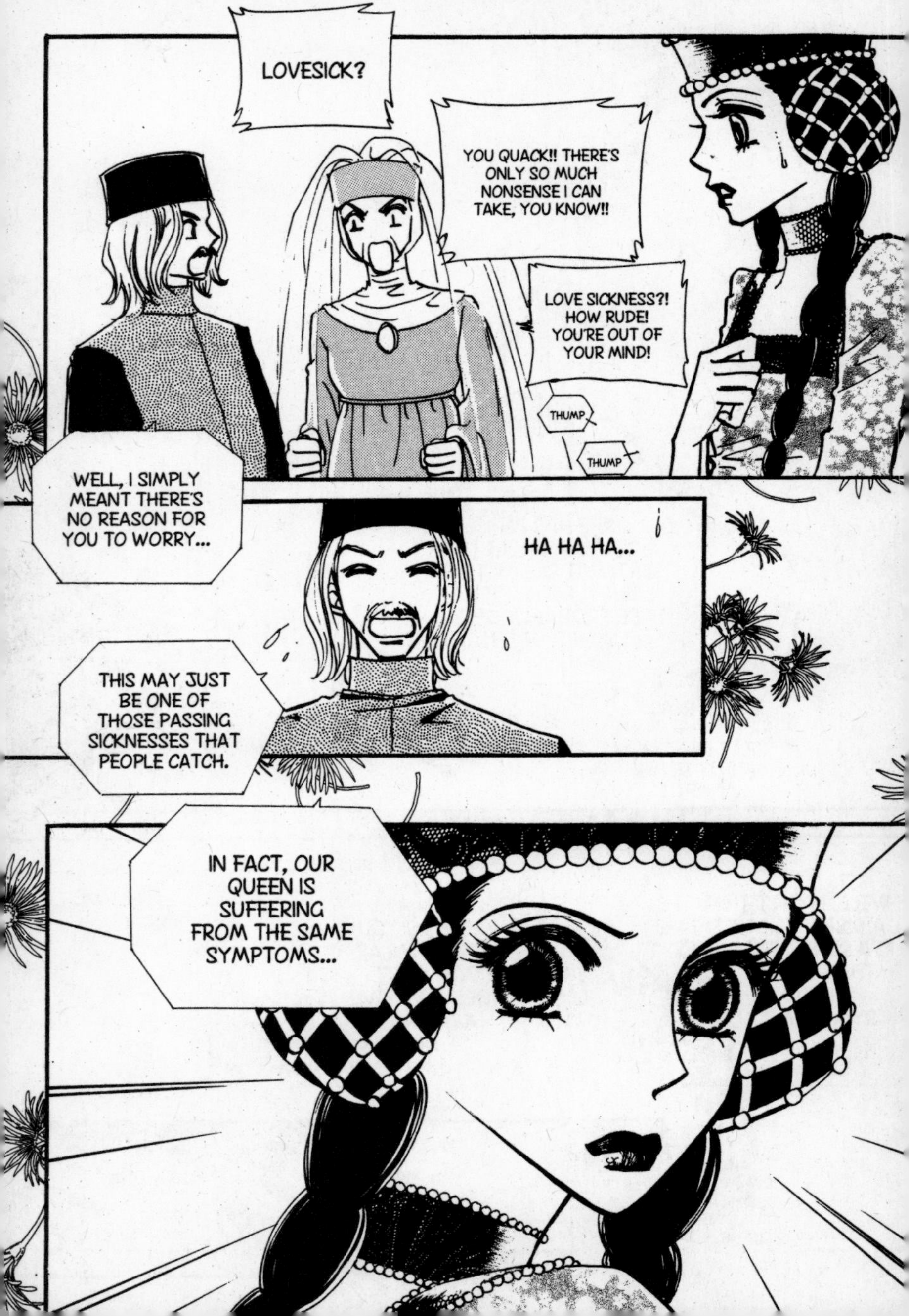
LOVESICK?
YOU QUACK!! THERE'S ONLY SO MUCH NONSENSE I CAN TAKE, YOU KNOW!!
LOVE SICKNESS?! HOW RUDE! YOU'RE OUT OF YOUR MIND!
THUMP
THUMP
WELL, I SIMPLY MEANT THERE'S NO REASON FOR YOU TO WORRY...
HA HA HA...
THIS MAY JUST BE ONE OF THOSE PASSING SICKNESSES THAT PEOPLE CATCH.
IN FACT, OUR QUEEN IS SUFFERING FROM THE SAME SYMPTOMS...

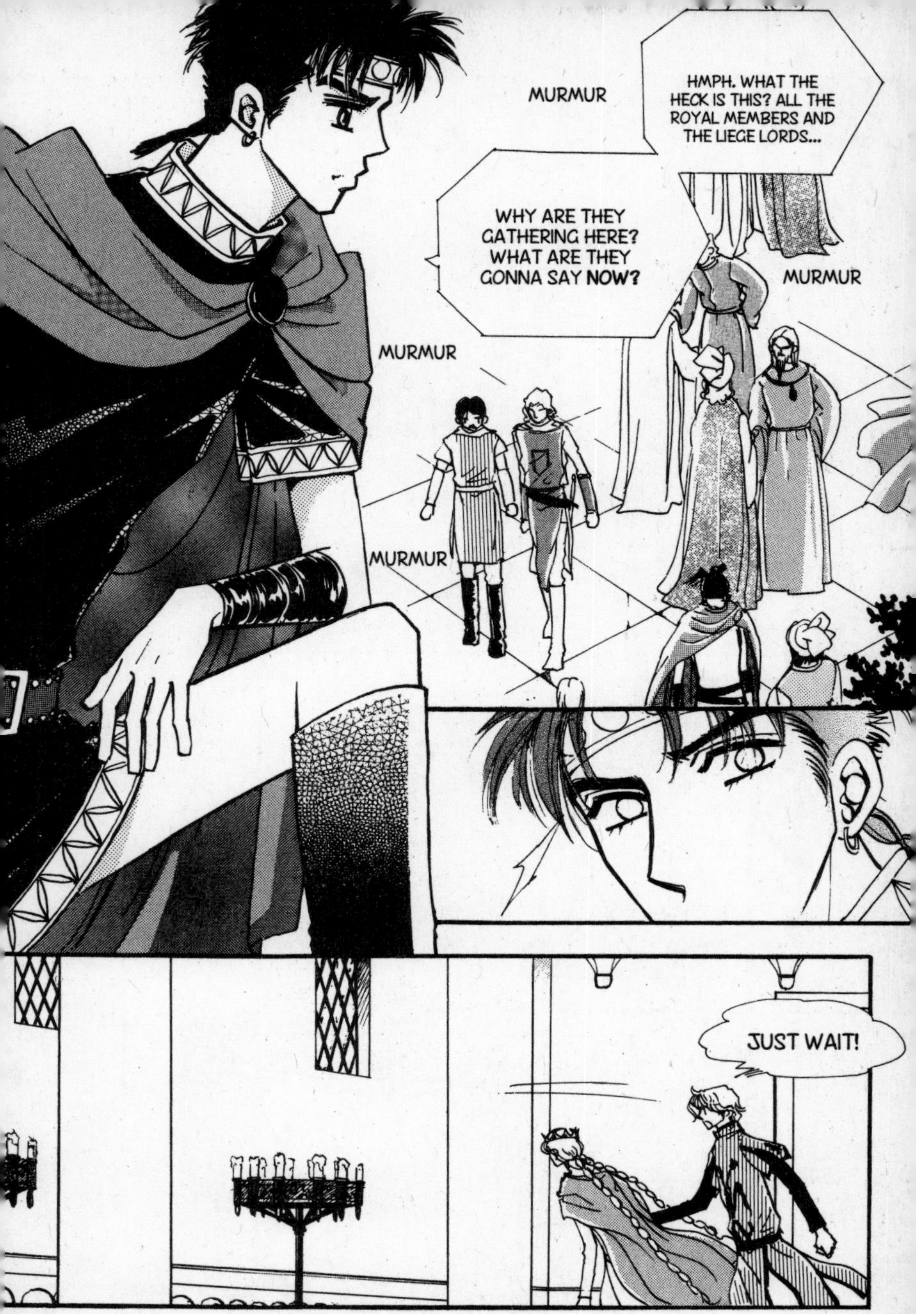
MURMUR
HMPH. WHAT THE HECK IS THIS? ALL THE ROYAL MEMBERS AND THE LIEGE LORDS...
WHY ARE THEY GATHERING HERE? WHAT ARE THEY GONNA SAY NOW?
MURMUR
MURMUR
MURMUR
JUST WAIT!

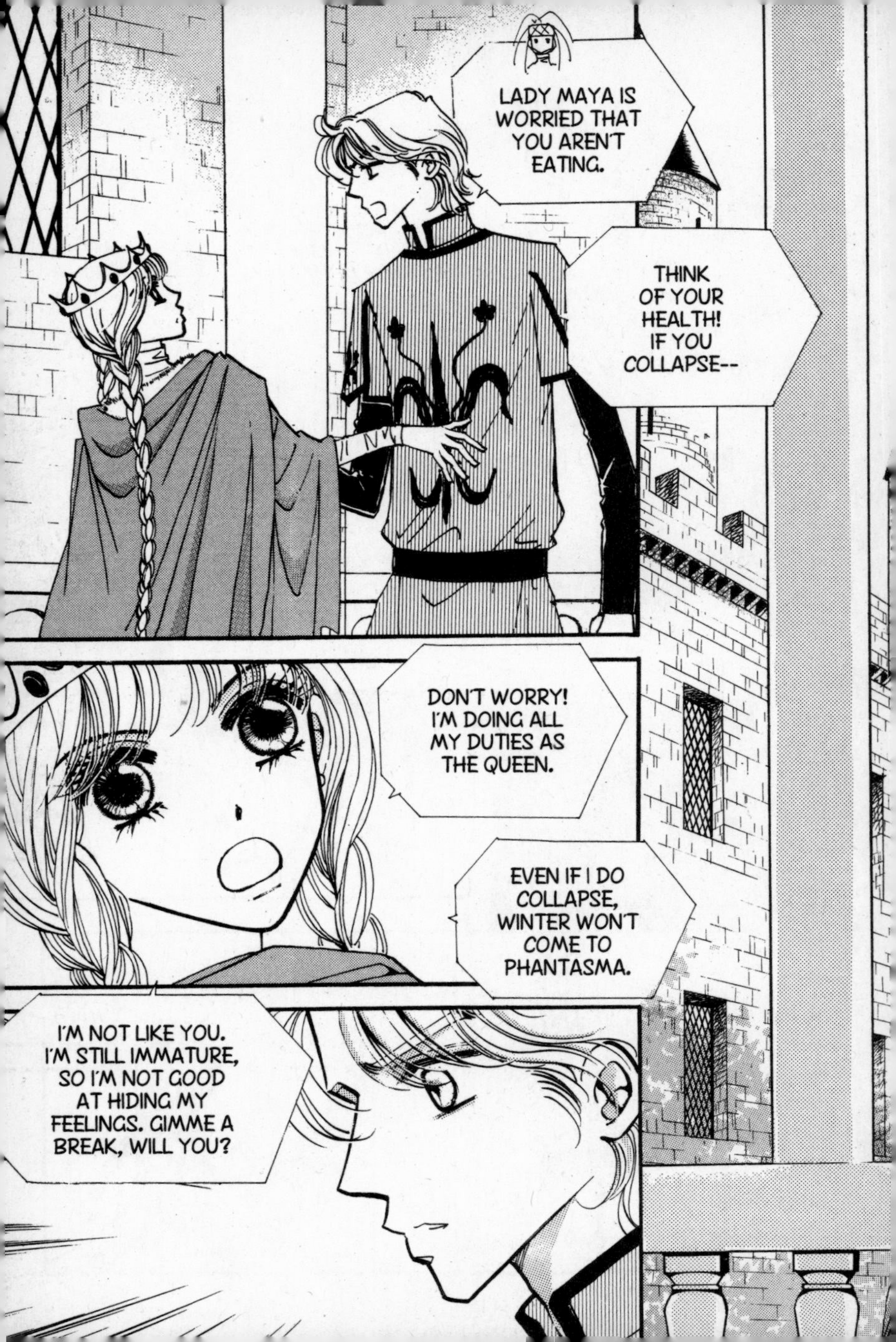
LADY MAYA IS WORRIED THAT YOU AREN'T EATING.
THINK OF YOUR HEALTH! IF YOU COLLAPSE--
DON'T WORRY! I'M DOING ALL MY DUTIES AS THE QUEEN.
EVEN IF I DO COLLAPSE, WINTER WON'T COME TO PHANTASMA.
I'M NOT LIKE YOU. I'M STILL IMMATURE, SO I'M NOT GOOD AT HIDING MY FEELINGS. GIMME A BREAK, WILL YOU?

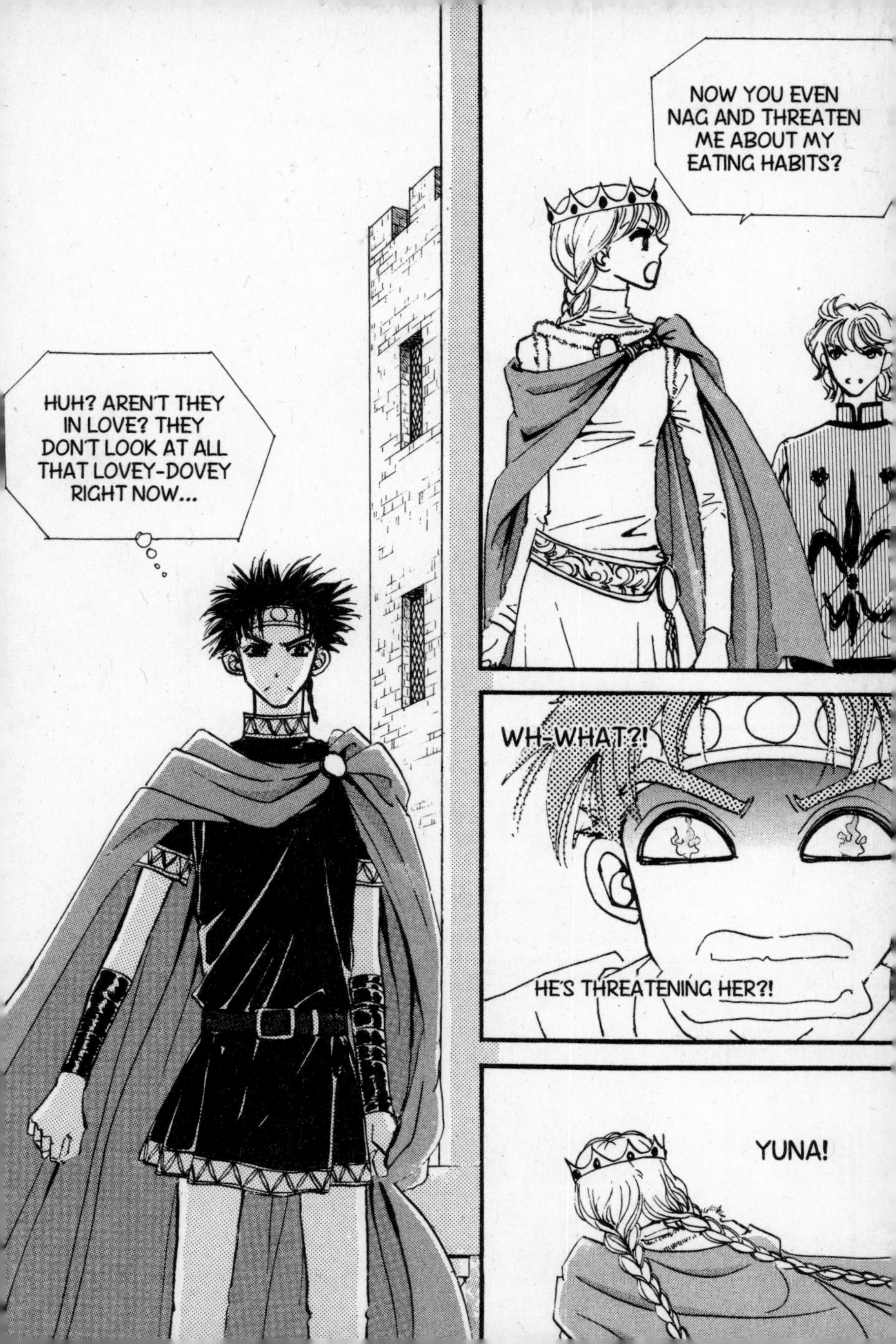
HUH? AREN'T THEY IN LOVE? THEY DON'T LOOK AT ALL THAT LOVEY-DOVEY RIGHT NOW...
NOW YOU EVEN NAG AND THREATEN ME ABOUT MY EATING HABITS?
WH-WHAT?!
HE'S THREATENING HER?!
YUNA!

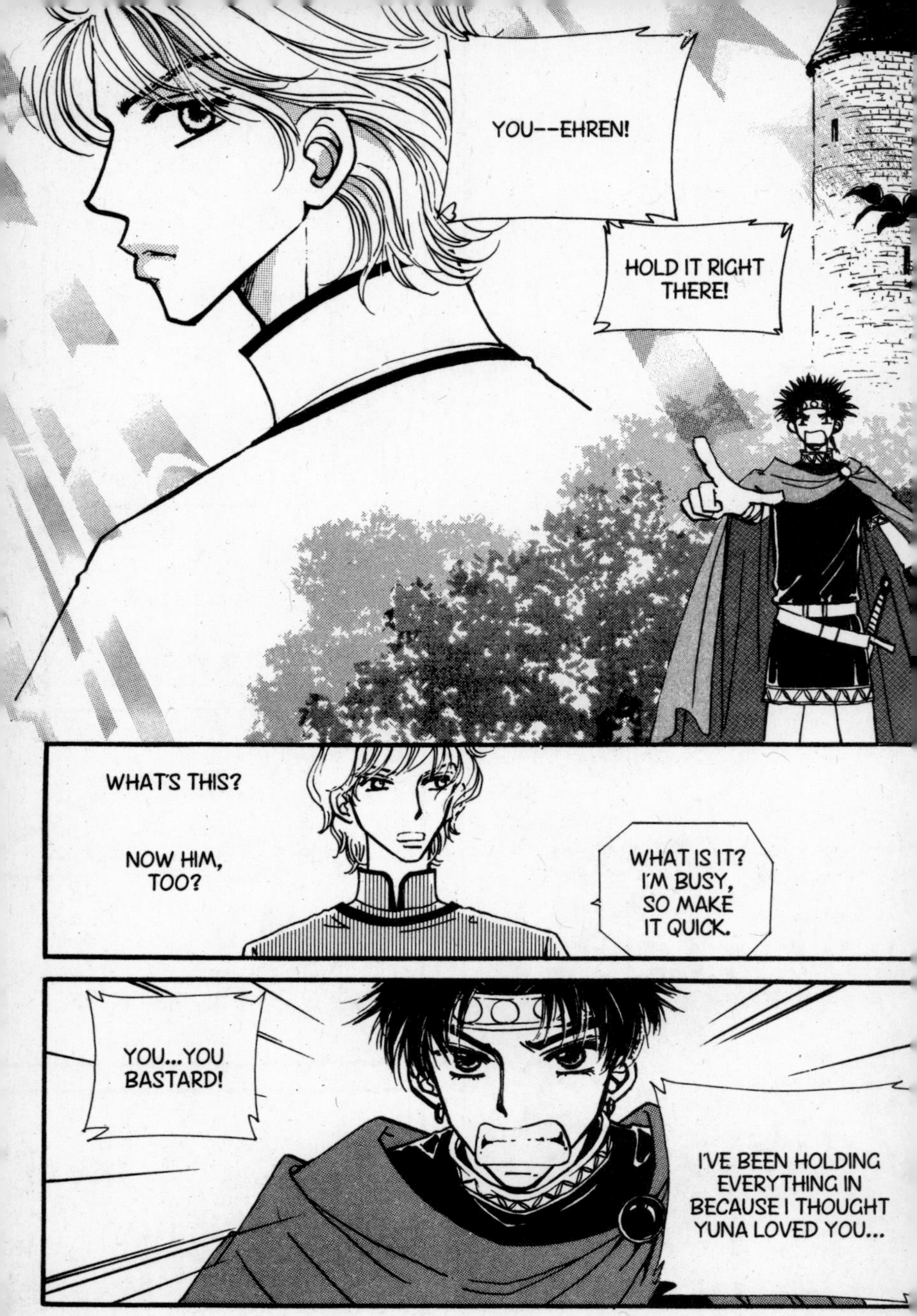
YOU--EHREN!
HOLD IT RIGHT THERE!
WHAT'S THIS?
NOW HIM, TOO?
WHAT IS IT? I'M BUSY, SO MAKE IT QUICK.
YOU...YOU BASTARD!
I'VE BEEN HOLDING EVERYTHING IN BECAUSE I THOUGHT YUNA LOVED YOU...

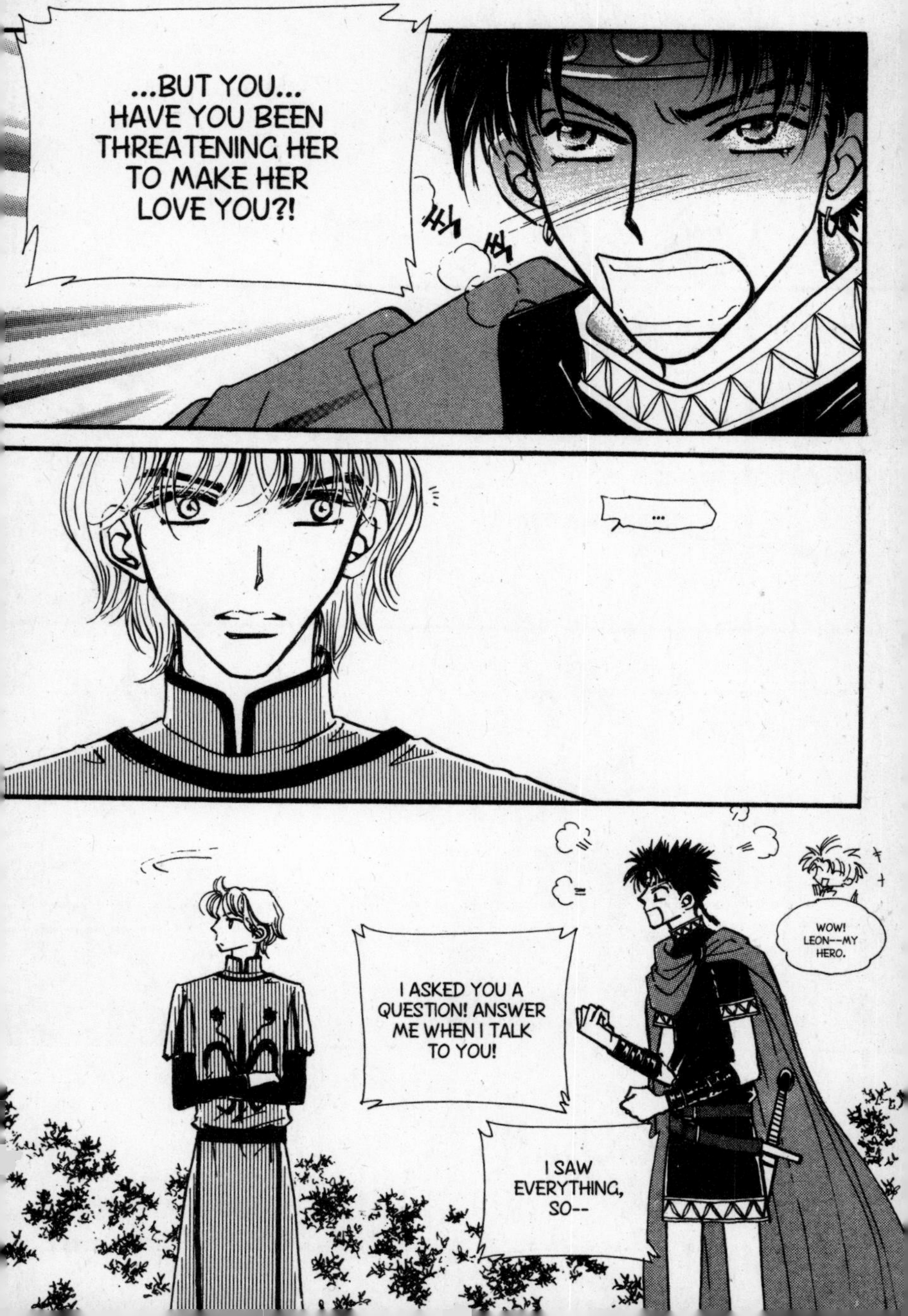
...BUT YOU... HAVE YOU BEEN THREATENING HER TO MAKE HER LOVE YOU?!
...
I ASKED YOU A QUESTION! ANSWER ME WHEN I TALK TO YOU!
WOW! LEON--MY HERO.
I SAW EVERYTHING, SO--

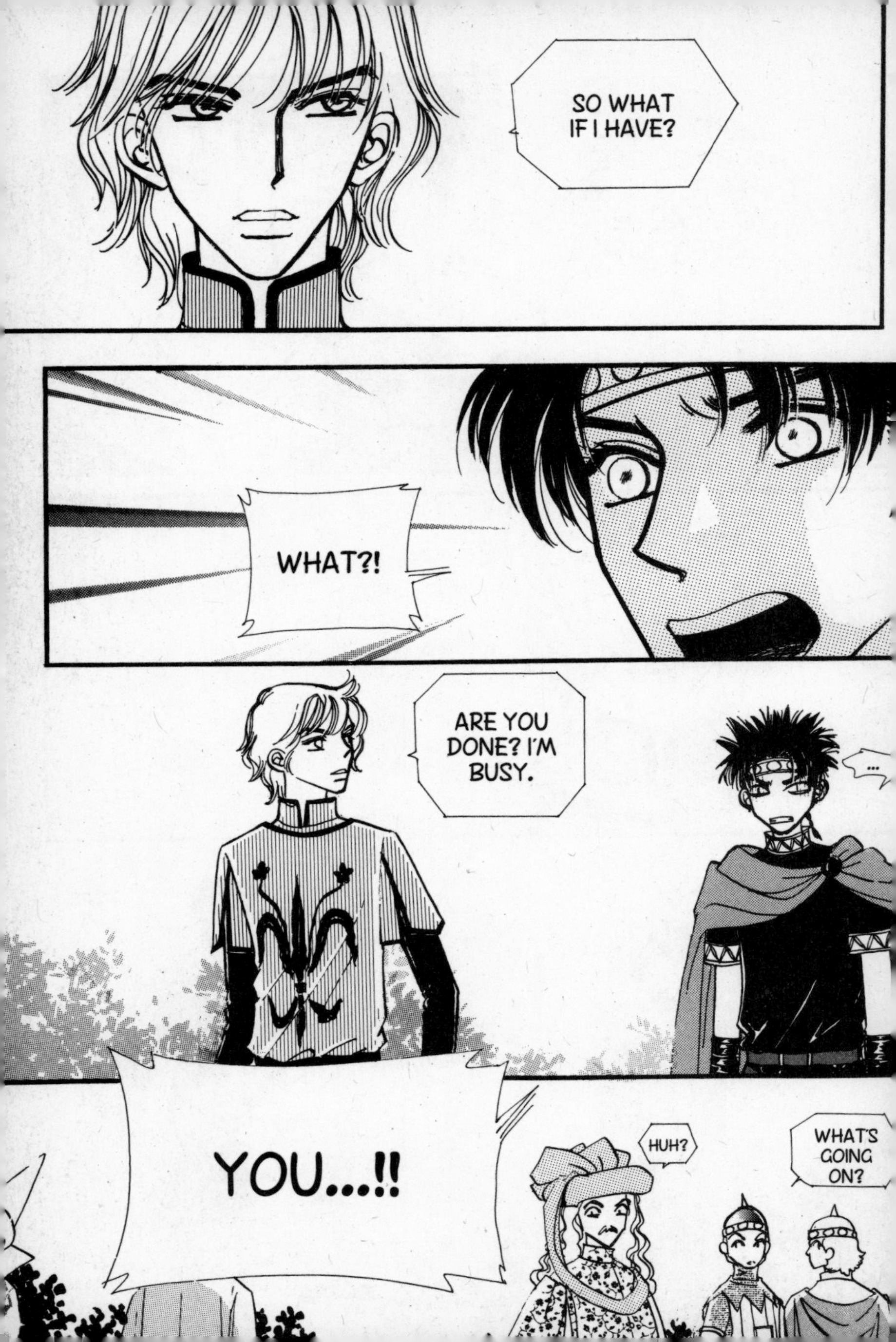

SO WHAT IF I HAVE?
WHAT?!
ARE YOU DONE? I'M BUSY.
...
YOU...!!
HUH?
WHAT'S GOING ON?

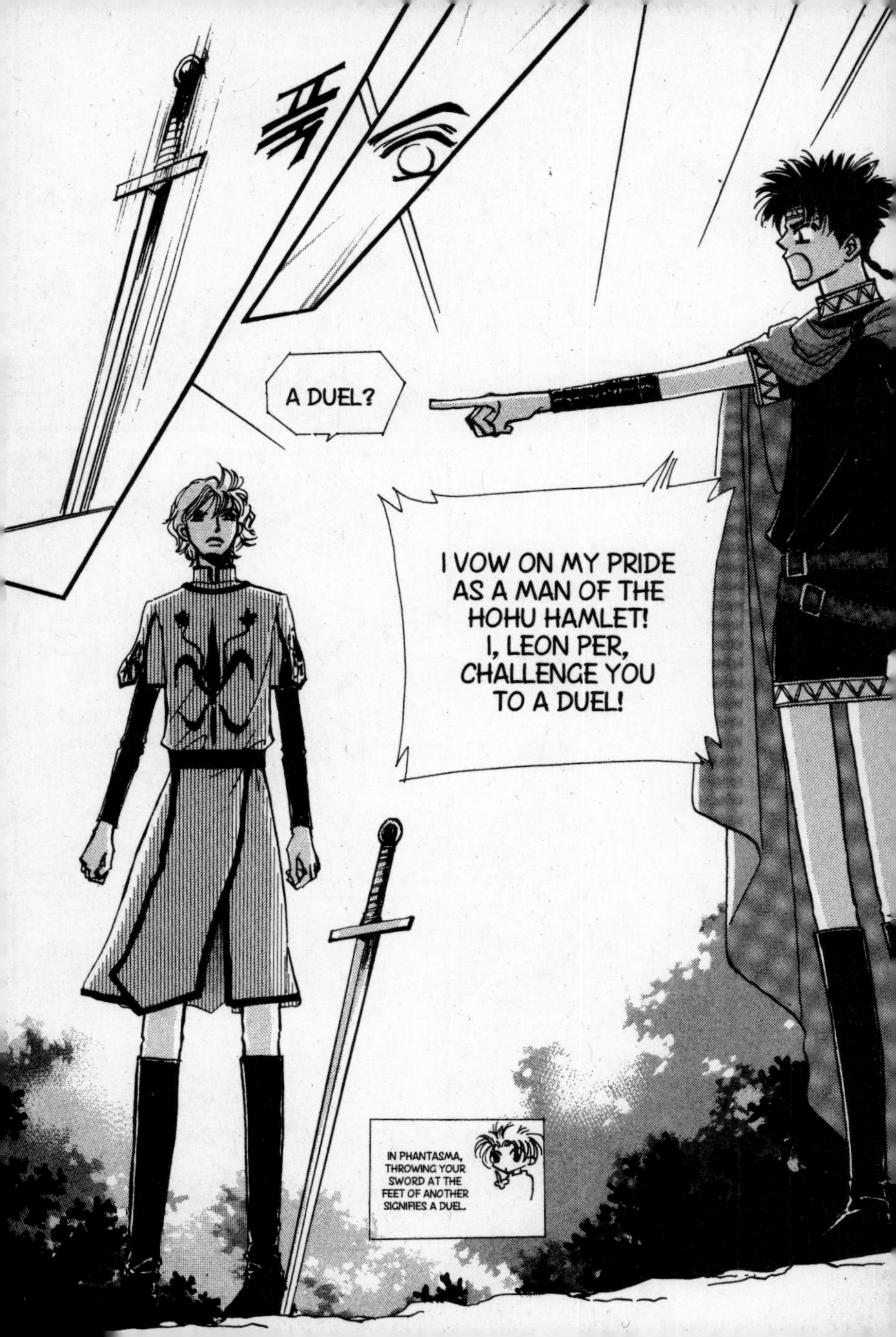

A DUEL?
I VOW ON MY PRIDE AS A MAN OF THE HOHU HAMLET! I, LEON PER, CHALLENGE YOU TO A DUEL!
IN PHANTASMA, THROWING YOUR SWORD AT THE FEET OF ANOTHER SIGNIFIES A DUEL.

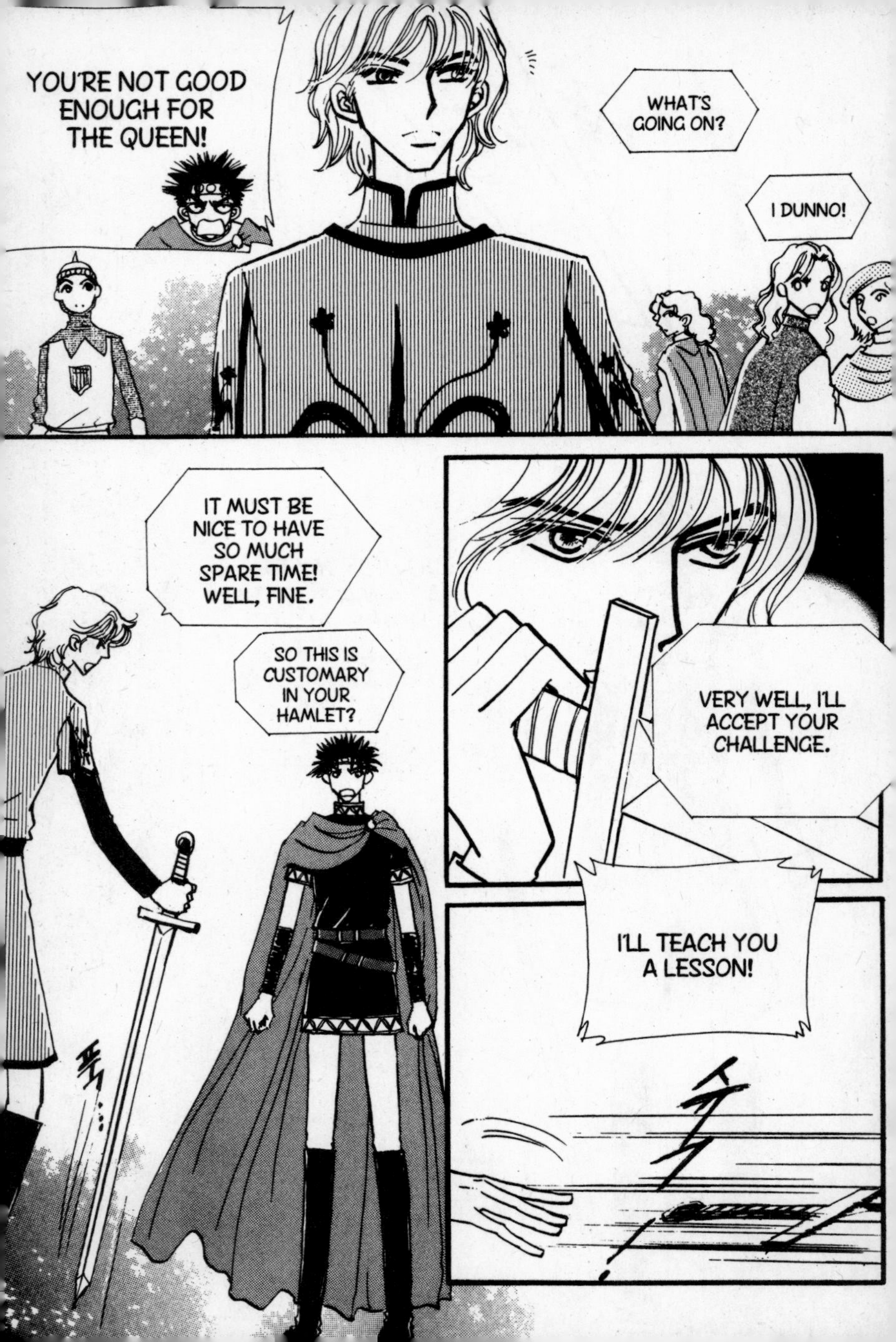
YOU'RE NOT GOOD ENOUGH FOR THE QUEEN!
WHAT'S GOING ON?
I DUNNO!
IT MUST BE NICE TO HAVE SO MUCH SPARE TIME! WELL, FINE.
SO THIS IS CUSTOMARY IN YOUR HAMLET?
VERY WELL, I'LL ACCEPT YOUR CHALLENGE.
I'LL TEACH YOU A LESSON!

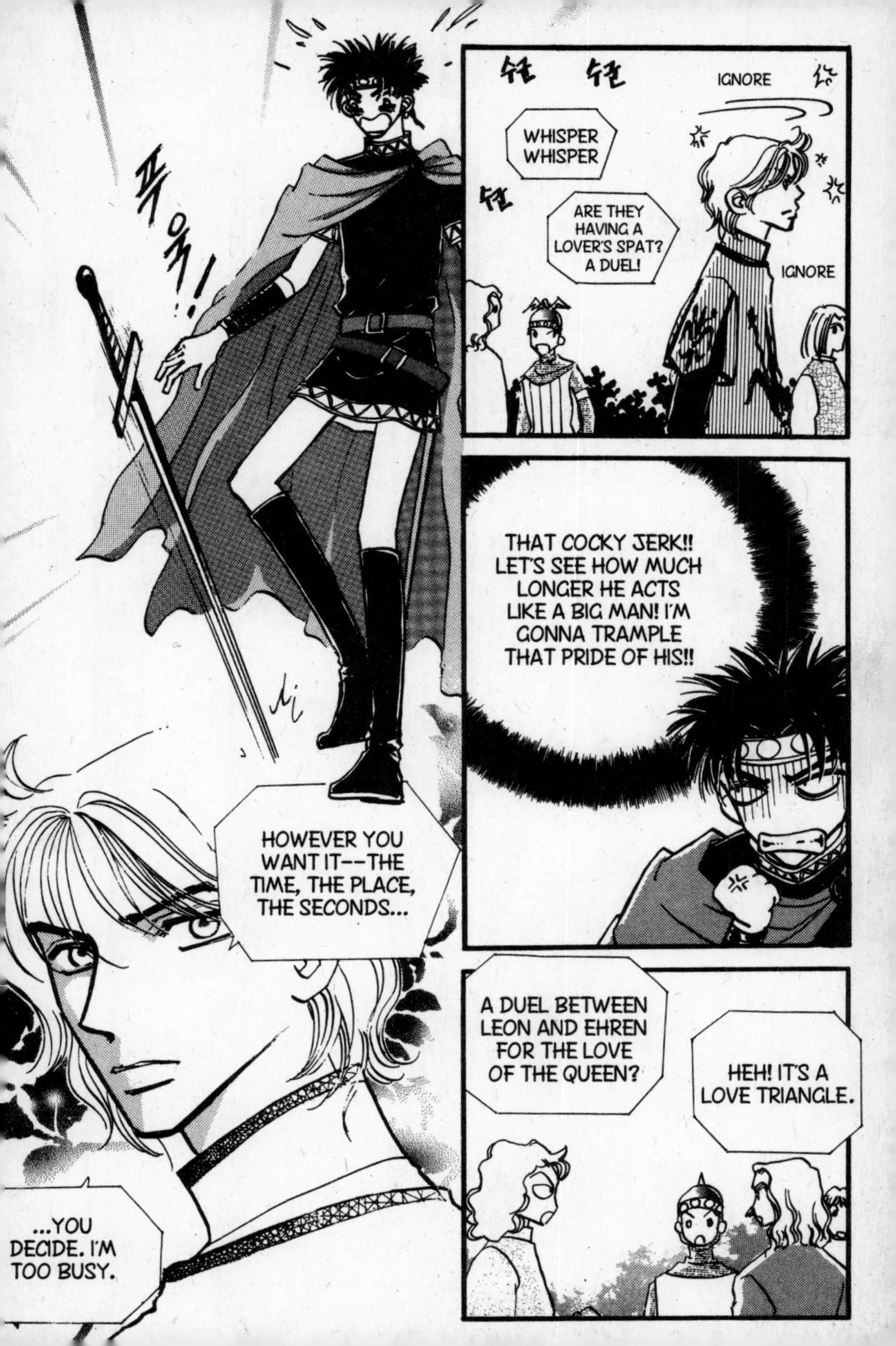

푸욱!!
HOWEVER YOU WANT IT--THE TIME, THE PLACE, THE SECONDS...
...YOU DECIDE. I'M TOO BUSY.
수군 수군
IGNORE
WHISPER WHISPER
수군
ARE THEY HAVING A LOVER'S SPAT? A DUEL!
IGNORE
THAT COCKY JERK!! LET'S SEE HOW MUCH LONGER HE ACTS LIKE A BIG MAN! I'M GONNA TRAMPLE THAT PRIDE OF HIS!!
A DUEL BETWEEN LEON AND EHREN FOR THE LOVE OF THE QUEEN?
HEH! IT'S A LOVE TRIANGLE.

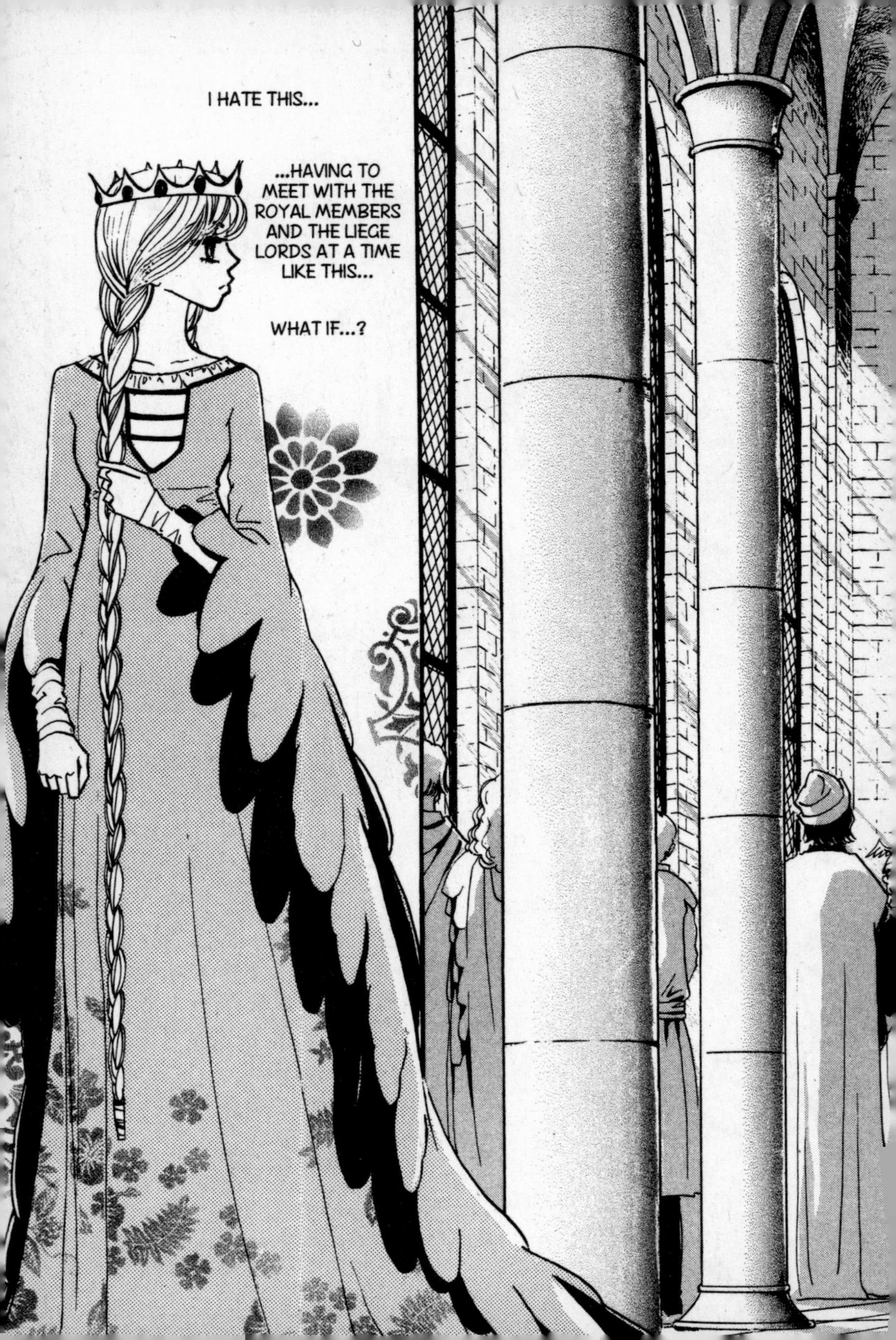
I HATE THIS...
...HAVING TO MEET WITH THE ROYAL MEMBERS AND THE LIEGE LORDS AT A TIME LIKE THIS...
WHAT IF...?

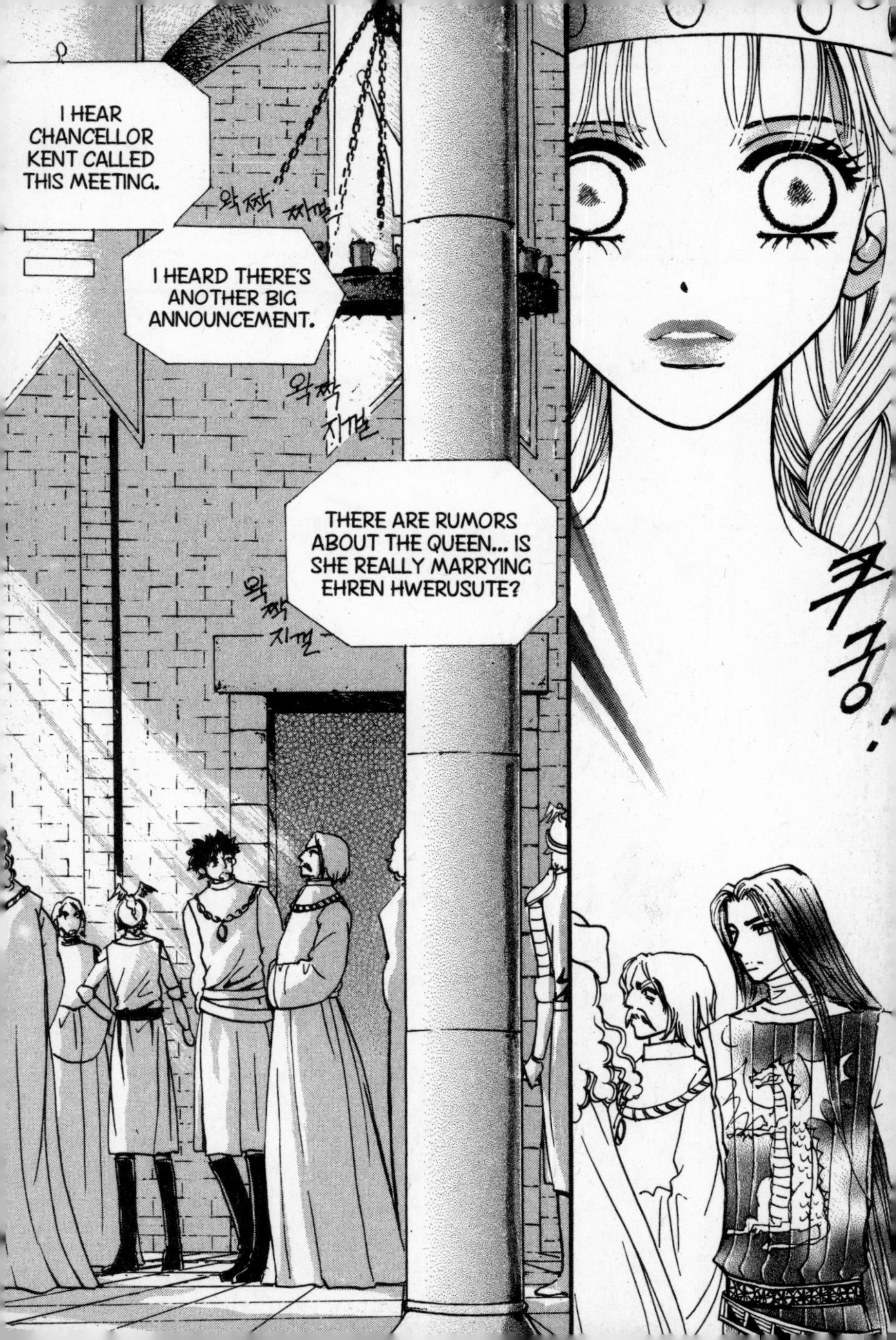
I HEAR CHANCELLOR KENT CALLED THIS MEETING.
I HEARD THERE'S ANOTHER BIG ANNOUNCEMENT.
THERE ARE RUMORS ABOUT THE QUEEN... IS SHE REALLY MARRYING EHREN HWERUSUTE?
쿠궁

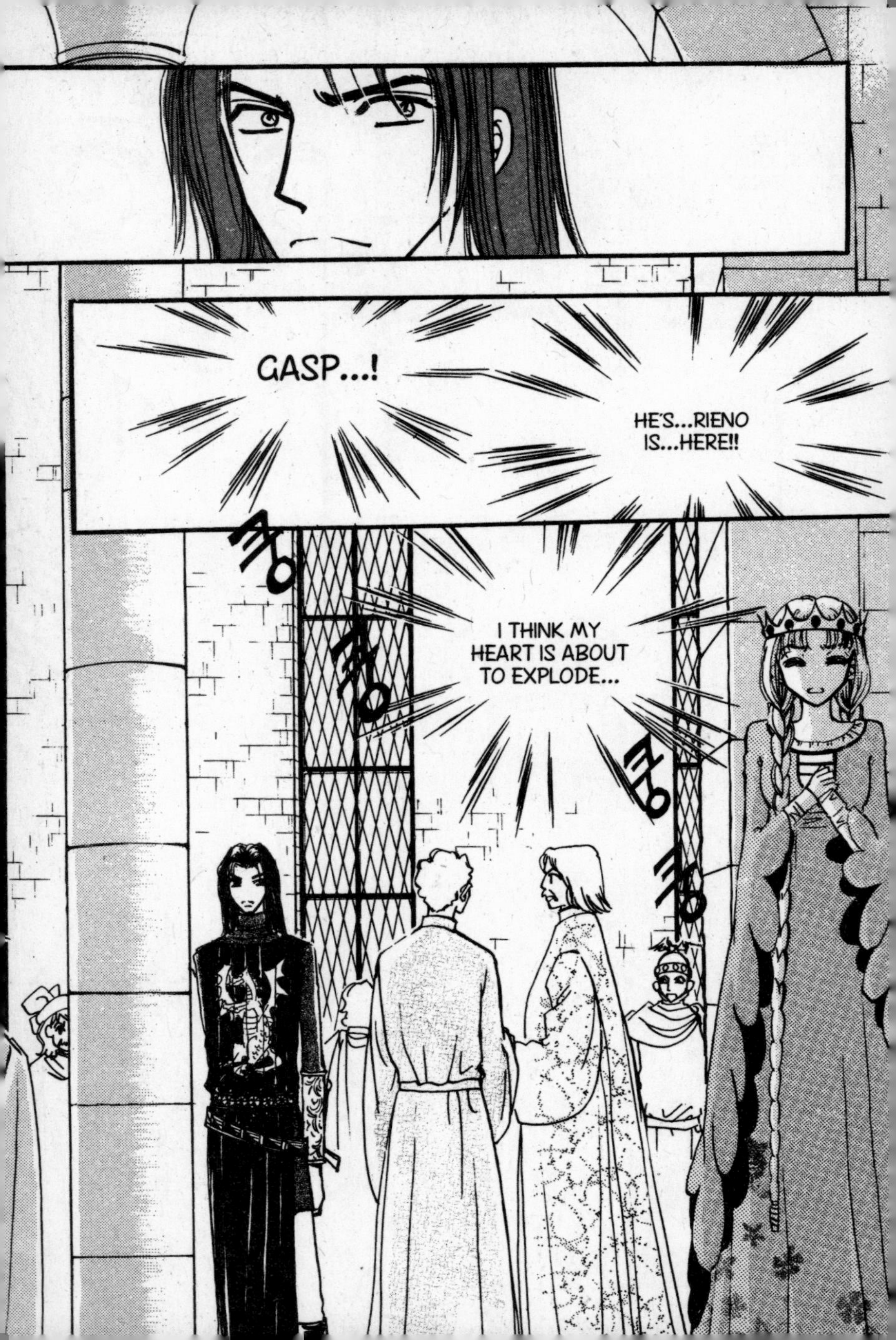
GASP...!
HE'S...RIENO IS...HERE!!
I THINK MY HEART IS ABOUT TO EXPLODE...

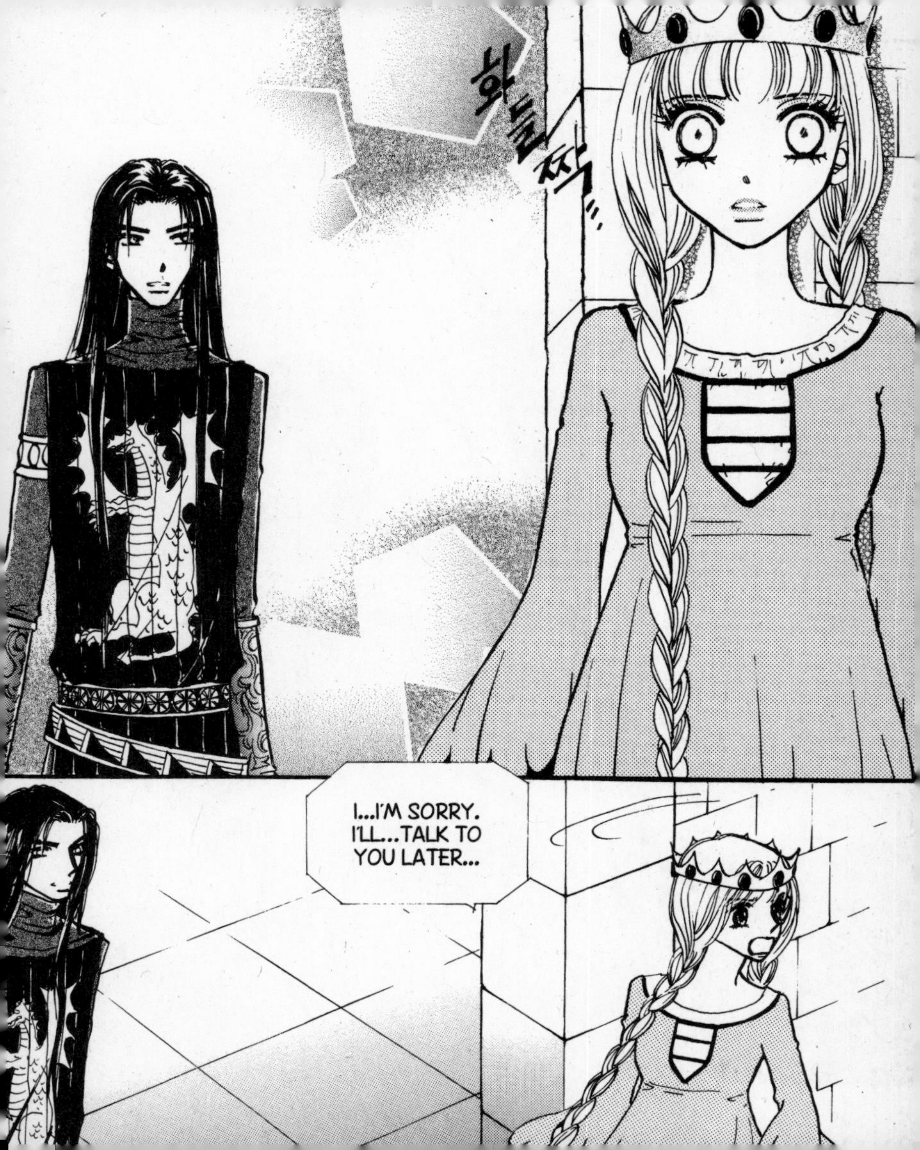
화들짝
I...I'M SORRY. I'LL...TALK TO YOU LATER...

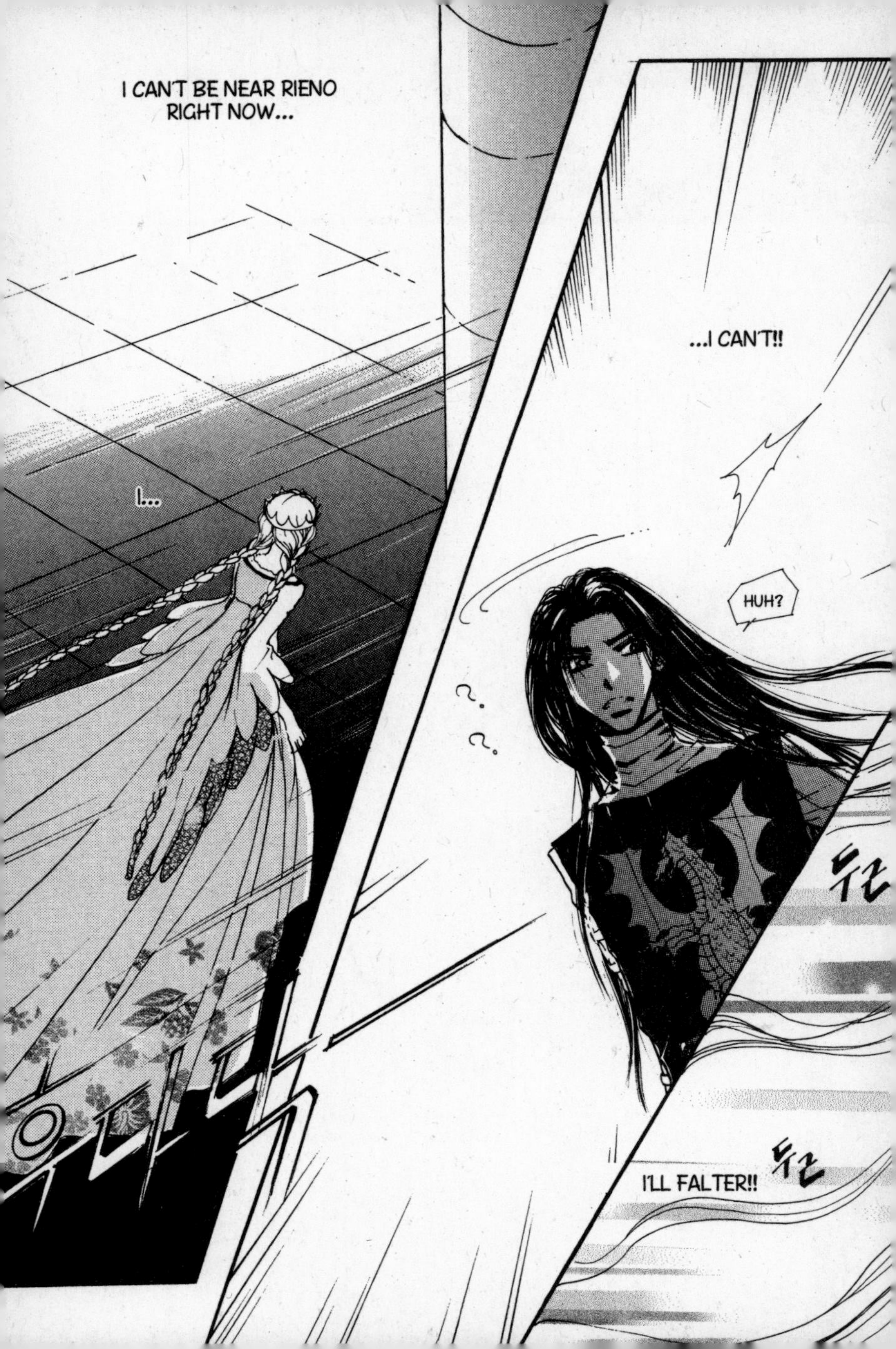
I CAN'T BE NEAR RIENO RIGHT NOW...
I...
...I CAN'T!!
HUH?
두근
I'LL FALTER!!
두근

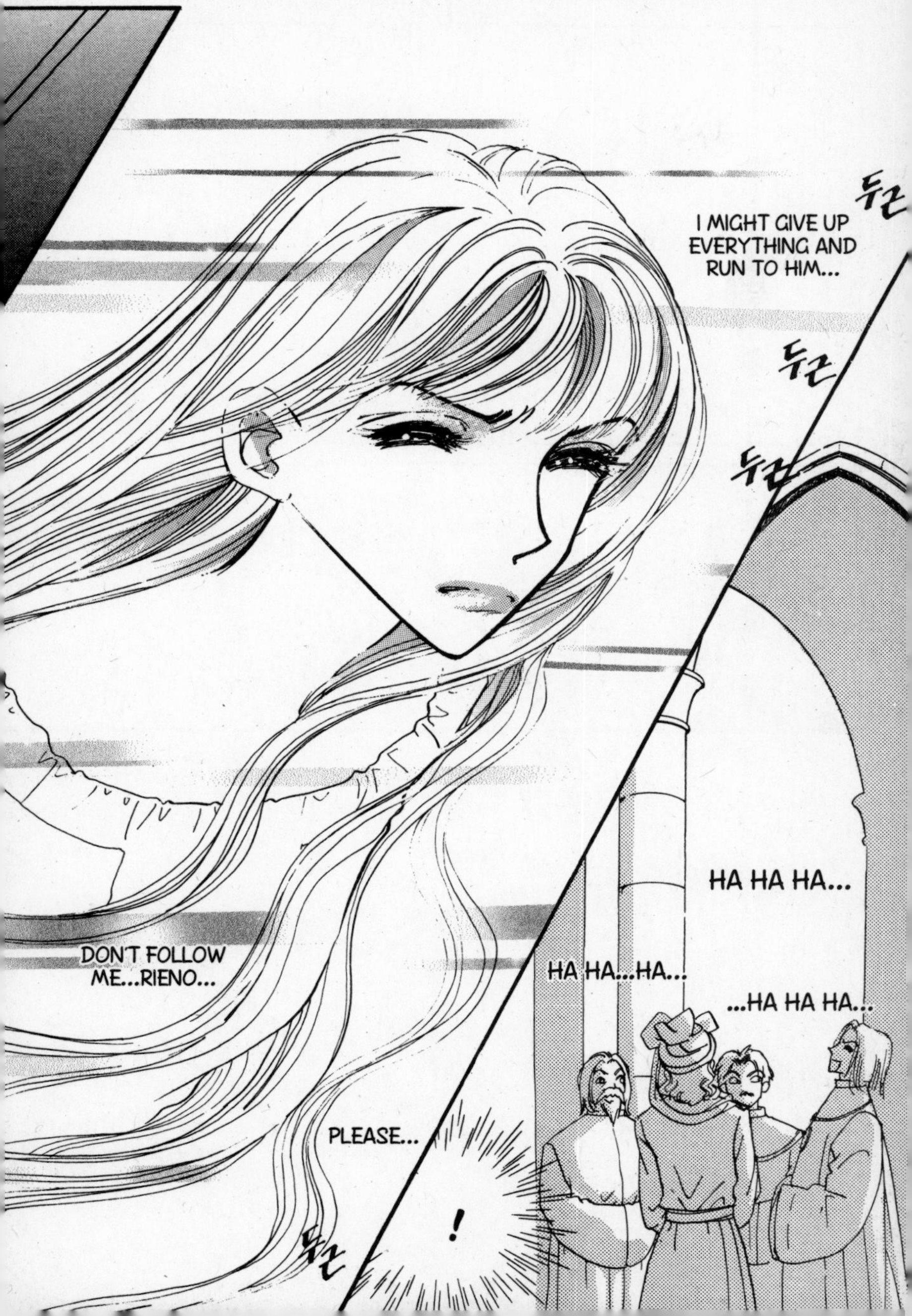
두근
I MIGHT GIVE UP EVERYTHING AND RUN TO HIM...
두근
두근
DON'T FOLLOW ME...RIENO...
PLEASE...
두근
HA HA HA...
HA HA...HA...
...HA HA HA...
!

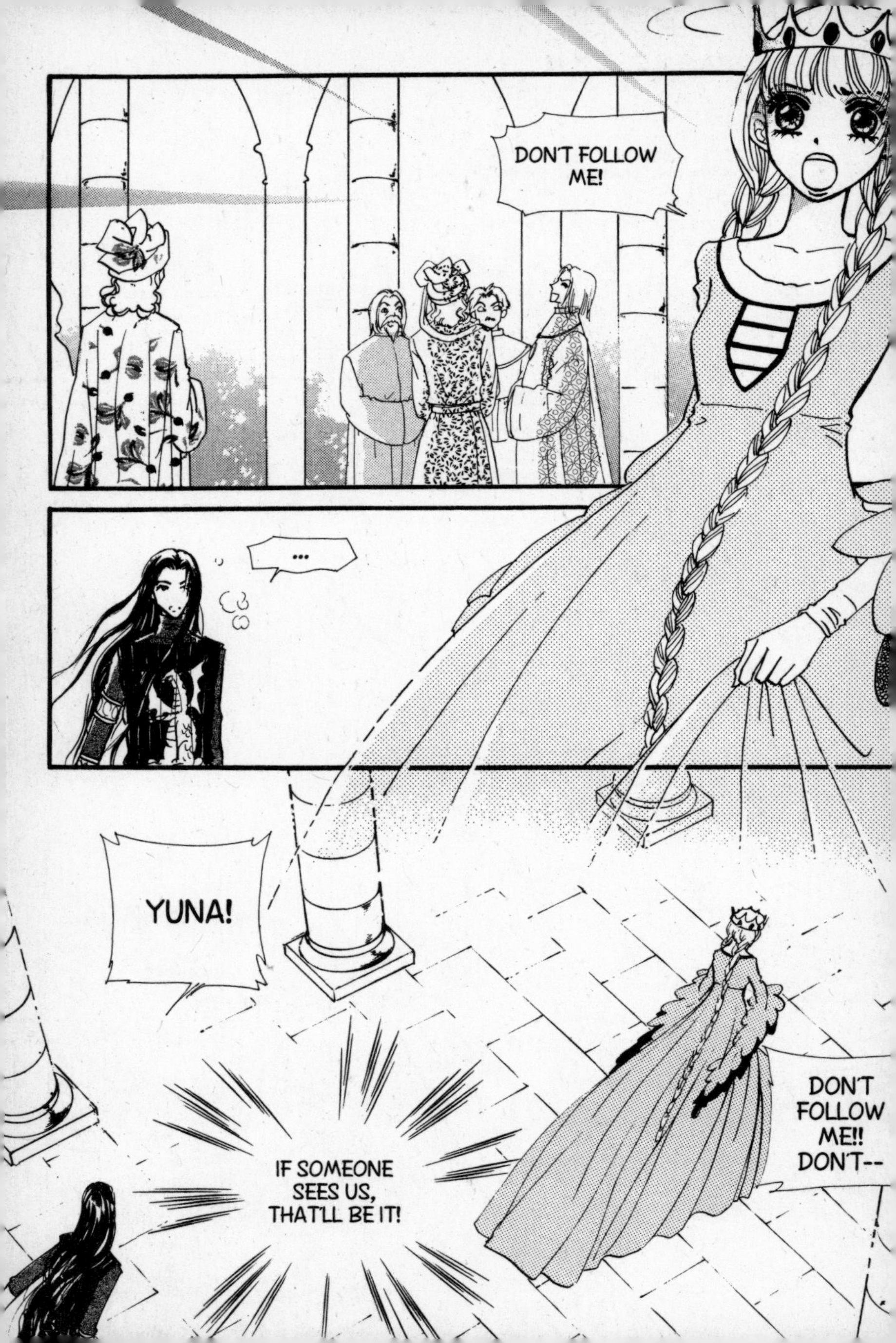
DON'T FOLLOW ME!
...
YUNA!
IF SOMEONE SEES US, THAT'LL BE IT!
DON'T FOLLOW ME!! DON'T--

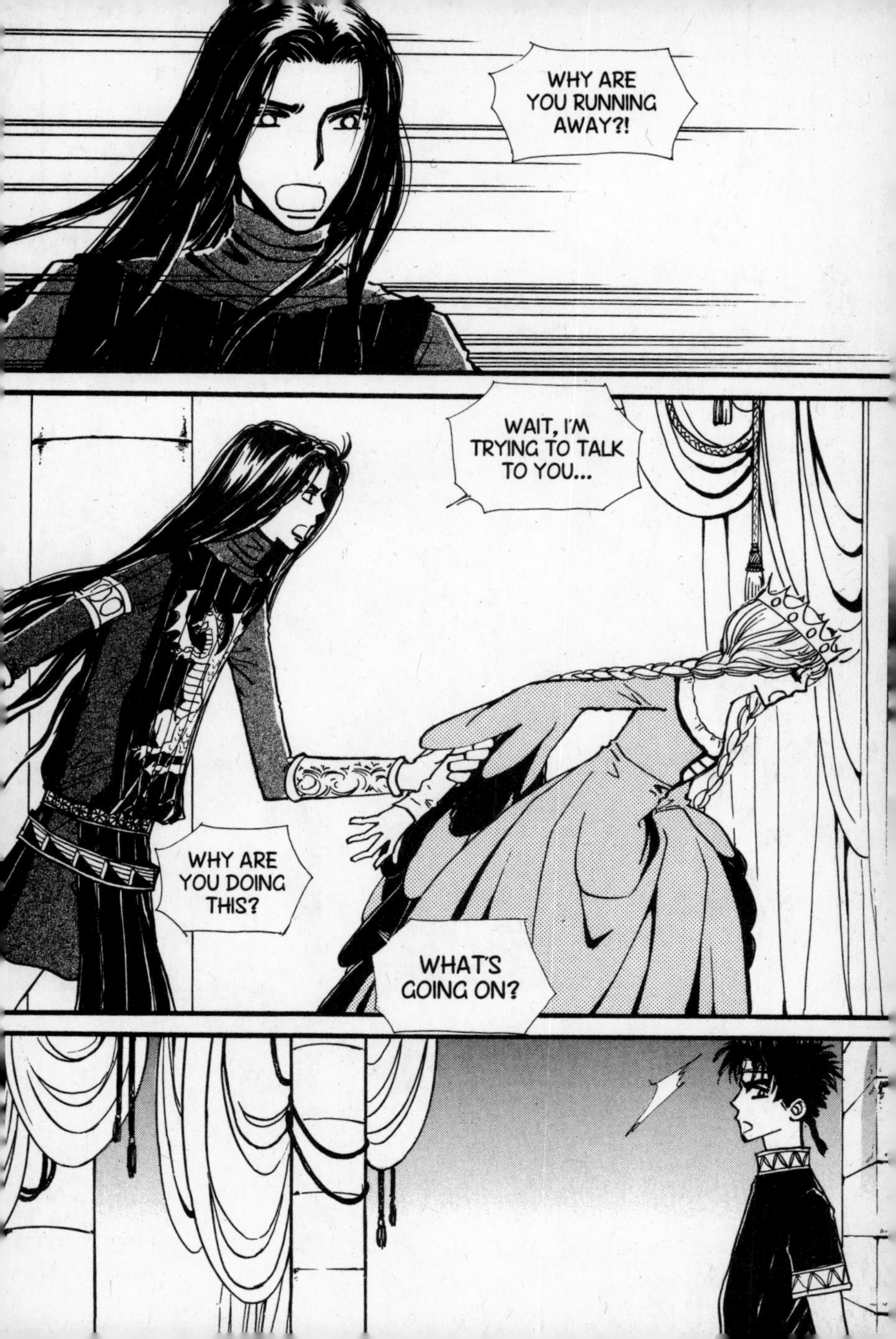
WHY ARE YOU RUNNING AWAY?!
WAIT, I'M TRYING TO TALK TO YOU...
WHY ARE YOU DOING THIS?
WHAT'S GOING ON?

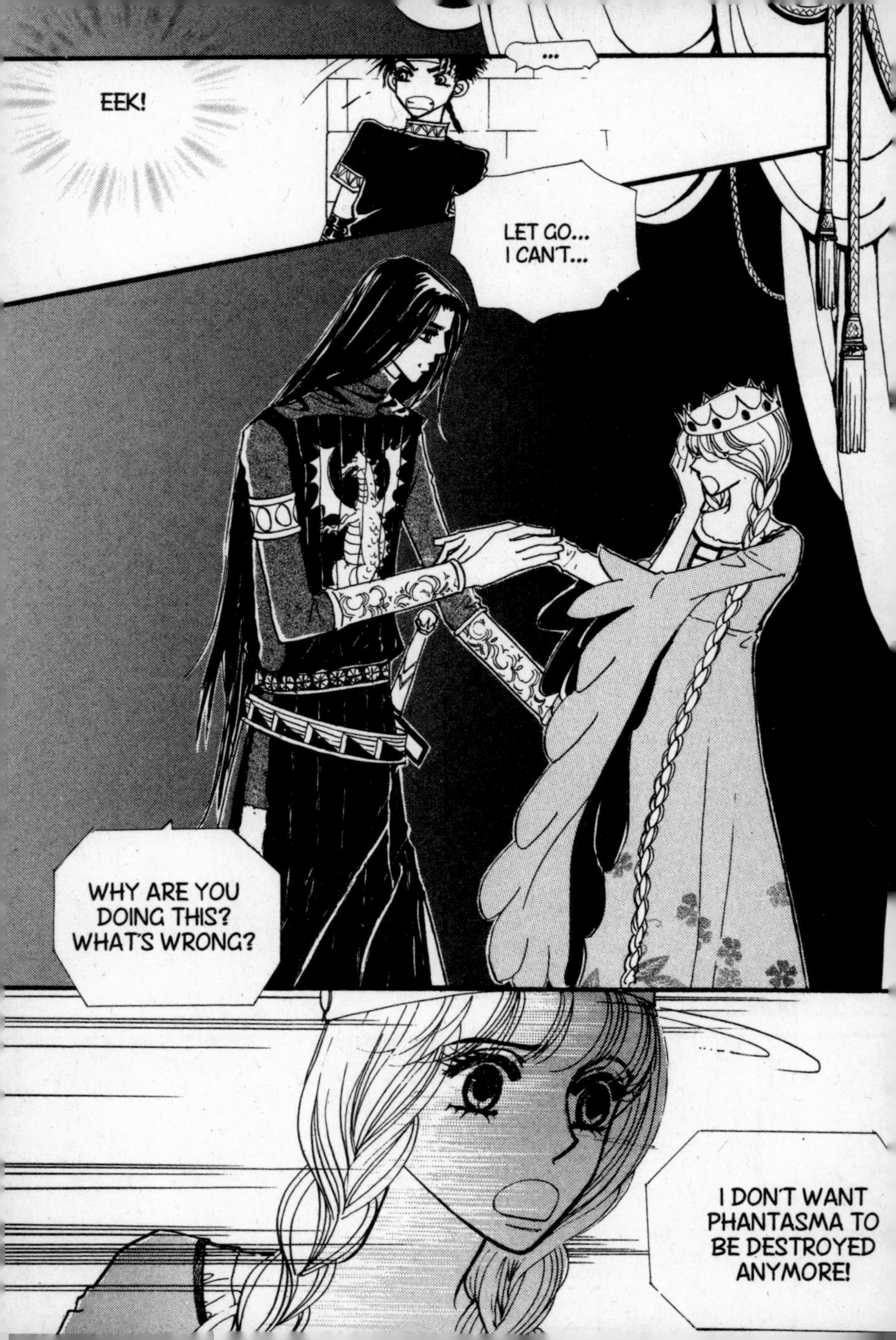
...
EEK!
LET GO...
I CAN'T...
WHY ARE YOU DOING THIS? WHAT'S WRONG?
...
I DON'T WANT PHANTASMA TO BE DESTROYED ANYMORE!

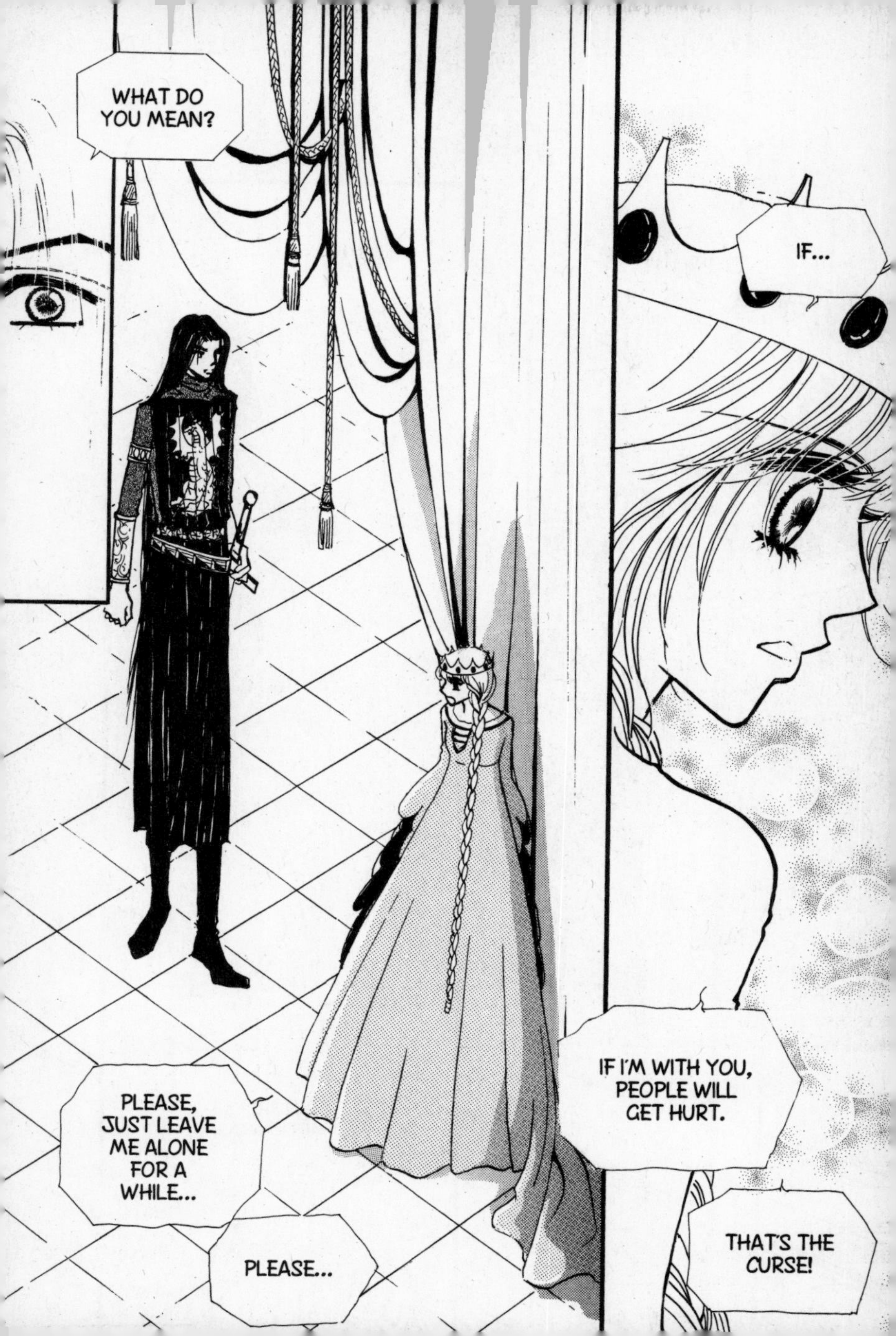
WHAT DO YOU MEAN?
PLEASE, JUST LEAVE ME ALONE FOR A WHILE...
PLEASE...
IF...
IF I'M WITH YOU, PEOPLE WILL GET HURT.
THAT'S THE CURSE!

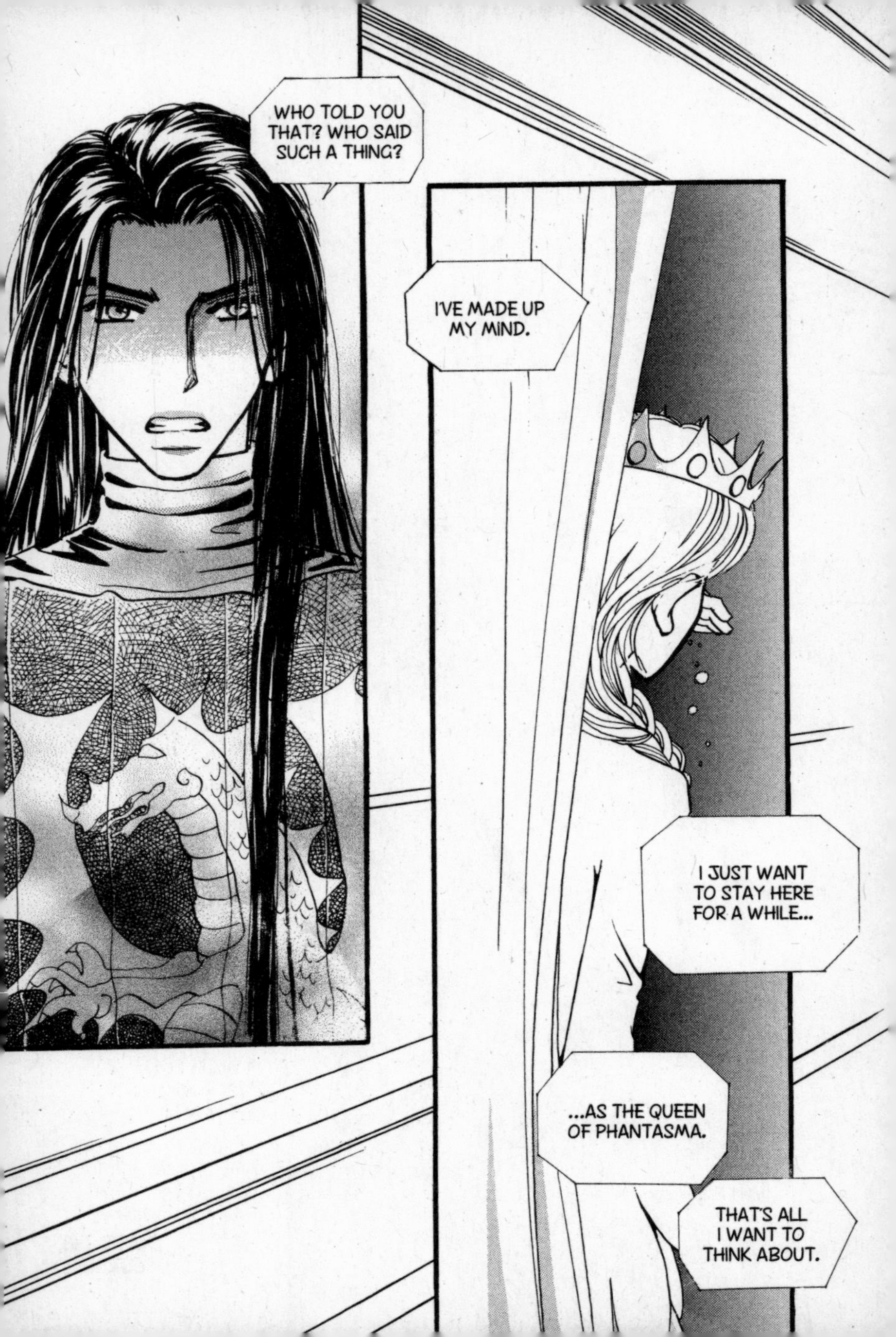
WHO TOLD YOU THAT? WHO SAID SUCH A THING?
I'VE MADE UP MY MIND.
I JUST WANT TO STAY HERE FOR A WHILE...
...AS THE QUEEN OF PHANTASMA.
THAT'S ALL I WANT TO THINK ABOUT.

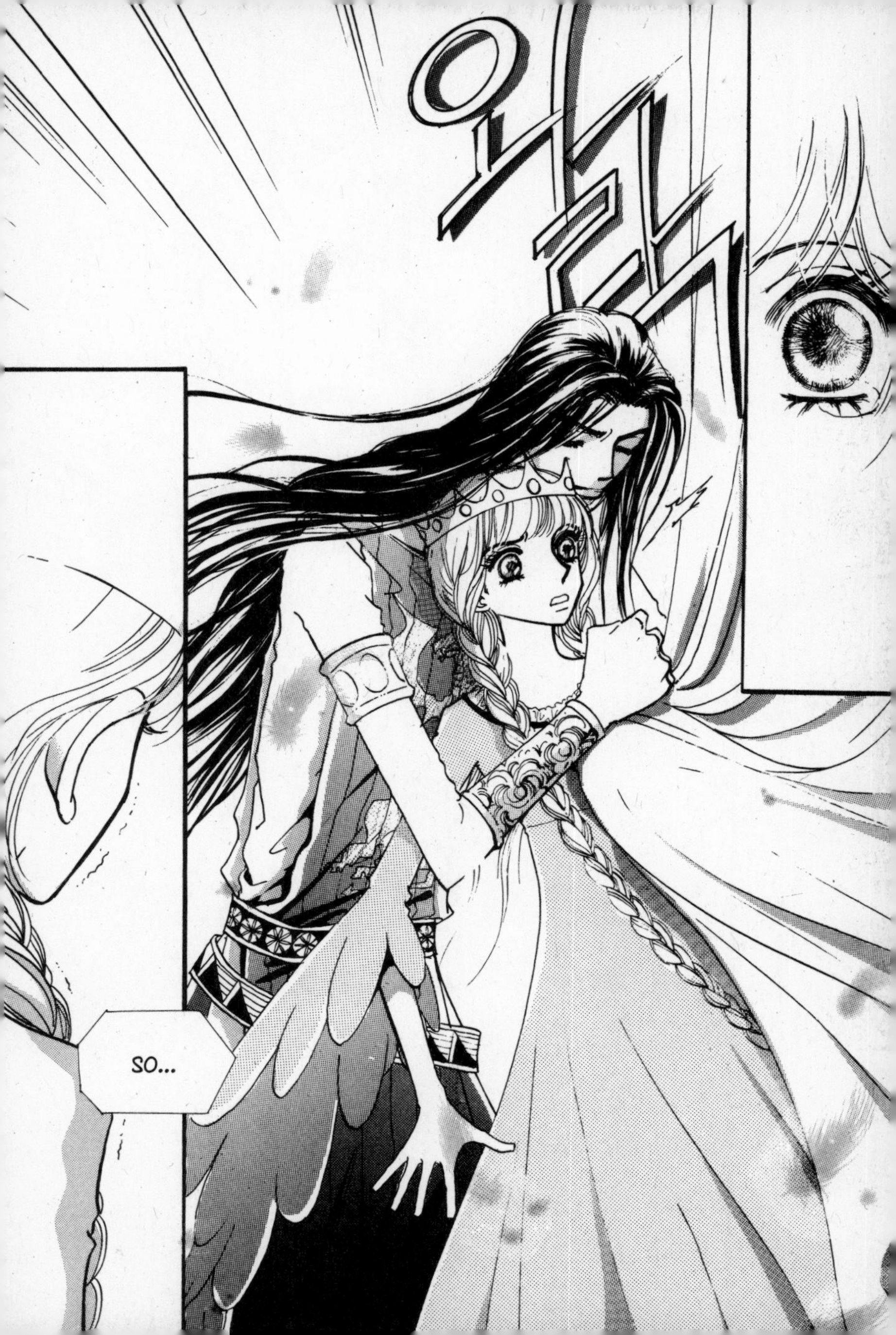
와락
SO...

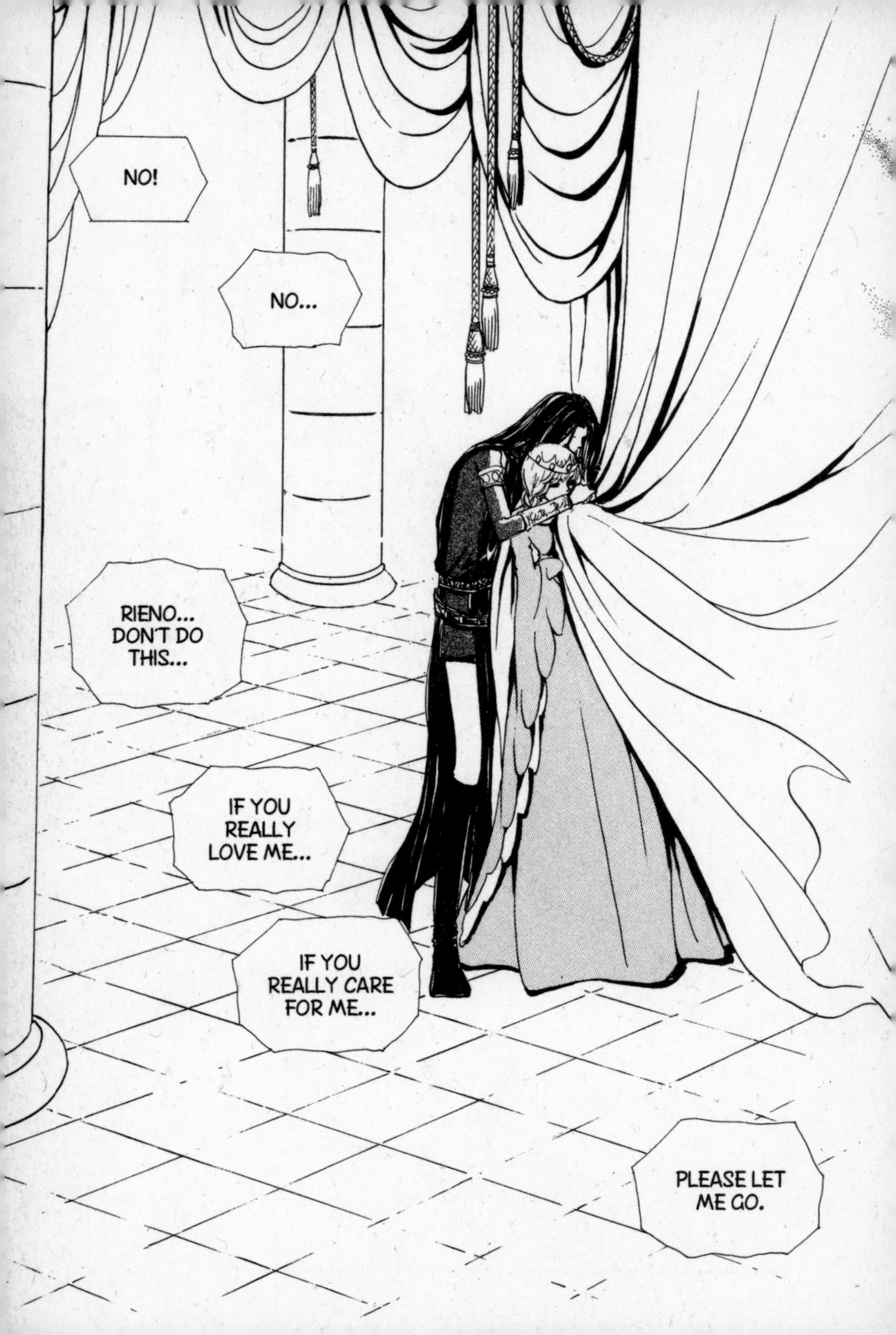
NO!
NO...
RIENO... DON'T DO THIS...
IF YOU REALLY LOVE ME...
IF YOU REALLY CARE FOR ME...
PLEASE LET ME GO.

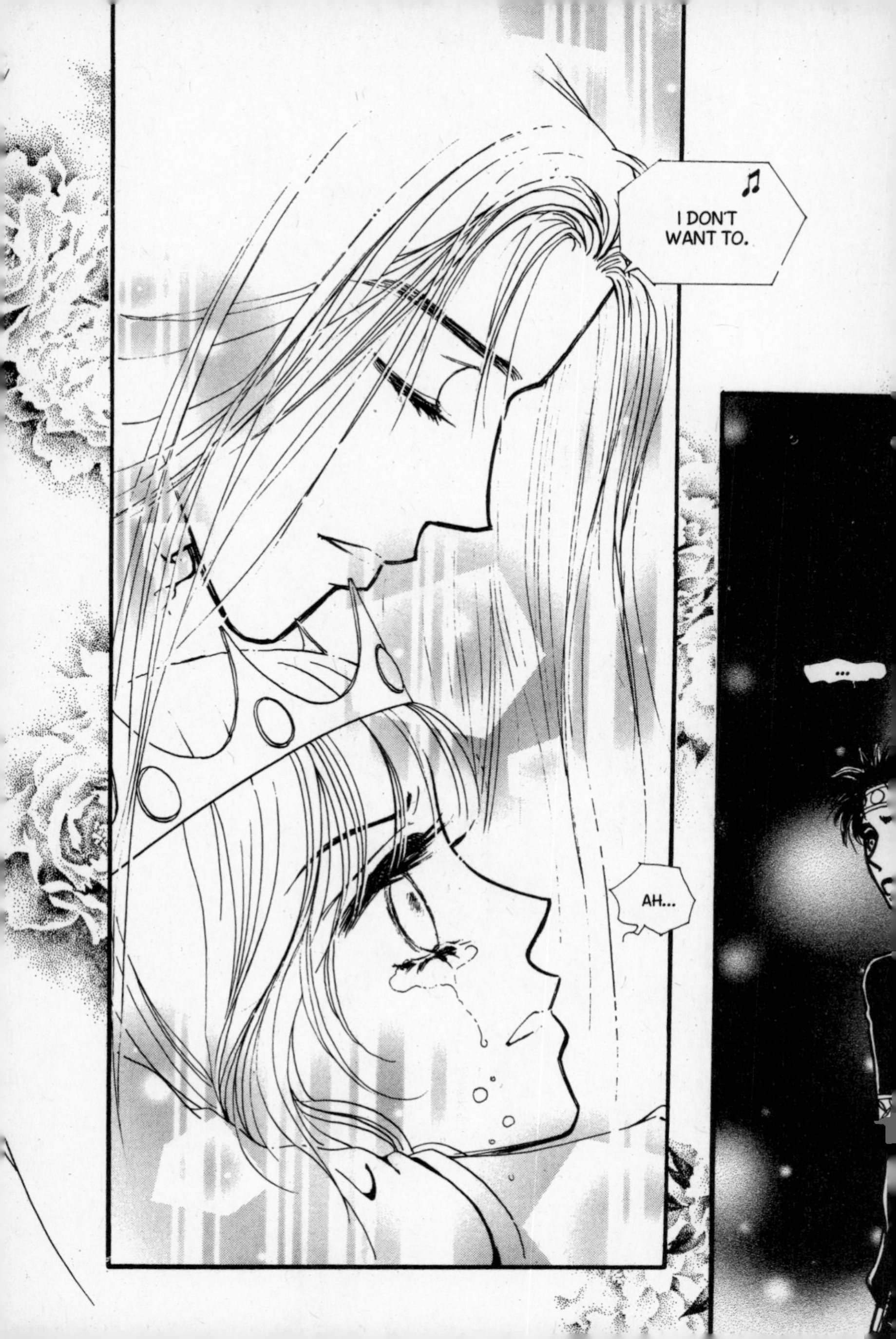
♫ I DON'T WANT TO.
AH...
...

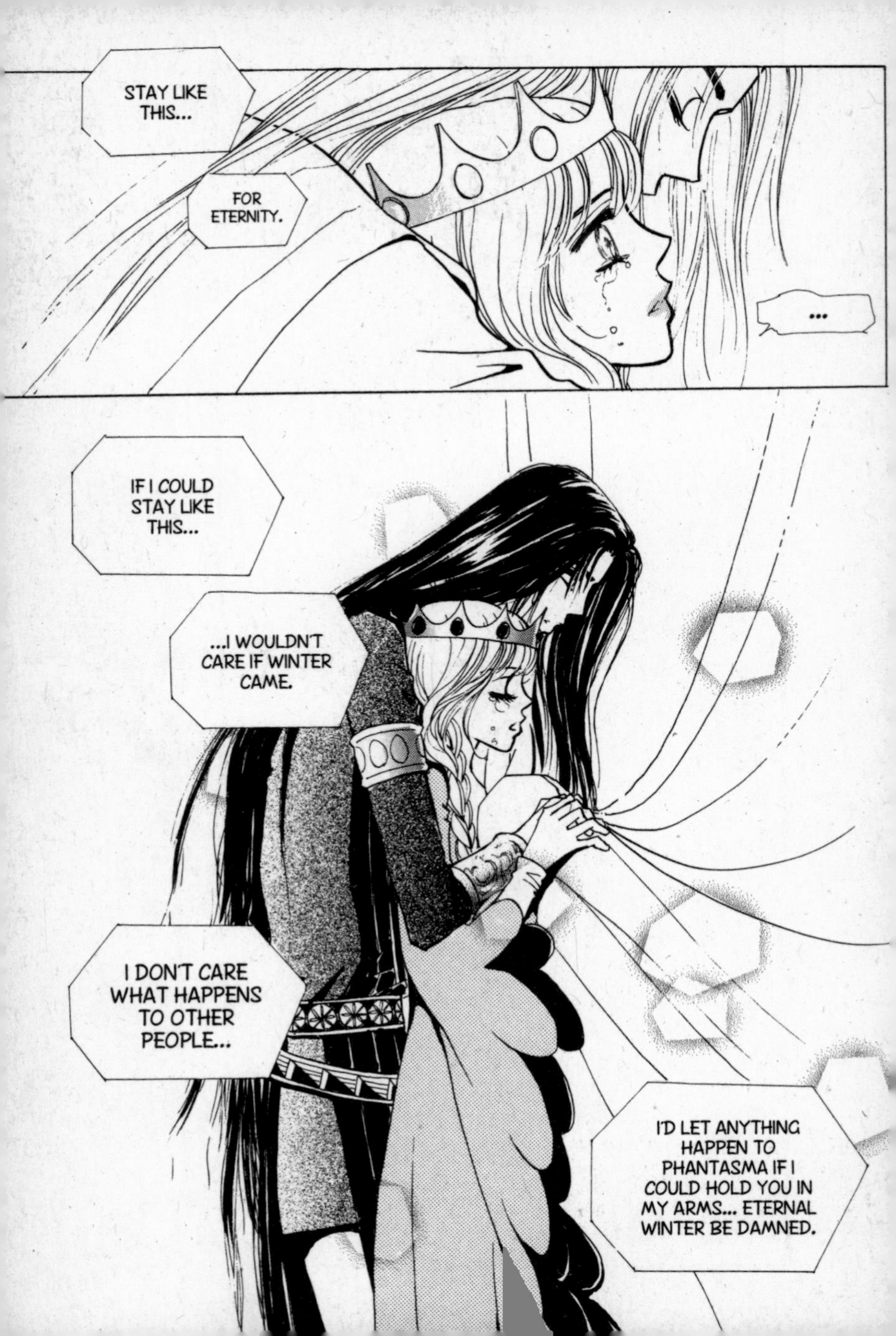
STAY LIKE THIS...
FOR ETERNITY.
...
IF I COULD STAY LIKE THIS...
...I WOULDN'T CARE IF WINTER CAME.
I DON'T CARE WHAT HAPPENS TO OTHER PEOPLE...
I'D LET ANYTHING HAPPEN TO PHANTASMA IF I COULD HOLD YOU IN MY ARMS... ETERNAL WINTER BE DAMNED.

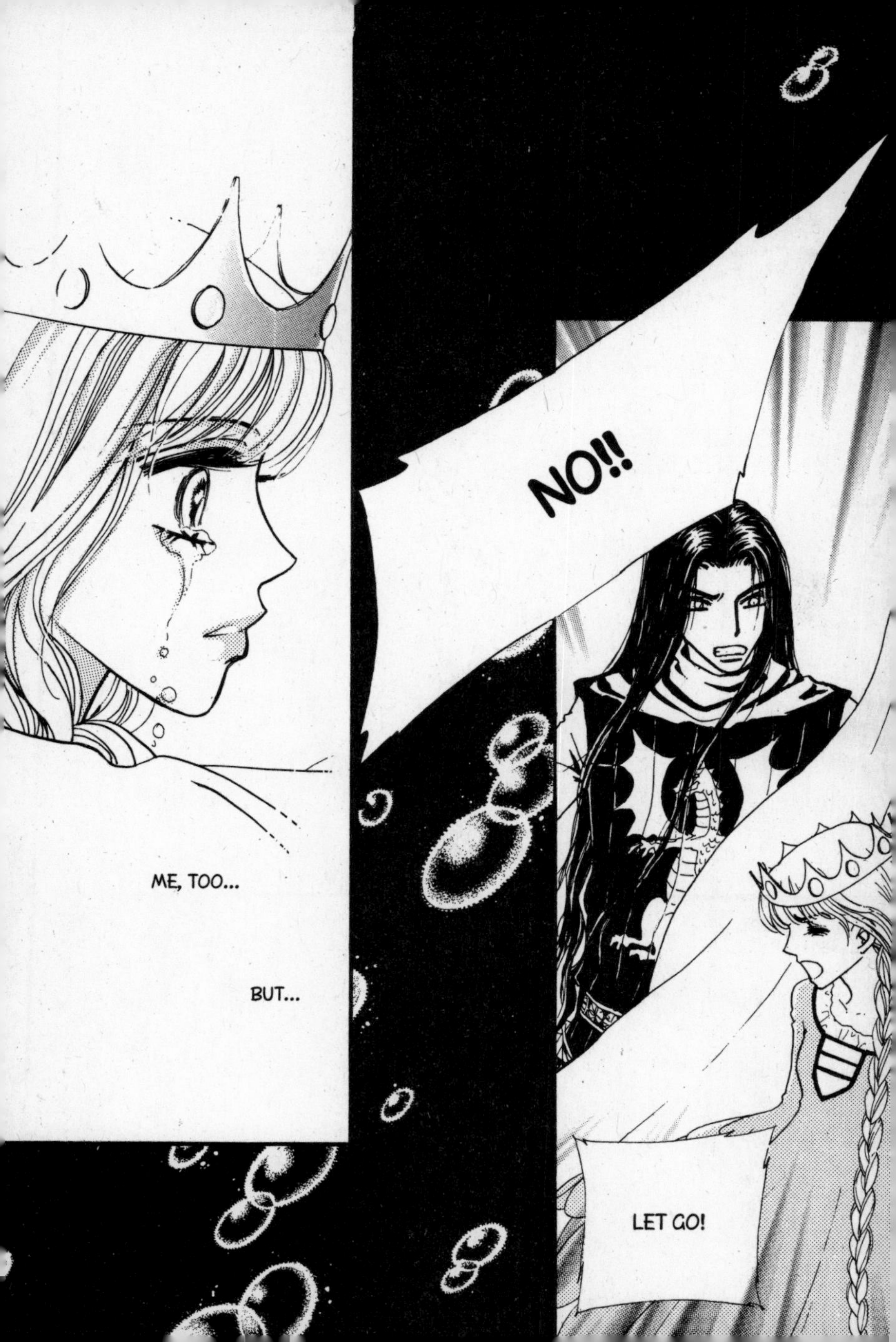
ME, TOO...
BUT...
NO!!
LET GO!

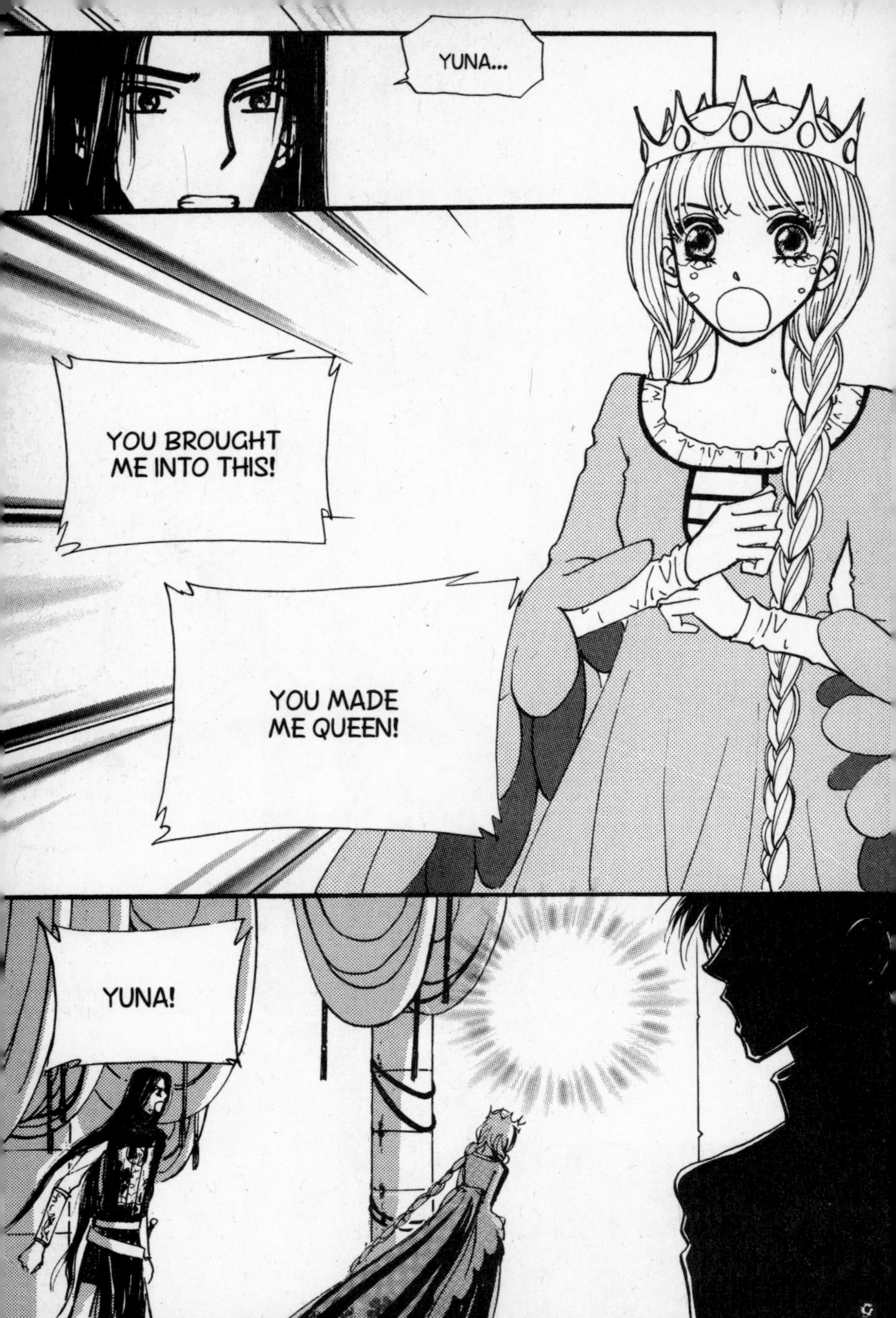
YUNA...
YOU BROUGHT ME INTO THIS!
YOU MADE ME QUEEN!
YUNA!

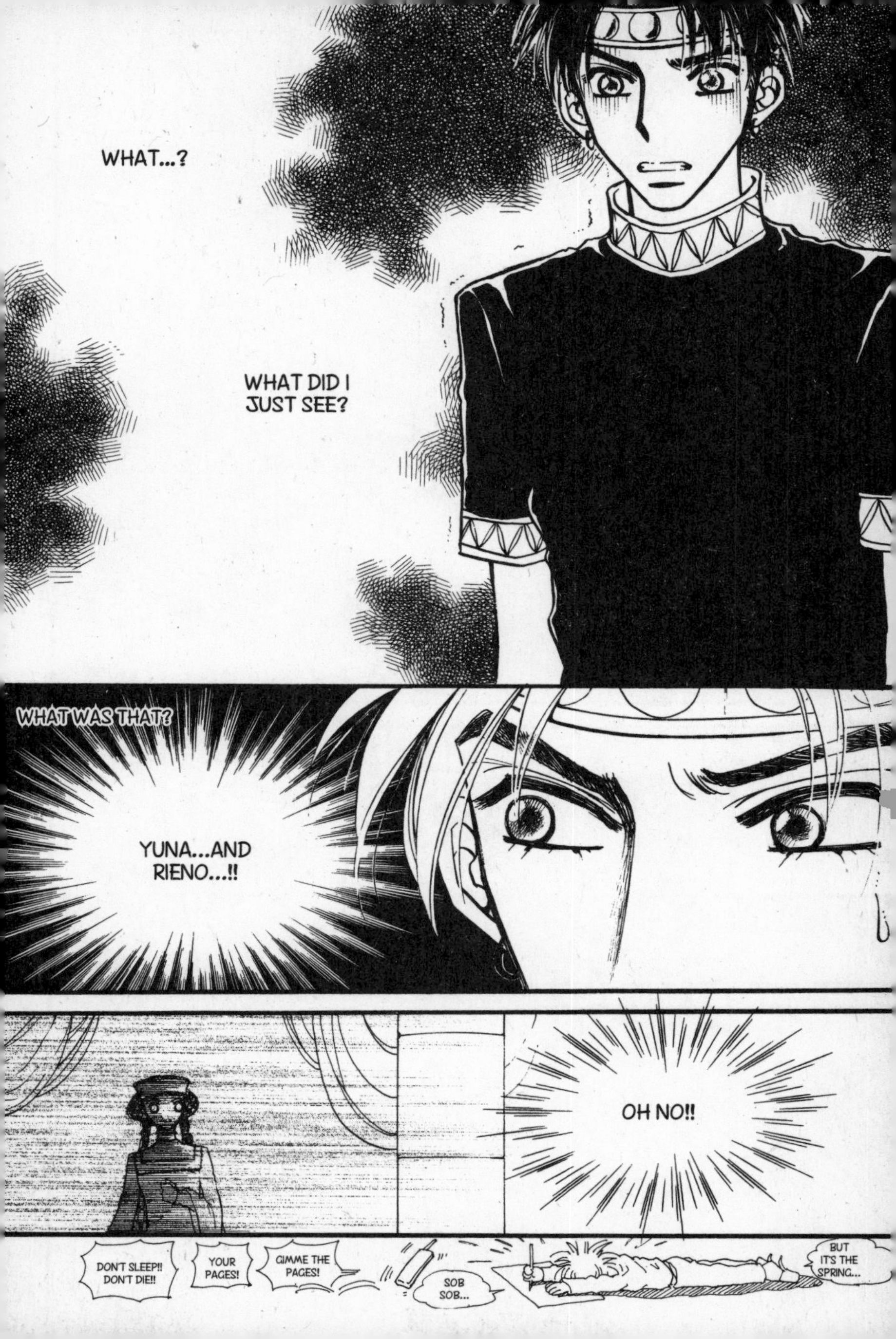
WHAT...?
WHAT DID I JUST SEE?
WHAT WAS THAT?
YUNA...AND RIENO...!!
OH NO!!
DONT SLEEP!! DONT DIE!!
YOUR PAGES!
GIMME THE PAGES!
SOB SOB...
BUT IT'S THE SPRING...

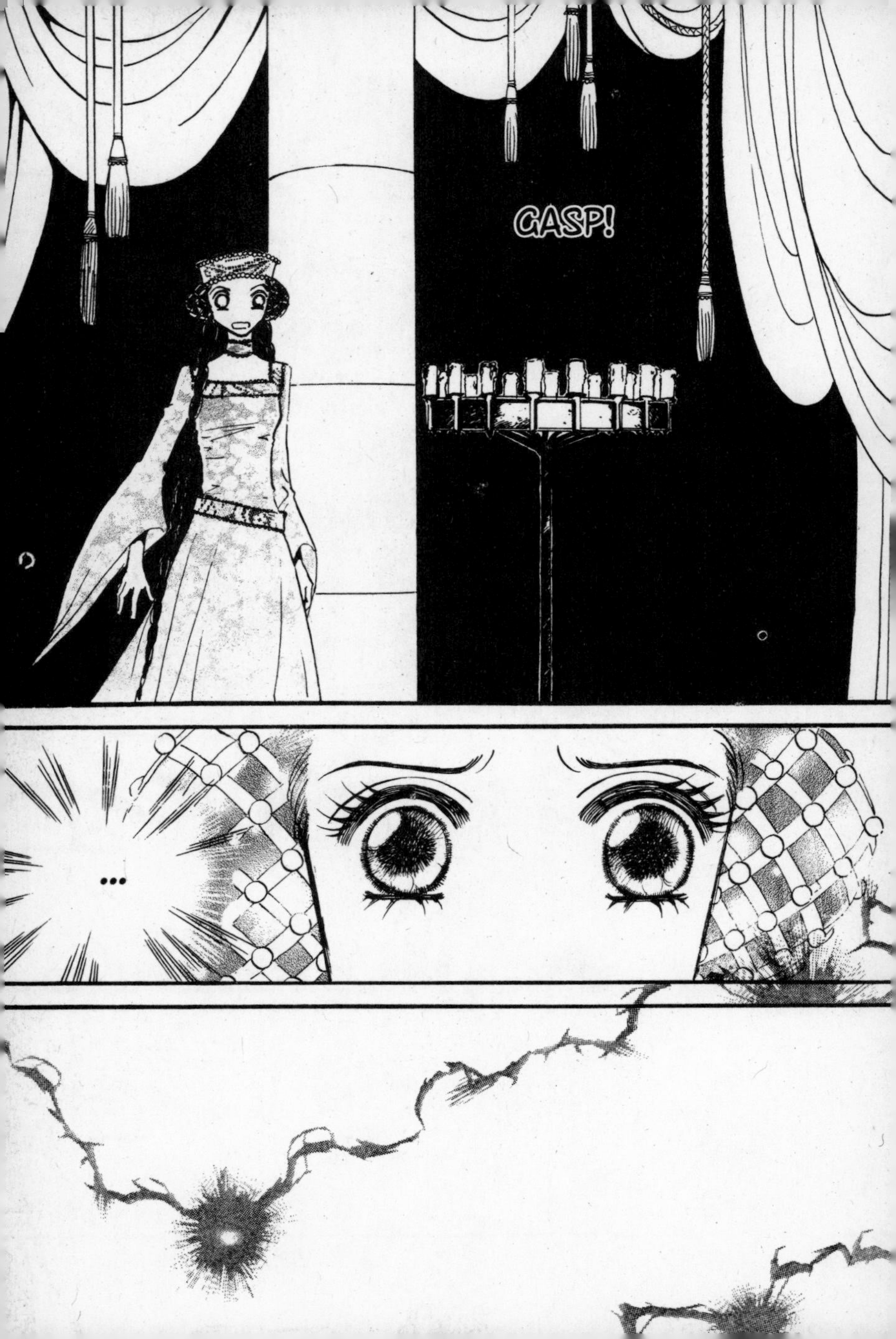
GASP!
...

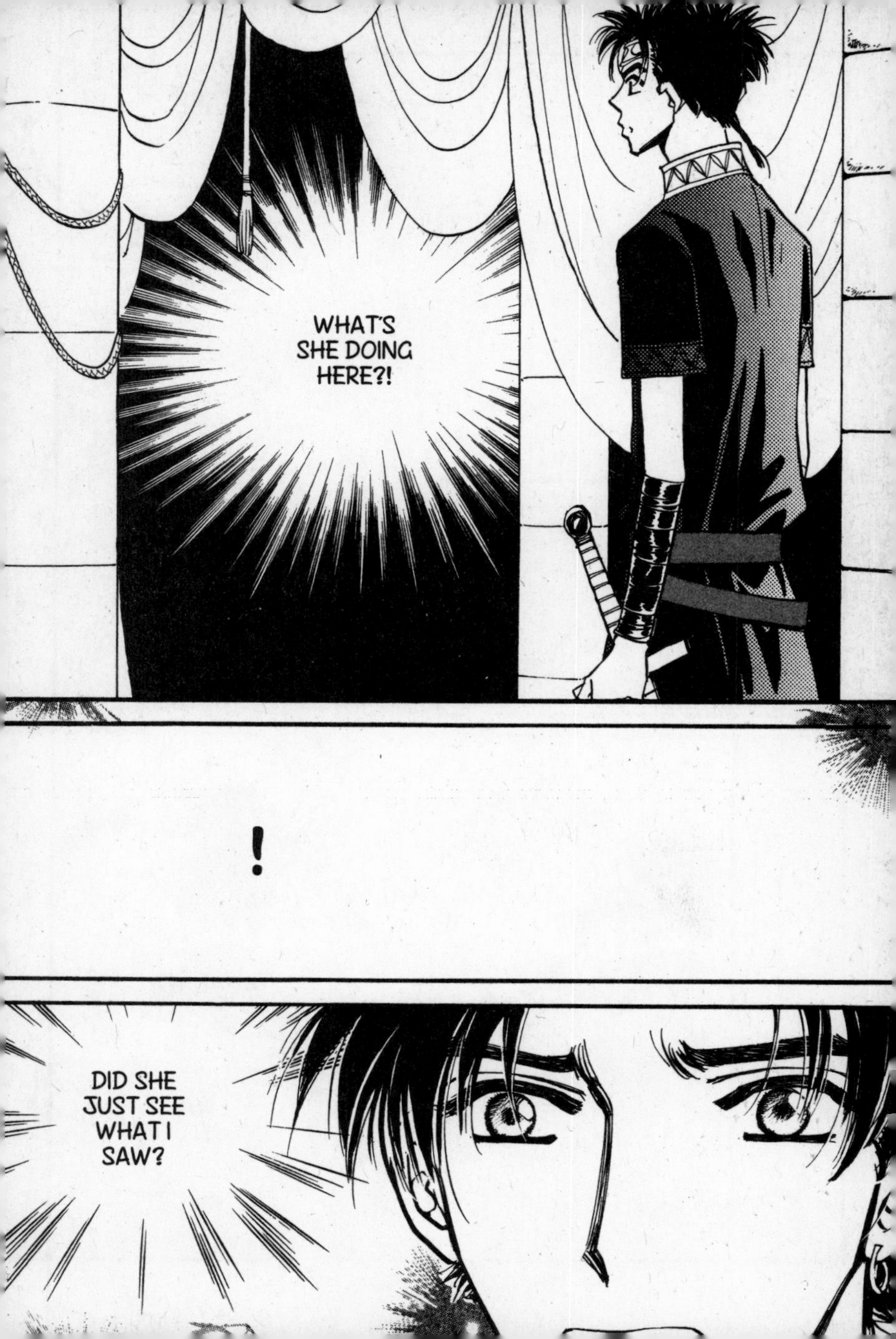
WHAT'S SHE DOING HERE?!
!
DID SHE JUST SEE WHAT I SAW?

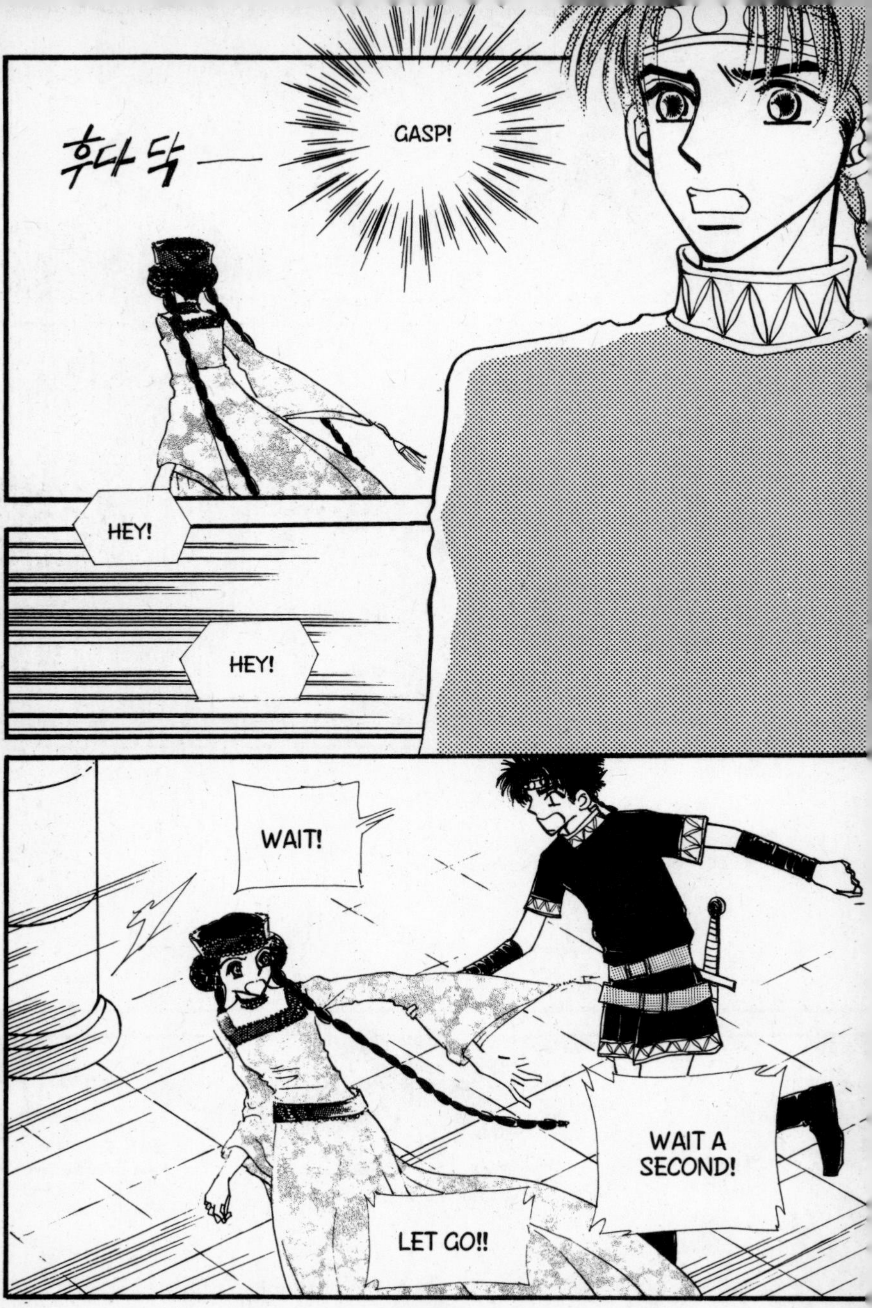
후다닥
GASP!
HEY!
HEY!
WAIT!
WAIT A SECOND!
LET GO!!

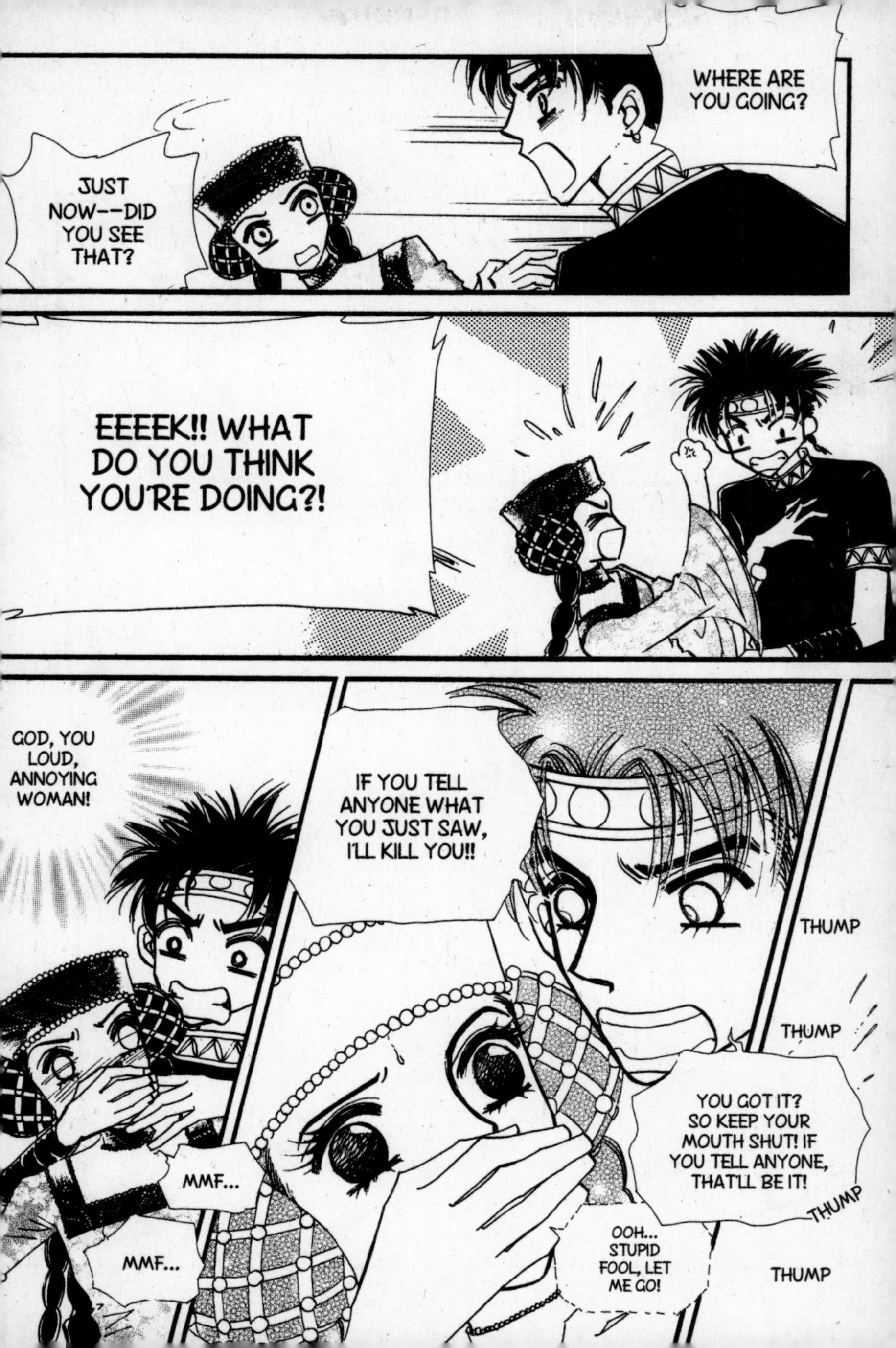
JUST NOW--DID YOU SEE THAT?
WHERE ARE YOU GOING?
EEEEK!! WHAT DO YOU THINK YOU'RE DOING?!
GOD, YOU LOUD, ANNOYING WOMAN!
MMF...
MMF...
IF YOU TELL ANYONE WHAT YOU JUST SAW, I'LL KILL YOU!!
THUMP
THUMP
YOU GOT IT? SO KEEP YOUR MOUTH SHUT! IF YOU TELL ANYONE, THAT'LL BE IT!
THUMP
OOH... STUPID FOOL, LET ME GO!
THUMP

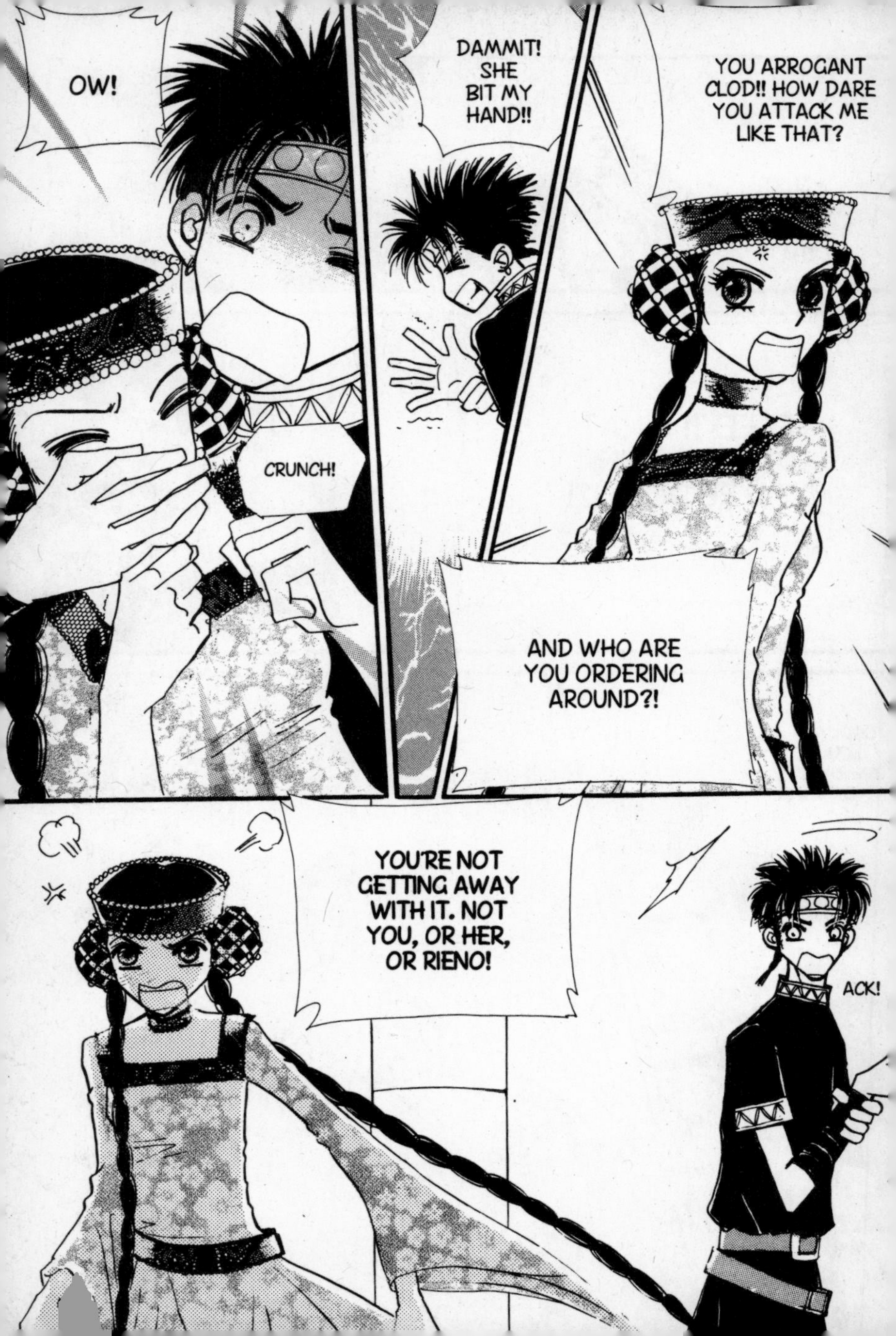
OW!
CRUNCH!
DAMMIT! SHE BIT MY HAND!!
YOU ARROGANT CLOD!! HOW DARE YOU ATTACK ME LIKE THAT?
AND WHO ARE YOU ORDERING AROUND?!
YOU'RE NOT GETTING AWAY WITH IT. NOT YOU, OR HER, OR RIENO!
ACK!

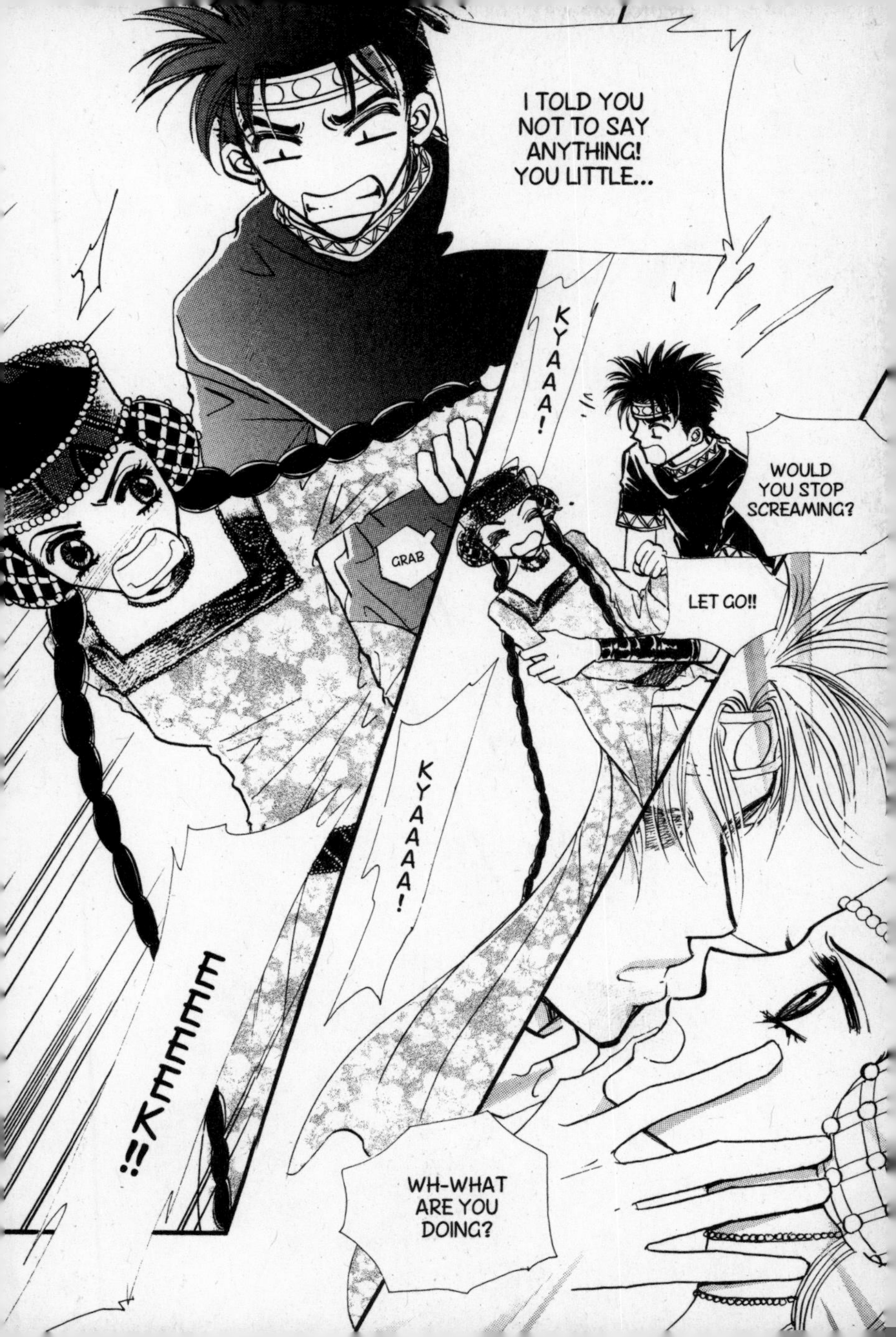
I TOLD YOU NOT TO SAY ANYTHING! YOU LITTLE...
GRAB
EEEEEEK!!
KYAAAA!
WOULD YOU STOP SCREAMING?
LET GO!!
KYAAAAA!
WH-WHAT ARE YOU DOING?

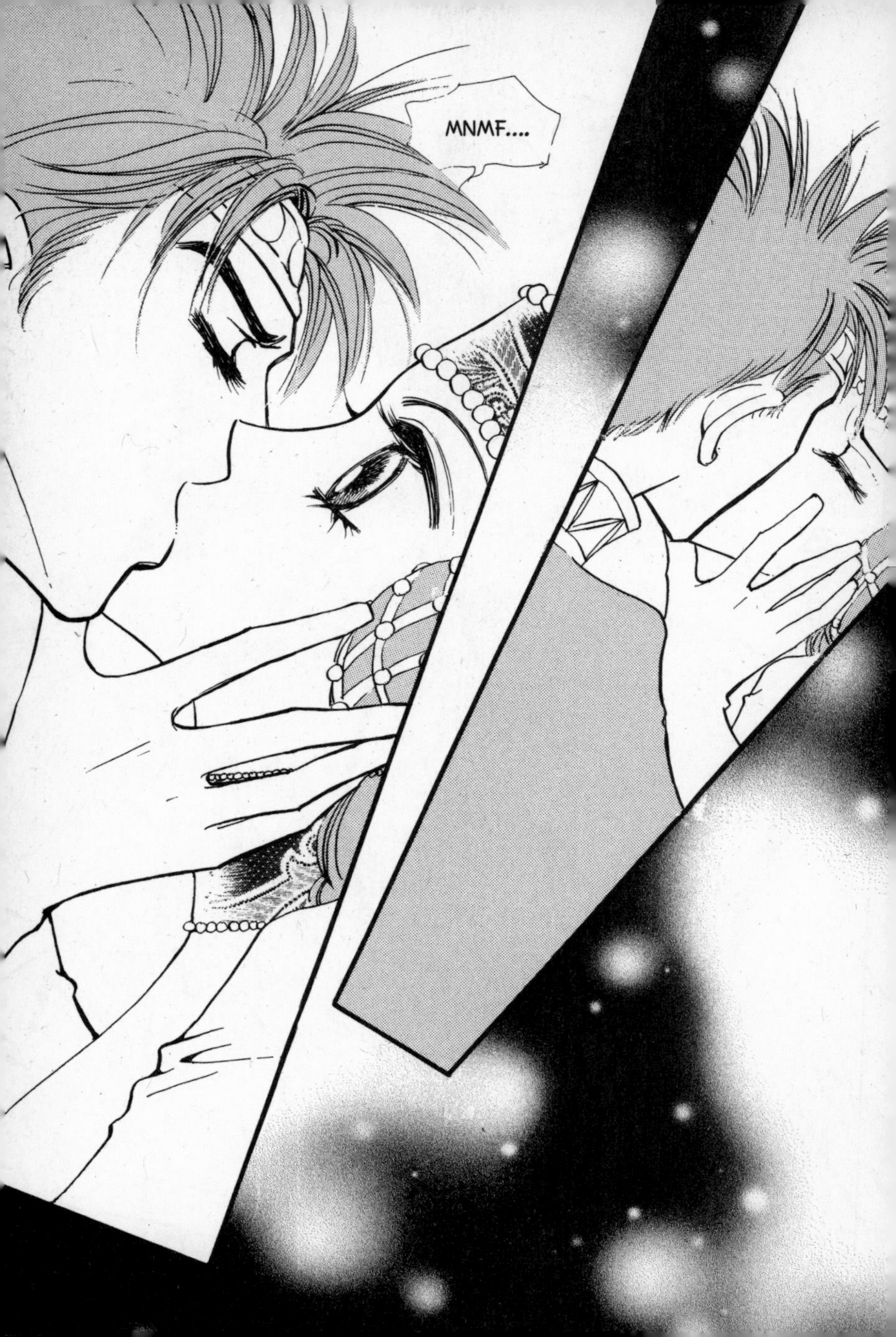
MNMF....

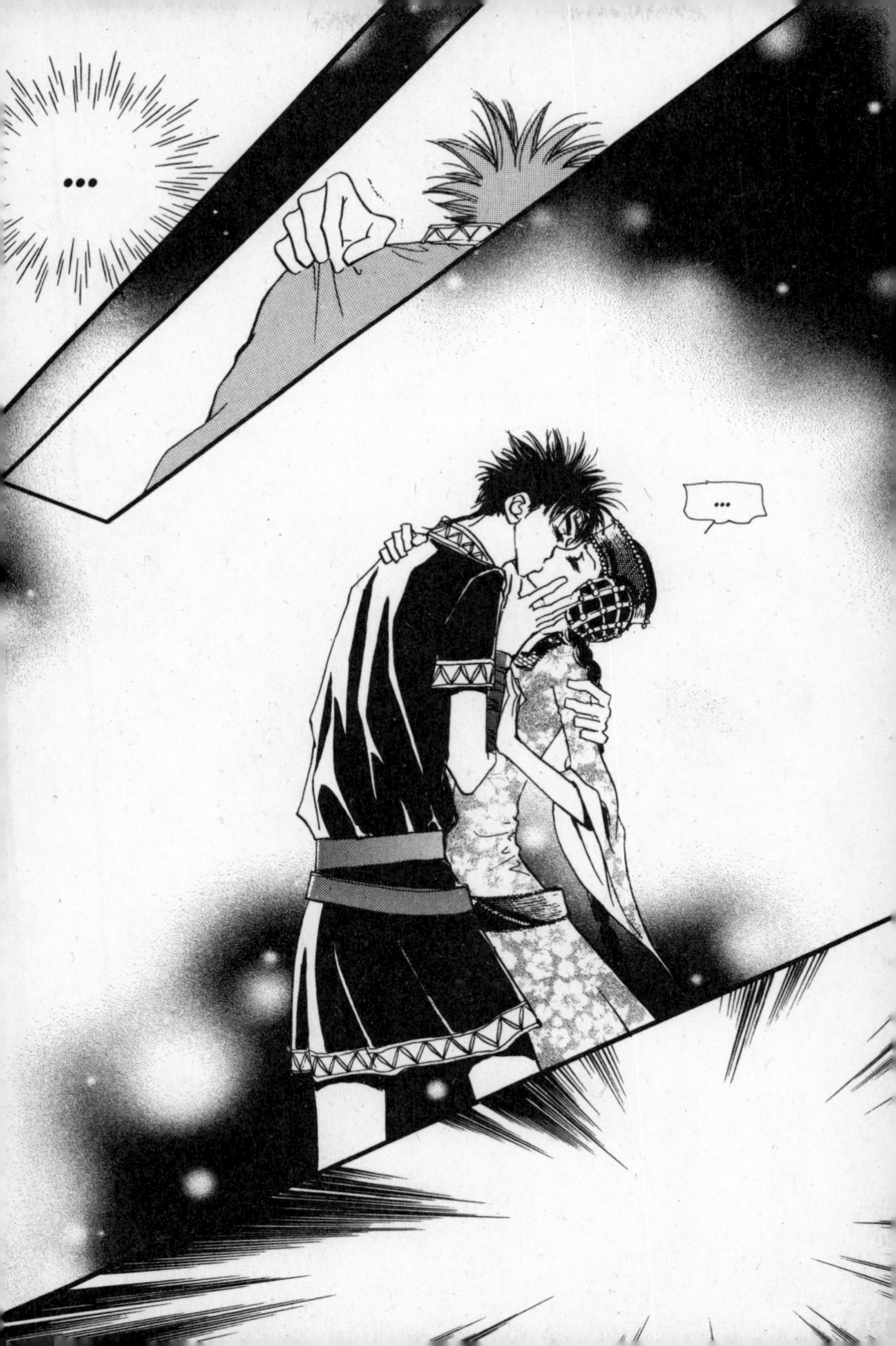
...
...

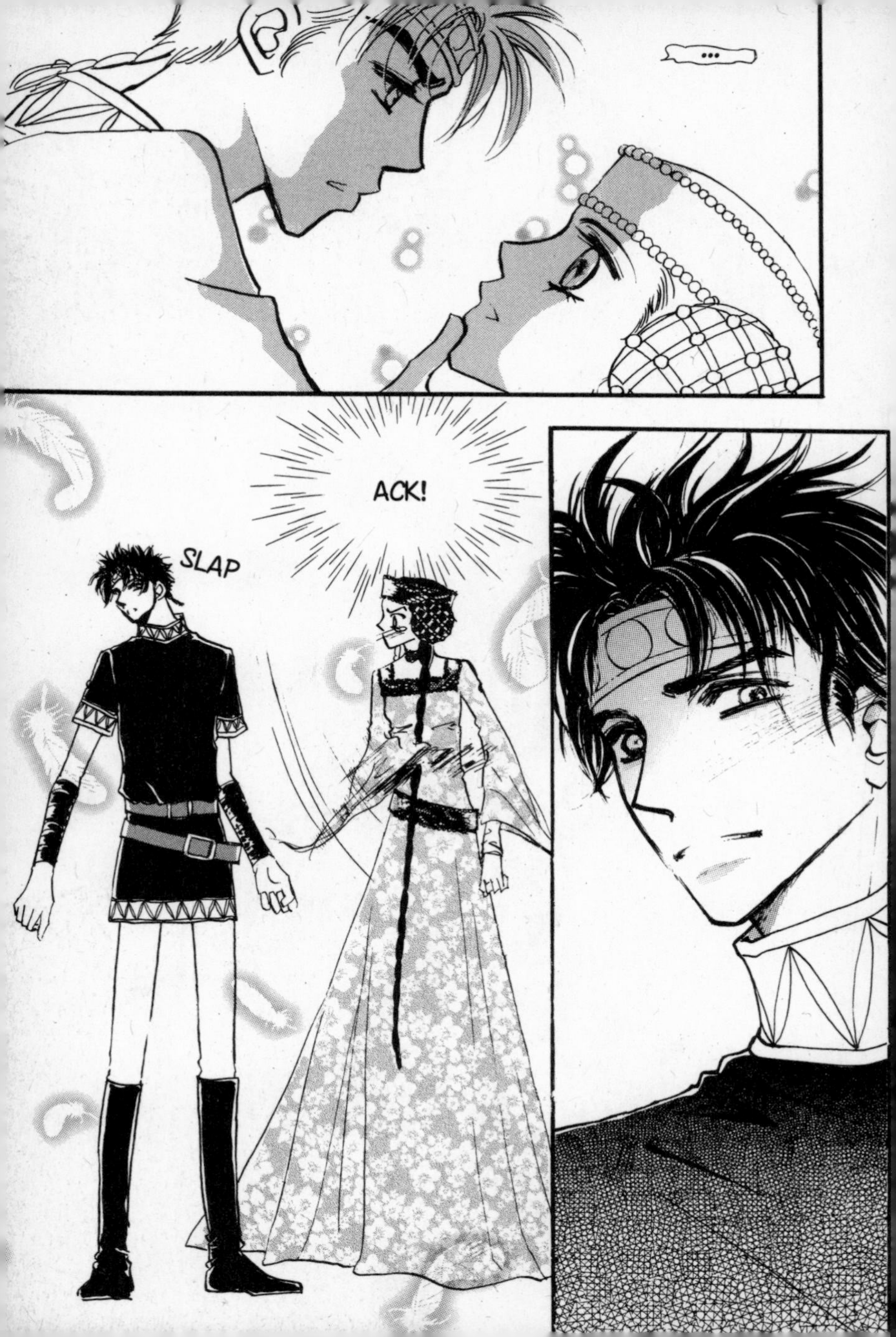
...
ACK!
SLAP

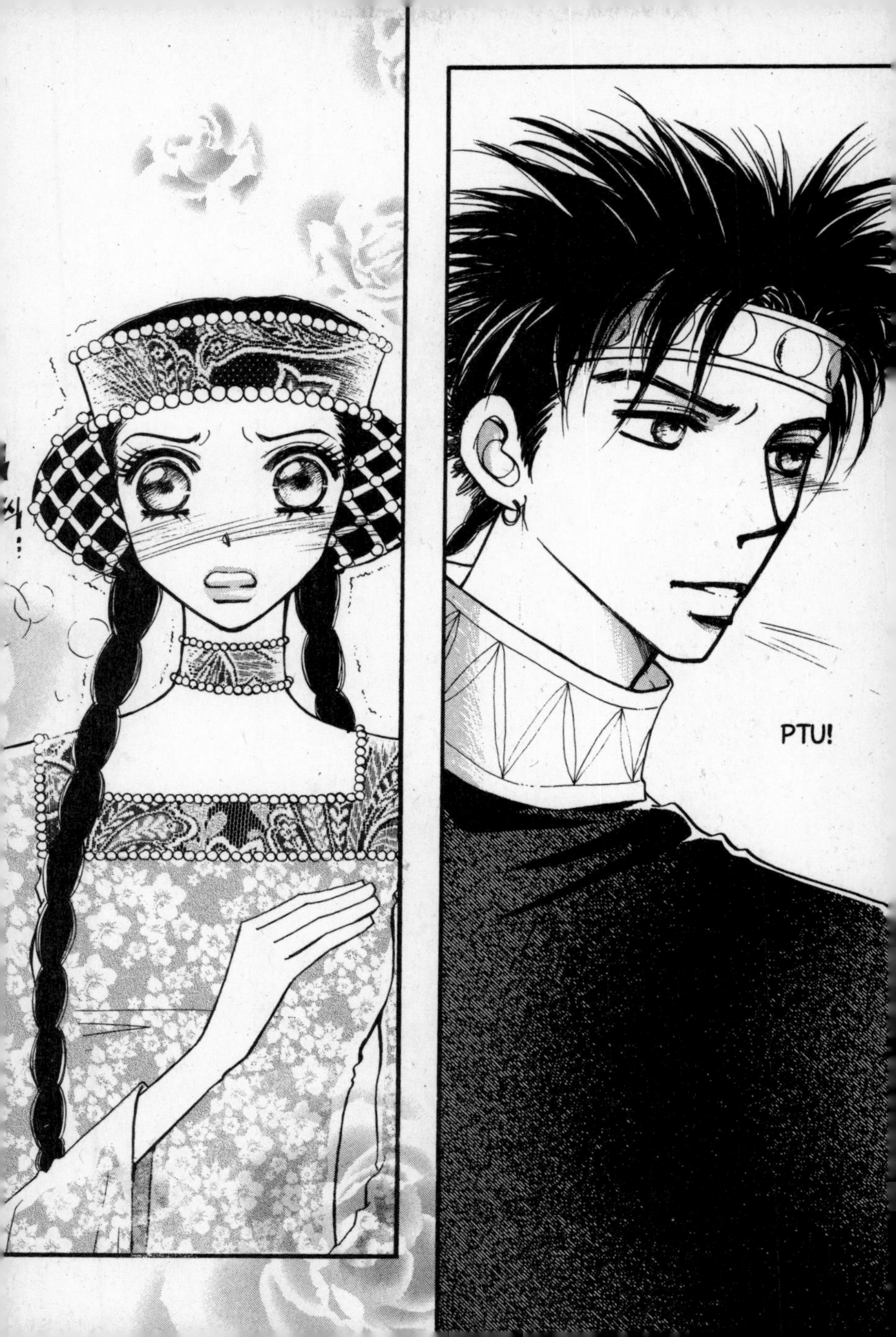PTU!

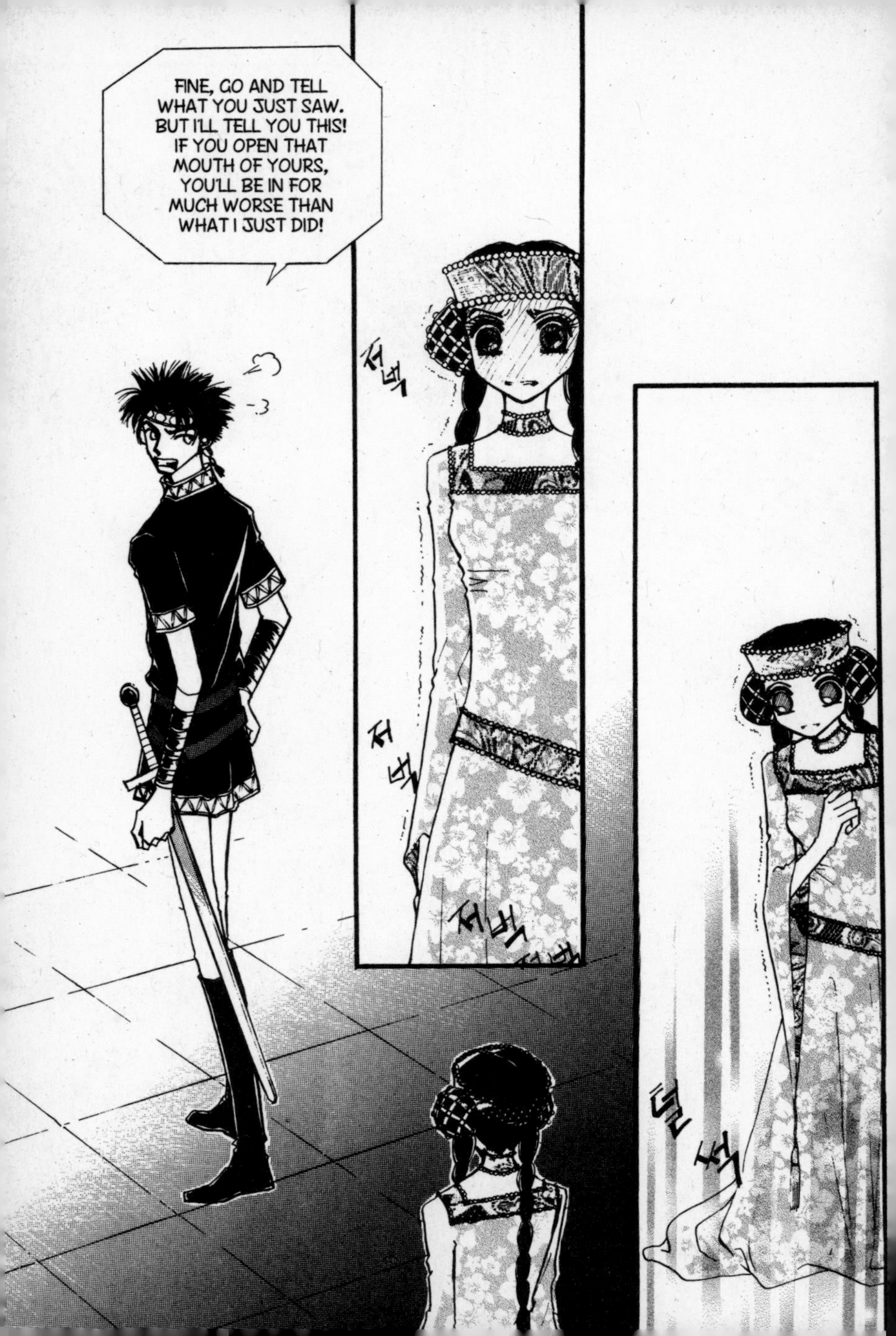
FINE, GO AND TELL WHAT YOU JUST SAW. BUT I'LL TELL YOU THIS! IF YOU OPEN THAT MOUTH OF YOURS, YOU'LL BE IN FOR MUCH WORSE THAN WHAT I JUST DID!
저벅
저벅
저벅

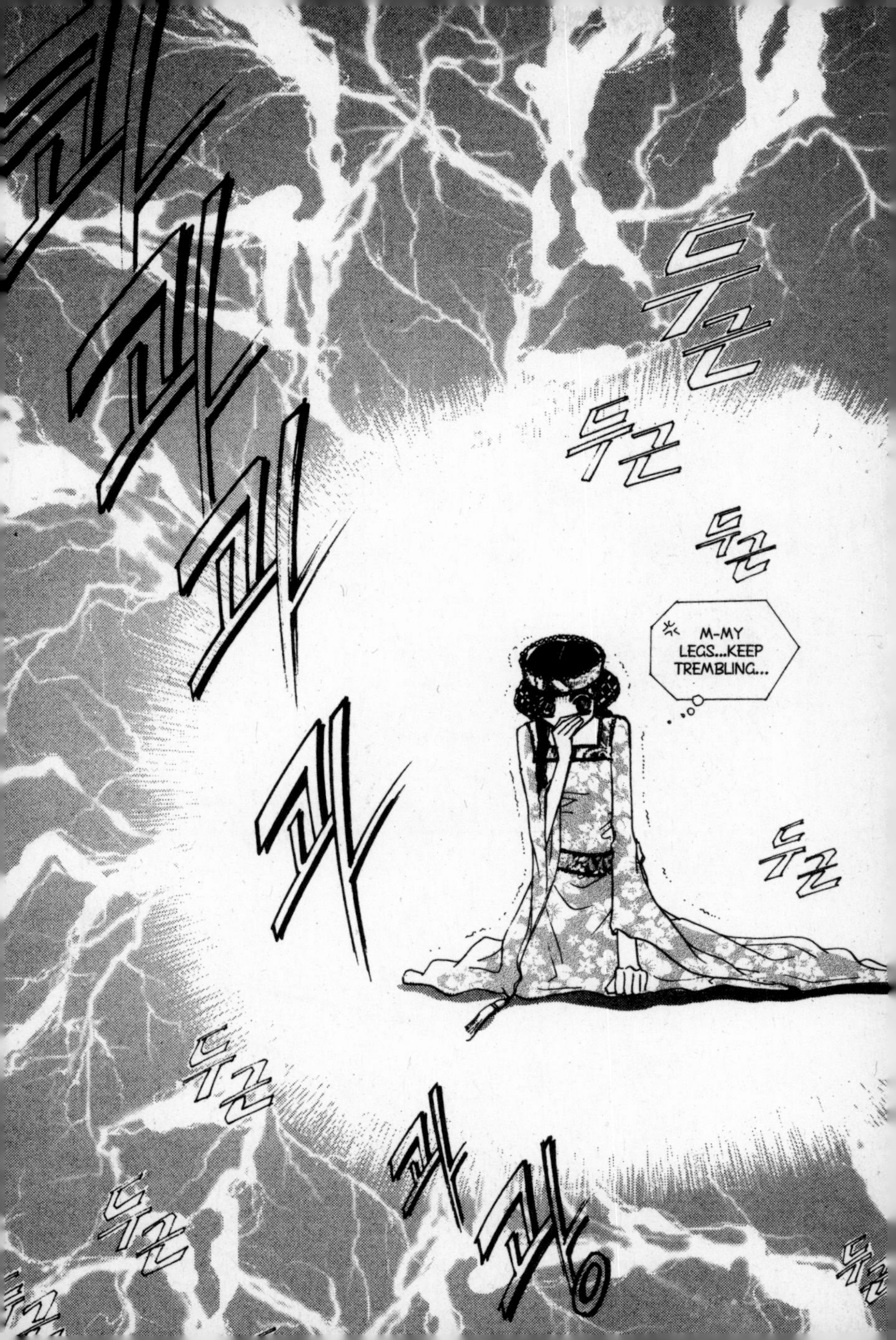
두근
두근
두근
M-MY LEGS...KEEP TREMBLING...
두근
두근
두근
두근

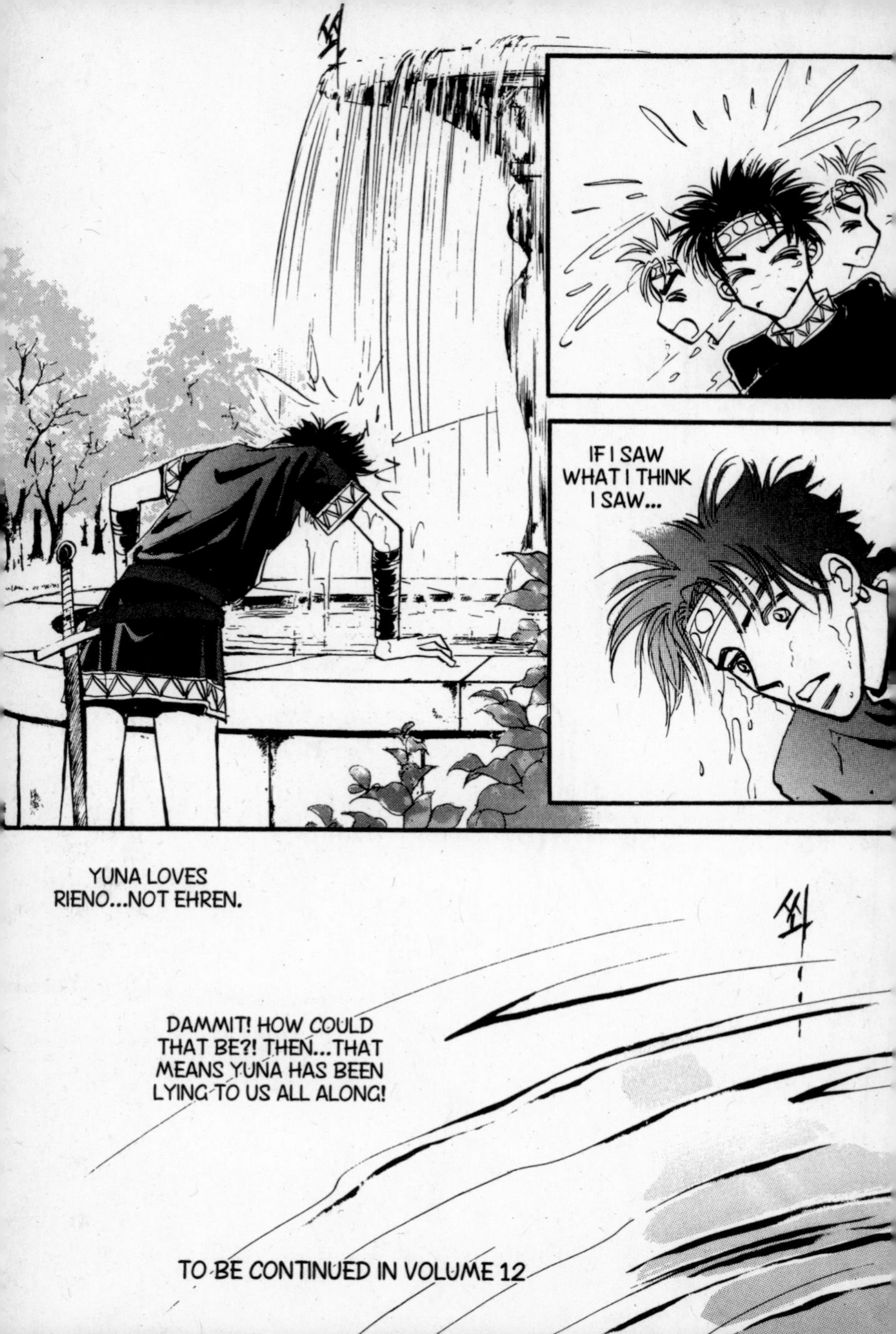
IF I SAW WHAT I THINK I SAW...
YUNA LOVES RIENO...NOT EHREN.
DAMMIT! HOW COULD THAT BE?! THEN...THAT MEANS YUNA HAS BEEN LYING TO US ALL ALONG!
TO BE CONTINUED IN VOLUME 12

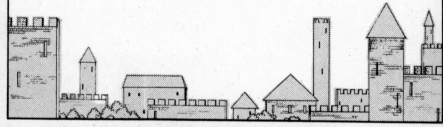

THE QUEEN'S KNIGHT
SHORT STORY

PRETTY BOY
CHANCELLOR KENT...

ONCE UPON A TIME, IN A LAND
CALLED PHANTASMA, THERE LIVED A
CHANCELLOR WHO WAS A LIEGE LORD
OF THE WEALTHY HAMLET OF TOYER.

THIS CHANCELLOR HAD TWO SONS, WHO WERE AS DIFFERENT AS LIGHT AND SHADOW...

THE HANDSOME BOY
EHREN, WHO RECEIVED
ALL THE GOOD GENES
OF THE FAMILY, WAS
BOTH CLEVER AND
GOOD-LOOKING.

KENT, WHO
RECEIVED ALL
THE BAD GENES
OF THE FAMILY,
WAS
ASTONISHINGLY
UGLY--WITH AN
OVERWHELMING
INFERIORITY
COMPLEX AND
A TENDENCY
TO ALWAYS
BE UPSET.

(AT THIS MOMENT
IN TIME, HE DID NOT
HAVE THE SELF-
MADE NICKNAME OF
"PRETTY BOY.")

THE STORY THAT I HAD PREPARED EVEN BEFORE VOLUME 1... FINALLY!
WE HEAR THE BEHIND STORY OF KENT! (HEE HEE HEE...)

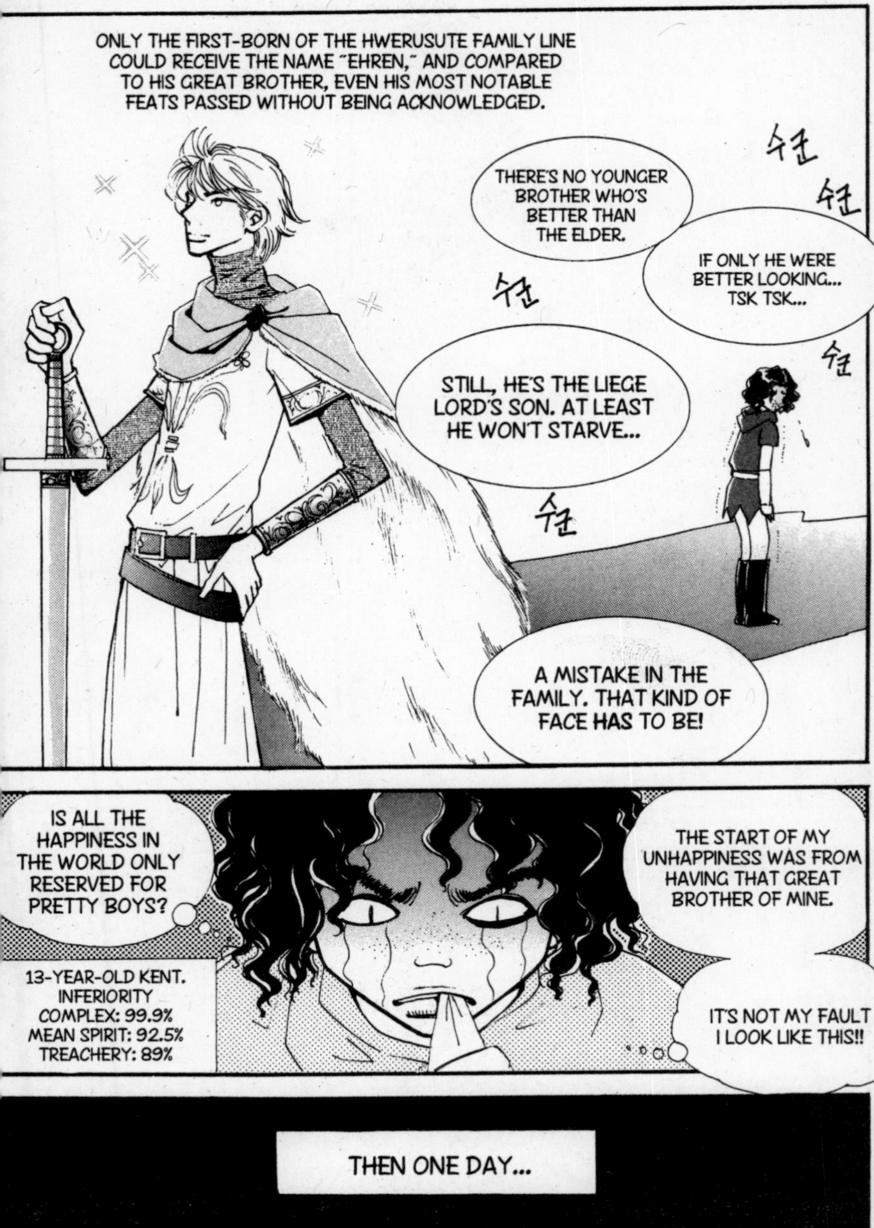
ONLY THE FIRST-BORN OF THE HWERUSUTE FAMILY LINE COULD RECEIVE THE NAME "EHREN," AND COMPARED TO HIS GREAT BROTHER, EVEN HIS MOST NOTABLE FEATS PASSED WITHOUT BEING ACKNOWLEDGED.
수군
수군
THERE'S NO YOUNGER BROTHER WHO'S BETTER THAN THE ELDER.
IF ONLY HE WERE BETTER LOOKING... TSK TSK...
수군
수군
STILL, HE'S THE LIEGE LORD'S SON. AT LEAST HE WON'T STARVE...
수군
A MISTAKE IN THE FAMILY. THAT KIND OF FACE HAS TO BE!
IS ALL THE HAPPINESS IN THE WORLD ONLY RESERVED FOR PRETTY BOYS?
13-YEAR-OLD KENT. INFERIORITY COMPLEX: 99.9% MEAN SPIRIT: 92.5% TREACHERY: 89%
THE START OF MY UNHAPPINESS WAS FROM HAVING THAT GREAT BROTHER OF MINE.
IT'S NOT MY FAULT I LOOK LIKE THIS!!
THEN ONE DAY...

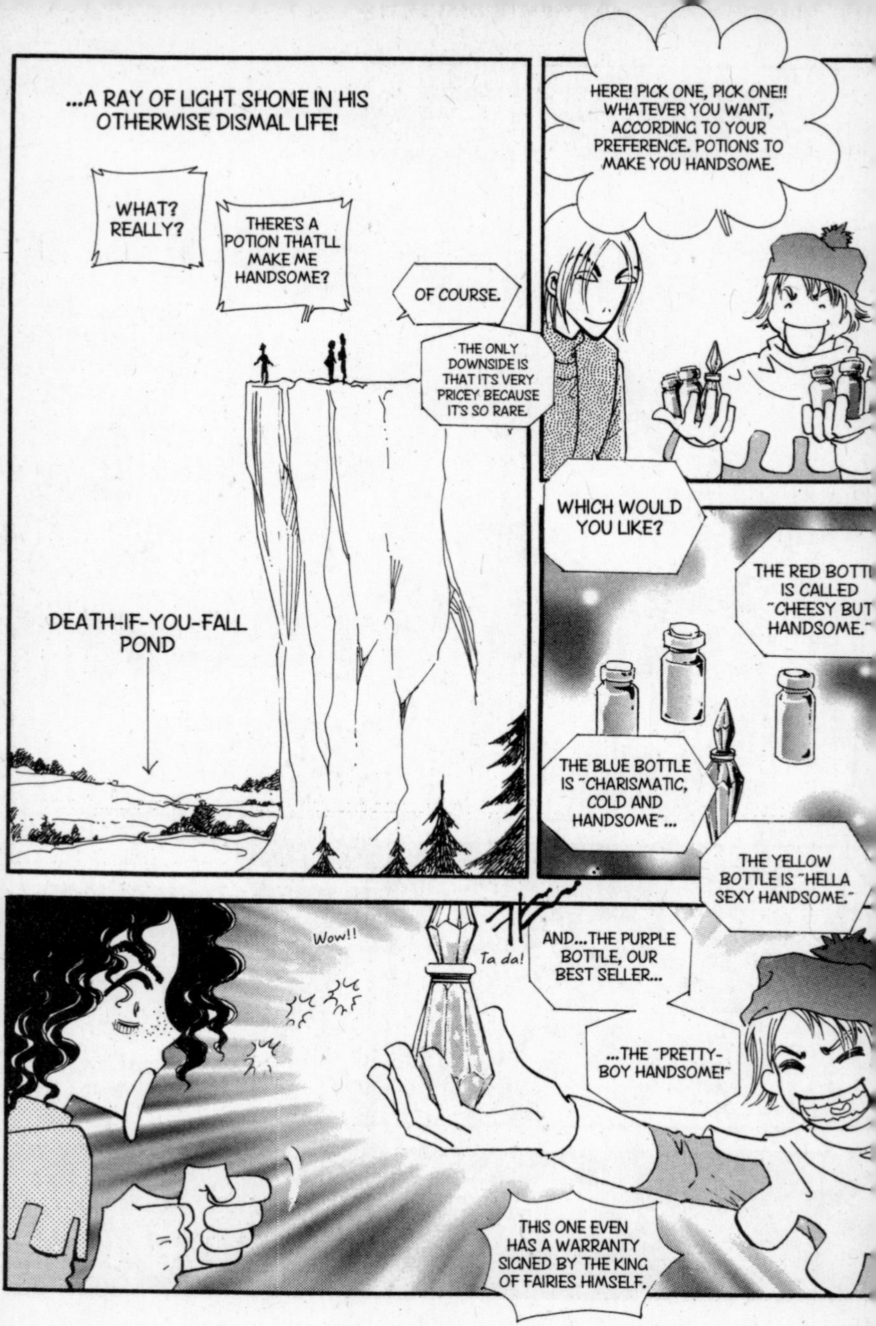
...A RAY OF LIGHT SHONE IN HIS OTHERWISE DISMAL LIFE!
WHAT? REALLY?
THERE'S A POTION THAT'LL MAKE ME HANDSOME?
OF COURSE.
THE ONLY DOWNSIDE IS THAT IT'S VERY PRICEY BECAUSE IT'S SO RARE.
DEATH-IF-YOU-FALL POND
HERE! PICK ONE, PICK ONE!! WHATEVER YOU WANT, ACCORDING TO YOUR PREFERENCE. POTIONS TO MAKE YOU HANDSOME.
WHICH WOULD YOU LIKE?
THE RED BOTT IS CALLED "CHEESY BUT HANDSOME."
THE BLUE BOTTLE IS "CHARISMATIC, COLD AND HANDSOME"...
THE YELLOW BOTTLE IS "HELLA SEXY HANDSOME."
Wow!!
Ta da!
AND...THE PURPLE BOTTLE, OUR BEST SELLER...
...THE "PRETTY-BOY HANDSOME!"
THIS ONE EVEN HAS A WARRANTY SIGNED BY THE KING OF FAIRIES HIMSELF.

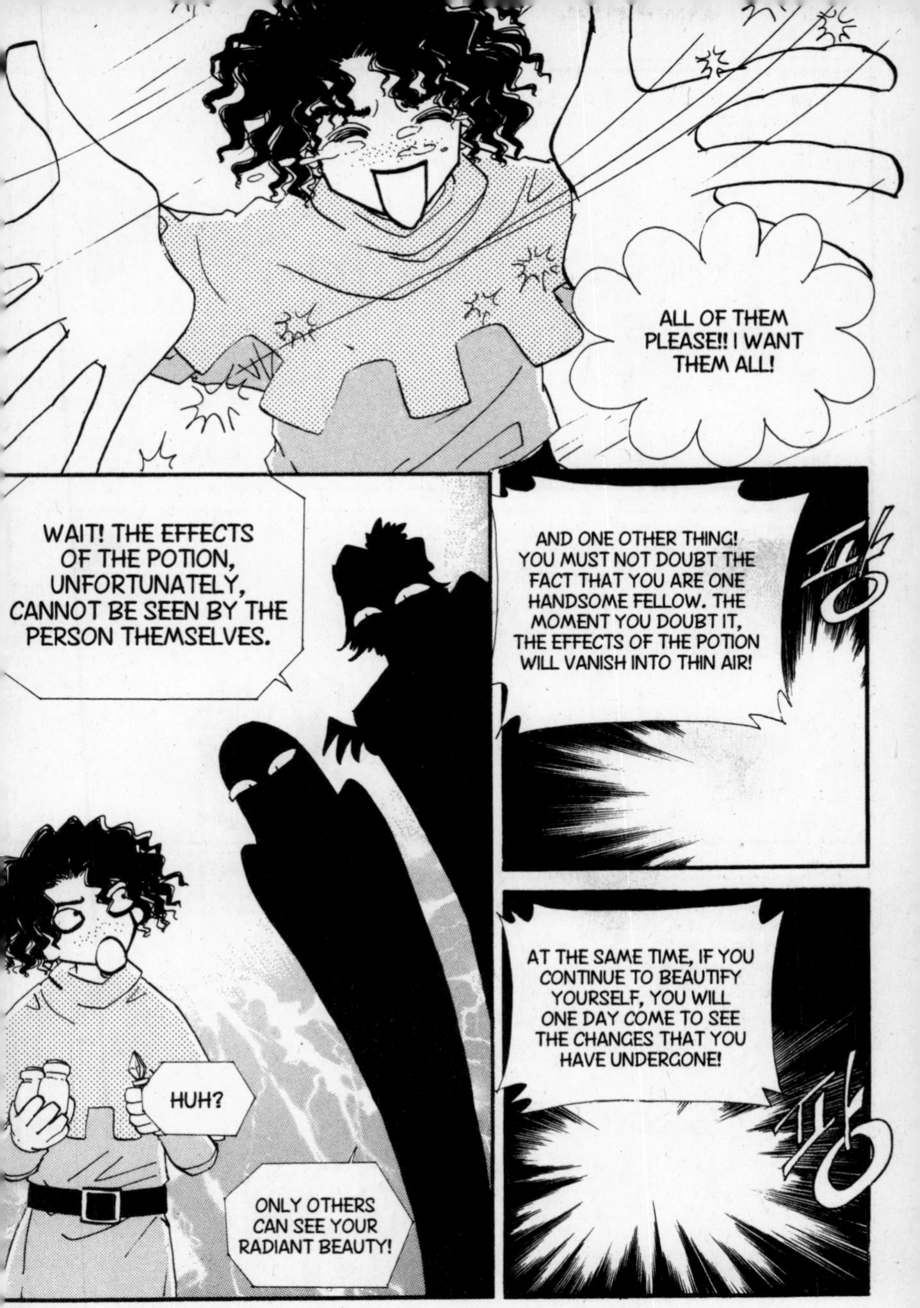
ALL OF THEM PLEASE!! I WANT THEM ALL!
WAIT! THE EFFECTS OF THE POTION, UNFORTUNATELY, CANNOT BE SEEN BY THE PERSON THEMSELVES.
HUH?
ONLY OTHERS CAN SEE YOUR RADIANT BEAUTY!
AND ONE OTHER THING! YOU MUST NOT DOUBT THE FACT THAT YOU ARE ONE HANDSOME FELLOW. THE MOMENT YOU DOUBT IT, THE EFFECTS OF THE POTION WILL VANISH INTO THIN AIR!
AT THE SAME TIME, IF YOU CONTINUE TO BEAUTIFY YOURSELF, YOU WILL ONE DAY COME TO SEE THE CHANGES THAT YOU HAVE UNDERGONE!

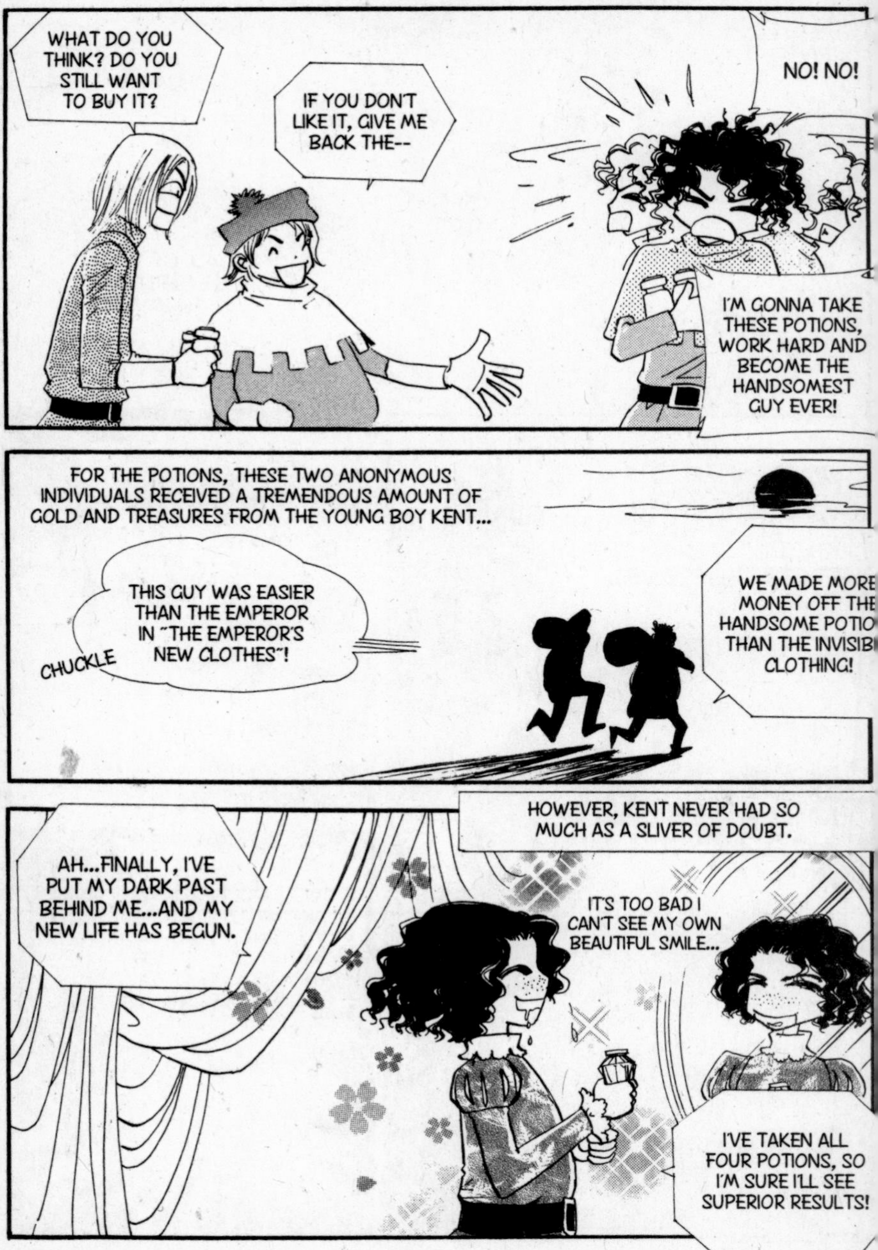
WHAT DO YOU THINK? DO YOU STILL WANT TO BUY IT?
IF YOU DON'T LIKE IT, GIVE ME BACK THE--
NO! NO!
I'M GONNA TAKE THESE POTIONS, WORK HARD AND BECOME THE HANDSOMEST GUY EVER!
FOR THE POTIONS, THESE TWO ANONYMOUS INDIVIDUALS RECEIVED A TREMENDOUS AMOUNT OF GOLD AND TREASURES FROM THE YOUNG BOY KENT...
THIS GUY WAS EASIER THAN THE EMPEROR IN "THE EMPEROR'S NEW CLOTHES"!
CHUCKLE
WE MADE MORE MONEY OFF THE HANDSOME POTIO THAN THE INVISIB CLOTHING!
AH...FINALLY, I'VE PUT MY DARK PAST BEHIND ME...AND MY NEW LIFE HAS BEGUN.
HOWEVER, KENT NEVER HAD SO MUCH AS A SLIVER OF DOUBT.
IT'S TOO BAD I CAN'T SEE MY OWN BEAUTIFUL SMILE...
I'VE TAKEN ALL FOUR POTIONS, SO I'M SURE I'LL SEE SUPERIOR RESULTS!

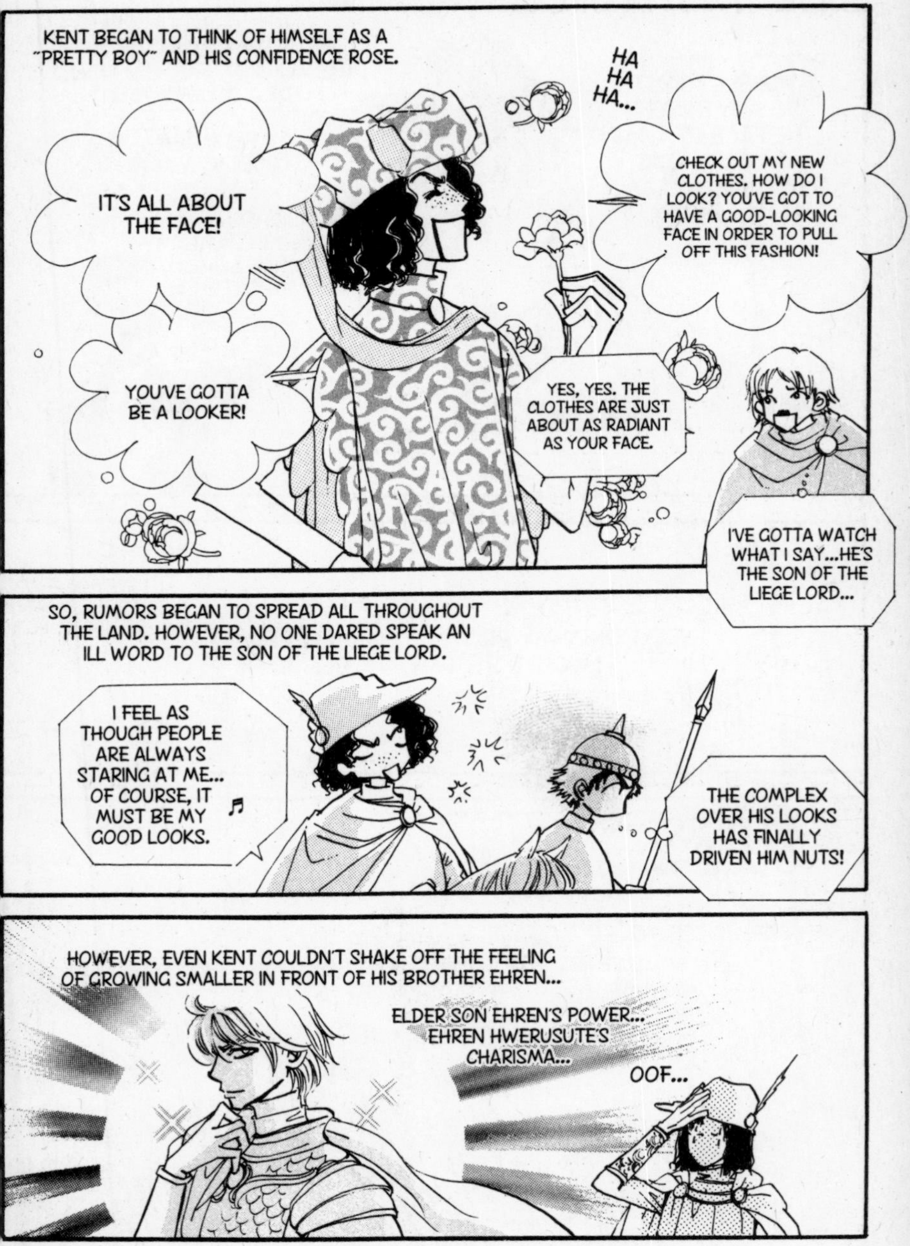
KENT BEGAN TO THINK OF HIMSELF AS A "PRETTY BOY" AND HIS CONFIDENCE ROSE.
HA HA HA...
IT'S ALL ABOUT THE FACE!
CHECK OUT MY NEW CLOTHES. HOW DO I LOOK? YOU'VE GOT TO HAVE A GOOD-LOOKING FACE IN ORDER TO PULL OFF THIS FASHION!
YOU'VE GOTTA BE A LOOKER!
YES, YES. THE CLOTHES ARE JUST ABOUT AS RADIANT AS YOUR FACE.
I'VE GOTTA WATCH WHAT I SAY...HE'S THE SON OF THE LIEGE LORD...
SO, RUMORS BEGAN TO SPREAD ALL THROUGHOUT THE LAND. HOWEVER, NO ONE DARED SPEAK AN ILL WORD TO THE SON OF THE LIEGE LORD.
I FEEL AS THOUGH PEOPLE ARE ALWAYS STARING AT ME... OF COURSE, IT MUST BE MY GOOD LOOKS. ♪
THE COMPLEX OVER HIS LOOKS HAS FINALLY DRIVEN HIM NUTS!
HOWEVER, EVEN KENT COULDN'T SHAKE OFF THE FEELING OF GROWING SMALLER IN FRONT OF HIS BROTHER EHREN...
ELDER SON EHREN'S POWER... EHREN HWERUSUTE'S CHARISMA...
OOF...

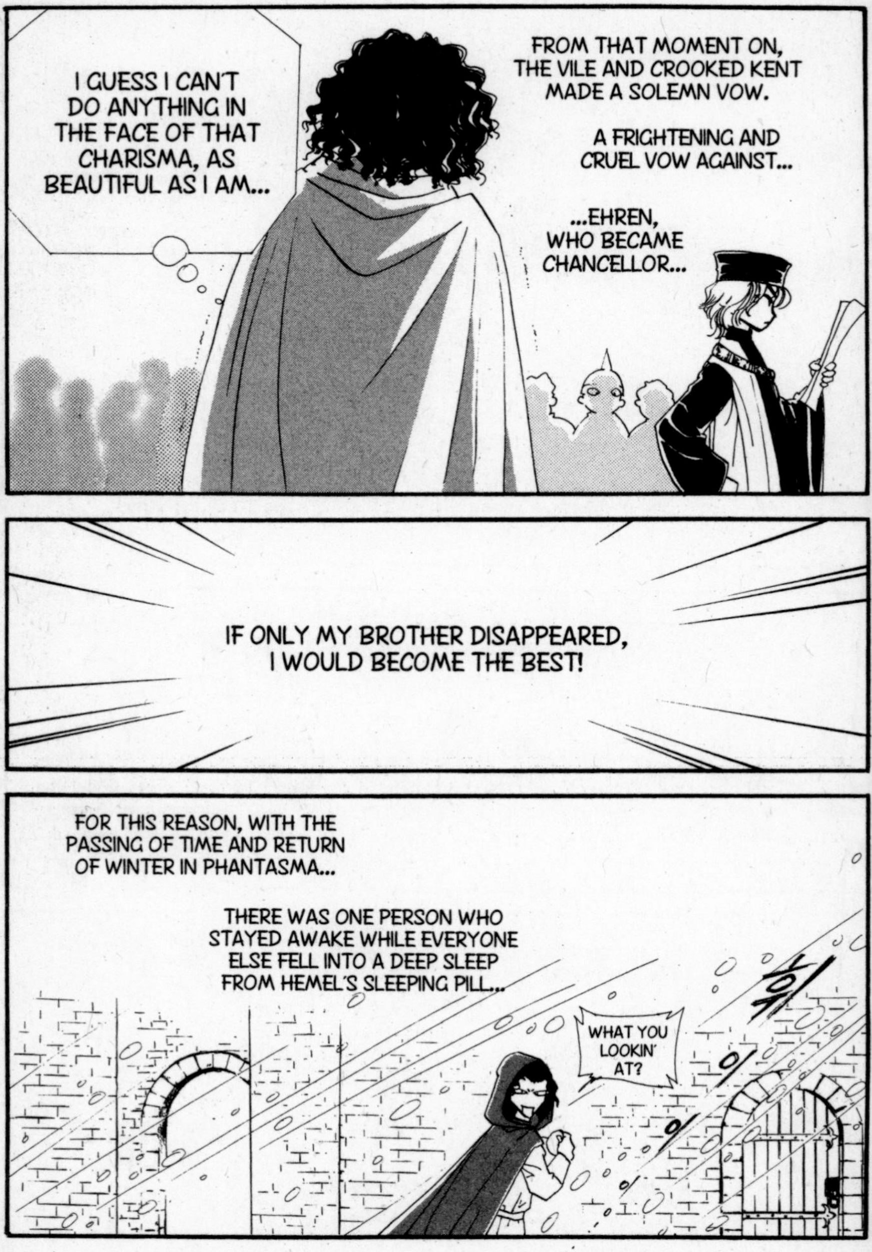
I GUESS I CAN'T DO ANYTHING IN THE FACE OF THAT CHARISMA, AS BEAUTIFUL AS I AM...
FROM THAT MOMENT ON, THE VILE AND CROOKED KENT MADE A SOLEMN VOW.
A FRIGHTENING AND CRUEL VOW AGAINST...
...EHREN, WHO BECAME CHANCELLOR...
IF ONLY MY BROTHER DISAPPEARED, I WOULD BECOME THE BEST!
FOR THIS REASON, WITH THE PASSING OF TIME AND RETURN OF WINTER IN PHANTASMA...
THERE WAS ONE PERSON WHO STAYED AWAKE WHILE EVERYONE ELSE FELL INTO A DEEP SLEEP FROM HEMEL'S SLEEPING PILL...
WHAT YOU LOOKIN' AT?

AS ALWAYS, SPRING RETURNED WITH THE RISE OF A NEW QUEEN...

ALL OF PHANTASMA'S CITIZENS AWOKE FROM THEIR SLUMBER...

EVEN YOUR FATHER AGED A BIT... BUT STILL...

CLARE...

KENT'S NEPHEW, EHREN...

AAAGH!! WHY DID I GET SO OLD?

DID I TAKE TOO MUCH OF HEMEL'S SLEEPING PILL?!

KENT'S MANOR

NO, NO...I MUSTN'T DOUBT MY BEAUTY...

IT DOESN'T MATTER IF I AGE BECAUSE I'M BEAUTIFUL ANYWAY!

I'M HANDSOME!!

I NEED TO GET A GRIP.

NOW KENT IS CHANCELLOR! NO ONE WOULD DARE STRIKE AT HIS COMPLEX. EXCEPT ONE PERSON...

HMPH! STUPID, UGLY, OLD DUDE...

WHAT?!

NO--I'M BEAUTIFUL...

I'M HANDSOME...

I WON'T FORGIVE THAT QUEEN!! HOW DARE SHE TALK ABOUT MY LOOKS...

I MUSTN'T GET MAD...ITS NOT GOOD FOR MY FACE...

EVEN SO, CHANCELLOR KENT...IS ALWAYS NERVOUS ABOUT HIS LOOKS.

PRETTY BOY CHANCELLOR KENT--THE END

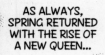

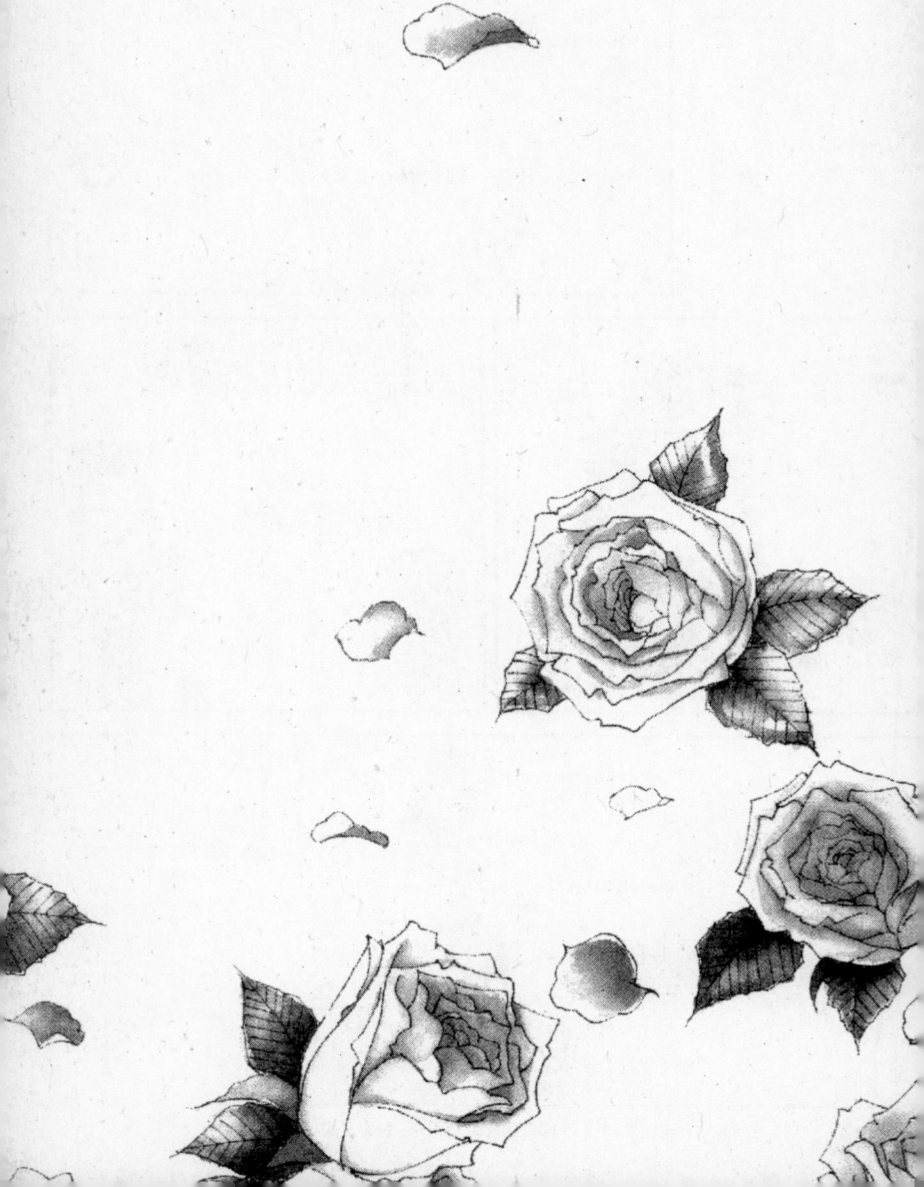

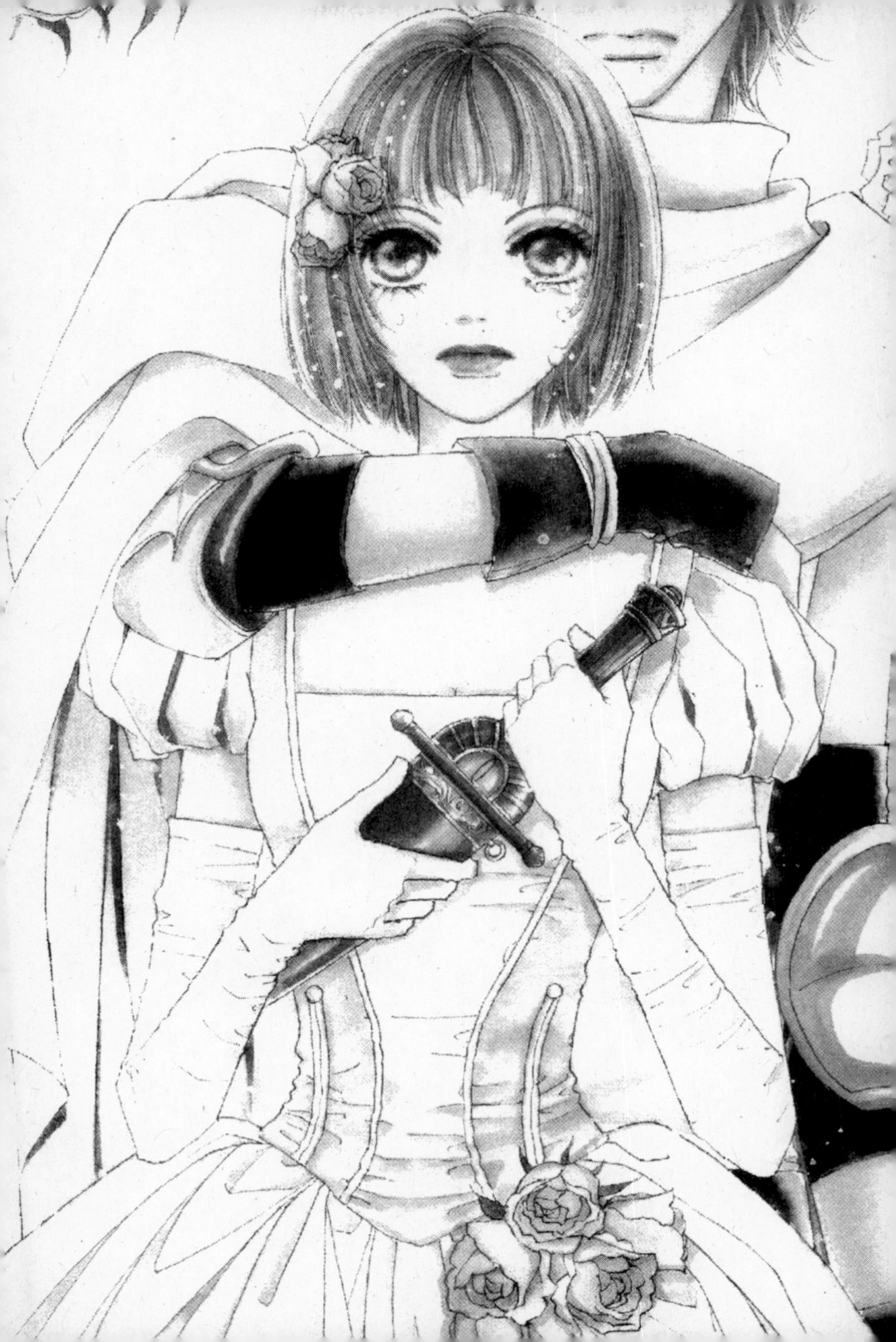

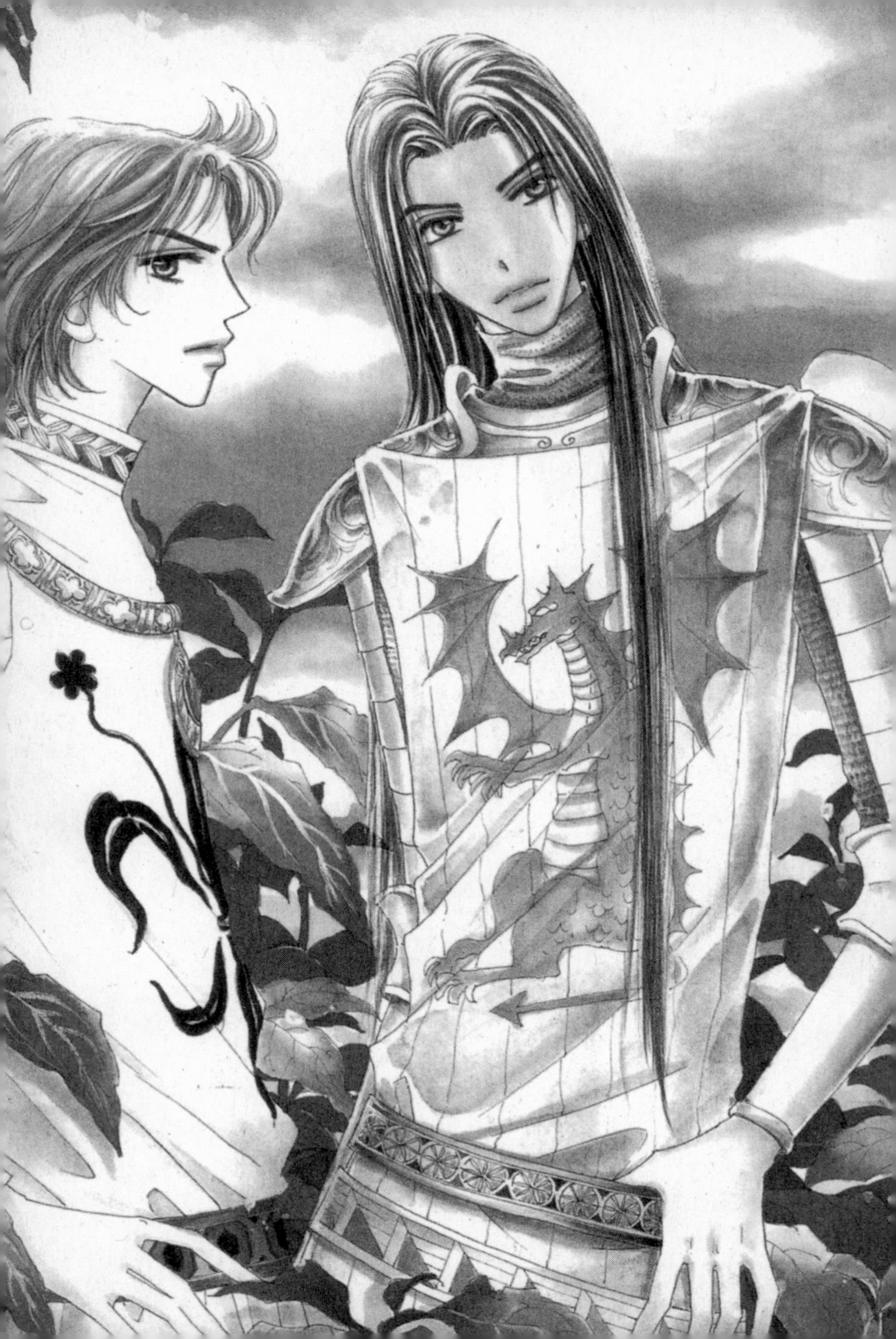

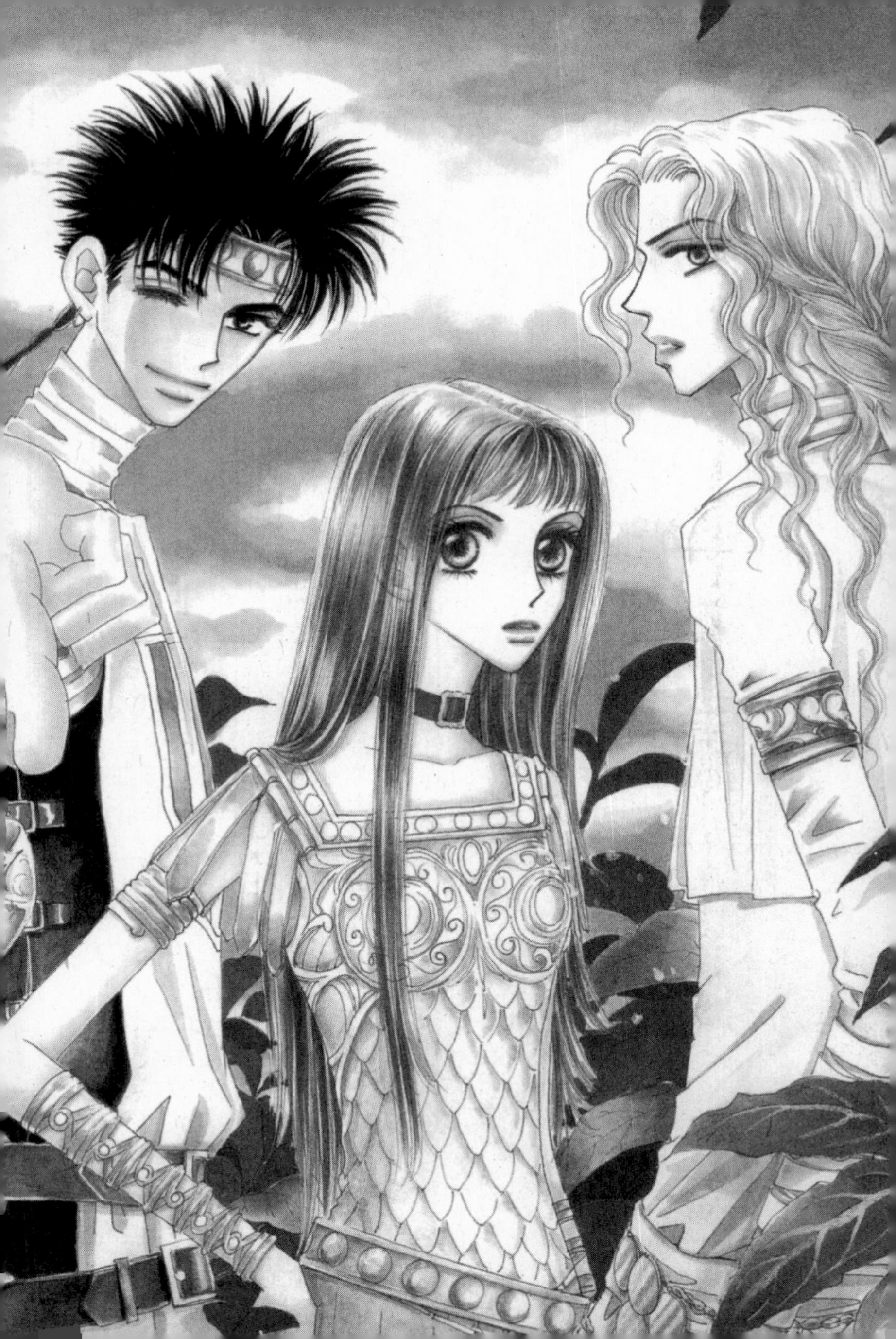

IN THE NEXT VOLUME OF...

THE QUEEN'S KNIGHT

THE SECRET LOVE OF RIENO AND YUNA'S HAS BEEN
DISCOVERED! PRINCESS LIBERA, DESPITE LEON'S WARNING,
TRIES TO DEPOSE THE QUEEN BY REVEALING YUNA'S
TRUE LOVE. THE KNIGHTS MAINTAIN SOME SEMBLANCE
OF LOYALTY TO YUNA, DECIDING THAT THEY WILL
DEFEND AND PROTECT HER FOR THE TIME BEING, SO
LIBERA'S PLAN COMPLETELY BACKFIRES. HOWEVER,
ONE THING LEADS TO ANOTHER AND AT THE END
OF IT ALL, THERE'S A BLOODY MASSACRE OF ALL THE
HIGH DIGNITARIES, LIEGE LORDS AND SOLDIERS...
HAVING WITNESSED THE TRAGEDY, WILL YUNA
FLEE FROM PHANTASMA AND THE DUTIES AS ITS
QUEEN? OR WILL SHE CEMENT HER COMMITMENT
TO THE KINGDOM SHE HAS GROWN TO LOVE BY
LETTING GO OF RIENO ONCE AND FOR ALL?

COMING SOON!